D1566022

Wrongful
Convictions
of Women

Wrongful
Convictions
of Women

When Innocence Isn't Enough

Marvin D. Free, Jr.
Mitch Ruesink

LYNNE
RIENNER
PUBLISHERS

BOULDER
LONDON

Published in the United States of America in 2016 by
Lynne Rienner Publishers, Inc.
1800 30th Street, Boulder, Colorado 80301
www.rienner.com

and in the United Kingdom by
Lynne Rienner Publishers, Inc.
3 Henrietta Street, Covent Garden, London WC2E 8LU

Library of Congress Cataloging-in-Publication Data
Names: Free, Marvin D., author. | Ruesink, Mitch, author.
Title: Wrongful convictions of women : when innocence isn't enough / Marvin
    D. Free, Jr., and Mitch Ruesink.
Description: Boulder, Colorado : Lynne Rienner Publishers, 2016. | Includes
    bibliographical references and index.
Identifiers: LCCN 2015037554 | ISBN 9781626375062 (hc : alk. paper)
Subjects: LCSH: Judicial error—United States—Cases. | Criminal justice,
    Administration of—United States—Cases. | False imprisonment—United
    States—Cases. | Women prisoners—United States—Cases. | Prosecutorial misconduct
    United States.
Classification: LCC KF9756 .F74 2016 | DDC 345.73/0122—dc23
LC record available at http://lccn.loc.gov/2015037554

British Cataloguing in Publication Data
A Cataloguing in Publication record for this book
is available from the British Library.

Printed and bound in the United States of America

 The paper used in this publication meets the requirements
of the American National Standard for Permanence of
Paper for Printed Library Materials Z39.48-1992.

5 4 3 2 1

Contents

Preface

dates back to 1932, when Edwin Borchard compiled data on sixty-five cases in which innocent individuals had been erroneously convicted. But sustained public interest in wrongful convictions was not immediately forthcoming. With improved forensics in general, and the use of DNA in particular, it became possible to reexamine evidence from earlier convictions to ascertain whether an innocent individual had been wrongly convicted. Although the vast majority of exonerations are not the result of DNA testing, the findings that some prisoners were innocent of the crimes for which they had been incarcerated began to catch the attention of the media. Organizations such as the Center on Wrongful Convictions at Northwestern University and the National Registry of Exonerations (a joint effort of Northwestern University and the University of Michigan) have brought greater awareness to these miscarriages of justice. The Innocence Project and its state and regional affiliates further disseminate information on false convictions, as does the Innocents Database (http://forejustice.org). Additionally, the Death Penalty Information Center tracks exonerated death row inmates.

Despite the increasing wealth of data on the subject, there has been relatively little publicity given to wrongly convicted women. The muted attention paid toward this population is perhaps somewhat understandable since women are considerably less likely than men to be involved in crimes such as murder and sexual assault, two of the larger categories making up wrongful convictions. Nevertheless, the preoccupation with male-dominated wrongful conviction statistics belies the problem facing women. The limited financial resources that often accompany wrongful convictions, through a lack of adequate legal counseling, are not restricted to men. Many women who are processed into prison come from impoverished backgrounds and share the problem of ineffective assistance of counsel. Moreover, because many of their crimes are not as serious as those of men and involve shorter prison sentences, programs designed to assist the wrongfully convicted are less likely to choose cases in which the defendants are women. The more carefully circumscribed gender roles of women make them more likely targets for overzealous prosecutors given cases involving child abuse. These perversions of societal expectations for mothers and caretakers are especially likely to be handled with haste as a prosecutor attempts to bring a perpetrator to justice. Drug use and violent behavior similarly may be perceived as more serious when they involve women because this behavior is more typically associated with men. Racial distinctions also permeate wrongful convictions involving women. As the chapters in this book reveal, black women are more likely to be wrongfully convicted of drug violations than white women whereas white women are more likely than black women to be wrongfully convicted of child abuse. And, similar to their male counterparts, black women are disproportionately found among those who have been erroneously convicted.

Even those women wrongfully convicted of less serious crimes may be treated harshly. Juries may be more easily convinced to convict since many of these crimes do not involve extended prison sentences. With more important crimes to prosecute, less time may be allocated to discovery of the facts. Furthermore, prosecutors may be more willing to extend a plea bargain, which can encourage defense counsel to have the client accept a lesser sentence rather than risk a conviction even if the client insists she is innocent. If the defendant is offered probation or a suspended sentence, she may reluctantly accept the offer rather than try to prove her innocence.

Because the field of wrongful convictions has been cast typically as a male-dominated social issue, we seek to bring to light the plight of women whose miscarriages of justice frequently go unnoticed. The 163 cases identified in the sample represent known wrongful convictions from the 1970s through 2012. Most of these individuals have been formally exonerated, although a few egregious cases, in which for various reasons the individual was not formally cleared, are included as well.

Our approach is to provide readers with a descriptive profile of the known wrongful convictions to capture the turmoil and human tragedy associated with these miscarriages of justice. For purposes of discussion, the cases are arranged according to the most serious offense for which these women were wrongly convicted. We attempt to offer a voice to those individuals whose cases might otherwise not be heard. And we hope that this exclusive focus on women will stimulate greater discussion of this facet of the wrongful conviction problem and will encourage further research into this area.

Wrongful Convictions of Women

1

Women and Wrongful Convictions

In February 1999, Victoria Bell Banks, a thirty-one-year-old black woman with an IQ of 40, was being held in the Choctaw County Jail in Butler, Alabama. As are many of the area's inhabitants, she was illiterate and poor. To gain her freedom early, she concocted a story that she was eight months pregnant and should be released because the jail had no accommodations for prenatal care. (Whether she originated this idea or a fellow inmate suggested it is open to debate given her diminished mental capacity.) She exhibited no physical signs of a pregnancy and refused to allow physicians to conduct a pelvic examination. Two doctors who later examined her failed to reach a consensus regarding her status. Nonetheless, authorities released Victoria on bond in May 1999 after she broached the possibility of a lawsuit for failure to provide adequate prenatal care.

On August 3, 1999, Choctaw County Sheriff Donald Lolley paid a visit to Victoria to inquire about her baby. She informed the sheriff that she had miscarried, whereupon he took her to the office of one of the physicians who had previously examined her. An examination failed to disclose any evidence of a pregnancy or a miscarriage. Victoria, along with her estranged husband, Medell Banks, Jr., and her sister, Dianne Tucker, were later questioned by authorities regarding the "missing" infant. They confirmed that Victoria had feigned the pregnancy to get out of jail and that she was incapable of becoming pregnant because she had her tubes tied in 1995. Nevertheless, after repeated interrogations Medell (whose IQ at 57 is only marginally higher than that of Victoria), having waived his right to counsel, reluctantly succumbed to the suggestion that perhaps he had heard a baby cry. All three eventually confessed to killing the baby, but their descriptions of the events were inconsistent and contradictory.

Once these confessions were obtained the prosecution went forward with trials for the so-called Choctaw Three. Originally indicted for murder of an infant, the charge was reduced to manslaughter in return for guilty pleas. Victoria was sentenced to fifteen years in prison in 2000 with Dianne and Medell receiving identical sentences in 2001. The three were convicted despite Victoria's physical inability to conceive a child, the absence of a body, questionable confessions, and the fact that no one ever reported seeing the supposed infant.

Dianne, who suffered from diminished mental capacity as well, was released on July 17, 2002, after being incarcerated for almost three years. New sentencing gave her credit for time served and included one day of probation. Further included was a provision that she could never appeal her original sentence nor could she pursue civil charges against the Alabama court system. On August 9, 2002, the Alabama Court of Appeals agreed to allow Medell to withdraw his original guilty plea. The Choctaw County prosecutor, however, refused to drop the charges, appealed the higher court's decision, and proceeded to charge him with murder. On January 10, 2003, during a pretrial hearing, Medell was finally released and his murder charge was dismissed in return for pleading guilty to tampering with unspecified evidence (despite the fact that there was no evidence). Finally, in early 2003 Victoria again testified that she had given birth to a baby in 1999. Because the prosecution had threatened to charge her with lying under oath if she didn't recant her earlier statement, her statement was given under duress. Victoria, who was serving a concurrent five-year sentence for an unrelated offense, was still incarcerated as of 2012 (Herbert, 2002; Reynolds, 2002; Russo, 2009; Sherrer, 2003).

The preceding account illustrates two features commonly associated with wrongful convictions. First, despite the presence of compelling evidence to the contrary, many prosecutors refuse to acknowledge that the offended party is innocent. Second, not all false convictions involve the actual commission of a crime. In a number of cases defendants are wrongly convicted of crimes that never occurred. This possibility increases significantly when the defendant is a woman. Between 1989 and 2012 almost 58 percent of female exonerees identified by the National Registry of Exonerations were convicted of crimes that never happened. Conversely, approximately 15 percent of their male counterparts were convicted of crimes that never occurred (National Registry of Exonerations, 2013).

Scholars differentiate between *legal* innocence and *factual* innocence. The former focuses on cases that are cleared through the discovery of procedural errors that violated the defendant's constitutionally protected rights. In contrast, the latter implies that the defendant is not guilty because either no crime was committed or the defendant did not commit the crime. In reality, however, these categories tend to overlap because convictions obtained through questionable legal procedures and practices enhance the probability that factually innocent individuals will be pronounced guilty. The case involving the Choctaw Three clearly illustrates the extent to which misbehavior exhibited by actors in the criminal justice system contributed to the false conviction of three factually innocent persons.

A Brief Historical Overview of
Wrongful Convictions in the United States

It is beyond the scope to this book to provide a complete accounting of wrongful convictions in the United States. Nevertheless, an abbreviated history of this miscarriage of justice is important to place the current cases to be discussed in some cultural and historical context. Any review of the history of wrongful convictions must begin with the Puritans' fascination with witches and their witch trials in which mainly women were alleged to have practiced witchcraft. According to John Murrin (2003), many of the witch trials exhibited similar characteristics.

> In most early New England trials, adult men brought accusations against post-menopausal women. In nearly every case within this pattern, the complaint involved maleficium, some evil deed that the victim attributed to the accused—a dead cow or pig, a child who suddenly took ill, or something of that kind. In New England, as in western Europe, witchcraft was overwhelmingly a female crime. Women accounted for more than 80 percent of the accused. Even many of the men who fell under suspicion were secondary targets who happened to be closely related to the primary suspect, a woman. (Murrin, 2003, p. 315)

Although the Salem witch trials are arguably the best known of these incidents of wrongful conviction, the first such trials occurred in Connecticut during the mid-1600s. On May 26, 1647, Alse Young (also referred to as Alice or Achsah) of Windsor was the first person in North America to be hanged as a witch. The following year, Mary Johnson of Wethersfield became the second person to be executed for being a witch. Though many of the trial records no longer exist, at least eleven individuals (nine women and two husbands of accused witches) were executed during this time in Connecticut (findingDulcinea, 2011; Klein 2012; Taylor 1908/1974; Witchcraft and Witches, n.d.). Given the limited documentation available on these trials, we proceed to a more detailed description of the events leading up to the infamous Salem witch trials in Massachusetts.

The Salem Witch Trials

By the time Samuel Parris accepted the position of minister in Salem, three others had occupied the position for varying lengths of time. Two of the three ministers—James Barley and George Burroughs—had left the position over money disputes. Their bad experiences had made the rounds in various New England communities. The third minister, Deodat Lawson, left after being denied the position of full minister. Parris delayed his decision while negotiating a larger salary. He was also concerned about how such a move would affect his social status. Another factor that was weighing heavily on his mind was the fact that Salem was known as a contentious place. Many families there were struggling just to survive. Bad weather could easily destroy the crops for the year, and a disease like smallpox could wipe out an entire family. It is not surprising that the Puritans believed that many of the tribulations they endured were directly caused by evil spirits.

Parris had studied theology at Harvard but left before he completed his studies. He inherited and managed his father's sugar trading company in Barbados, but bad luck seemed to follow him from the start of this enterprise. Sugar prices were low and a hurricane destroyed the company warehouse. Parris stayed in Barbados for eight years, but ultimately decided to move to Boston, where he attempted another business venture that failed. At this point he turned his attention toward the pulpit. He started applying for positions, but Salem was the only response he received.

While John Putnam, an influential elder, was pressuring Parris to move to Salem, he was also feuding with the Towne family over property rights. Putnam, a farmer, was the head of one of the largest families in Salem. He also had disagreements with the Porter family, one of the wealthiest in town. In 1672 a dam and sawmill owned by the Porter family flooded the Putnam farm, later resulting in a lawsuit.

Parris arrived in Salem with his family, including his wife, Elizabeth, his daughter, Betty, and his niece, Abigail Williams. He brought two slaves from Barbados—Tituba and John Indian. It was unusual to see slaves in New England, and the Puritan community viewed the slaves suspiciously and wondered if they were associated with the devil.

The two girls, Betty Parris and Abigail Williams, had different personalities. Betty was a quiet child who obeyed her parents and was very afraid of the devil. Abigail was bolder and believed that her association with Reverend Parris would be enough to save her from harm.

Parris saw people in black-and-white terms. Either they were very good or very evil. His sermons, filled with fire and brimstone, repeatedly urged his parishioners to reward him with what he believed was his due, including more pay. He held strict standards for those joining his church. While other area congregations were starting to ease their standards, members who wanted to join his flock had to be baptized and make a public declaration of faith. It was not long before Parris had a faction in Salem against him.

The Puritans believed in a life focused on work and not on leisure. Often, by the time Puritan children were around the age of seven years, they were expected to share in the many chores that came with running a household.

Betty and Abigail did not have much time for games, instead spending their time helping Tituba with daily chores such as cooking and cleaning. When the girls did have spare time, they listened intently to Tituba's stories about growing up. Frequently the stories involved voodoo or magic, which was viewed as the devil's work in Puritan society. The girls found themselves pulled between disobeying their family and therefore going against their faith and their fascination with voodoo and magic. They probably had heard about Elizabeth Knapp, who exhibited signs of possession in 1671, and the Goodwin children, who displayed similar signs in 1684.

During the long winter of 1691, Betty and Abigail decided that they would try their hand at fortune-telling. The girls were curious about their future mates and their occupations. They saw it as an innocent game to play, not knowing that it would set off what became the Salem witch trials. The girls used what was known as a "venus glass," something they probably learned from Tituba. The object was to put an egg white into a glass of hot water and then wait until a shape appeared. On one occasion Betty saw an image that looked like a coffin, instead of the usual face or shape. A short time later, she started acting strangely. She forgot things, had a hard time concentrating, and was often in her own world. As her behavior became more unusual, she started barking and screaming, and threw a Bible across the room. It was not long before Abigail was acting in the same strange manner. Reverend Parris wanted to help his daughter and niece. Both girls complained about being pinched and poked, babbled on end, and acted as if they were being choked. They continued to behave strangely, and Parris became desperate to find the cause. He prayed and fasted, but this had little effect on the girls' behavior.

Eventually, four others—Elizabeth Hubbard, Ann Putnam, Mercy Lewis, and Mary Walcott—began to exhibit similar symptoms. A neighbor, Mary Sibley, who was also the aunt of Mary Walcott, suggested that a "witch's cake" should be made to determine the real witch. The cake consisted of batter and urine of the affected girls. The mixture was then fed to a dog, whereupon it was believed that the identity of the witch would be disclosed since the particles of the witch would be in the cake. This method did not reveal anything and only served to further infuriate Reverend Parris, who beat Tituba until she confessed to being a witch.

By mid-February, Parris asked a friend, Dr. William Griggs, to take a look at the girls. It quickly became apparent that the physician could not find a disease that would account for their bizarre behavior. During this time, when doctors could not diagnose a disease, the problem was often attributed to witchcraft. It is unlikely that this diagnosis would have been questioned, since most Puritans believed that witches especially liked to target children.

It did not take long before the villagers of Salem were hunting for witches. The girls were questioned by ministers and town leaders and pressured to reveal who had put a curse on them. Betty immediately identified Tituba. The girls also identified Sarah Osborne, an elderly and frail woman who needed assistance even to stand before the town officials. Osborne spent most of her time in bed due to poor health and as a result had not attended church for three years, a sin in Puritan society. The third person identified was Sarah Good, a pipe smoker and homeless beggar who went door to door looking for handouts. When she was refused a handout, she would leave, muttering under her breath. Villagers, who already eyed the ill-tempered woman suspiciously, believed she was putting curses on them. Good had been accused previously of witchcraft and villagers believed that she was responsible for livestock deaths in the area.

Sarah Good was born the daughter of John Solart, a successful innkeeper. When she was nineteen, her father committed suicide by drowning himself. From that point forward, it seems that her life continued on a downward spiral. It was not very long before the thirty-year-old woman looked many years older. The estate, worth £500, was divided between the two oldest sons and Mrs. Solart. It was stipulated that Sarah and her sisters would each get a share when they came of age. Sarah's mother remarried and soon her husband had control of most of the estate.

Sarah married Daniel Poole, a laborer who was constantly looking for work and died in debt in 1686. When Sarah later married William Good, a portion of her land was sold to pay off some debt. The remainder of the land was sold shortly thereafter, so the couple would have some cash on which to live. William worked as a laborer in exchange for lodging and food. Consequently, the family stayed in various locations throughout the village, until villagers became hesitant to hire him and deal with his unpleasant wife. At this point, most of the village would have been happy to be rid of Sarah Good. As the witch trials began in March 1692, she was the first person to be tried. She answered her accusers by stating that she was not a witch, but that Tituba and Sarah Osborne were. Her husband and four-year-old daughter were brought in to testify against her. William testified that his wife might be a witch and their daughter, Dorcus, said that her mom was a witch and she was, too. As a result the young child spent nine months in jail and was permanently scarred from the experience.

Sarah Osborne was an outcast from Puritan society for different reasons, including not attending church because she was very ill. In 1662 she married her second husband, Robert Prince, who bought a 150-acre farm next to his brother-in-law, John Putnam. Twelve years later, in the winter of 1674, Robert died and Sarah became involved in a dispute over the land. Her husband's will stated that upon his death the land was to be given to his two sons, James and Joseph, who were ages two and six at the time. Robert had appointed Thomas Putnam and John Putnam to supervise this process. With three small children and a farm to take care of, Sarah hired an indentured servant, Alexander Osborne. He had paid for his trip from Ireland by indenturing himself for a certain period of time. The villagers thought that the two were living together, a sin that was punishable by whipping. Nevertheless, it was not long before Sarah paid off Alexander's indenture and decided to marry him. By this time, however, the damage had been done. The villagers of Salem looked down on Alexander for living with Sarah outside of marriage, his low status, and his Irish ethnicity. After the marriage, the couple tried to change Robert's will so that they could claim all of the land. By 1692 the dispute was still unsettled and Sarah had become bedridden. This conflict pitted her against the powerful Putnam family, who went on to accuse many of their enemies of being witches.

Each of the first three women arrested for witchcraft—Tituba, Sarah Good, and Sarah Osborne—were women who lived outside the accepted practices of Puritan society. The women were, for one reason or another, outcasts who, in a time of crisis, were most likely to be singled out for causing trouble. It was not until nearly a month later, when Martha

Corey was accused of witchcraft, that every citizen of the village of Salem realized that they could be accused next. In all, nineteen people, including five men, were hung at Gallows Hill in 1692 from June through September. At least four people died in prison and one, Martha Corey's husband, Giles, was executed by being crushed to death.

Martha Corey was sixty-five when she was the fourth person to be accused of witchcraft. She was the third wife of Giles Corey, a prosperous landowner, who attended church on a regular basis and was a respected member of the Salem community. Martha, nonetheless, did have a skeleton in her closet. When she was younger, she gave birth to an illegitimate mulatto child, Benoni, whom she raised. She was unafraid of letting people know that she believed the witchcraft accusers were lying. Word spread about her disbelief, and a short while later Martha was accused by Ann Putnam of practicing witchcraft. Giles, certain that his wife was telling the truth, defended her by speaking out against the girls making the accusations. Before long he, too, was arrested. He was part of the Porter faction of the village that opposed the Putnams, making an accusation more probable. Meanwhile, Reverend Parris, who played a major role in the ongoing hysteria, gave a sermon addressing the issue of witchcraft and condemning Martha and Rebecca Nurse for their actions.

On September 9, 1692, Martha Corey was convicted and sentenced to hang. The following day Giles was brought to court. When he was younger, he had a bad reputation as a thief based on two incidents. Once he married Martha, however, he turned his life around and remained committed to the church. He knew that he was innocent and refused to be tried by refusing to plead guilty or innocent. At this point Giles must have known that he did not have a case and that it was very likely he would be found guilty. He further knew that the penalty for refusing to accept a trial is being crushed by heavy stones (pressed) over a period of days. According to records, this was the only time this punishment was inflicted. Giles was stripped naked and a board placed on his chest. Those watching saw heavy rocks, one after another, piled on the board. He could have ended the process by yielding, but instead asked for more heavy rocks so that he would not suffer. After two days he died at the age of eighty.

When Giles died on September 19, 1692, the witch trials were already beginning to wind down. Just one month later, the English government gave all men the right to sit on a jury. Before this change, only church members could be part of a jury. In January 1693, thirty accused people were brought before the court and had their charges dismissed, since it was found that there was no basis for prosecution. By May of that year, all of those accused had been released. Tituba had been in jail the longest—over a year. The other two accused with her had died: Sarah Good by hanging and Sarah Osborne while incarcerated. After her release, Tituba was sold to a new owner. Reverend Parris tried to win back the support of the village, without success. Instead of admitting his culpability in the witch hunts, along with the Putnams, he blamed Satan. He managed to stay in Salem until September 1697, when a council of ministers told him that he must give up his position and leave town.

Today, Salem is a city of approximately 41,000 people. There is a memorial built in 1992 to commemorate "those innocents who died during the Salem village witchcraft hysteria of 1692." Squad cars in Salem sport a witch logo that identifies the city. One of the elementary schools is known as Witchcraft Heights, and the high school teams are called the Witches. Gallows Hill, where Sarah Good and eighteen others were hanged, is now the site of an athletic field.

Even though the Salem witch trials ended over 300 years ago, events such as the Holocaust and the McCarthy era suggest that as humans, we will find new ways to cast blame on others in the name of removing evil. The child sex abuse hysteria cases of the 1980s and 1990s (discussed in Chapter 2) are more recent reminders of the extent to which unfounded accusations by children can lead to gross miscarriages of justice (Hill, 1995, 2000; Linder, 2014; Norton, 2002; Roach, 1996, 2013; Saari and Shaw, 2001; "The Salem witch trials, 1692," 2014).

Early Wrongful Murder Convictions

Documentation of early wrongful convictions for murder in America is largely unreliable or unavailable. Nevertheless, any historical discussion of wrongful convictions would be remiss without the inclusion of several cases. In this section, wrongful convictions involving two women and two men from the eighteenth and nineteenth centuries are analyzed.

Elizabeth Wilson. One of two children, Elizabeth Wilson was born in East Marlborough Township in Pennsylvania. Her father, John Wilson, was a farmer with a good reputation, although much of his property had been confiscated after the American Revolution since he had sided with the British. Elizabeth's biological mother died when she was young. When her father remarried, Elizabeth's stepmother never showed any affection toward her or her brother, William. Described in the literature as an attractive woman, Elizabeth was alternately portrayed as a devout

Christian who fell prey to an unscrupulous man who exploited her sexually or as a promiscuous woman had given birth to three illegitimate children. Regardless of which account was more accurate, Elizabeth developed a romantic interest in a man named Joseph Deshong while visiting Philadelphia. With promises of marriage, she became pregnant with twin boys. After their birth, she demanded financial support from Joseph when it became apparent that he was not going to marry her. He became incensed and killed the infants by trampling them with his boot. Shortly thereafter a hunter came on their bodies, which had been hidden in the woods. Elizabeth was charged with their deaths despite her claim that she had abandoned the infants by the side of a public road.

Her trial began in June 1785 with Judge William Augustus Atlee presiding. When Elizabeth was asked to enter a plea, she remained silent, so the judge entered a "not guilty" plea on her behalf. Because she remained reticent throughout the proceedings, her defense counsel requested and received a postponement. When the trial resumed in the fall of that year, the case against her was largely circumstantial. With the defendant's unwillingness to refute the charges, the jury reluctantly rendered a guilty verdict. She was sentenced to hang at Gallows Hills on December 7, 1785. Shortly thereafter, her father and stepmother abandoned her. Only her brother chose to remain by her side.

When William saw Elizabeth in jail on December 3, 1785, she acknowledged for the first time the role that Joseph had played in the twin's deaths. According to her confession, Joseph demanded that Elizabeth end their lives, but she refused. Consequently, he killed them and threatened to kill her if she ever disclosed what had happened. With the date for the execution drawing near, William hurriedly arranged for Judge Atlee and several other highly respected individuals to hear his sister's story. He immediately took the signed confession to the Supreme Executive Council on December 6, 1785. The council, whose president was none other than Benjamin Franklin, consented to postpone the execution until January 3, 1786, so that her case could be scrutinized more thoroughly.

With more time to devote to his sister's case, William began searching for Joseph. He eventually located him on a farm in New Jersey, whereupon Joseph denied ever having known Elizabeth. Unsuccessful in his attempt to get a confession of guilt from the victims' father, he proceeded to Philadelphia where he sought witnesses who could corroborate Elizabeth's story about her fling with Joseph. On the day prior to her scheduled hanging, William was again able to secure a postponement from the Supreme Executive Council. Armed with a note from

Charles Biddle, the vice president of the council, he began his ride to Chester, some fifteen miles from Philadelphia. When he finally arrived, he found that Elizabeth had been hung just minutes earlier. Had the ferry across the Schuylkill River been operating, he would have been on time to prevent her execution. Moreover, members of the Supreme Executive Council believed that Elizabeth was innocent and were considering granting her a full pardon. Saddened by the loss of his only sibling, William lived the rest of his life as a recluse (Executed Today, 2011).

Margaret Houghtaling. On October 17, 1817, a prostitute named Margaret Houghtaling (alias Peggy Densmore) was executed by hanging in Hudson, New York. Allegedly she had poisoned fifteen-month-old Lewis Spencer, who had been left in her care by his mother. According to a September 23, 1817, edition of the New York *Evening Post*, the child was "apparently in convulsions, its tongue protruded from the mouth, and covered with erosions." The mother, Caty Ostrander, also a prostitute, accused Margaret of killing her child. Despite her repeated claims of innocence, Margaret was swiftly brought to trial and convicted of murder. The hanging was a public spectacle attracting between 5,000 and 15,000 people. Just before she was to be hanged, Margaret reiterated her innocence by proclaiming, "God forgive you all for hanging me, but I am innocent, and my only prayer is that someday it may be proved and the black spot taken off my name and memory."

As is typical of these early wrongful convictions, multiple stories exist in the folklore to explain this miscarriage of justice. One scenario is that Caty, who later died of a sexually transmitted disease, eventually admitted that she had been responsible for poisoning Lewis and that she had falsely accused Margaret to avoid suspicion. A second scenario suggests that Lewis was actually Margaret's son and that another (unnamed) woman had poisoned him in order to seek revenge on Margaret, who had gotten the better of her in a quest for a suitor. Whether either account is accurate is impossible to ascertain, although public indignation, along with Margaret's devalued status in society, made a just trial highly improbable during this historical period (Druse, 1887; Executed Today, 2014; Jenkins, 1979).

Jesse and Stephen Boorn. These two brothers were suspected of murder when their brother-in-law Russell Colvin disappeared from Manchester, Vermont, in 1812. When bone fragments thought to be Russell's remains were discovered in 1819, Jesse was arrested. A warrant was issued for Stephen, who had relocated to New York.

Meanwhile, a jailhouse snitch falsely testified that Jesse had admitted to killing Russell and had also implicated his brother and his uncle, Amos Boorn. In return for his testimony, the informant was released from jail. Jesse eventually confessed to the murder but placed the primary onus on his brother. When Stephen unexpectedly returned to Vermont, Jesse recanted his testimony. Stephen, in the belief that he could somehow avoid the death penalty, also confessed, claiming that he acted in self-defense. Prior to the start of the trial, the two physicians who had identified the bone fragments as human recanted their earlier testimony. Nonetheless, both men were found guilty and sentenced to death. Although Jesse had his sentence commuted to life in prison, Stephen remained on death row until, through a series of fortuitous events, the supposed murder victim, who was alive and living in another state, reappeared to prevent the miscarriage of justice (Bluhm Legal Clinic, n.d. a).

Gary Dotson:
First Man to be Exonerated through DNA Analysis

In 1977 in Illinois, a sixteen-year-old girl claimed that she had been abducted by three men, one of whom raped her. Her rape kit contained several hairs found in her stained underpants, along with a vaginal swab. She assisted the police in drawing a composite sketch of the assailant, which portrayed a young, clean-shaved white man with long hair. While viewing photographs, the victim later identified Gary Dotson as the perpetrator. When taken into custody five days after the alleged incident, he had a prominent mustache that could not have been grown since the crime was committed. Nonetheless, he was sentenced in 1979 to concurrent sentences of twenty-five to fifty years for rape and aggravated kidnapping. In 1985 the victim recanted her story after admitting that she concocted it to hide the fact that she and her boyfriend had engaged in sexual relations and she was afraid that she was pregnant. Although the governor commuted Dotson's sentence to time served and placed him on parole, he was in and out of prison until August 14, 1989, when DNA testing positively excluded him as the contributor of the semen and all charges against him were dropped. On January 9, 2003, he received a full pardon from the state (Warden n.d. b).

Paula Gray:
First Woman to Be Exonerated through DNA Analysis

Seven years after DNA testing cleared Gary Dotson of any wrongdoing, Paula Gray became the first US woman to be exonerated through this procedure. Although this case is discussed in greater detail in Chapter 3, a brief synopsis of the events leading up to her wrongful conviction is included in this section.

Paula was a seventeen-year-old mildly intellectually challenged African American teenager in May 1978 when a white couple was abducted from a gasoline station in Homewood, Illinois. Their bodies were discovered the following day in Ford Heights. Both had been shot, and the woman had been raped multiple times. Four African American men were arrested based on a false tip, and Paula was brought in for questioning. After being held for two days without benefit of an attorney, she falsely confessed to being involved in the crime along with the four men. One month later, during her preliminary hearing, she recanted her story but to no avail. She was later found guilty of murder, rape, and perjury and received a sentence of fifty years. In return for the promise of early release she later testified against her codefendants. In 1996 DNA testing excluded all five defendants of involvement in the murders and rape and eventually resulted in the arrest and conviction of the actual perpetrators, who were still alive. The four men became known as the "Ford Heights Four." Paula was granted a pardon based on innocence in November 2002. Six years later she was awarded $4 million for her wrongful conviction (National Registry of Exonerations, n.d. e).

Kirk Bloodsworth:
First Death Row Inmate to Be Exonerated by DNA Testing

Just a few years after Dotson was exonerated with DNA testing, Kirk Bloodsworth was exonerated of a 1984 rape and murder using DNA testing, marking the first time in the United States an individual previously on death row was cleared through this process. Accused of raping and killing nine-year-old Dawn Hamilton in Baltimore County, Maryland, he was convicted partly on forensic evidence that matched his shoes to marks found on the child's body. Though the Maryland Court of Appeals overturned his conviction in 1986, he was subsequently retried and given two life sentences. Centurion Ministries was successful in having the DNA evidence examined by two laboratories. Their tests concluded that Bloodsworth could not have been the assailant. Released in June 1993, he received a full pardon in December 1994 (Bluhm Legal Clinic, n.d. c; Jankin, 2004).

Sabrina Butler and Debra Milke:
The Only Women on Death Row to Be Exonerated

As of this writing, no US woman on death row has been exonerated using DNA analysis. This may be at least partially attributed to the fact that women constitute less than 2 percent of those on death row. Nonetheless, two death row women—Sabrina Butler and Debra Milke— have been released and exonerated of their crimes. Sabrina was cleared in 1995 and Debra was exonerated in 2015. Their stories appear below.

In 1989 Sabrina Butler, an African American, was a teenage mother with a nine-month-old son, Walter. On April 12 of that year, she discovered her son unable to breathe. Attempts to resuscitate him were unsuccessful and shortly after her arrival at a Columbus, Mississippi, hospital the infant was pronounced dead. The hospital staff was suspicious of the circumstances because the baby had internal injuries as well. An obviously distressed Sabrina gave several different accounts of the events leading up to her son's death. She eventually signed a confession in which she claimed that she had struck her son in the abdomen because she couldn't get him to stop crying. Within a day of his death, Sabrina was officially charged with his murder.

Her trial began on March 8, 1990. The prosecutor based his case on Sabrina's sworn confession and an autopsy that disclosed numerous internal injuries and the presence of peritonitis, an internal infection. No witnesses were called to testify on her behalf. One week later a jury found her guilty and she was sentenced to death, making her the only woman on Mississippi's death row. In 1992 the Mississippi Supreme Court heard her case and vacated her conviction and sentence because the prosecutor had improperly commented on Sabrina's decision to refrain from testifying.

With a change of venue, Sabrina's second trial began in December 1995. Unlike the previous trial, testimony was presented from neighbors who corroborated Sabrina's story that she attempted to perform CPR on her son. They further acknowledged that one of the neighbors also attempted to revive the infant through CPR. Her defense also brought in a medical expert to testify that the injuries could have been the result of futile efforts to resuscitate the boy. The physician responsible for the autopsy also admitted that he had not been as thorough as he should have. Consequently, the jury acquitted Sabrina of the murder on December 17, 1995. Sometime later she received $50,000 from the state for her wrongful conviction (Asistio, 2012; Perlstein, 2003; Possley, 2015b).

Shortly after twenty-five-year-old Debra Milke received her divorce, she agreed to move in with a family friend, forty-two-year-old James Styers. At the time she was accompanied by her son, four-year-old Christopher. On December 2, 1989, James asked to use Debra's car to run some errands. Since he was going to also stop at a Phoenix shopping mall, Christopher pleaded to go with him to visit Santa Claus. Debra agreed to let him go since James had previously babysat Christopher. That afternoon around 3 p.m. Debra received a disturbing phone call from James who said that he didn't know where Christopher was, as he lost him in the mall. He assured her that he had the mall's security guards looking for him. When an hour passed and Debra had not heard back from James, she called the police, who initially suspected a possible kidnapping. Meanwhile, at the mall James and his friend, Roger Scott, were being questioned by the police.

The next day Roger was questioned by Phoenix Detective Armando Saldate, Jr. During the interrogation Roger confided the location of the child's body, some twenty miles in the desert. There the police found Christopher's bullet-ridden body. Three bullets had pierced his skull. According to Saldate, Roger confessed that he and James killed Christopher with Debra's knowledge to collect on a $5,000 insurance policy.

Saldate later interrogated Debra while she was visiting her father in Florence, Arizona. During that interrogation, which was not recorded or witnessed by any other parties, Saldate claimed Debra admitted to conspiring to have her son killed. During the trial he also testified that she let him see her breasts and offered sex in return for releasing her. Although there was no physical or forensic evidence connecting her to the crime, in October 1990 Debra was convicted by a jury of capital murder, child abuse, kidnapping, and conspiracy and sentenced to death. In separate trials, James and Roger were also found guilty and sentenced to death.

The possibility of being found innocent seemed remote in 1993 when the Arizona Supreme Court upheld her convictions and sentence. It wasn't until March 2013 that Debra finally received some good news. The US Court of Appeals for the Ninth Circuit set aside her convictions and sentence and ordered a new trial after it was discovered that Saldate had lied under oath about the confession and had a history of lying. He had even received a five-day suspension for lying to his superiors when he took "liberties" with a female motorist whom he had stopped. Although the prosecution was aware of the transgressions of its star witness, no knowledge of the officer's past was made available to Debra's defense counsel during the trial.

Debra was released on bond in September 2013, but her ordeal was not over. When it became apparent that the Maricopa County District Attorney's office intended to retry her case, her attorneys filed a motion to dismiss the charges. They contended that to retry her would be tantamount to double jeopardy given the serious nature of the prosecutorial misconduct. In January 2014 the Maricopa County Superior Court denied the motion. Later that same year the Arizona Court of Appeals overturned the Superior Court's decision and ordered the charges dropped. With only one option left, prosecutors appealed to the Arizona Supreme Court, which refused to review the case. Finally, Debra was officially exonerated when Superior Court Judge Rosa Mroz dismissed the charges against her on March 23, 2015.

Now fifty-one years of age, Debra, who spent twenty-two years of her life on death row, struggles to find a peaceful resolution to her life. A psychiatrist is helping her come to grips with her circumstances. Nonetheless, she admits that she feels "like a stranger in her own city" as she attempts to adjust to the changes in society that occurred during her absence (Ahmed and Botelho, 2015; Associated Press, 2015; Kiefer, 2015; Possley, 2015a).

The Prevalence of Wrongful Convictions in the United States

Any attempt to count wrongful convictions in the United States is subject to uncertainty. Because programs such as the Innocence Project tend to focus on cases involving murder and rape, which are more likely than other offenses to elicit strong sanctions, many wrongful convictions involving less serious offenses are undoubtedly overlooked. Furthermore, preoccupation with these male-dominated crimes decreases the probability that the defendant will be a woman. Because a conviction for a less serious crime may culminate in probation or a suspended sentence, a wrongly convicted defendant may have little incentive to seek redress (Gross et al., 2005). Additionally, if the wrongly convicted defendant has a checkered past, a legal remedy may not appear to be a realistic option. Even the use of statistics on successful appeals to approximate the frequency of wrongful convictions is problematic. As Marvin Free and Mitch Ruesink (2012) note: "innocence alone does not guarantee a successful appeal and a successful appeal does not necessarily demonstrate *factual innocence*, given that convictions may be overturned on the basis of procedural errors alone" (p. 4).

Determining the extent to which these miscarriages of justice permeate the US criminal justice system is made even more arduous because scholars have used different definitions, employed different methodologies, and made different assumptions in estimating the scope of the problem. While the actual number of wrongful convictions is unknowable, many scholars have estimated that from 3 to 5 percent of all convictions may involve a faulty finding of guilty (Gould and Leo, 2010). Because the known wrongful convictions tend to be concentrated among murders and rapes, we know relatively little about convictions for lesser crimes. Although Samuel Gross (2008) suggests that errors may be less common among the less serious offenses, Jon Gould and Richard Leo (2010) argue that errors may be more pronounced in cases involving less serious felonies and misdemeanors. They speculate "that errors are more common, and more commonly accepted, in cases where neither police nor prosecutors have as much time, resources, or pressure to investigate cases thoroughly and in which the lesser stakes of punishment do not command as many or as zealous advocates to investigate postconviction" (Gould and Leo, 2010, p. 836).

Known cases of wrongful convictions in the United States can be obtained from several sources. The Innocence Project, for instance, contains data on DNA exonerations. According to that website, 316 individuals have been exonerated through DNA testing as of April 2014. Eighteen of the exonerations involved cases in which the defendant had received a death sentence. African Americans were disproportionately represented among the DNA exonerations: over 60 percent of the cases involved African American defendants (Innocence Project n.d. d).

The Death Penalty Information Center (DPIC) contains information on Americans on death row who have "been acquitted of all charges related to the crime that placed them on death row, or had all charges related to the crime that placed them on death row dismissed by the prosecution, or been granted a complete pardon based on evidence of innocence" since 1973 (Death Penalty Information Center, n.d.). As of April 2014, the DPIC lists the exoneration of 144 individuals who were serving time on death row. Slightly over half of the wrongfully convicted inmates were African American.

Created by Hans Sherrer in 1997, the forejustice.org website contains in excess of 4,600 wrongful conviction cases from more than 110 countries. Almost 2,800 cases are from the United States, some dating back to the early seventeenth century. Approximately 60 percent of the US cases involve wrongful convictions for murder and rape/sexual assault (Forejustice, 2014).

The Center on Wrongful Convictions at Northwestern University has tracked wrongful convictions since its inception in 1998. A list of known exonerations from the United States is broken down by state and the District of Columbia, although little information is available on most of the cases listed at the website.

Arguably the most complete listing of US exonerations since 1989 is available from the National Registry of Exonerations (NRE), a joint effort between the law schools of the University of Michigan and Northwestern University. Launched in May 2012, the NRE lists 1,325 exonerees—only 8 percent of which were women—as of March 2014. African Americans composed 46 percent of those exonerated. Slightly over three-fourths of the wrongful convictions were for either homicide or sexual assault, and 28 percent of the cases were exonerated at least in part by DNA evidence (National Registry of Exonerations, n.d. f).

Factors Associated with Wrongful Convictions

The wrongful conviction literature has typically ignored issues of gender and race. Consequently, the underlying causes have not been adequately addressed. Societal issues such as the marginalization of women and minorities and institutional racism are potential explanatory variables that have been mostly unexplored by scholars in the field. Thus legislation that is neither gender- nor race-neutral, selective law enforcement, the underrepresentation of women in the areas of policing and judicial positions of authority, and the societal double standard that imposes greater responsibility on women for the protection and care of their offspring may precede a false conviction by disproportionately involving these individuals in the judicial system. Drug legislation, in particular, has adversely affected women and minorities (Beckett et al., 2006; Bush-Baskette, 1998; Lurigio and Loose, 2008; Mauer, 1999; Tonry 1994, 1995, 2010, 2011). Although these issues are important precursors to wrongful convictions, researchers have tended to focus on those factors that enhance the probability of a wrongful conviction *after* the individual has come to the attention of the criminal justice system. Among the more frequently documented factors are witness errors (including mistaken and deliberate misidentification), false confessions, prosecutorial and police misconduct, use of informants or snitches, perjury by criminal justice officials, forensic errors (including misrepresentation of forensic findings and the use of junk science), ineffective assistance of counsel, and insufficient evidence to support a conviction.

Witness Error

Research suggests that witness error is the most common factor in many wrongful convictions (Scheck et al., 2003). According to the Innocence Project (n.d. e), witness error was a factor in approximately three-fourths of all convictions that were overturned through DNA evidence.

However, the extent to which witness error accompanies wrongful convictions may vary by type of offense and the gender of the defendant. Witness error was a recurring theme in almost 93 percent of the wrongful rape and sexual assault convictions but only 43 percent of the wrongful murder convictions of African American men (Free and Ruesink, 2012). In contrast, an examination of wrongly convicted women by Mitch Ruesink and Marvin Free (2005) revealed that witness error was present in less than one-fifth of their cases.

The misidentification of suspects is a problem that is recognized by many professionals in criminal justice. C. Ronald Huff, Arye Rattner, and Edward Sagarin (1996) found that witness error was perceived as the most important factor associated with wrongful convictions by criminal justice personnel in their survey. Unintentional witness error can be influenced by psychological, systemic, societal, and cultural factors. For instance, exposure time, level of illumination, observer distance, amount of violence, and postevent factors are psychological variables affecting the accuracy of the identification. Some of the systemic factors that can affect one's perception include lineups in which only one person resembles the alleged perpetrator and lineups in which the suspect is of a different race than others. Personal prejudice, stereotypes, and expectations based on past experience represent potentially important societal and cultural influences (Ruesink and Free, 2005). Cross-racial identifications are especially problematic. Many misidentifications have occurred when white eyewitnesses have attempted to identify black subjects (Meissner and Brigham, 2001; Rutledge, 2001).

False Confessions

False confessions represent another factor that commonly appears in the wrongful conviction scholarship (Gould and Leo, 2010; Leo and Davis, 2010; Ofshe and Leo, 1997). The degree to which false confessions contribute to wrongful convictions varies considerably in the research. An investigation in Illinois revealed that false confessions played a role in over half of the wrongful convictions (Warden and Fredrickson, 2012). Nationally, approximately a fourth of all DNA exonerations are the result of false confessions (Innocence Project, n.d. f). Yet false confessions are less prevalent when non-DNA wrongful convictions are examined. The National Registry of Exonerations reports that false confessions were present in only 16 percent of the exonerations in the United States from 1989 to 2012 (Gross and Shaffer, 2012). Apparently, the importance of this factor also varies according to the type of offense with which the defendant is charged. False confessions were a contributing factor to wrongful murder convictions in 18.4 percent of the cases involving African American men, whereas they were found in only 10 percent of the cases involving rape and sexual assault (Free and Ruesink, 2012).

Scholars have observed a number of factors that may affect the probability of a false confession. The age and mental capacity of the defendant appear to be associated with the likelihood of falsely confessing. Samuel Gross and Michael Shaffer (2012) found that juveniles were five times more likely than were adults to confess falsely. Similarly, mentally challenged defendants were nine times more likely than those without such deficiencies to confess to a crime they did not commit. Extended interrogations are also more likely to produce false confessions. In addition, duress, coercion, intoxication, a misunderstanding of the law, fear of the police, threat of a long sentence if a confession is not forthcoming, and a misunderstanding of the situation may increase the probability of a false confession (Innocence Project, n.d. f).

Prosecutorial and Police Misconduct

Prosecutorial and police misconduct are among the most frequently encountered factors associated with wrongful convictions. Barry Scheck, Peter Neufeld, and Jim Dwyer (2003) report that prosecutorial misconduct was present in 42 percent of the DNA exonerations they investigated. Furthermore, police misconduct was a factor in half of the cases. An extensive analysis of over 4,000 state and federal appellate rulings in California from 1997 through 2009 by the Northern California Innocence Project disclosed that prosecutorial misconduct was present in 707 cases. In about 20 percent of these cases prosecutorial misconduct was deemed so harmful to the defendants that the courts "set aside the conviction or sentence, declared a mistrial, or barred evidence" (Ridolfi and Possley, 2010, p. 4). More recently, an examination of wrongly convicted African American men revealed that prosecutorial and police misconduct were present in 36.2 percent and 38.5 percent of the murder cases, respectively. Less prevalent in sexual assault cases, prosecutorial misconduct and police misconduct occurred in approximately 15 percent and approximately 23 percent of the cases, respectively (Free and Ruesink, 2012).

Nevertheless, the full impact of prosecutorial misconduct cannot be ascertained by merely analyzing known wrongful convictions. In numerous instances it goes undetected or, if detected, it is tolerated without penalty. The doctrine of "harmless error" has been used to allow trials to continue or to uphold convictions (Weinberg, 2003). The

Northern California Innocence Project, for instance, found that approximately 80 percent of their prosecutorial misconduct cases resulted in rulings that the misconduct was harmless and the defendant still received a fair trial (Ridolfi and Possley, 2010).

Prosecutorial misconduct can manifest itself in myriad ways, the most typical of which involves withholding exculpatory evidence (Gould and Leo, 2010). Many illustrations of this kind of misconduct exist in the literature. For example, it may involve inappropriate behavior during grand jury proceedings; dismissal of potential jurors based on their race, ethnicity, or gender; harassment or bias toward the defendant or defense attorney; use of known false or misleading evidence; withholding relevant information about the prosecution's witness (e.g., the witness received immunity or other incentives in return for testifying); and the use of improper closing arguments (Gershman, 1991; Huff et al., 1996; Weinberg, 2003). Additionally, prosecutors may mischaracterize the facts or evidence of the case, mishandle evidence, and badger, threaten, or tamper with witnesses (Davis, 2007). In contrast, police misconduct may involve "coaching" the witness in identifying a particular suspect during a lineup; use of deceit, force, threat, or brutality to secure a confession; planting evidence at a crime scene; mishandling physical evidence; and threatening a potential witness for the defense (Free and Ruesink, 2012).

Use of Informants or Snitches
The use of an informant or snitch has been implicated in a number of wrongful convictions, although the pervasiveness of this problem appears to vary considerably in the literature. For instance, the Innocence Project reports that informant testimony was a factor in over 15 percent of the wrongful conviction cases involving DNA evidence (Innocence Project, n.d. h). In many cases the jury had not been informed that the informant/snitch had been paid to testify against the defendant or had been released from prison in exchange for the testimony and therefore had an incentive to lie. Data from the Center on Wrongful Convictions suggest that the problem of using testimony from an informant/snitch is even more prevalent. Of the 111 death row exonerations examined in their report, snitch testimony was present in almost 46 percent of the cases, making it the most common factor in death penalty wrongful convictions (Warden, 2005). When wrongly convicted cases are restricted to African American men, the extent to which the use of informants/snitches results in wrongful convictions varies by type of offense. Informant/snitch testimony was present in one-third of the

black male wrongful murder convictions but in only one case involving wrongful sexual assault convictions (Free and Ruesink, 2012).

Racial disparity in drug enforcement is exacerbated by police use of informants/snitches. Loyola University Law Professor Alexandra Natapoff (2009) contends that because the police tend to focus their attention on high-crime urban communities, which are typically heavily populated with people of color, minority citizens are under closer scrutiny than their more affluent white counterparts residing in the suburbs. Since many police informants also reside in these high-crime areas and since they often have an incentive to lie, they are frequently unreliable sources of information. The overexposure of these minority inhabitants means that "false accusations, mistaken warrants, erroneous raids, and wrongful convictions associated with snitches will be more frequent in communities in which the practice is prevalent" (Natapoff, 2009, p. 113).

Perjury by Criminal Justice Officials
Perjured testimony from law enforcement, attorneys, and judges either before or during a trial has been identified as a factor in some wrongful convictions. Although not exclusively the province of wrongful drug convictions, some of the more notable mass drug arrests in the United States have been the product of perjury by criminal justice officials. In 1999 in the small town of Tulia, Texas, for example, forty-six people (thirty-nine of whom were African American) were arrested on drug-related charges based solely on the perjured testimony of Tom Coleman, an undercover police officer. Although none of the suspects possessed drugs at the time of the arrests, some received sentences of up to ninety years (Blakeslee, 2002). Coleman was eventually convicted of aggravated perjury and sentenced to ten years of probation (Stecklein, 2009). The impact of this failed drug bust on women is discussed in greater detail in Chapter 4.

Another miscarriage of justice involving perjured testimony occurred in 2005 in Mansfield, Ohio, where twenty-three people were arrested on alleged drug transactions set up by a paid informant, Jerrell Bray. By May 2007, seventeen of those arrested had been convicted on federal drug charges and sentenced to prison (sixteen of those convicted were African American). Bray was later arrested for an unrelated crime and while incarcerated confessed that he and Lee Lucas, a longtime Drug Enforcement Administration (DEA) agent, fabricated their stories to secure convictions. Bray was eventually charged with two counts of perjury and five counts of deprivation of civil rights and received a fifteen-year sentence. In contrast, Lucas, who had also been suspected of lying in some Florida drug cases when he was assigned to the Miami DEA office, received an eighteen-count indictment by a federal grand jury for perjury, making false statements, and violating the civil rights of three people. In 2010 Lucas was acquitted of all charges. That same month, Richland County, Ohio, sheriff's deputy Chuck Metcalf was found guilty of perjury for lying during the trial of one of the individuals convicted. He was subsequently sentenced to twelve weekends in jail for his role in the frame-up (Caniglia, 2009; Kroll, 2008e; Krouse, 2010a, 2010b; Love, 2009; Turner, 2009).

Forensic Errors

Flawed analysis of the biological evidence, misleading or false interpretations of the results, the mishandling of forensic evidence, and the use of questionable forensic evidence have all contributed to wrongful convictions. Fingerprinting analysis, traditionally one of the most common practices for identifying suspects, has recently been criticized for "a lack of validity testing and an absence of validated standards for declaring a match" (Gould and Leo, 2010, p. 852). Bite mark analysis, hair comparison analysis, and serology analysis (used to determine if a suspect and the perpetrator share the same blood type) are also unreliable. Furthermore, DNA testing can result in a false positive. Large-scale errors in forensic testing have been reported by the Federal Bureau of Investigation ("Errors at F.B.I.," 2003) and the US Army Criminal Investigation Laboratory (Taylor and Doyle, 2011). Several states have also discovered such problems as "contaminated evidence, mislabeled blood samples, falsified DNA data, inflated statistical matches of DNA evidence, and questionable testimony by forensic experts or laboratory managers" (Free and Ruesink, 2012, p. 10).

The role of forensic errors in wrongful convictions appears to fluctuate depending on the offense. An examination of US exonerations from 1989 through 2012 disclosed that false or misleading forensic evidence was present in 37 percent of the sexual assault cases, 23 percent of the homicide cases, and 21 percent of the child sex abuse cases. Forensic errors were additionally present in 17 percent of other violent crimes. Conversely, forensic problems were present in only 6 percent of the wrongful convictions for robbery and 3 percent of the wrongful convictions for nonviolent offenses (Gross and Shaffer, 2012). Forensic issues are also frequently among the factors cited in DNA exonerations. The Innocence Project (n.d. g) found that unvalidated or improper forensic science was present in about half of the false convictions overturned by DNA evidence.

Ineffective Assistance of Counsel

Incompetent lawyering by the defense counsel can take many forms. Some of the more common manifestations of ineffective assistance of counsel include failure to appear for hearings, falling asleep during the trial, failure to investigate alibis, and failure to consult experts on forensic issues. The Innocence Project reports that in one case, legal representation by the defense counsel was so inadequate that an attorney was disbarred after completing a capital case (Innocence Project, n.d. b). Among the factors that may contribute to ineffective legal representation are inadequate funding for indigent clients, a failure to monitor the quality of legal representation provided by defense attorneys, a lack of motivation, and the presumption of guilt that pervades the criminal justice system (Bernhard, 2001; Gould and Leo, 2010).

The prevalence of ineffective assistance of counsel is probably minimized in much of the wrongful conviction research because it is difficult to demonstrate when appealing a decision. In 1984 the use of this argument was further diminished when the US Supreme Court ruled in *Strickland v. Washington* (466 US 668, 104 S. Ct. 2052 [1984]) that for ineffective assistance of counsel to be the grounds for an appeal, the appellate court must be convinced that if the defense attorney had pursued a more rigorous course of action the verdict would have been different. Moreover, the justices ruled that in ascertaining the effectiveness of counsel, "A court must indulge a strong presumption that counsel's performance was within the wide range of reasonable professional assistance." A recent investigation of DNA exonerations in which potentially innocent defendants raised claims of ineffective assistance of counsel reveals the extent to which these claims are rejected by appellate courts. Of the fifty-four cases that qualified, forty-four were rejected. Three additional cases were either deemed harmless errors or were remanded to lower courts for further review. Only seven cases (13 percent) resulted in the appellate courts concurring with the appellants (West, 2010).

The extent to which ineffective legal counsel appears in the literature varies considerably. Whereas Hugo Bedau and Michael Radelet (1987) found this problem in less than 3 percent of their wrongful convictions, an investigation of capital appeals revealed that ineffective assistance of counsel was the primary contributing factor to false convictions (Liebman et al., 2000). Moreover, Scheck and colleagues (2003) observed ineffective assistance of counsel in 27 percent of the cases exonerated through DNA evidence. Free and Ruesink (2012) found that ineffective lawyering was present in 11.5 percent and 11 percent of wrongful murder convictions and wrongful sexual assault/rape convictions, respectively, in their study of wrongly convicted African American men.

Insufficient Evidence to Support a Conviction
Though considerably less prevalent than the preceding factors, insufficient evidence to support a conviction is a possible factor in wrongful convictions. This factor is easily overlooked, in part because wrongful conviction research tends to focus on high-profile cases such as murder and rape that may have ample evidence. It may also be undercounted because a determination of the sufficiency of the evidence is more subjective than many of the other factors discussed here. Regardless, there are documented instances in which appellate courts have acknowledged that a defendant was found guilty without enough evidence to support the conviction. The limited scholarship examining this factor suggests that both the offense and the race of the defendant may be important. Whereas insufficient evidence was a factor in 5.7 percent of the wrongful murder convictions involving African American men, it represented less than 1 percent of the wrongful convictions for rape and sexual assault among this population (Free and Ruesink, 2012). Among women, distinct racial differences have been observed. Ruesink and Free (2005) found that insufficient evidence did not appear among the list of factors for any of the African American women in their sample, yet insufficient evidence was present in 15 percent of the cases involving white women.

The Special Case of Wrongfully Convicted Women

Despite recent growth of scholarship in this area, little research has focused on potential gender differences among wrongful convictions. Because the most egregious wrongful convictions have involved murder and rape—offenses that are predominantly the domain of men—the issue has been framed as a male problem.[1] The occasional female wrongful conviction to come to light is thus seen as the exception rather than the rule. Consequently, the potential significance of wrongful convictions involving women has been largely ignored by scholars until recently.

Although most of the literature has concentrated on wrongly convicted men,[2] the limited scholarship in this area points to nuanced differences between men and women who have been wrongly convicted. As noted already, female exonerees are considerably more likely than their male counterparts to be wrongly convicted of nonexistent crimes. In a recent NRE study, only 15 percent of the male exonerees and 58 percent of the female exonerees had been convicted of a crime that never occurred. NRE data further reveal that women are much more likely than men to be wrongly convicted of violent crimes against children: over half versus 18 percent, respectively (National Registry of Exonerations, 2013).

Another area in which wrongful convictions of men and women differ involves the availability of DNA evidence from the crime scene. Women, for instance, are more likely than men to be incarcerated for offenses in which biological evidence that could be used to verify their innocence is unavailable. Whereas DNA evidence is routinely gathered in male-dominated murder and rape cases, it is not typically collected in drug offenses and nonviolent crimes for which female prisoners are more likely to be incarcerated (Konvisser, 2012; Smith and Hattery, 2011). Since the Innocent Project accepts only those cases in which DNA evidence can be tested to prove innocence, the probability of a wrongful conviction involving a woman being selected is substantially lower than that involving a man.

Nor are all female wrongful convictions alike. Although the scholarship in this area is sparse, it appears that there are racial differences in the types of crimes which lead to wrongful conviction. In particular, white women are more likely than black women to be wrongfully convicted for some form of child abuse. Conversely, black women are more likely than their white counterparts to be falsely convicted for drug offenses (Free and Ruesink, forthcoming; Konvisser, 2012; Ruesink and Free, 2005). Racial differences have also been observed regarding the relative importance of the factors associated with wrongful convictions. Perjury by criminal justice officials, for example, appears to be a more frequent factor associated with wrongful convictions among black women than among white women. In a recent study perjury by criminal justice officials was found in 53 percent of the wrongful convictions involving black women. In contrast, this factor was found in only 4 percent of the cases in which white women had been wrongly convicted (Ruesink and Free, 2005).

The significance of race in wrongful convictions varies along gender lines as well. Black women constituted 28 percent (Konvisser, 2012) and 35.7 percent (Ruesink and Free, 2005) of the total number of wrongfully convicted women in two investigations. However, an NRE investigation primarily composed of men found that 47.3 of the exonerees were black (National Registry of Exonerations, 2013). It thus appears that black males are more likely than their female counterparts to be found among the known cases of wrongful conviction.

The Study

Identifying and Researching the Cases

The Internet is replete with websites purporting to exhibit cases involving wrongful convictions, yet the inability to ascertain the veracity of the data through independent sources inhibits the utility of these websites. To maximize the probability of including only those cases in which convicted defendants are factually innocent, the wrongful convictions analyzed in this book were primarily obtained from six websites that are frequently cited in the wrongful conviction scholarship. Databases from the Center on Wrongful Convictions, the Innocence Project, the Death Penalty Information Center, the National Registry of Exonerations, and forejustice.org were critically scrutinized for wrongful conviction cases from the United States in which the defendant was a woman. In addition, *Justice Denied*, an electronic and print magazine devoted exclusively to false convictions, was examined to supplement information obtained from the previous sources. Although the websites have limitations, collectively they represent a reliable repository of information on known wrongful convictions in the United States.

Computer searches were used to identify magazine and newspaper articles pertaining to the cases. When feasible, we sought to reconcile contradictory information and/or incomplete data by contacting journalists and attorneys familiar with the false convictions. To locate wrongful convictions that were excluded from the six main websites, we also conducted several computer searches using generic terms (e.g., wrongful conviction, false conviction, innocent) to identify individuals who were factually innocent but not formally cleared of their charges. After the case identification phase was terminated in 2013, a select number were investigated in greater depth through phone conversations with the individual who had been erroneously convicted. (The terms "false convictions" and "erroneous convictions" are used interchangeably to refer to wrongful convictions.) To limit the sample to more contemporary cases, only known false convictions since 1970 were selected. This resulted in a usable sample of 163 women. For more detailed information on the methodology and selection of websites, please refer to Appendix A.

Characteristics of the Sample

Table 1.1 contains a detailed breakdown of the sample characteristics. The 25.8 percent representation by black women in the sample compares favorably to the 28 percent figure reported by Konvisser (2012), although it is considerably lower than the 37 percent figure reported by Ruesink and Free (2005). However, if only those cases in which it was

Table 1.1 Sample Characteristics and Findings (*N* = 163)

Characteristic	Percentage of Cases
Race	
White	57.0
Black	25.8
Other	4.3
Unknown	12.9
Most Serious Charge	
Murder	36.8
Child abuse	27
Drugs	12.3
Fraud	3.1
Manslaughter	2.5
Arson	1.2
Burglary	1.2
Rape	<1
Robbery	<1
Other	14.7
Sentence	
Not sentenced	6.1
Probation	6.1
Fine only	1.2
Fine and community service	<1
Suspended sentence	1.2
<1 year	3.7
1–5 years	11
6–10 years	13.5
11–15 years	4.3
16–20 years	5.5
>20 years	13.5
Life	24.5
Death	3.7
Other	<1
Unknown	4.3
Years in Jail/Prison	
0	14.7
<1 year	8.6
1–5 years	38.7
6–10 years	12.9
11–15 years	4.3
16–20 years	6.7
>20 years	2.5
Incarcerated	5.5
Unknown	5.5[a]
Age When Convicted	
Mean age: 33 years old	
Range: 11–61 years old	
Unknown	16%

Table 1.1 Continued

Characteristic	Percentage of Cases
Age When Released	
Mean age: 39.1 years old	
Range: 14–69 years old	
Not released	6.1
Executed	<1
Not applicable	15.3
Unknown	12.3
Exonerated Through DNA Testing	
Yes	4.3
No	95.7
Factors Related to the Wrongful Conviction	
Prosecutorial misconduct	40.5
Police misconduct	30.1
Eyewitness error	23.9
Forensic errors	21.5
Perjury by criminal justice officials	20.2
Ineffective assistance of counsel	19
False confession	17.2
Informant/snitch	13.5
Insufficient evidence	13.5
Other	28.2
Unknown	<1

Note: a. There was one case involving nine years of house arrest.

possible to determine the racial identity of the innocent are used in ascertaining the racial breakdown of the sample, then black women constituted 29.6 percent of the sample, a figure that lies between that recorded by Konvisser (2012) and Ruesink and Free (2005).

An analysis of the most serious charge among the sample reveals that murder and child abuse are the two most common offenses resulting in a false conviction. Collectively, they compose nearly two-thirds of the cases in the sample. The third most common charge involved drugs but it was present in only about one-eighth of the cases. A particularly interesting characteristic of the female wrongful convictions is the diversity of the offenses with which women are charged. Almost 15 percent of the women were charged with crimes not included among the nine offense categories selected for the study. Hence female wrongful convictions tend to exhibit greater offense diversity than those typically attributed to male wrongful convictions.

The most common sentence among the falsely convicted women was a life sentence. Virtually one of every four cases involved this sentence. An additional 13.5 percent received sentences in excess of twenty years. The death sentence was very rare, occurring in less than 4 percent of the cases. Though 6.1 percent of the sample was either not sentenced or placed on some form of probation, the overall distribution of sentences reveals that wrongly convicted women typically received rather harsh sanctions for their alleged transgressions.

Despite the somewhat lengthy sentences that many women received, the actual jail and prison time was typically short. Almost 15 percent of the women were never incarcerated, and an additional 8.6 percent were incarcerated for less than one year. The most common period of incarceration was one to five years. Practically one in four women in the sample fell into this category. In other words, 62 percent of the women spent zero to five years in jail or prison even though their sentences were frequently long. These findings notwithstanding, four women (2.5 percent) were falsely imprisoned for over twenty years and nine women (5.5 percent) remained in prison during the time of the investigation.

It was possible to determine the age at conviction for 84 percent of the sample. Those cases revealed a mean age of thirty-three years with a range from eleven to sixty-one years of age. The mean age, nevertheless, was somewhat misleading as the most common age was twenty-nine ($n = 11$), followed by twenty-three ($n = 9$) and twenty-six ($n = 8$). Moreover, the largest category was women in their twenties ($n = 48$). Women in their thirties made up the second largest category with forty cases.

The age at release was additionally calculated. Excluded from this analysis were those cases in which individuals were never incarcerated, those cases in which individuals remained incarcerated, a single case in which the woman had been executed, and cases in which it was impossible to establish the age at release. Of the remaining 107 women, the mean age at release was 39.1 years old and the range of ages extended from 14 to 69 years. The most common age was thirty-seven ($n = 8$), followed by forty-four ($n = 7$) and thirty-three ($n = 6$). A further breakdown of the data discloses that the largest category was women in their thirties ($n = 39$), and the second largest category was women in their forties ($n = 27$).

The role of DNA testing in the exonerations was also examined. DNA evidence was at least partially responsible for the determination of innocence in only 4.3 percent of the cases. Conversely, almost 96 percent of the women were cleared without the advantage of DNA testing. This finding suggests that future female wrongful conviction cases will not be the beneficiaries of increased reliance on DNA evidence to prove innocence to any great extent.

The Findings

Gender Differences. As in male false convictions, female false convictions frequently result from multiple factors that coalesce to produce the erroneous conviction. An examination of the factors related to the wrongful convictions discloses that prosecutorial misconduct (40.5 percent) tops the list. This percentage approximates the 42 percent figure reported by Scheck and colleagues (2003) in their examination of predominantly male DNA exonerations. The second most frequent contributing factor to female wrongful convictions is police misconduct, present in 30.1 percent of the cases. When contrasted with the DNA exoneration study mentioned previously, it appears that police misconduct plays a more instrumental role in male false convictions. The earlier study found that police misconduct contributed to the miscarriage of justice in half of the DNA exonerations.

Eyewitness error was present in almost one-fourth of the cases in the sample, making it the third most frequently occurring factor. This number compares favorably with an earlier study by Ruesink and Free (2005) that reported the presence of eyewitness error in 19 percent of female wrongful convictions. When compared to the recent findings by Gross and Shaffer (2012), however, eyewitness error appears to be more problematic in male wrongful convictions than in female wrongful convictions. Their investigation of predominantly male exonerations disclosed that mistaken witness identification was a contributing factor in 43 percent of their cases. Eyewitness error may exert an even greater impact on false rape and sexual assault convictions involving African American men. Free and Ruesink (2012) report that eyewitness error was present in almost 93 percent of the cases in which African American men had been wrongly convicted of rape and sexual assault. Furthermore, eyewitness error was present in almost 43 percent of their wrongful murder convictions, making this the most common factor among wrongly convicted black men for both offense categories.

Forensic errors represent the fourth most frequently occurring factor in the sample, being found in 21.5 percent of the cases. A comparable figure was reported by Gross and Shaffer (2012) in their predominantly male sample. Closely following forensic errors are perjury by criminal justice officials, which prevailed in 20.2 percent of the cases. Ineffective assistance of counsel was present in 19 percent of the cases. The extent to which gender differences exist between these two factors is unclear. Gross and Shaffer (2012), for instance, report that perjury or false accusations were present in over half of their exonerations, although their variable was more broadly conceived than that used in this investigation. Moreover, as observed earlier, because of its subjective nature, ineffective assistance of counsel tends to be underreported, thereby precluding an analysis of gender distinctions.

The seventh most common factor associated with wrongful convictions in the sample was false confessions. Slightly over 17 percent of the cases included this factor. Whereas a much smaller percentage was reported by Ruesink and Free (2005) in their investigation of falsely convicted women, this percentage is close to the 15 percent found in exonerees in the study by Gross and Shaffer (2012). The importance of false confessions in male wrongful convictions, however, appears to vary by offense (Free and Ruesink, 2012; Gross and Shaffer, 2012).

Of the major factors associated with false convictions, the use of an informant/snitch and insufficient evidence to support a conviction were present in the smallest number of cases. Each factor appeared in 13.5 percent of the wrongful convictions. Whereas a slightly lower percentage of incidents involving an informant/snitch was documented by Ruesink and Free (2005) in their investigation of wrongfully convicted women, the frequency with which this occurs in studies analyzing predominantly male wrongful convictions has varied widely (see, for example, Innocence Project, n.d. h; Warden, 2005).

The extent to which gender differences exist in cases in which there is insufficient evidence to support a conviction is difficult to evaluate. It is likely that much of the wrongful conviction literature neglects this factor given its tendency to focus on high-profile cases such as murder and rape in which there is potentially a greater abundance of evidence. Nonetheless, some evidence suggests that falsely convicted men are less likely than falsely convicted women to be affected by this problem. In Free and Ruesink's (2012) study of wrongfully convicted African American men, for example, insufficient evidence to support a conviction was present in only 5.7 percent of the murder convictions and less than 1 percent of the rape and sexual assault convictions.

Of special interest in this investigation is the fact that factors other than those commonly examined in the literature were present in 28.2 percent of the female false convictions. The variety of factors indicates a greater constellation of factors are responsible for the wrongful conviction of women than for men. The results of this investigation thereby suggest the need to expand the range of factors examined in female wrongful convictions beyond those typically associated with this miscarriage of justice.

Racial Differences. Some interesting results emerge when racial differences are examined (see Table 1.2). Two particularly noteworthy findings involve racial differences in drug violations and child abuse offenses. While 38.1 percent of the black women were falsely convicted of drug violations, only 3.2 percent of their white counterparts were falsely convicted of this offense. Huge racial differences were apparent among wrongful child abuse convictions as well. Almost 38 percent of the white women were charged with this offense compared to slightly over 2 percent of the black women. Although modest differences prevailed among the remaining offenses, the miscellaneous category (other) exhibits racial differences. Whereas slightly over one of every ten white women was falsely convicted for a crime that fell outside the nine offense categories used in this research, almost one of every five black women was falsely convicted of a miscellaneous crime.

A breakdown of the sentences for wrongfully convicted white and black women discloses some racial differences as well. White women were more likely than their black counterparts to receive long sentences. For instance, 16.1 percent of the white women received a sentence in excess of twenty years. The comparable figure for black women was 11.9 percent. Moreover, nearly one-third of the white women in the sample were sentenced to life in prison compared to less than one-eighth of the black women in the sample. The greater presence of white women in these categories is largely a function of their greater representation among the cases involving murder and child abuse, offenses that are likely to elicit harsh sanctions. Nevertheless, white and black women had similar chances of receiving a death sentence: 4.3 percent of the white women and 4.8 percent of the black women were sentenced to death.

When the analysis turns to cases in which women received some form of probation or incarceration for less than a year, white women again fared worse than their black counterparts. Almost 12 percent of the black women received probation compared to only 4.3 percent of the white women. When the data are further disaggregated, it is discovered that this discrepancy is due primarily to a high concentration of drug cases among black women. Four of the five black probation cases involved violations of drug laws. White women were additionally less likely than black women to receive sentences of less than one year. A

Table 1.2 Comparative Statistics for White and Black Women
(*N* = 135; white = 93; black = 42)

	White	Black
Most Serious Charge		
Murder	39.8%	33.3%
Child abuse	37.6%	2.4%
Drugs	3.2%	38.1%
Fraud	4.3%	—
Manslaughter	1.1%	4.8%
Arson	1.1%	2.4%
Burglary	1.1%	—
Rape	1.1%	—
Robbery	—	—
Other	10.8%	19.0%
Sentence		
Not sentenced	3.2%	7.1%
Probation	4.3%	11.9%
Fine only	1.1%	2.4%
Fine and community service	1.1%	—
Suspended sentence	2.2%	2.4%
<1 year	1.1%	9.5%
1-5 years	10.8%	9.5%
6-10 years	12.9%	11.9%
11-15 years	2.2%	7.1%
16-20 years	5.4%	9.5%
>20 years	16.1%	11.9%
Life	32.2%	11.9%
Death	4.3%	4.8%
Other	—	—
Unknown	3.2%	—
Years in Jail/Prison		
0	12.9%	16.7%
<1 year	4.3%	21.4%
1-5 years	40.9%	35.7%
6-10 years	16.1%	4.8%
11-15 years	6.5%	—
16-20 years	5.4%	11.9%
>20 years	3.2%	2.4%
Incarcerated	7.5%	7.1%
Unknown	3.2%	—
Age When Convicted		
Mean age	34.9 years old	29.4 years old
Range	16–61 years old	11–57 years old
Unknown	16.1%	—
Age When Released		
Mean age	41.9 years old	35.8 years old
Range	19–69 years old	14–57 years old
Not released	7.5%	7.1%
Executed	—	2.4%
Not applicable	14.0%	21.4%
Unknown	12.9%	—

Table 1.2 Continued

	White	Black
Exonerated Through DNA Testing		
Yes	5.4%	2.4%
No	94.6%	97.6%
Factors Related to the Wrongful Conviction		
Prosecutorial misconduct	36.6%	57.1%
Police misconduct	34.4%	33.3%
Eyewitness error	26.9%	16.7%
Forensic errors	28.0%	11.9%
Perjury by criminal justice officials	14.0%	42.9%
Ineffective assistance of counsel	18.3%	21.4%
False confession	19.4%	11.9%
Informant/snitch	15.1%	16.7%
Insufficient evidence	9.7%	14.3%
Other	34.4%	16.7%
Unknown	—	—

scant 1.1 percent of the falsely convicted white women received this sentence, whereas 9.5 percent of the black women received an identical sentence.

In general black women were more likely than white women to be incarcerated for shorter periods of time. Over 38 percent of the wrongfully convicted black women spent either no time in jail or prison or less than one year. In contrast, only 17.2 percent of the wrongfully convicted white women fell into one of these categories. Although white women were somewhat more likely than black women to be released within one to five years, the percentage of white women spending six to ten years, eleven to fifteen years, and more than twenty years in prison exceeded that of black women. Despite these apparent racial differences, the probability of white and black women remaining incarcerated was virtually the same: 7.5 percent of the white women versus 7.1 percent of the black women were still in prison at the time of the investigation.

Table 1.2 further discloses that black women are convicted at younger ages than their white counterparts. The average age at conviction for black women was 29.4 years; the average age for white women was 34.9 years. Overall, almost 60 percent of the black women in the study were convicted prior to turning thirty. In contrast, 27.9 percent of the white women in the investigation were less than thirty when convicted. Similarly, among those released black women were released at an earlier age than their white counterparts. The mean age at which black women were released was 35.8 years, whereas the mean age at which white women were released was 41.9 years. Furthermore, 47.6 percent of the black women were released prior to turning forty, compared with 32.3 percent of the white women released prior to their fortieth birthday.

Because DNA testing is increasingly being used to exonerate the innocent, the sample was examined to determine the extent to which DNA evidence contributed to the exoneration of innocent women. DNA tests were responsible for only a small fraction of all known female wrongful convictions. Slightly over 5 percent of the white women and only 2.4 percent of the black women were cleared through DNA technology. These low figures reflect gender differences in the offenses for which wrongly convicted men and women are charged. False convictions of men typically involve murder or rape, offenses for which the collection of usable DNA is more likely to occur. Although DNA is likely to be found in child abuse cases involving sexual abuse, but because many instances of such abuse did not actually occur, there is no DNA to use for ascertaining innocence. Collectively, these low percentages indicate that wrongful convictions of women have not benefited from the increased reliance on DNA testing to the degree that male wrongful convictions have. Nor are they likely to in the immediate future, given gender differences in offending.

Racial differences also exist when factors related to the wrongful conviction are examined. While prosecutorial misconduct was the single most common factor in both female false convictions, this factor was more prominent among black women than white women. Prosecutorial misconduct was present in 57.1 percent of all black cases compared to 36.6 percent of all white cases. Perjury by criminal justice officials was also more prevalent among cases involving black women. Whereas perjury by criminal justice officials was found in only 14 percent of the white wrongful convictions, it appeared as a factor in 42.9 percent of the black wrongful convictions. The enhanced presence of this factor among black women was largely attributable to cases involving drug violations. Furthermore, insufficient evidence to support a conviction was slightly more noticeable among black false convictions.

In contrast, eyewitness error was more likely to be found among white wrongful convictions than among black wrongful convictions. Present in almost 27 percent of the white cases, eyewitness error was a factor in only 16.7 percent of the black cases. The difference is primarily attributable to the large number of child abuse cases involving white women in which easily manipulated children were used as eyewitnesses to the alleged crime. False confessions were also more prevalent among wrongly convicted white women. This factor appeared in almost 20 percent of the white cases but less than 12 percent of the black cases. Similarly, forensic errors were more prominent in white wrongful convictions. Forensic errors were factors in 28 percent of the white false convictions compared to almost 12 percent of the black false convictions. This factor was primarily associated with wrongful murder convictions for both groups. All of the black wrongful convictions in which forensic errors were found involved murder and almost 70 percent of the white wrongful convictions in which forensic errors were found involved murder.

Factors related to the false convictions of women exhibited some similarities as well. For instance, police misconduct was nearly identical for both groups: 34.4 percent of the white wrongful convictions versus 33.3 percent of the black wrongful convictions. The use of an informant or snitch, moreover, was present in 15.1 percent of the white false convictions and 16.7 percent of the black false convictions. An often overlooked variable—ineffective assistance of counsel—was additionally present in similar percentages for white and black women. Ineffective assistance of counsel was a factor in 18.3 percent of the miscarriages of justice involving white women and 21.4 percent of those involving black women.

Of special significance is the extent to which factors not typically examined in the wrongful conviction literature appeared among the wrongly convicted women in this study. Factors other than those enumerated were present in 34.4 percent of the white false convictions but only 16.7 percent of the black false convictions. These figures suggest the need to expand the number of factors examined in wrongful convictions when analyzing women, especially when the defendants are white women.

Focus and Scope of the Book

Throughout the book, cases involving falsely convicted women in the United States are critically examined to enhance the reader's comprehension of the dynamics through which these women have come to be wrongfully convicted. With an emphasis on gender and racial differences, the discussions focus on both the nuanced differences and similarities between these women and other known false convictions. Through an in-depth examination of numerous wrongful convictions, the reader is exposed to the diversity of circumstances surrounding these miscarriages of justice. To personalize the experience that these women

underwent, some analyses include personal statements from the innocents themselves. It is hoped that cumulatively these findings will pro-
mote a clearer understanding of the intricate nature of female wrongful
convictions while concomitantly encouraging further exploration of this
topic.

It is also important to note what this book isn't. It is not meant to be
a theoretical essay since the research in this area is still in its infancy.
Furthermore, it is not meant to be an exhaustive investigation of all
wrongly convicted women in the United States since 1970, as only
known false convictions available electronically were included in the
sample. Because many wrongful convictions involving women are
unknown and many more may not be obtainable through computer-
based searches, there are limitations to the sample. That being said, the
websites utilized and the supplemental information make this sample
arguably one of the most exhaustive searches of female wrongful convictions currently available.

In this chapter the reader was exposed to some background information on wrongful convictions. We began with a discussion of the
Choctaw Three in Alabama and highlighted the history of wrongful convictions in the United States. The chapter then examined the prevalence
of false convictions and looked at the factors commonly associated with
them. Finally, we concluded with an analysis of 163 female wrongful
convictions by examining gender and racial differences.

Chapter 2 focuses on women who have been wrongfully convicted
of some form of child abuse. Perhaps nowhere is the contrast between
male and female wrongful convictions more apparent than in the examination of offenses associated with the abuse of children. Although relatively few men have been falsely convicted of these abuses, a much
larger number of women appear in the wrongful conviction scholarship.
A strong racial divide exists among the women erroneously convicted of
this offense. Whites greatly outnumber their black counterparts. Chapter
2 analyzes this phenomenon from a gender and race perspective.

One area where there is overlap between male and female wrongful
convictions involves murder. Although criminal justice data for any
given year reflect the fact that arrests for murder predominantly involve
males, an appreciable number of women in the study were erroneously
convicted of this crime. Chapter 3 examines those cases in which
women were wrongfully convicted of murders they did not commit.
When women kill, it is often someone they know intimately, making
their murders (and convictions) qualitatively different from that of many
men. This chapter scrutinizes the circumstances surrounding the cases
and examines similarities and differences between men and women.

For many decades the United States has been aggressively waging a war on drugs. Only recently has the nation begun to reconsider the wisdom of this approach. Although typically the individuals appearing in the wrongful drug convictions have been men, many women (particularly black women) have become victims of this country's preoccupation with drug prevention and use. Contrasts between wrongful drug convictions involving men and women are discussed in Chapter 4. Racial distinctions among the women in the study are also analyzed.

Chapter 5 explores cases in which women have been falsely convicted for crimes not delineated in the previous chapters and reviews numerous offenses for which women have been erroneously convicted. The diversity of these crimes demonstrates the need for investigations of wrongfully convicted women to go beyond the typical offenses of murder, rape, and drugs which permeate much of the literature of their male counterparts.

Finally, Chapter 6 summarizes the major findings and suggests directions for future scholarship in this area. Similarities as well as differences between wrongly convicted men and women are discussed, as are racial differences within female wrongful convictions.

The book additionally contains two appendixes. Appendix A includes a more detailed discussion of the research methodology employed in the study. Appendix B enumerates the entire sample of wrongfully convicted women analyzed herein. A succinct overview of the main characteristics of each case accompanies each entry.

Notes

1. Perhaps nowhere is this more self-evident visually than in the book *The Innocents* (Simon et al., 2003). Prominently appearing on the dust jacket are pictures of forty-five individuals who have been wrongfully convicted and whose stories appear in the book. Buried among the photographs of the forty-four falsely convicted men is a single photograph of a falsely convicted woman.

2. Some contemporary books that have examined wrongful convictions involving men include Connery (1996), Protess and Warden (1998), Scheck et al. (2000), Mello (2001), Johnson and Hampikian (2003), Edds (2003), Cohen (2003), Jankin (2004), Grisham (2007), Budd and Budd (2010), Burns (2011), Rooney (2011), Masters and Lehto (2012), and Free and Ruesink (2012). Particularly noteworthy among this collection is *The Innocent Man*, authored by John Grisham. Although Grisham is best known for his legal fiction novels, this *New York Times* bestseller is a true story involving a wrongly convicted Oklahoma man.

2

Child Abuse

Sandra Craig, mother of three, opened a day care facility in Clarksville, Maryland, in 1981. Her nightmare began in April 1985 when her fifteen-year-old son, Jamal, was accused of being sexually promiscuous with a five-year-old girl at his mother's day care center. Although the charges were dropped after Jamal consented to undergo counseling and to avoid visiting the center when children were present, the stage was set for a series of events that forever affected the Craig family.

In June 1986, the parents of two children who attended the day care alleged that their children had been physically and sexually abused by Sandra and Jamal. After a state investigation, two more children came forward with similar claims of abuse. Later that year, the facility was ordered closed by the health department. As the scope of the state investigation into these allegations expanded, child abuse hysteria became prevalent. By October 1986 Sandra found herself indicted on charges of child abuse, first- and second-degree sexual offense, perverted practice, and assault and battery that allegedly covered a two-year period. In December 1986 the judge decided that the thirteen indictments would be tried separately. Jamal was also indicted on eight counts of child abuse and rape, although his case was later dismissed.

Sandra was convicted by a jury for the sexual abuse of Brooke Etze and sentenced to a ten-year prison term in April 1987. The main evidence used to convict her was the one-way closed-circuit television testimony of the little girl who was four to six years old when the alleged events occurred. Brooke claimed that Sandra had inserted a stick in her "private parts" and pierced her arms and hands with thumbtacks. There was no physical evidence to suggest that thumbtacks had been pushed into her arms and hands, and a vaginal infection at the time of the trial precluded a definitive determination of the causes of the scarring of tissue in her vagina. She also accused the child care operator of killing a rabbit by hitting it with a hammer. Her testimony was corroborated by four-year-old Justin Peeples, five-year-old Jessie Sue Smith, and five-year-old Drew Woodbury, who claimed to have various objects stuck in their anuses sometime during the previous two years. Testimony was also heard at trial that Sandra had buried one of the children in a cage in a hole that she had dug near the playground, despite no evidence that this event ever transpired.

Sandra's attorneys—William H. Murphy, Jr., and M. Christina Gutierrez—moved for a new trial on the grounds of ineffective assistance of counsel by her earlier attorney and the withholding of exculpatory evidence by the prosecution. Copious notes from Brooke's therapist, Mary Burke, which were available to the prosecution, raised questions regarding the extent to which Brooke could differentiate reality from fantasy. There was also evidence that Brooke would sometimes confuse Sandra with her daughter Zena and Sandra's husband with her son, Jamal. In later therapy sessions, Justin denied that he had been penetrated in the anus with a screwdriver or any other object. When Justin was asked by the therapist where Sandra had touched him, he motioned toward his ears. Justin's brother, Elliott, who was not a student at the facility, claimed to have had a screwdriver inserted into his penis. Thus, the children had made numerous inconsistent statements that undermined their credibility, yet none of the inconsistent statements were presented at trial. Moreover, Brooke's vaginal scarring could have been inflicted by other children or self-inflicted. In fact, during one of her therapy sessions Brooke mentioned that children would bring sticks to school and place them on chairs and that "maybe that is how she (Brooke) got hurt" (Murphy, 1989).

After Circuit Court Judge Raymond Kane, Jr., rejected Sandra's motion for a new trial, her attorneys began preparing her appeal. Meanwhile, the Craig family's financial status steadily deteriorated. Financial institutions soon foreclosed on their home and their child care center. After sentencing and while out on bail awaiting the results of the appeal, the family moved to Newark, New Jersey, where they rented a house and Sandra took a job as restaurant manager to help pay the family's bills. Because of her frequent trips to Maryland to deal with legal issues regarding her case, she was eventually fired. Jamal later dropped out of college due to his parents' financial circumstances. Her younger daughter found it difficult to make friends since her mother was perceived by many as a child molester.

Two years after she was sentenced, the Maryland Court of Appeals reversed the earlier conviction. By a unanimous decision, the justices ruled that her right to confront a hostile witness had been violated as the trial judge should have conducted pretrial interviews with Brooke to determine if the girl could testify at the trial. Instead, the judge had accepted the opinions of therapists in making the decision to use a one-way closed-circuit television for the testimony. Dissatisfied with this outcome, the Maryland Attorney General's Office appealed the decision to the US Supreme Court, which eventually remanded the case back to the Maryland Court of Appeals. In 1991, for a second time, the appellate court ordered a new trial, stating that whenever possible hostile witnesses should be expected to appear in court. In the event that a closed-circuit television was used, however, it should be a two-way closed-circuit television so that both parties could see each other.

When prosecutors decided not to retry Sandra's case on July 2, 1991, her five-year ordeal finally came to an end. Now forty-four years old, Sandra was never tried on the remaining indictments. Nevertheless, the strain it placed on Sandra and her family was evident. With legal fees of $200,000 and more, she had ambivalent feelings knowing that she would not be appearing in court anymore. In a 1991 interview she commented that she was saddened by the fact that "after all this, my name isn't cleared. I still have to start from scratch. All of this was for naught." Concomitantly, she expressed a feeling of relief. She said that she "felt very good that it's all over . . . I can't quite believe it" (Buckley, 1991; Clark, 1991; Leff, 1987; Murphy, 1989; West and Samuels, 1991).

The case involving Sandra Craig is in many ways a prototype of the child abuse hysteria that gripped the United States during the 1980s and 1990s. Many of the cases from this era included a number of common themes. After unsubstantiated claims of sexual and physical abuse, an investigation ensues. The investigation discloses even more cases of abuse, often after the children have spent considerable time with therapists and/or police officers who may have intentionally or inadvertently planted these ideas in the children's minds. This is immediately followed by overcharging on the part of the prosecutor. (Sandra was originally charged with fifty-three counts of child pornography and sexual and physical abuse of nine children.) The prosecutor withholds exculpatory evidence from the defense, typically in the form of inconsistent statements by the children or statements suggesting that nothing actually occurred or someone else was responsible for the alleged crime. Finally, despite a lack of physical evidence to support the charges, the defendants are primarily convicted on the testimony of impressionable children. This scenario played out numerous times during the height of the child abuse hysteria in the United States.

Child Abuse Hysteria in the United States

This section highlights some of the more highly publicized child abuse cases involving day care centers or large groups of alleged child sex offenders from the 1980s and 1990s. The hysteria that prevailed in many of these cases is reminiscent of the Salem witch trials discussed in Chapter 1.

Kern County and the Pitts Seven

The San Joaquin Valley in California is probably best known for its collection of oil wells and fruit trees. In the valley lies Bakersfield, the largest of the cities that make up primarily rural Kern County. The county prides itself in being the antithesis of Los Angeles, with its attendant social problems. Bakersfield is inhabited by many settlers from the South who hold strong Christian beliefs and believe in the importance of law and order. But in the 1980s Bakersfield was torn asunder by accusations of child abuse, child sex abuse, and satanic rituals. In 1982, Kern County had arrests for child molestation that were twice as high as the state average (Mathews, 1989). Between 1984 and 1986 the county convicted at least thirty individuals of some form of child abuse and sentenced them to extensive periods of imprisonment. Eight other people agreed to plea bargains to avoid incarceration. Their accusers—sometimes as young as four years of age—had been coerced into testifying that they had been the victims of child abuse. By 2005, twenty of the wrongly convicted individuals had been exonerated (Gross, n.d. c). Nor was the child abuse hysteria confined to Kern County. One estimate places the number of individuals falsely accused of some form of child abuse in 1985 at one million (Pride, 1986). During this wave of child abuse hysteria, the case known as the Pitts Seven occurred.

The story begins in January 1984 when six-year-old Brian Pitts and several other children were detected engaging in sexually inappropriate behavior at their school. After talking with a school counselor, Brian intimated that he had been sexually abused by his mother, Marcella Pitts. As a result, Child Protective Services (CPS) and the police began intensively interviewing Brian and his two older brothers. For several months the police repeatedly questioned the boys. As the number of interviews increased, so did the seriousness of their accusations. The alleged members of a child sex ring now expanded to include Rick Pitts, Marcella's husband, who was a former bartender and truck driver, and

Marcella's siblings, Colleen Dill Forsythe and Wayne Dill, Jr. Also implicated were Grace Dill, Marcella's mother, and Colleen's husband, Wayne Forsythe. One nonfamily member—Gina Miller—was additionally accused of child abuse.

On June 4, 1984, Marcella, Rick, and Colleen were arrested and eventually charged with conspiracy; forcible, lewd, and lascivious acts on children under fourteen years of age; use of children for pornography; child endangerment; and assault. By August that year the remaining four members of the alleged sex ring had been arrested and charged with similar crimes. Because of the interrelatedness of the offenses, a decision was made to try all seven together and on December 13, 1984, the trial of the Pitts Seven began.

Six children testified that they had been the victims of child abuse, and two children denied any wrongdoing on the part of the defendants during the trial. To discredit the children who testified for the defense, the prosecution offered testimony from a physician that there was physical evidence that the two children had been molested. Among the allegations leveled against the seven defendants were that the children were administered drugs, forced to drink urine and alcohol, and forced to have sexual relations with both adults and other children while being videotaped. Throughout the trial parallels were drawn between these events and the Holocaust. One prosecutor even claimed that the children's testimony was corroborated by Christ. As Judge Gary T. Friedman announced the sentences for each of the defendants, he commented, "I doubt if our friends in the animal kingdom would treat their young in such a fashion."

Despite protestations of innocence by the seven defendants, all were found guilty during the seven-month trial. Gina Miller, a fast-food employee who was nursing her infant at the time, was originally offered a lighter sentence if she would testify against the other defendants. She refused, saying, "People think I was crazy for not taking that deal, but how could I take responsibility for all these people?" (Mathews, 1989). Although only two children identified her in a lineup, Gina was sentenced to 405 years in prison. Grace Dill and Wayne Dill, Jr., were also sentenced to 405 years. Rick and Marcella Pitts and Colleen Dill Forsythe were given the second longest sentence: 373 years in prison. Wayne Forsythe received the shortest sentence: 285 years in prison. Collectively the Pitts Seven received sentences totaling 2,619 years, thereby establishing a child abuse case record for the state of California (Mathews, 1989). Yet no adults had witnessed the alleged crimes, there were no videotapes to substantiate the accusations that these events were recorded, and the medical evidence used to convict was controversial at best.

Convicted of a total of 377 counts, the defendants began serving their sentences in summer 1985. They appealed their case on the grounds of prosecutorial misconduct. Before the California Court of Appeals heard their case in 1990, two children had already recanted their testimony. One child—Christina Hayes—recalled being interviewed for hours on end by Carol Darling, a social worker who later retired citing excessive mental and emotional problems, as well as other investigators who fed her information on what the other children had supposedly said. Christina was also threatened with placement in a foster home if she didn't cooperate with the investigation. The Court of Appeals immediately reversed the convictions, citing numerous examples of prosecutorial misconduct, finding that prosecutors had made inappropriate comments that were likely to have prejudiced jurors and had coerced the children into making false statements. Because of the seriousness of the misconduct, the court required the original court of jurisdiction to dismiss specific counts. By 1991 the remaining counts were dismissed, and by 1994 all of the witnesses had recanted their stories of abuse and admitted that their testimony had been coerced (Gross, n.d. d; Mathews, 1989).

Kern County and the "Child Sex Ring" of the Early 1980s

The case of Debbie and Alvin McCuan and Brenda and Scott Kniffen in Kern County, California, represents perhaps the earliest example of the child abuse hysteria epidemic that swept the United States during the latter part of the twentieth century. Although the events of this case preceded those of the Pitts Seven, the exoneration of the innocent did not occur until later. Although there were fewer supposed victims involved in this case, the circumstances surrounding this miscarriage of justice soon became all too familiar.

In 1980 Becky McCuan, daughter of Debbie and Alvin McCuan, claimed that her grandfather, Rod Phelps, had sexually abused her, a claim that was later substantiated by the family physician. Although the grandfather was not charged with any offense, Becky was placed under the supervision of a therapist. Mary Ann Barbour, Debbie's stepmother, who struggled with mental issues, was upset that not enough was being done to protect her grandchildren, Becky and Dawn. Mary Ann unsuccessfully tried to have Debbie's day care license revoked. When she learned that Debbie and Alvin had taken their daughters to see their abusive grandfather and their grandmother on a supervised visit, she had a psychotic episode and had to be hospitalized. She eventually recovered and in March 1982, amid allegations that Debbie and Alvin participated in a sex ring involving children, she gained custody of Becky and Dawn.

After multiple interrogations by authorities, both girls testified that they had been sexually abused by their grandfather. They further claimed that their father had molested them. No other individuals were implicated in the incidents. It was only after being in the custody of their grandmother, who was convinced that a child sex ring existed, that the girls began to tell bizarre stories of abuse. Among the alleged incidents were belt whippings, involvement in child porn movies, hanging from hooks, and being rented to strangers in motels. During group therapy the girls additionally told of satanic rituals in which infants were killed. Becky and Dawn began implicating individuals other than their parents in this sex ring: their grandparents, an uncle, a coworker of their father, three social workers, and Brenda and Scott Kniffen, who were family friends. Despite these wild accusations, no physical evidence to corroborate their stories was ever found.

The Kniffens' sons, Brian and Brandon, were interrogated on multiple occasions using highly suggestive techniques. During the interrogations the boys were told that they could go home if they testified about the abuse. Each was falsely informed that the other brother had confessed to being sexually abused by his parents and the other individuals supposedly participating in the sex ring. Only after these repeated interrogations did the boys acquiesce and confess to being abused by their parents and others.

Although she was not permitted to testify during the trial, Brandon's grandmother, during a supervised visit, asked him whether the events he described actually happened. Brandon admitted to her that he had never been sexually abused and the events were fictitious. When it was discovered that his grandmother had talked to Brandon about the case, she was arrested and had her visitation rights terminated.

For over a year Debbie and Alvin McCuan and Brenda and Scott Kniffen remained in jail awaiting their trial, and on one occasion held a hunger strike to draw publicity to their case. On May 16, 1984, all four defendants were convicted of child sex abuse based on the testimony of their daughters and sons. Prosecutors also had Dr. Bruce Woodling testify that his physical examination of the children had disclosed a "wink response" when he touched their anuses with a swab. He argued that this reaction suggested that the children had been victims of anal copulation. Debbie was subsequently sentenced to 252 years in prison and Alvin received a 268-year sentence. Brenda and Scott received sentences of 240 years each.

In 1992, Brian and Brandon recanted their testimony, stating that they were cajoled and intimidated into testifying by police and prosecutors. The following year the four defendants filed petitions for writs of habeas corpus and provided new research that found that "wink responses" are present in both abused and nonabused children. While the petitions were denied in 1994 by the Kern County Superior Court, on August 12, 1996, the California Court of Appeals dismissed their convictions based on the recantations of Brian and Brandon, misconduct by the police and prosecution, and erroneous forensic evidence. The McCuans and Kniffens were immediately released, and all charges were dropped shortly thereafter.

The true dimensions of these wrongful convictions go well beyond the fourteen years Debbie, Alvin, Brenda, and Scott spent behind bars. During that time the spouses remained isolated from each other and wondered if they would ever be vindicated of their charges. Becky and Dawn McCuan never recanted their testimony and have probably developed false memories of events that never happened. The girls have not seen their parents since the original trial. Until turning thirteen years of age and being placed in the custody of his grandparents, Brian Kniffen resided in sixteen different foster homes, including some that were abusive. For many years Brandon Kniffen was convinced that he had been forsaken. In an interview at the age of twenty-three, he commented, "For a long time I felt deserted by my family. . . . I didn't know that all along they were trying to see me, get custody. I just thought they had forgotten about me" (Gross, n.d. b, n.d. c; Robinson, 2005).

East Valley YMCA Day Care Facility

Another bizarre case of child abuse unfolded at the East Valley YMCA day care center in El Paso, Texas. Although more limited in scope, the similarities between this case and the Pitts Seven are intriguing. In both cases the defendants were convicted based on the testimony of young, impressionable children who had been interviewed using coercive and suggestive techniques. In both cases, the defendants were convicted primarily on the testimony of witnesses who weren't physically present during the trials. Evidence of prosecutorial misconduct was present in both cases as well.

The investigation began in June 1985 when a four-year-old child attending the East Valley YMCA in El Paso used an inappropriate word at home. Upset by this, the parents began to focus on the day care center as the source of the problem. Two teachers—Michelle Noble, age thirty-four, and Gayle Stickler Dove, age forty—were implicated. Using questions obtained from the McMartin preschool child abuse investigation,[1] the two teachers were indicted on multiple counts of sexual molestation and child sexual assault. In March 1986 Michelle was sentenced to life plus 311 years. Later that year Gayle was sentenced to three life terms plus sixty years.

In both trials, videotapes of five girls and two boys were presented in which the accusers described situations involving sexual assault, child pornography, spankings with a tennis racket, and being kissed by Michelle and twelve-foot-tall monsters, all while being held captive at Michelle's home several blocks from the day care facility. The children testified that they were warned not to tell anyone or they would be eaten. They additionally said they had been forced to eat body parts and watch the killing of animals. Finally, the children stated that they had pennies placed on their "peepees" and had pencils as well as other objects stuck in their anuses.

In November 1987, Michelle's verdict was overturned when an appellate court ruled that videotaped confessions by the children violated her constitutional right to confront hostile witnesses. During her second trial in April 1988, she was acquitted after some of the witnesses withdrew from the case and an expert witness asserted that the interviews and interrogations of the children had resulted in false memories due to the suggestive and coercive nature of the technique.

Gayle's verdict was overturned in March 1987 because the jury had viewed evidence that was never admitted at trial. At her new trial that same year, she was convicted on a single count of aggravated battery and sentenced to twenty years. On March 31, 1989, an appellate court overturned that conviction based on the prosecution's reliance on hearsay and inadmissible evidence. The charges were formally dismissed in April 1990 (Newton, 1996; Possley, n.d. c).

Fells Acres Day School

Malden, Massachusetts, a seven-mile drive from Boston, was settled by the Puritans and named after Maldon, England. Cited by *Bloomberg Businessweek* in 2009 as the "Best Place to Raise Your Kids" in Massachusetts, the city was the site of yet another case of child sex abuse hysteria in the mid-1980s. The Fells Acres Day School had operated in Malden for eighteen years when false accusations of child sex molestation prompted its closure in 1984. Begun in 1966 by Violet Amirault, a single mom trying to raise two children, Fells Acres grew from a small day care facility in a basement to a thriving day care center that could accommodate over seventy students. By the time of the alleged crimes, Violet had surrendered her teaching responsibilities and assumed the role of school principal. Her daughter, Cheryl Amirault LeFave, taught one toddler class, and her son, Gerald Amirault, performed various functions at the school.

The precipitating incident occurred in April 1984 when a newly admitted student wet his pants during nap time. Because the teacher was busy, Gerald agreed to take the boy to the bathroom to dry him off and change him into his spare clothes. According to the child's mother, whose marriage was on the rocks, the boy began to experience behavioral problems, including bedwetting, masturbation, hostility, lying, and acting out sexually. Disturbed by this behavior, she asked her brother, who had been sexually abused during his youth, to talk to his nephew. It was during a walk in the park that the boy informed his uncle that Gerald had touched his penis. The boy eventually revealed that there was a "secret room" at school where Gerald would blindfold and sexually abuse him. Consequently, his mother alerted authorities and the school was officially shut down three days after Gerald's arrest.

On September 12, 1984, the local police convened about sixty-five parents whose children attended the school to warn them about the situation. Parents were encouraged to aggressively seek out additional information about these incidents from their daughters and sons. They were told specifically to inquire about "magic rooms," "secret rooms," and clowns (Gerald supposedly dressed as a clown during some of the alleged incidents). Police further informed the parents that bedwetting, nightmares, and loss of appetite are some of the symptoms associated with child abuse. The parents were also warned, "God forbid you say anything good about the people (the Amiraults) or your children will never tell you anything" ("A Fells Acres chronology," n.d.).

It was only after this meeting that other children began to tell bizarre stories of child sex abuse at the school. Some of those stories were quite graphic. A little girl accused Gerald of inserting a foot-long knife into her anus. Others claimed that they were tied to trees while nude and then photographed, forced to watch the mutilation of animals, and raped by a clown. All told, forty-one children between the ages of three and six accused Gerald, Violet, and Cheryl of sexually inappropriate behavior. Gerald was charged with sexually abusing nineteen children, whereas Violet and Cheryl were charged with sexually abusing ten children.

Gerald's trial began on April 29, 1986. Although one child testified via videotape, the other child witnesses were positioned in small plastic chairs directly in front of the jury, where they were unable to view

Gerald. On July 8, 1986, the jury began its deliberations. After an epic 64.5 hours of deliberation, the jury found him guilty on all counts. The next month Judge Elizabeth Dolan sentenced Gerald to thirty to forty years in prison. After an unsuccessful attempt to secure a new trial, the Supreme Judicial Court on March 6, 1989, unanimously rejected his appeal. Gerald didn't receive his freedom until the parole board of the state of Massachusetts granted his request for parole. He was finally released on April 30, 2004.

Violet and Cheryl were tried together beginning on June 1, 1987. As with the earlier trial involving Gerald, the child witnesses were placed in front of the jury with their backs toward Violet and Cheryl. During the trial, children testified that they were forced to eat feces, stripped of their clothes and tied to a tree while observing a squirrel mutilation, raped by clowns and lobsters, and threatened by a robot that resembled R2-D2, among other things. On June 13, 1987, Violet and Cheryl were found guilty on all counts, and two days later they were each sentenced to eight to twenty years in prison.

After spending eight years in prison Violet and Cheryl's future began to look brighter when their convictions were temporarily overturned based on a ruling that the arrangement of the chairs containing the child witnesses prevented the defendants from having an "eye to eye" view of their hostile witnesses, which was a violation of their constitutional rights to confront their accusers. Unfortunately, their freedom was short-lived. On March 24, 1997, their convictions were reinstated by the Supreme Judicial Court in a six-to-one decision in which the court acknowledged that some of their rights might have been violated but the conviction must stand because "the community's interest in finality" must take precedence ("A Fells Acres chronology," n.d.).

After the Supreme Judicial Court refused to reconsider its decision, their lawyer began the task of requesting a new trial on the basis of ineffective assistance of counsel. Judge Isaac Borenstein granted a new trial to the two women and was highly critical of the original trial, arguing that the investigators were "overzealous" and had created a "climate of panic, if not hysteria" (Possley, n.d. s). Before the trial could conclude, Violet died of stomach cancer. Consequently, the charges against her were dismissed posthumously on June 28, 1998.

On October 21, 1999, Cheryl's attorneys were able to reach an agreement with Assistant District Attorney Lynn Rooney in which Cheryl's sentence would be modified to the time already served in prison with certain stipulations. Among the conditions were that she was to have no contact with any of the alleged victims or their families and only could have contact with a child under the age of sixteen if being supervised. She could not benefit monetarily from any future publication of the case, and she would remain under supervised probation for an additional ten years. The most controversial conditions of the agreement, which was ratified by Judge Paul Chernoff, were the requirements that she must cease attempting to clear her name through legal channels and she must not openly talk about the case for a minimum of ten years. After hearing these conditions one reporter commented, "That's outrageous. This is America," whereupon one of Cheryl's lawyers, Charles Ogletree, a Harvard Law School professor, responded, "This is Middlesex County" (Estrin, 1999; "A Fells Acres chronology," n.d.; "The Fells Acres scandal," n.d.; Leung, 2004a, 2004b; Newton, 1999; PBS *Frontline*, 1997; Possley, n.d. s).

Wee Care Day Nursery
In life one's choices frequently define an individual. In the case of Margaret Kelly Michaels, her decision to briefly work at the Wee Care Nursery in Maplewood, New Jersey, had profound ramifications for her life that she could not have fathomed. Kelly, twenty-two years old at the time, was interested in acting and had taken classes in fine arts and drama while in college. Wanting to live near New York City, she began employment in 1984 at the Wee Care Day Nursery in nearby New Jersey to help pay her rent. Being the oldest child in a large family and a frequent babysitter, Kelly knew how to properly care for the young children at the center and soon was promoted from a teacher's aide to a preschool teacher. But the excessive workload and lack of supervision led to her discontent. After working there for seven months, she accepted a teaching position at a more upscale facility in East Orange, New Jersey. While working there, the events that defined her life began to play out.

While getting ready for work on May 6, 1985, Kelly heard a knock on her apartment door. "At first I thought it was because I was playing my music too loud," she said. As she opened her door she saw two men—a police sergeant and an investigator. "When they told me they were investigating an allegation of child abuse, that's when I remember not being able to breathe" ("Rush to judgement," 1993). She learned that three boys from the Wee Care Day Nursery had accused her of sexually abusing them. After waiving her Miranda rights, Kelly underwent nine hours of intense questioning and agreed to take a polygraph test, which she passed. Yet the investigation was just getting started.

On June 6, 1985, Kelly was indicted after an investigation concluded that she abused all fifty-one children under her care. Some of the accusations included having the children lick peanut butter off her genitals, inserting knives and forks into the children's anuses and vaginas, forcing the children to eat feces and drink urine, taking pictures of nude children, forcing nude children to jump on top of her while she was naked, and forcing nude children to jump on one another while she accompanied them on the piano.

The emotionally charged trial lasted approximately eleven months and at a cost of $3 million. As in many other child sex abuse cases, the children were not physically present at the trial. All nineteen witnesses were allowed by Judge William Harth to testify in his chambers on closed-circuit television. The children would agree with whichever attorney was questioning them, suggesting that they were unreliable witnesses. For instance, one of the young witnesses said that "We chopped our penises off" and then later exclaimed, "It's all lies" (Manning, 2007). Nor was there any substantial evidence to support the claims. There were no nude photographs of the children, and no physical evidence that the children had been penetrated with knives and forks. But Peg Foster of the Child Abuse Diagnostic and Treatment Center at Children's Hospital of New Jersey did find a jar of peanut butter in the Wee Care Day Nursery kitchen, which was used to corroborate some of the children's accusations. A verse from one of Kelly's favorite songs ("Both Sides Now" by Joni Mitchell), which she had written in her Wee Care attendance book, was sung by one of the prosecutors during the closing arguments to intimate that Kelly had a dark side that she was hiding: "I've looked at life from both sides now / From up and down / And still somehow / It's life's illusions I recall."

The jury deliberated for thirteen days before finding Kelly guilty of 115 of 163 counts of sex abuse of children between the ages of three and five. Kelly later reflected on that moment, saying, "You're finished. Your life is over. You're dead. For all intents and purposes, you're dead. And I remember just looking at the jury and saying, 'Why?'" On August 2, 1988, she was sentenced to forty-seven years in prison and denied bail while awaiting her appeal.

After she served five years of her sentence, the New Jersey Superior Appellate Court reversed her conviction on March 26, 1993. The court was especially critical of the expert testimony called by the prosecution. According to the appellate court, the expert witness "was permitted to lead the jury to believe that the (interviewing) process was rooted in science and thus was a reliable means of determining sex abuse" (Possley, n.d. g). Freed on $75,000 bail four days later, Kelly was initially prohibited from setting foot in New Jersey and being near children under the age of thirteen, conditions that were later dismissed.

On June 23, 1994, the New Jersey Supreme Court unanimously upheld the decision of the appellate court. Prior to any new trial, the court ruled that a pretrial hearing was required to ascertain the reliability of the children's testimony. Writing for the court, Justice Alan Handler stated, "We find that the interrogations that occurred in this case were improper and there is a substantial likelihood that the evidence derived from them is unreliable" (Nieves, 1994).

Finally, on December 2, 1994, Essex County Prosecutor Clifford Minor reversed an earlier decision to seek a retrial and announced he would dismiss the charges and not retry the case. When interviewed about the new decision, Kelly responded, "I am greatly relieved to have this terrible nightmare finally over. And above all, I praise God for the returning of my rightful freedom and good name and the right to live a quiet and decent life" (Manning, 2007; Nieves, 1994; PBS *Frontline*, 1997; Possley, n.d. g).

The Little Rascals Day Care Center
Edenton is a town of approximately 5,000 residents and is part of North Carolina's Inner Banks region. The first colonial capital of that state, Edenton has been recognized by Forbes as one of America's Prettiest Towns. With its large array of eighteenth-century houses, Edenton stands as a reminder of an earlier time period. But the child abuse hysteria that gripped this city in the last decade of the twentieth century tarnished the image of this tourist attraction and retirement community. As with earlier cases, it all began with accusations of child abuse from a single child at a day care facility.

The Little Rascals day care center of Edenton began accepting children in summer 1986. Run by Betsy Kelly, with the assistance of her husband, Bob Kelly, a part-time plumber and golf pro, the facility prospered, moving from its original location on Court Street to a new location on East Eden Street. Less than three years later it was closed, another victim of child sex abuse hysteria.

The narrative begins on January 19, 1989, when a mother filed a complaint with the Department of Social Services alleging that her son was abused while attending Little Rascals. A police officer and social workers began investigating the allegations. By February, three additional children came forward with similar stories of abuse; on April 14, 1989, Bob was arrested and charged with child sex abuse. His bail was set at $1.5 million. Four and a half months later Betsy was arrested, and bail was set at $1.8 million.

Meanwhile, the police notified parents and suggested that they take their children to therapists to determine if they had been abused. Some children were treated by local therapists who believed in the existence of satanic rituals; others were taken to therapists from outside Edenton who professed no such belief. All of the children who received assistance from the local therapists eventually claimed to have suffered some type of satanic abuse, whereas none of the children who received assistance from therapists in a neighboring town reported any type of abuse. Overall, ninety children accused twenty adults of 429 instances of child sex abuse in Edenton. Nor were these accusations confined to individuals working at the preschool—both the mayor and the sheriff were implicated in the bizarre acts.

Seven individuals were eventually arrested as a result of these allegations. In addition to Bob and Betsy, Kathryn Dawn Wilson (the center's cook), Robin Byrum (a teacher), Shelly Stone (a teacher), and two persons not affiliated with the day care (Willard Scott Privott, who owned the local video store, and Darlene Harris, who was employed at Head Start). Charges were later dropped against Robin, Shelly, and Darlene, though Robin was incarcerated for a year while waiting for her trial. Willard, who was incarcerated for three and a half years while awaiting trial, pleaded no contest to thirty-seven counts of child abuse and received probation.

Bob Kelly's trial was moved to Farmville, some sixty miles away because of the extensive publicity, both local and national, surrounding the case.[2] On July 22, 1991, jury selection began. Originally charged with 248 counts of child sex abuse, a number of counts were later dropped and by the time of the trial Bob was facing 100 counts. Among the accusations made by the children were being sexually abused in a back room of a store, which would have been easily visible to customers, and being flown to outer space in hot air balloons where they were sexually abused. Other accusations included watching newborn babies being thrown into a pool of sharks in the ocean; participating in satanic rituals; taking trips on pirate ships; having forced sex with other children; having to watch adults have sex, defecate, and urinate; watching a baby being murdered; and being placed in microwave ovens. No physical evidence to support these claims was ever found.

On April 23, 1992, Bob was convicted on 99 of the 100 counts of child sex abuse. He was subsequently sentenced to twelve consecutive life sentences based on the testimony of twelve children between the ages of four to seven and the results of physical and psychological tests submitted by the prosecution. The trial, which lasted eight months, was the longest and most expensive trial in that state's history.

In May 1995 a North Carolina appellate court overturned his conviction, and in September of that year the North Carolina Supreme Court
upheld the appellate court's decision. Nevertheless, on April 29, 1996,
after dismissing the charges stemming from the Little Rascals investigation, prosecutors indicted him on unrelated charges of raping a ten-
year-old girl. The prosecution finally dismissed the rape charges three
years later.

After having been jailed on pretrial detention for two years, Betsy
recognized the futility of going to trial and decided to plead no contest
to the thirty counts of child abuse. She was given a seven-year sentence
for her involvement in the alleged scandal and began serving her sentence on January 28, 1994. Later that year she was placed on parole. The
following year, Betsy and Bob formally separated.

On November 2, 1992, Kathryn Wilson's trial began in Hertford,
North Carolina, approximately fifteen miles from Edenton. She was convicted on January 26, 1993, and given a life sentence. While serving her
sentence, she gave birth to a son. In September 1993 she was released on
$250,000 bail while awaiting the outcome of her appeal. During that time
she was placed under house arrest. On May 2, 1995, the Appellate Court
of North Carolina dismissed her conviction, and four months later the
North Carolina Supreme Court upheld the decision of the appellate court.
Although Dawn's house arrest ended on October 5, 1995, it wasn't until
May 22, 1997, that charges against her were formally dropped by the
prosecution, thus bringing to a close this travesty of justice ("Little
Rascals day care sexual abuse trial," 2013; PBS *Frontline*, 1998; Possley,
n.d. e; Robinson, 2003; Smothers, 1991).[3]

The Wenatchee Child Sex Abuse Scandal

When Bob Perez took over the Wenatchee, Washington, sex crimes unit
in January 1994, he had approximately one week of training for the job.
This was not unusual, since the job was awarded on a rotating basis. By
the time Perez assumed this position, he had been on the police force for
eleven years. Perhaps as important to him as his police work was the
foster children's Christmas party he was in charge of each year. During
each holiday season, Perez would purchase gifts for the children, wrap
them, and then pass out the presents while case workers, parents, and
officers looked on.

By 1987, Robert Devereux was fifty years old and an executive with
an insurance company. He and his wife, Maxine, took in their first foster
child in 1987. After a neighbor woman committed suicide, the
Devereuxs took in her son to live with them. Over the next four years,

the two were foster parents for more than 200 children, until their marriage ended in 1991. After Maxine left, Robert let five of the girls remain in the house. Most of the girls were between the ages of six and twelve and were previous victims of sexual abuse. It seemed suspicious to some that he was still letting young girls live with him.

Things started unraveling in Wenatchee in February 1992. Seven-year-old Ann Everett started acting strangely after claiming that two boys in her class had trapped her in an alley and touched her genitals. Ann and her brother, who saw what happened, told their mother, Idella, who reported the incident to a social worker. There was concern that Idella was covering up for her husband, Harold. This suspicion led to questioning by Child Protective Services and police officials, as well as examinations by at least two physicians. One doctor found no evidence of sexual abuse, while a second found signs of possible sexual abuse.

When Idella said that Harold could not have abused their daughter, social workers assumed that Harold and Idella were both involved and wanted to remove Ann from their home. Harold, who is illiterate, and Idella, who has an IQ of 68, did not understand that they could contest this decision. Consequently, they signed a "voluntary placement agreement," consenting to Ann's removal from their home. After she was taken from them, she was questioned several times and finally named a family friend, Abel Lopez, as an abuser. When Abel was questioned, he denied any wrongdoing. However, he did not understand English and ultimately signed a confession. Within a year of being placed in therapy, Ann told authorities that Harold had used a belt on the children. After hearing this, CPS made certain that Harold was no longer in the home.

At this point the first priority for authorities was to place the children in a safe location. The boys, Robert and Stephen, were placed in separate foster homes. Ann was placed as a foster child with Robert Devereux.

About a month before Ann was placed in Devereux's home, Sid and Laura Holt had a domestic dispute, after Laura found a hotel receipt belonging to Sid. She confronted him, and he retaliated by telling her that not only was he seeing someone else, but that he was also having sex with their ten-year-old daughter, Pam. Laura immediately reported this to the police. Sid was arrested, charged with three counts of child rape, and sentenced to fourteen years at the Washington State Penitentiary.

A few weeks after Ann Everett was placed with Robert Devereux, Cherie Town knew that she needed to do something about her husband. Cherie, despite her IQ of 77, realized that her husband, Gene, was fooling around with other women. She may have been pushed over the edge when he started bragging about this to others in town. She wanted revenge for this and she got it when she called the Rape Crisis Center to report that her husband had been molesting their two young sons. The boys were interviewed by police and confirmed what their mother had claimed but also said that she had been sexually abusing them. When Perez interviewed Cherie, she confessed under duress and was charged, along with her husband. Gene received eighteen years in prison and Cherie, ten years. Their children were placed in foster care.

Shortly after Perez assumed his new position, Laura Holt took Pam to him to report another crime. As he listened to Pam, Perez also started questioning Laura's motives. She was subsequently arrested after Pam disclosed that Laura had molested her.

Doris Green was also under suspicion after a landlady told Perez that Doris had probably been leaving her children with the Holts. Perez contacted Doris by telephone but said that he could not discuss this matter over the phone. Instead, he asked Doris to come to the station to meet with him personally. Indeed, Doris did meet with Perez and, after four hours, was being held in a jail cell. Doris was eventually convicted of three counts of child rape and one count of child molestation and sentenced to twenty-three years in prison.

Meanwhile, Devereux was experiencing more problems with his foster children. He had grounded one girl, Kate Sanchez, and she retaliated by trying to poison him with iodine. Perez interviewed the girl in juvenile hall, where she claimed that Devereux had molested her. The other girls staying in the house, however, did not corroborate her story. Later Kate said that Perez had coerced her into making an accusation. Nevertheless, the police arrested Devereux and, after a long interview with another girl who stayed with him, were successful in obtaining another accusation.

This modern-day witch hunt continued and the children of Wenatchee, with the strong-arm tactics of Bob Perez, pointed fingers at all available adults in the community. Before it was over, forty-three adults—including a church pastor and his wife—were arrested on 29,726 charges of child sex abuse involving more than sixty children. An example of Perez's questionable tactics is illustrated by an event in which he drove around the town accompanied by ten-year-old Ann Everett.[4] By this point, she claimed to have been abused by just about every adult she had encountered. As they made their way around Wenatchee, Ann told Perez where she and others were supposedly raped and molested. She identified twenty-two places where the abusive acts had taken place. By now Perez was convinced that he had uncovered a huge child sex ring in Wenatchee, even though he never recorded his conversations or took notes.

One of the individuals that Ann mentioned was her half-sister, Donna Hildago, a home health aide and orchard worker. Problems started for Donna and her husband, Manuel Hildago Rodriguez, when Ann stated that she had been assaulted several times by a man named Manuel. This presented a dilemma since there were two men around Ann's house with the same name. Although Rodriguez was not the person she was talking about, Ann also named Donna as one of the abusers. Perez interrogated Donna and was able to coerce a confession. She was initially charged with 416 counts of child rape of four half-siblings, although a plea bargain later reduced it to a single count of incest. Donna served all fourteen months of her sentence before being released.

Another person named by Ann was Linda Miller, a welfare mother who lived with her children. After interrogating her for hours, Perez had a confession. Originally charged with 3,200 counts of child molestation, Linda was convicted of eight counts and received a thirty-three-year sentence.

Things were getting progressively worse in Wenatchee for Ann's parents. After confessing, Idella faced 1,586 counts of rape and 4,836 counts of aiding and abetting the sexual abuse of ten children. Unfortunately, she was too developmentally disabled to assist in her own defense. Hence, she pleaded guilty to two counts of child molestation and received four years, eight months in prison. Harold stood accused of 6,422 counts of rape against eight children. He, too, pleaded guilty but to eight counts of rape and molestation. For his alleged involvement in the child sex ring he received a sentence of twenty-three years.

Two months later, Jessica Cunningham named her father, Henry, as an abuser. Henry and Connie Cunningham lived in Wenatchee with their daughters, Jennifer, Sarah, and Jessica. Henry was a vocational rehabilitation counselor and Connie was a homemaker. In many ways, they were living a typical middle-class existence. However, Henry had a bipolar disorder and was under the care of a psychiatrist. In May 1994 Jessica was sent to Pinecrest Hospital after attempting suicide. Over the course of her treatment, she claimed that her father had sexually abused her. Any Pinecrest employee who learns of possible sex abuse is mandated by law to report it to Child Protective Services. Soon the Wenatchee police department and Bob Perez were involved in the case. A month later, Henry and Connie Cunningham were both arrested.

Connie was later sentenced to 46.5 years in prison and Henry received a sentence of 47 years.

The Cunninghams were good friends with another family in Wenatchee, Mark and Carol Doggett. When Henry and Connie were sent to prison, Mark and Carol took custody of their daughters. The Doggetts also had five children of their own: Ashley, Melinda, Jeremy, Lisa, and Sarah. Before long the Doggetts became part of the city-wide investigation and were ultimately charged with sex crimes. They were having problems with Jeremy and reported that he had molested one of their daughters, hoping that the police would place him in custody until they could arrange for therapy. After Perez failed to take action, Jeremy was sent to live with a relative. At this juncture Perez interceded, believing that the Doggetts were trying to hide something. He questioned Jeremy and then his siblings until they named their parents as abusers. Both parents were arrested and interrogated by Perez. Even though neither Mark nor Carol admitted any guilt, they were held and charged. The children, who had endured several more rounds of questioning by Perez, caseworkers, and therapists, vacillated in their statements regarding their parents' involvement in these alleged activities. In court the children also said that Perez had forced confessions from them.

Perez did not have to work very hard to get a confession from Sharon Ann Filbeck. Sharon and her husband, Gary, may not have even understood the charges against them. Sharon, who has an IQ around 70, and Gary, who is illiterate, were intimidated by Perez and provided him with confessions. They agreed to testify against others. In return for their assistance, Sharon and Gary were placed on probation.

Sadie Hughes, who was severely mentally disabled, was yet another individual wrongfully convicted during the Wenatchee child sex abuse scandal. Originally charged with multiple counts of rape and molestation, she pleaded guilty to one count of first-degree child molestation. Sentenced in 1995 to five years, eight months in prison, she was released after being given credit for time served.

Then there was Barb Garass, whom Ann had pointed out during her tour of the city. Barb was familiar with Ann because she lived across the street from her. Barb had four children who were taken from their home and interrogated about possible sex crimes. They, too, eventually named their parents as the perpetrators. Perez then interrogated Barb and her husband, Ralph Gausvik, without getting a confession. But like many others who preceded them, they were charged and placed in jail. In 1995, Barb was found guilty of child sex abuse and sentenced to twenty-six months in prison. Ralph was convicted of three counts of child rape and molestation and received a twenty-three-year sentence.

In the end, the Wenatchee child sex ring was the result of what Perez and the team of social workers that he convinced, without any physical evidence, believed. The people he targeted all shared similar backgrounds—namely, living on welfare assistance. Many of those accused were also developmentally disabled, making it less likely that they would be competent to defend themselves against the charges. To the community of Wenatchee, those charged were already viewed with distrust. When their day in court arrived, many of the Wenatchee parents received sentences in excess of twenty years. By 1998, as more people became aware of the bizarre allegations, a group of forty attorneys and twenty-five law students joined in conjunction with the Innocence Project Northwest (IPN) to help those who were convicted and sitting in prison. In short duration, those convicted regained their freedom. By 2000 the IPN had wrapped up all of the cases. More than a dozen civil lawsuits were eventually filed against the city of Wenatchee. Perez retired from the police department in 1998 (Beck, 2004; Innocence Project Northwest, 2013; Kershner, 1996; Leatherman, 2012; Lyon, 1998; Porterfield, 1999; Schneider and Barber, 2008; Williams and Norton, 1995).

All in the Family: Individual Cases of Child Abuse

Many instances of wrongful conviction involve alleged child abuse within a family. This section examines some of these situations. Although the typical defendant in these cases is the mother, the first case appearing in this section deviates from that scenario. The case involves a sixteen-year-old girl who was wrongly convicted of sexually abusing her younger sister.

Dayna Christoph

Dayna Christoph had a horrendous childhood. She was born with fetal alcohol syndrome and experienced both physical and sexual abuse as a child. She was sexually abused by an uncle, her cousins, and her alcoholic mother's boyfriends by the age of five. Three years later her mother put her and her younger sister up for adoption. In addition to her dysfunctional family background, Dayna was mentally disabled and emotionally disturbed. By the age of sixteen she had been to sixty-four different foster homes and mental institutions. She was living at a group home when she was accused by her adoptive mother of having sexually abused her younger sister.

Unable to fully comprehend the seriousness of the allegations and confusing her own victimization with that of which she was accused,

Dayna falsely confessed to sexually abusing her sister one hundred times over approximately a three-year period. As a result the prosecution charged her with first-degree rape on July 10, 1995. The next month she signed a confession admitting guilt and was placed in a juvenile facility until she turned eighteen on August 13, 1996.

The case laid dormant until the Innocence Project Northwest came to Dayna's rescue in 1999. A motion was filed to dismiss the guilty plea because she had not received proper legal counsel and there was no evidence suggesting that her sister had been victimized. The ineffective assistance of counsel was particularly egregious: her attorney had devoted less than two hours to her case and failed to review Dayna's medical records or talk to the supposed victim. The police were remiss as well because they never bothered to interview her sister. Dayna later admitted that she had confessed to the accusations because she felt pressured during the interrogation and had developed false memories of the alleged incident due to her own abuse as a young child.

The Spokane County Superior Court dismissed Dayna's conviction on January 14, 2000, citing that this was a case of "manifest injustice." Later that year the Washington Court of Appeals concurred after concluding that "a minimally adequate investigation would have discovered Ms. Christoph's documented long-term mental and emotional difficulties and sufficient exculpatory evidence to warrant dismissal" ("A few of Washington's wrongfully convicted," 2013; Possley, n.d. b).

Shirley Souza

Slightly more than thirty miles from Boston lies the city of Lowell, Massachusetts, a working-class community of 100,000-plus people. Here is where Shirley and Ray Souza raised five children—Sharon, Scott, Tommy, David, and Shirley Ann. To properly provide for their children, both worked: Shirley as a part-time nurse and Ray as a lineman with the electric company. This close-knit family often spent considerable time together even after the children became adults. Sharon lived just two doors down from her parents and frequently ate meals at their house. Scott lived with his parents for an extended period of time, and Tommy used his parents' basement to play drums. David spent considerably less time with his parents because his wife, Heather, didn't like her mother-in-law. Shirley Ann, the youngest, was traumatized by an attempted sexual assault during a date. That near rape and trial precipitated the events that eventually culminated in a gross miscarriage of justice.

In 1990 as a result of a recurring dream in which she envisioned herself being raped by her parents, Shirley Ann began seeing a therapist, who persuaded her to seek out repressed incest memories. The therapist had been strongly influenced by *The Courage to Heal* by Ellen Bass and Laura Davis, a now largely discredited self-help book that was supposed to assist sexually abused individuals in reconstructing memories of their earlier abuse. In her dream, Shirley Ann was missing her limbs, her mother possessed a penis, and her father would place a crucifix inside her vagina. Although the dream lacked realism, Shirley Ann was convinced it meant that she had been molested as a child. She proceeded to telephone her sister-in-law Heather to tell her of her revelation. At this point she implored Heather to "keep your children away from mom and dad" (Pendergrast, 1996).

Heather, who already had disdain for her mother-in-law, immediately took her five-year-old daughter to visit a therapist. The therapist was unconvinced the girl had been victimized and raised questions about the pressure Heather was placing on her to recall past events. Dissatisfied with the therapist's conclusions, Heather found a second therapist, who after a single session determined that the child was suffering from post-traumatic stress disorder (PTSD) that was probably the result of prior abuse. Heather interpreted this diagnosis as confirmation that her mother-in-law and father-in-law had been molesting her daughter. The daughter later accused her father, David Souza, of similar abuse.

Sharon, also a recipient of a telephone call from a distraught Shirley Ann, did not originally suspect any trouble. Nonetheless, when her four-year-old daughter began experiencing nightmares involving her grandparents and began refusing to visit them, Sharon became concerned. She finally decided to take her daughter to a therapist and chose the same one that had been treating Heather's child. After some sessions with the therapist, Sharon, too, became convinced of her parents' guilt.

As the accusations of child abuse began to accumulate, Shirley and Ray needed a temporary break from their problems. A trip to Florida during the dreary month of February 1991 seemed to be a good way to alleviate their discomfort. Unfortunately, when they returned on March 1, their problems again became apparent. While in Florida their house had been vandalized by one of their children. Family photographs had been removed from the walls, broken glass was strewn on the floor, and a threatening note greeted their arrival. The note, apparently written by one of their daughters, said, "Who are you? What are you? Don't try to contact us or we'll take legal action against you" ("Rush to judgement," 1993).

After numerous delays, the Souzas went on trial in January 1993. Upon advice from their attorney, Shirley and Ray elected to have a bench trial, fearing that a jury might be more easily influenced by their children's testimony. As luck had it, their judge was Elizabeth Dolan, who had presided over the Fells Acres case and believed everything that a young child said was true without exception. By the time the trial commenced, the two child witnesses had been questioned by their parents, therapists, and court personnel for two and a half years, plenty of time to solidify their false memories of abuse.

The case revolved around the testimony of the two children, their symptoms of abuse, and the testimony of experts for the defense and prosecution. As the trial proceeded, inconsistencies in the testimony of the girls were overlooked by the judge. Moreover, descriptions of sexual abuse that defied reality were not viewed as possible evidence of misplaced recollections. Dolan was overtly hostile to the defense's expert witness, Dr. Richard Gardner, a Columbia University psychiatrist, who was skeptical of the interviewing techniques used to elicit these past events. Gardner additionally criticized the use of anatomically correct dolls. He noted that the dolls "sexualize the interview, they draw the child's fantasies into sexual realms" (Pendergrast, 1996).

The prosecution countered with Dr. Leslie Campis, a staff psychologist at Children's Hospital in Boston. She reassured the judge that only on rare occasions will a child falsely disclose. Also testifying on behalf of the prosecution was Dr. Andrea Vandeven, a staff pediatrician at the same hospital. Her physical examination of the girls revealed no irregularities in their vaginas. Nevertheless, she claims to have found an "anal wink," which she stated was "consistent with anal penetration," a conclusion she later qualified (Pendergrast, 1996).

When it came time for Shirley and Ray to testify, it became apparent that their attorney had ill prepared them for cross-examination. Instead, they appeared to be angry and defensive whenever questions regarding their involvement in child abuse were raised. Although they had character witnesses testify on their behalf, the judge summarily dismissed this testimony as "window dressing" (Pendergrast, 1996).

Their defense attorney neglected to call Heather's first therapist, who didn't believe her daughter had been abused and felt that Heather had been pressuring the girl too much. Nor was a medical expert consulted to counter Vandeven's suggestion that anal penetration had occurred. He never challenged the credentials of Jeanine Hemstead, a then-unlicensed social worker, who conducted the initial interviews of the children. Consequently, the Souzas were convicted and sentenced to nine to fifteen years in prison. Pending appeal, Shirley and Ray were permitted to remain under house arrest wearing ankle bracelets and using a telephone monitoring system.

It is unclear why Judge Dolan allowed the Souzas to remain in their house pending their appeal. Perhaps she began to have second thoughts about their guilt or felt that the sixty-one-year-old defendants posed little risk. She also did not impose restrictions on home visitations, and friends of the family frequently brought their children with them while visiting Shirley and Ray. Furthermore, the judge later revised their sentence to nine years retroactive to May 10, 1993, despite turning down their appeals on two occasions.

In April 2002 Shirley and Ray completed their sentence, although they were never exonerated of molesting their two grandchildren. Five years later Ray passed away from complications arising from Alzheimer's. As of 2009 Shirley continued to be a registered sex offender in Massachusetts (Friends of Justice, 2010; Pendergrast, 1996; "Rush to judgement," 1993).

Mary Ann Elizondo

Antecedent to this wrongful conviction was a school-related problem involving ten-year-old Robert Bienvenue who lived in Port Arthur, Texas. He got in trouble when his teacher discovered a sexually explicit drawing he made of a kangaroo. He also possessed a sexually suggestive note from one of the girls in his class. As his father and police officers questioned him about these items, he asserted that he had been sexually abused by his twenty-seven-year-old remarried mother, Mary Ann Elizondo, and her forty-nine-year-old husband, Joe Elizondo. His eight-year-old brother later admitted that he, too, had been sexually abused by Mary Ann and Joe.

After the couple was arrested and charged with sexual abuse of a child on September 23, 1983, their one-year-old daughter was taken from them and later adopted by another family. The outcome for Joe looked especially bleak because he had a history of public intoxication and driving under the influence of alcohol. He was additionally on probation for marijuana possession. Mary Ann and Joe were tried separately in 1984. Joe received a life sentence for aggravated sexual assault and was fined $10,000. Mary Ann received a twenty-year sentence for the sexual abuse of Robert and entered a plea of no contest to a second charge, which resulted in a thirty-five-year sentence. The sentences were to be served concurrently.

During Joe's trial Robert told the jury that he and Richard were forced into having oral sex with Joe, anal sex with both Mary Ann and Joe, and oral contact with Mary Ann's breast. He further claimed that the two boys were required to watch sex videos and occasionally had another man and two women join in their sexual activities. The jury was also informed of the materials confiscated during school. The boys' stepmother confirmed that Robert and Richard had told her the same stories of sexual abuse that they were testifying to during the trial.

After their trial, Mary Ann and Joe did not have any contact with Robert or Richard until Robert's seventeenth birthday in 1988, when he learned for the first time that his mother and stepfather were still incarcerated. Then he wrote to authorities that he had lied about the sexual abuse and at a hearing in 1995 he testified that his father had threatened them with physical punishment if he didn't testify against them. He went on to say that his father wanted to punish his mother for remarrying. His brother also testified that the accusations were false, although he denied that their father had forced them to testify.

Joe received his freedom from prison on June 23, 1997, when the district attorney dropped the charges. His freedom, however, was short-lived as his health deteriorated. In 2003, six years after his release, Joe died.

In 1991 Mary Ann was released on parole. Two conditions of her parole—to confess to sexually abusing her sons and to attend group therapy—were intolerable because she was innocent of the charges. She declined to submit to these conditions and was placed back in jail for six months before gaining her release.

Mary Ann's desire to be exonerated of the charges was eventually realized in November 2005 when the Texas Court of Criminal Appeals vacated her conviction and the charges were dismissed. After divorcing Joe, Mary Ann remarried and filed for compensation for her wrongful conviction. By 2012 she had received over $500,000 in remuneration (Possley, n.d. i).

Sloppy Housekeepers and Child Abuse

Our society traditionally places primary responsibility for childrearing on women. If she fails to live up to those expectations, she is often viewed with disdain and contempt. In some cases she may even have her children taken from her custody. The gender double standard is quite prominent when examining incarcerated mothers and fathers. Incarcerated mothers are more likely than incarcerated fathers to have the courts terminate their parental rights. Furthermore, incarcerated women are more likely than their male counterparts to be sanctioned for minor prison rule infractions (Berger et al., 2009; McClellan, 1994; Pearson, 1997).

But do filthy houses and inept housekeeping constitute punishable offenses? The following stories recount the wrongful convictions of four women who were found guilty of felonies for essentially being sloppy housekeepers.

Judith Scruggs

New England is replete with quaint little towns and Meriden, Connecticut, qualifies as one of these. This is the setting for a trial that acted as a springboard for a national movement against bullying. But this story is about more than bullying; it is about the extent to which poor housekeeping can constitute a punishable felony.

Judith Scruggs, a single mother in her fifties, was working sixty hours a week at two jobs when her twelve-year-old son, Daniel, committed suicide by hanging himself with a necktie in his closet. Kicked, punched, and spat on by his classmates in middle school and ridiculed for his bad breath and body odor, Daniel took his life on January 2, 2002. To avoid the criticism and physical abuse he faced at school, he was frequently truant. In fact, he had been absent for forty-four of the last seventy-eight school days prior to his suicide. He sometimes soiled his own clothes so he would have an excuse to return home. The bullying was so severe that a few days before his death, the Connecticut Department of Children and Families had recommended that he remain at home until he could transfer to a new school.

When the police came to investigate Daniel's death, they found a house that was cluttered with clothes, boxes, papers, and debris. In court one police officer later testified that upon entering the house he detected "an odor of garbage" and the house generally smelled like a "dirty clothes hamper." The police also found several large knives in Daniel's bedroom, which he kept there because of recent burglaries in the neighborhood.

In October 2003 Judith was found guilty of one felony count of providing a "home living environment that was unhealthy and unsafe" despite the fact that no psychologist or therapist testified that her son's suicide was the result of a poor home environment (Salzman, 2004). Although the jury acquitted her of cruelty to persons and risk of injury to a minor, in May 2004 she received a suspended eighteen-month sentence, was placed on probation for five years, and was required to work one hundred hours of community service while undergoing counseling. Judge Stephen Frazzini, who presided over her trial, in pronouncing the sentence chastised her for not exhibiting remorse and for not accepting responsibility for her actions. Afterward Judith explained, "I wasn't trying to push off responsibility. I was trying to get to the point where . . . the kids would help around the house" (Salzman, 2004). She remained steadfast in her belief that her son's suicide was the result of merciless bullying he experienced at school. In the CBS program *60 Minutes II* Judith commented, "I tried to convince Daniel that, you know, go to counseling." However, "You have to fix the problem [bullying] first before you can . . . address the illness" (Santora, 2003).

Two years later the Connecticut Supreme Court cleared Judith of criminal liability and brought national attention to the problem of bullying. In a unanimous decision the court acknowledged the lack of "objective standards for determining the point at which housekeeping becomes so poor that an ordinary person should know that it poses an unacceptable risk to the mental health of a child" (Salzman, 2006a). Moreover, the court noted that the Connecticut Department of Children and Families had inspected Judith's home prior to the suicide and had closed the case. Justice David Borden further observed, "Indeed, the department's message was that the defendant should keep Daniel home from school in the very conditions that the same state of Connecticut, through its criminal prosecutorial arm, later charged created an unreasonable risk to his mental health" (Christofferson, 2006).

After her conviction was overturned, Judith was asked if the court decision made her feel better. She replied, "It helps, but the damage has already been done. It relieves the stigma of being a convicted felon. But all the pain and anguish I've gone through will never go away." She additionally commented, "I miss him [Daniel] every day. The pain is always there" (Christofferson, 2006). Her attorney further acknowledged that as a result of her conviction she was evicted from her house and "No one has been willing to hire her because she's been a convicted felon up until now" (Salzman, 2006b).

One offshoot of the trial and its attendant publicity has been the greater visibility given to the problem of bullying. As a result of Daniel's death, the Advocacy Group for Parents of Children Affected by Bullying was founded on September 25, 2002. The group was successful in getting legislation passed in Connecticut that made schools more responsible for controlling bullying and made it easier for students who are bullied to report such incidents (Christofferson, 2006; "Mother's conviction thrown out by court," 2006; Salzman, 2004, 2006a, 2006b; Santora, 2003).

Michelle Wesson

Jimmy Alford was not a typical fourteen-year-old boy. He was born with a chromosomal abnormality that affected his immune system. As such he was extremely susceptible to illness from germs that are found virtually everywhere. Furthermore, he was developmentally delayed, having the mental understanding of a three-year-old child. His single mother, Michelle Alford Wesson, had limited financial means and was known for her poor housekeeping. Occasionally she had been visited by the Florida Department of Children and Family Services and informed that she needed to clean her house or face possible loss of custody of her children. Indeed, she did briefly lose custody of her children in 1996, although they never experienced any health issues despite a filthy house.

On the morning of November 11, 2001, Michelle could not awaken Jimmy, who was lying on a mattress on the floor. He had apparently passed away sometime during the early morning hours due to septicemia (blood poisoning). An autopsy later disclosed that unknown bacteria were responsible for Jimmy's death. On August 9, 2002, thirty-three-year-old Michelle was arrested and charged with child neglect. The following year she was convicted of child neglect causing great bodily harm, a second-degree felony, and sentenced to five years in prison.

Although Michelle was held criminally responsible for her son's death, the actual cause of his death could not be determined. The evening before his tragic demise Michelle and Jimmy had visited Geraldine Alford, her former stepmother. While there, Jimmy ate some raw oysters and later complained of having a stomachache. The prior night he had spent some time at his uncle's house. At the trial her defense attorney argued that the raw oysters were the most likely culprits leading to Jimmy's septicemia. Conversely, the state contended that it was the result of an unsanitary home environment and pointed out that the house was cluttered with pet and human feces, spoiled food, insects, unclean bathtub water, and dirty dishes. Although it was true that the house was unclean, an inoperable toilet, which was being repaired by Michelle's father, had led to soiled toilet paper being placed in a trash can that had been overturned.

During the trial none of the experts testified that the lethal bacteria were more likely to have come from Michelle's house than any of the other possible venues. Furthermore, the medical examiner's mishandling of the specimens and the decomposition of the body prohibited any further determination of the cause of death. By his own admission, the medical examiner could not ascertain if the harmful organism had entered Jimmy's body through his nose, mouth, or open sores on his skin. Nor did the state show through expert testimony why Jimmy was only now affected by the unsanitary conditions that had existed in his home for years. The state's two expert witnesses were at odds regarding the possibility of the raw oysters being the cause of the septicemia: one discounted it as a causal agent; the other testified that raw oysters were more likely than a filthy house to result in blood poisoning.

In 2005 a panel of three judges reviewed Michelle's conviction. The judges of the First District Court of Appeal ruled that the state had failed to prove its argument that Jimmy's death was the direct result of living in unsanitary conditions. At best, the state showed that the conditions of the household were merely a "possible" contributing cause to his death. Pointing out the inconsistencies of the prosecution's expert witnesses and the places where the boy had been and could have contracted the germs that led to the development of the lethal bacteria, the court unanimously concluded that the lower court had neglected to prove its case "beyond a reasonable doubt" and reversed the decision (Associated Press, 2005a; Rominger Legal, 2005).

Nancy Baker-Krofft

Salem is the second largest city in Oregon and its capital. Nancy Baker-Krofft lived there with her husband and eleven-year-old son. While inspecting her home, a compliance officer from the municipal health department saw what he deemed to be unsanitary conditions. At the time of his arrival, Nancy was at work, but her husband and son were home. As the officer proceeded through the house, he observed cluttered areas and an odor resembling mold and mildew. Moreover, the house did not contain any operable smoke detectors, and there were several fire hazards in the home and backyard, where they ran an extension cord to a space heater in their chicken coop. Nevertheless, there was no evidence of rodents or other pests on the property, and the child appeared to be healthy and well fed. Upon completion of his inspection, the officer concluded that Nancy and her husband were in violation of a local public health ordinance and cited them for having a public nuisance. Believing that the conditions of the home were unsafe for their child, he notified the local police.

When two detectives from the Salem Police Department arrived, they were greeted by Nancy's husband and received his consent to search the home. They observed fire hazards, clutter, an overfilled garbage can, a loose railing on the stairs, and a refrigerator that exuded the pungent smell of expired milk. After the detectives had finished their inspection of the house and surroundings, they requested that Nancy immediately return home, whereupon they arrested her and her husband despite the fact that their son was, from all appearances, not suffering from ill health or lack of attention to his physical needs. In short, they were arrested for having an unclean and apparently unsafe house.

Charged with second-degree criminal mistreatment, Nancy's husband pleaded guilty to the charge and agreed to testify for the prosecution at the upcoming trial. Nancy, who was also charged with second-degree criminal mistreatment based on "withhold[ing] necessary and adequate physical care," contested the charge and went to trial. During the trial the prosecution called the compliance officer, the two detectives, and the defendant's husband to the stand. A jury found her guilty.

In September 2009 her appeal was heard in the Court of Appeals of the state of Oregon. The main issue separating the state and the defendant was the meaning of the phrase, "withholds necessary and adequate physical care." This phrase was not defined in the criminal statute and was therefore subject to various interpretations. Nancy maintained that her home environment did not violate the intent of the statute since the law was intended to include only care "that poses a significant likelihood of serious harm" to minor children. She further noted that her home did not contain any pests or illegal drugs and her son was well fed and appropriately dressed. The state argued that in passing this bill the legislature intended to have it interpreted more broadly to include even less serious infractions. The Court of Appeals agreed with the trial court and concluded that even the presence of fire hazards was sufficient to constitute a violation of that criminal statute. Consequently, the trial court was correct in denying her motion for acquittal based on insufficient evidence.

In 2010, the Oregon Supreme Court agreed to review the Court of Appeals decisions involving Nancy and two other defendants (Cynthia Geneva Walker and Timothy Lee McCants). Nancy was represented by the deputy public defender and the chief defender. These cases revolved around what constitutes "withholding necessary and adequate physical care." Critical of both statutes (one involved first-degree criminal mistreatment; the other, second-degree criminal mistreatment) the justices commented that they overlapped with civil statutes that were intended to remedy the problem through the intervention of the juvenile court. Furthermore, the civil statutes were passed with the prospect of reuniting the child with his or her family once the child's safety had been properly provided. The justices additionally noted that although Nancy was not an exemplary parent, her son was in good health and there was no evidence that she had not provided for his physical needs. Regarding the issue of his safety, the justices argued that her son was never in any immediate harm's way. At best, the danger of fire was only a possible future risk. While the conditions might have warranted some intervention on the part of the juvenile court to remedy the problem, the conditions did not constitute criminal liability. As a result, on April 19, 2010, the Oregon Supreme Court reversed the judgment of the circuit court and barred a retrial of her case (Oregon Judicial Department Appellate Court Opinions, 2009, 2010).

Cynthia Geneva Walker

In another case regarding withholding necessary and adequate physical care, Cynthia Geneva Walker was charged with three counts of first-degree criminal mistreatment of her three children based solely on the condition of her household. In many ways this case parallels the earlier one involving Baker-Krofft.

The story begins on the afternoon of April 12, 2006, when two Salem police officers were dispatched to Cynthia's house based on a tip of suspected drug activity. Cynthia lived in a rental house with her significant other, Timothy McCants, and their three children, ages three years, two years, and five and a half months. When the officers arrived, they noticed garbage near the garage and clutter on the enclosed porch. They detected the aroma of garbage and dirty laundry from outside the house. Looking in the front window, they further observed a couch littered with laundry as well as soiled diapers and garbage on the living room floor. When the officers asked to enter the residence to resolve the alleged drug activity, Timothy refused admittance. While talking to Timothy, one of the officers noticed that children lived there. Timothy assured the officer that the children were "okay" even though the house was unkempt. Concerned for the welfare of the children, the officers arrested Cynthia and Timothy and charged them with first-degree criminal mistreatment.

The defendants agreed to allow the officers to search their domicile. Of particular concern by the police was the presence of small toys that represented potential choking hazards. One officer observed the two-year-old trying to insert a small toy into his mouth. One bedroom was partially blocked by a cabinet, which the officers construed as a fire hazard. The kitchen had an overfull garbage can and apparently a problem with ants. However, the refrigerator was well stocked with food and clean, and the bathroom was relatively clean. The officers were informed that a door leading to the garage was kept locked to prevent the children from playing there, although when the officers went into the garage the two oldest children followed, which caused the officers to disbelieve Cynthia and Timothy. There was the smell of mildew and mold emanating from the vicinity of the laundry. Cynthia reported that approximately a month earlier a rat had taken residence

Box 2.1 Spotlight on Julie Baumer

Julie Baumer was interviewed by Mitch Ruesink on June 4, 2014. The following story is based on that interview and other documents obtained during the data collection phase of this research.

Julie Baumer could not have imagined that she would be convicted of child abuse and sent to jail after she took her infant nephew, Philipp, to the hospital. Julie's younger sister, Victoria, was a crack addict when Philipp was born. Victoria, who had previously given up one child for adoption, knew that she would not be able to provide for the infant, so Julie agreed to a family adoption. Victoria's pregnancy was complicated by the fact that she was using drugs. Julie found out during her second trial that this can lead to a vitamin D deficiency, which was likely a contributing factor to Philipp's medical problems. Labor was induced two weeks before the due date, and the baby was small at birth.

After Philipp was born he was listless, so they transferred him to a neonatal intensive care unit for a week and fed him with a feeding tube. After his release, Julie was able to get him to eat a little at a time for about four weeks. By the fifth week, Philipp had problems keeping his formula down for more than a few hours. By October 3, 2003, according to Julie, "After 12 hours of him taking a feeding and not keeping it down, I contacted his pediatrician and I asked her what we should do since I do not want him to become dehydrated, can I bring him in?" Her doctor agreed that she should bring Philipp to the hospital.

Julie found out during her second trial that the physician in the ER had ordered an MRI, which was never taken because Philipp was transferred before the MRI could be done. Julie notes, "Had that order been fulfilled, they would have realized right then and there that he was actually stroking at the hospital."

Philipp was transferred to Children's Hospital in Detroit so they could better ascertain the condition of his health. According to Julie, "They were suspecting that he had some form of virus but they felt that [by] transferring him to a children's hospital, they would be able to narrow it down better." While Philipp was there, the attending nurse noticed that his head size had grown considerably. This time they did a CAT scan and an MRI, whereupon they discovered that he had bleeding in his brain. They performed emergency surgery to relieve the bleeding. On October 5, 2003, Julie received a call from the sheriff's office. She believed that the call was in reference to her sister, Victoria, who was using drugs again. Symptoms like listlessness, poor appetite, and bleeding of the brain are also associated with shaken baby syndrome (SBS) and the workers at the hospital believed that Philipp was a victim of SBS. After being interviewed at the sheriff's office for about twenty minutes, Julie realized they suspected her of child abuse. "So I immediately became, not defensive, but shut them down and they mistook my demeanor as being guilty."

Considering how the interview went, Julie was relieved she was not taken into custody. However, her problems were not over. She was brought in for a second interview, and this time they were playing the good cop/bad cop routine. The bad cop was a woman, and the first thing she said was "How dare you, you know that child has broken bones and bruises all over," to which Julie replied, "Excuse me, and I'm sorry if I sound offensive, but do you have me mixed up with someone else? You must have me mixed up with somebody else, because what you are telling me is completely inaccurate."

Unable to get a confession out of her, the police requested that she take a lie detector test and, since she still had some faith in the law, she consented. For Julie, the lie detector test could prove once and for all that she was innocent. It did not take long for this simple request to turn into a nightmare. As Julie observed,

> Well, I will tell you, that experience was absolutely horrific. Nobody could ever be prepared for that type of interrogation. You know, they sat me down in a very small room; they had me looking straight ahead. I couldn't move; they told me not to move, they told me to keep looking straight ahead and for three hours I was under full-blown interrogation.

As the test was drawing to a close, Julie was told that she had failed. She said "Nope. That's absolutely incorrect. I want to retake the test." She was informed that they could not let her do that and, with that, her request was dropped.

Three months passed between the lie detector test and the call that Julie received from her attorney telling her that they were going to press charges and that she had seventy hours to turn herself in. Her attorney, who practiced family law, advised her to get a criminal attorney. At this point she was in shock, hardly able to comprehend what was going on. Julie called her parents, family, and friends to let them know what was happening and to get some support.

A close friend recommended a bail bondsman who would probably know a good criminal defense attorney. The bondsman recommended Elias Muawad, who interviewed Julie over the phone and invited her into his office. After talking to her, Muawad recommended that she turn herself in and said that he believed that she would do a year in prison. Julie knew that she was innocent and wanted to fight the charges. The reality was that she had only three days to surrender to authorities, so she turned herself in. Despite being a model citizen before all of this occurred and belonging to several service organizations, she was arraigned and bail was set at $100,000.

Things started sinking in after her family was able to raise the standard 10 percent necessary to release her from jail. She still believed that the truth would prevail. Julie and her family knew that Philipp's injuries were likely from birth because of the early delivery and the second dose of pitocin to start labor. Her defense against the charges of child abuse was going to be birth trauma. After eighteen months of preparation, the trial started on September 13, 2005.

Although before the trial Julie believed that her defense was going to be birth trauma, she was shocked when her attorney gave his opening statement and said, "All I can tell you guys, it didn't happen on her watch." Muawad was referring to child abuse, which is what the prosecution was claiming Julie did. At this point, Julie had lost the heart of her defense, and she knew that the trial was over before it had really started. "My own lawyer did not have faith in me."

The trial turned out to be longer and more complicated than Muawad or Julie had anticipated. She recalls, "So after a four-week trial, I was completely railroaded. I wasn't allowed any expert defense, expert witnesses. I wasn't allowed any personal characteristic people, no character witnesses. I did have one expert witness, however, I couldn't afford her."

During the trial, two doctors testified against Julie. One testified that Philipp had suffered blunt force trauma; the other stated that he had suffered from SBS. Julie's attorney never presented contradictory evidence that Philipp's injuries were the result of natural causes. Instead, he argued that the state needed to prove that Julie had intended to shake the baby. The prosecution wanted to portray her as some sort of monster, and that is what the jury believed. Julie was found guilty on September 29, 2005.

Looking back, Julie believes her attorney should have gone to the court and asked for funds that could have been used to pay expert witnesses. He never did, so the jury heard a very one-sided view of things. After being convicted, Julie was shocked again when she was sentenced to ten to fifteen years in prison. She had expected a sentence of one to four years based on presentencing guidelines and the fact that she did not have a criminal record. Typically, the only reason a judge would give a harsher sentence in a case such as this one is because there is evidence compelling enough to justify it.

Julie's first appeal was unsuccessful. By the time she made a second appeal, she had very few resources left. She lost that appeal as well and was left sitting in prison with nobody left to help her. It seemed that all was lost. During her first few years she was very bitter about what happened. She was living in a small cell with a roommate, on lockdown for sixteen hours a day. Julie relied on her strong faith, asking God why this was happening, and what she should do next. She started writing attorneys, asking if they would help on a pro bono basis.

In fall of 2007 an answer came to her when Sister Lois, a nun from the Felician Sisters, came to visit for the first time. Julie's name was on a prayer list, and Sister Lois wanted to visit her and pray with her. As the visit was ending, the nun asked Julie to share the details of her case. Sister Lois additionally asked Julie if she needed an attorney. She offered to give Julie's name and information to Charles Lugosi, an attorney and visiting instructor of law at the Ava Maria School of Law. Sister Lois gave the case to Lugosi so his law students could use it for a class project.

It was a few months before Julie heard from Lugosi, who wrote her and said, "If you are guilty, I don't think that you got enough time; if you are innocent, I am going to get you out of there, so please forward your transcripts." Lugosi agreed to take the case and received support through the law school. It was not long before it became apparent that more help would be needed if they were going to be successful.

Two attorneys agreed to work on the case pro bono. The first was Heather Kirkwood, a Seattle-based attorney who specializes in child abuse defenses. A Michigan attorney, Carl Marlinga, also agreed to work on the case, along with the Michigan Innocence Project. Kirkwood was able to get a medical expert to look at Philipp's CAT scan and confirm that it was a stroke. His conclusion was, "This is a stroke. There is no way that this lady did anything." This was the defense Julie had been seeking.

A motion was filed for a relief from judgment based on newly discovered evidence. Ironically, the new motion was filed with Julie's original trial judge, James Biernat, who granted her a new trial. Julie had a bond hearing in November 2009 and was able to be released. The state decided to recharge her, although the second trial did not begin for almost another year.

Julie was out of prison, but she was not free from the stigma that follows anyone accused of a crime. After being released, she did not have anywhere to go. Her siblings were spread out, a few had left the state, and her parents had moved into a senior complex. She spent her first night out of prison in a homeless shelter. The next day she was asked to leave after an article appeared in the local paper about her. The director of the shelter was concerned that the residents and donors would be uneasy if she stayed.

A judge allowed Julie to live with her brother, who was further away. The second trial was scheduled in ten months. She had a strong legal team this time and possessed the evidence she needed to prove her innocence. Nonetheless, waiting for her day in court again was extremely difficult. She was also dealing with the death of her mother, who had a stroke and died two weeks after her release. The first time Julie went to trial she was confident that she would be found innocent. After being found guilty and sent to prison, Julie was timid and afraid before the second trial. The trial lasted four weeks and on October 15, 2010, the jury came back with a not guilty verdict and Julie was finally exonerated.

Julie had spent over four years in prison. Even though she was no longer behind bars, it took time before she actually felt that she was free. She was still dealing with the trauma of incarceration for something she did not do. She explains it by saying, "when you are convicted and thrown into prison, your identity is taken from you. There are so many things that you are stripped of, internally and emotionally, and . . . you are dehumanized."

One morning, after about four months of being free, Julie went for a walk. Nobody was there to stop her. In prison, she was told where she could go and when she could use the bathroom. After taking the walk, Julie realized that she was really free again.

When she was exonerated, Julie received a handshake and an apology from the judge. However, the prosecutor avoided her. Her family was ecstatic, but in four years, she had lost the connections she once had with family and friends. After she was convicted, people went on with their lives, and the people who knew her believed that she would not be back for at least fifteen years. Julie reluctantly recalls, "I have contact with all of my family, but sad to say, we're estranged. We don't have the connection that we once had. This is an issue that I am working through but I feel like I was abandoned by my family."

Julie did not receive any money from the state since Michigan does not offer any financial remuneration for a wrongful conviction. Despite being found innocent, she could not simply pick up where she left off. When she would seek employment, prospective employers would ask what she had been doing for the past four years. Over several months, Julie applied for several positions. Although she had letters stating that she was exonerated of any wrongdoing, she did not hear back from potential employers. "I would interview very well for various positions, but nobody called me back. So, after several months of not getting called back, and pushing a broom in a hospital, I realized that maybe I should bury this part of my life 'cause, obviously, people are not accepting it as I thought they would. A lot of people are close-minded." Julie found a job as an orderly so that she would be financially solvent. She also started working on a degree in criminal justice, hoping to change the system so that other women would not have to go through the same ordeal.

When Julie reflects back on these events, she laments the fact that she will never see Philipp again.

> I will never get back what I have lost. Never. Starting from them taking Philipp on. . . . Philipp was adopted out before my first trial started . . . I remember when we had gotten notice, after he was released from the hospital [and] he was placed in foster care. My parents were denied access because they said, "You're supportive of your daughter, you're supportive of your other daughter, and we don't want either of them to have contact with him [Philipp]. . . ." I had a sister down in Florida who was . . . a social worker for the state of Florida and even with her credentials, with her husband backing her up, to move up to Michigan and rent an apartment for the length of however long this was going to take, so that she could watch Philipp, they denied her.

Julie has not seen Philipp since the first trial. He is a special needs child who suffers from cerebral palsy. This has been especially difficult for her, since Philipp's adoptive parents still believe she is guilty. Julie has not initiated any contact and has not heard from his parents.

After two years of struggling, Julie was able to obtain a good job that has allowed her to get where she needs to be. She also authored a novel, *An Undeserved Sentence*, which was published in 2012. Despite the adversity and hardship she has faced, Julie continues to strive to rebuild her life.

in the roof above the garage. They had set rat traps and informed their landlord of the problem to no avail. The police failed to find any controlled substances during their sweep of the house. Cynthia's house was later declared a "public nuisance" by a compliance officer from the local health department who had been summoned by the police, although the unsanitary and unsafe conditions had been remedied within two weeks.

During their joint bench trial, Cynthia agreed that the small toys (doll accessories) represented potential choking hazards for the younger children, but mentioned that they were usually kept in a locked closet and played with when the younger children were not present. She further contended that the oldest child had taken the toys out just prior to the officers' arrival. In closing, the defendants' lawyer argued that the prosecution had failed to prove that their behavior constituted withholding necessary and adequate physical care. Unimpressed, the judge found Cynthia and Timothy guilty of three counts of first-degree criminal mistreatment. In handing down the guilty verdicts, the judge concluded that "this is just not a dirty house, and it's not a house that got this dirty over two days of [Walker] being sick. This house is absolutely filthy, and I consider it a danger to those children" (Oregon Judicial Department Appellate Court Opinions, 2009). In 2009 the state Court of Appeals affirmed the circuit court's ruling.

The following year their case was heard by the Oregon Supreme Court. Cynthia and Timothy were represented by the deputy public defender of Salem. He was assisted by the chief defender in preparation of the legal brief. Their case was joined with that of Nancy Baker-Krofft, given the similarities of the circumstances. On August 19, 2010, the court overturned the earlier convictions and prohibited a retrial of their case (Oregon Judicial Department of Appellate Court Opinions, 2009, 2010; Oregon Supreme Court, media release, 2010).

Shaken Baby Syndrome and Child Abuse

During the 1980s and 1990s, shaken baby syndrome (SBS) was a commonly accepted diagnosis for infants exhibiting subdural and retinal hemorrhaging and swelling of the brain. Today there is considerably less consensus among forensic, medical, and legal scholars. The triad of symptoms that were assumed to be the result of child abuse can result from a number of maladies including blood disorders and vitamin deficiencies.

Red-haired Brandy Briggs, a mother of two, grew up in east Texas and later moved to Highlands, Texas, an unincorporated rural area near Houston. She had become pregnant with her son Daniel while attending an alternative school after dropping out of high school. On May 5, 1999, she noticed that her two-month-old son was barely breathing and unconscious, so she immediately called 911. The infant was taken to the hospital, where a breathing tube was inadvertently inserted into his stomach, therefore depriving his lungs of oxygen for over forty minutes. Daniel died in Brandy's arms four days later on Mother's Day.

Dr. Patricia Moore, who was later questioned about a number of her diagnoses, performed an autopsy on Daniel and determined that the cause of death was SBS caused by severely shaking the infant. Brandy was subsequently arrested and charged with first-degree felony injury to a child. Unable to afford adequate legal representation and the expense associated with securing experts to testify on her behalf, she was told by her attorney to admit to shaking her baby and accept a plea bargain. Under that arrangement she would be charged with second-degree felony injury to a child, which her counsel assured her would result in probation. But such was not to be. Instead, the judge sentenced her to seventeen years in prison. At the young age of nineteen years, Brandy's life seemed to be falling apart. In addition to the death of Daniel, her other son, Joseph, was taken from her and placed in state custody.

Though the Texas Court of Appeals denied her motion for a new trial in 2002, her new appellate attorneys began to achieve some measure of success. They located two pediatricians who testified that the child's death was the result of a urinary tract infection. Questions were also being raised about the objectivity of Dr. Moore. The new medical examiner for Harris County found Moore's work to be "defective and improper" and to be slanted in favor of the police and prosecution. Upon reexamination of the evidence, the new medical examiner rejected the notion that SBS played a role in the infant's death. He also discovered that the boy had been deprived of oxygen for an extended period of time when his breathing tube had been incorrectly placed in his stomach.

In December 14, 2005, the Texas Court of Criminal Appeals overturned the verdict based on ineffective assistance of counsel. According to the court, her attorney "did not reflect reasonable professional judgment" when he failed to explore the infant's medical history. According to Brandy's new attorney, "They put an oxygen tube down the kid's throat, missed his lungs, went into his stomach, and for 42 minutes they pumped oxygen into the child's stomach. Had her attorney or the prosecutor read these medical records, they would have found this" (ABC

News, 2005). Brandy was released just before Christmas on $20,000 bail while the state decided whether to retry her case.

On December 25, 2005—after serving five years of her sentence—Brandy was reunited with her other son, Joseph. When interviewed she said, "It was wonderful. It was the best feeling. I've been waiting a long time just for that touch, to be able to hold him and kiss him and tell him I love him" (ABC News, 2005). Nevertheless, Brandy could not get comfortable because she still faced the possibility of a new trial.

Finally, nine months after her release on bail, Brandy learned that the state would not pursue her case. Yet as is frequent in overturned convictions, the prosecutors stopped short of saying that she was innocent. In lieu of pronouncing her innocent, the district attorney said that charges would be dropped due to insufficient evidence to retry her. Brandy, who indicated a desire to return to school, commented, "It's been difficult, not knowing what's going to happen one day to the next, knots in my stomach all the time. I had to take leave of absence from school. I just couldn't concentrate." She continued, "I know that I am innocent. The evidence is right there in their face. Why can't they see it?" (ABC News, 2005; Associated Press, 2005c; Gavett, 2011; Gross, n.d. a; Kever, 2006; Lezon, 2005; O'Hare, 2006)

Munchausen Syndrome by Proxy

According to the Merriam-Webster online dictionary, Munchausen syndrome by proxy (MSBP) refers to "a psychological disorder in which a parent and typically a mother harms her child (as by poisoning), falsifies the child's medical history, or tampers with the child's medical specimens in order to create a situation that requires or seems to require medical attention." In extreme cases this disorder can result in the death or near-death of a child. The diagnosis of the malady is often controversial because it is rare and little is known about its exact cause. This psychological disorder was not officially recognized by the American Psychiatric Association until the publication of the fifth edition of the *Diagnostic and Statistical Manual* (DSM) in 2013.

Yvonne Eldridge lived in a house in Walnut Creek, California, with her husband, Dennis, and their three daughters, Tamara, Amber, and Chandra. All three children were honor students and by all appearances a close-knit family. In 1987 Yvonne and Dennis, who had an impeccable record as foster parents, were asked by the San Francisco Department of Social Services to participate in a pilot program involving high-risk and medically fragile infants. Because of the nature of the program, all five family members consented to this request. Under this program they were to become a foster family to infants who were addicted to drugs, had AIDS, or suffered from some severe medical problem.

In spring 1987 the Eldridges welcomed a terminally ill infant into their household. Infected with HIV, Glenisha required special attention that her parents had been incapable of giving. She soon died of complications from AIDS. Later that year, Tasha was accepted into their home. Seven-month-old Tasha weighed less than eight pounds and could not roll over or sit up without assistance. In 1988 in recognition of their excellent service in the Baby Moms Program, Yvonne and Dennis received national recognition as one of the "Great American Families" and were later rewarded with a trip to the White House and a chance to meet Nancy Reagan. But Yvonne's troubles were just about to commence.

Denisha, another infant from the Baby Moms Program, became part of the Eldridge household in January 1991. As with Tasha, Dr. Marc Usatin became her primary care doctor and pediatrician. Usatin was part of their HMO. During some of their visits, Yvonne and her teenage daughter began receiving unsolicited sexual advances, which they immediately rebuked. As a result, Usatin turned Yvonne into the Contra Costa Children's Protective Services for alleged misbehavior. After an extensive review, the agency determined that the charges were unfounded. Usatin's attempt to get a district attorney to prosecute was also unsuccessful. Several months later, Amber had her first baby, a little boy. While she was still in her hospital room, two police officers accompanied a social worker who took custody of the infant. Amber was later informed that her son would be placed in a foster home unless she signed a document declaring that she would move out of her mom's house with her son, never allow her son to be left unattended with her mom, and confess that her mom had a mental disorder known as MSBP. Outraged, Amber refused to sign the statement, although she was eventually given temporary custody of her baby.

But Usatin was not finished with Yvonne. In November 1992 he and another physician were successful in getting Joyce Blair from the state Attorney General's Office to reopen the case. The next year investigators seeking to revoke her foster care license claimed that Yvonne's actions were responsible for three deaths and the harming of eight other children between the years 1987 and 1991. While the medically fragile infants in the Baby Moms Program often died of their illnesses, the state was intent on proving that Yvonne had hastened their demise.

As the accusations leveled against Yvonne by Usatin began receiving air time on television, the Eldridges began to feel the wrath of a misinformed public. Yvonne's three daughters became social pariahs at school. Chandra, the youngest of the three, had to see a school psychiatrist. Threatening and obscene phone calls, as well as rocks and other projectiles thrown at their house, made their life one of constant fear. Consequently, they moved to Eugene, Oregon, to begin a new life. But on a cool February morning in 1994, several police officers appeared at their doorstep, one of whom had a search warrant. A social worker also took custody of Amber's son, who was now eleven months old. Usatin and another physician had informed the police that upon entering the home they should immediately remove Amber's son because they "would most likely find [Amber's son] to be in dire need of medical attention." Yet as the social worker picked up the baby she exclaimed, "This baby looks perfectly healthy to me" ("Yvonne Eldridge falsely accused of harming children," n.d.). When Amber inquired as to why her son was being taken, she was told that she had missed a hearing in the Walnut Creek juvenile court, something for which she had never received notification. Although Amber later regained custody of her son, he spent five months in a foster home.

In November 1994 Yvonne was informed that Joyce Blair was going forward with a case against her and would be seeking an indictment from a grand jury shortly. She was to be charged with child endangerment, which was the result of MSBP. Because the prosecuting attorney decides what evidence the grand jury will hear and since the defense is not permitted to cross-examine witnesses or call their own witnesses, the grand jury indicted Yvonne on one count of child endangerment for Tasha and one count for Denisha.

Her trial began on May 8, 1996, in the Contra Costa Superior Court. While preparing for the trial, the prosecutor removed the original medical records of Denisha and Tasha from local hospitals, rather than making copies. Furthermore, the prosecutor made it difficult for Yvonne's court-appointed attorney to have access to the files. She kept the files in her private office and would only release copies when Yvonne consented to pay for them. Furthermore, Denisha and Tasha were removed from the Eldridge residence and Yvonne's parents, who lived separately from Yvonne, had their foster children taken into custody even though they were never charged with any crime.

As the trial progressed, the prosecutor selectively released excerpts of the 10,000 pages of medical records to the jury. One of the expert witnesses for the state testified that Yvonne suffered from MSBP based on a thirty-minute interview in his office.[5] The ineptness of her public defender did not help her cause. Her attorney failed to call any expert witnesses or character witnesses to offset the barrage of false accusations. Only Yvonne was called to the stand, but by then her testimony had been sufficiently impeached so as to be useless. It is unknown whether her public defender ever read the complete records since much of the information in the medical records contradicted the testimony of the doctors who testified against her. Yvonne was found guilty and sentenced to forty months in prison on July 10, 1996. She was placed on a $100,000 property bond and granted her freedom while she pursued health care for Dennis, who suffered from amyotrophic lateral sclerosis and was confined to a wheelchair.

Meanwhile Yvonne sought the assistance of two new attorneys, who filed a motion for a new trial based on ineffective assistance of counsel. They also discovered that one of the physicians who testified for the state was responsible for the investigation of Yvonne and had a pattern of accusing foster parents of being abusive. After a new trial was ordered on January 16, 1998, the prosecution appealed the ruling. The First District Court of Appeals remanded the case back to the lower court with the request to determine whether the public defender's legal representation constituted ineffective assistance of counsel.

In September 2000 the lower court judge heard arguments about the ineffectiveness of Yvonne's legal counsel. It was additionally noted that Usatin, who had testified in both the grand jury investigation and the trial, had made sexual advances to other patients and hospital employees and had a tendency to accuse women of suffering from MSBP. Consequently, a new trial was granted on December 21, 2000. The state appealed but was unsuccessful. Finally, on January 8, 2003, the charges against Yvonne were dismissed (Goodyear, 2000; Gross, n.d. f; "Yvonne Eldridge falsely accused of harming children," n.d.).

Summary

The plethora of child sex abuse cases at preschools and other facilities during the 1980s and 1990s accentuates the significance of studying wrongful convictions involving alleged child abuse. Although the convictions were not confined to women, the harm they produced for the accusers and the accused extends well beyond these two decades. Frequently these cases began with an unsubstantiated claim of child abuse and proliferated as false memories were implanted into the children by therapists and social workers. During the latter twentieth century, it was typically believed that children could not be manipulated into telling falsehoods; hence, if they spoke of sexual or ritual abuse, then it must have happened. Add to this mix some overzealous prosecutors who conveniently overlooked inconsistencies in the stories the children were telling and withheld exculpatory evidence and you have the makings of a wrongful conviction. Even when some of the children later recanted their stories and told of how they were pressured to say the things they said, prosecutors were reluctant to admit to their errors. At that point, the damage had been done. The lives of the alleged child molesters were never the same and an unknown number of children continued to hold steadfast to their inaccurate beliefs that they had been victimized.

The cases of sloppy housekeepers are especially interesting. While the descriptions suggest a household that goes beyond the term "dirty," the criminalization of such behavior reveals the excessive reach into the personal lives of women who are seen to have the primary responsibility for raising their children. Moreover, it would seem that this intrusion into their lives would not have occurred if they had not been poor. Since social workers are infrequently summoned to investigate the personal lives of wealthier individuals, a middle- or upper-class woman with an excessively unkempt household is unlikely to come to the attention of authorities. (Not to mention the fact that the woman of greater financial means can afford to hire someone to clean the home.) Failure to reflect middle-class standards likely enhanced their probability of being singled out for these convictions. In two of the four cases, for instance, the defendants were single mothers; in another case the defendant lived with her significant other. Only one of the wrongful convictions involved a woman whose husband was physically present in the household.

Shaken baby syndrome, briefly mentioned in this chapter, is addressed in greater depth in Chapter 3. Once accepted by the forensic and medical communities, SBS has been questioned more of late. In particular, some doubt exists whether the symptoms thought to be associated with SBS can occur without some external signs (e.g., bruising and scars) of excessive shaking. Since women are usually the primary caregivers, this syndrome is most likely to be used to convict women of harm to their infants. As more is learned about SBS, additional wrongful convictions are likely to be forthcoming.

Munchausen syndrome by proxy (MSBP) is another questionable diagnosis with serious ramifications for the wrongful conviction of women. Considered to be rare, this diagnosis is less likely to be used than SBS to convict women of possible child abuse. Only a single case of MSBP was identified in the sample of women charged with some form of child abuse.

Several common threads permeate the child abuse cases. As might be expected, the most common factor associated with these false convictions is eyewitness error. Eyewitness error was present in nearly seven out of every ten of these cases. In the majority of the cases, the eyewitness was an impressionable child who had been influenced by a therapist, social worker, or police officer into believing that he or she had been sexually or physically victimized by the defendant. Prosecutorial misconduct and police misconduct were equally present in these wrongful convictions: each was found in 36 percent of the child abuse cases. None of the other factors investigated in this study consistently contributed to this miscarriage of justice, although ineffective assistance of counsel was probably undercounted given the subjective nature of this factor.

One disparity was particularly apparent in these statistics: the overrepresentation of white women among the wrongfully convicted child abuse cases. Only one (2.8 percent) of the thirty-six cases in which it was possible to identify the race of the defendant involved an African American woman. This racial differential raises some intriguing questions regarding its existence. Does this disparity reflect racial differences in actual child abuse? If not, what accounts for this huge racial disparity?

In answer to the first query, it is informative to know that the US Department of Health and Human Services (2009) reported that African American children are nearly twice as likely as their white counterparts to be found in verified reports of child abuse and neglect. Moreover, in 2010 the US Census Bureau reported that only 12.6 percent of the US population self-reported its race as "Black or African American" (Humes et al., 2011). Although it is impossible to ascertain the exact racial dimensions of the child abuse and neglect problem, one can conservatively conclude that African American women should represent more than 12.6 percent of the child abuse cases. Hence, the 2.8 percent figure (or a single case) of black child abuse cases mentioned earlier is well below what one would expect if wrongful convictions reflected known cases of child abuse and neglect. Unfortunately, calculating an exact figure is complicated by the fact that many of the reported and verified child abuse and neglect cases may not be prosecuted.

Turning now to the second question, it is necessary to acknowledge the precursors to the wrongful convictions examined here. Trials resulting in wrongful convictions are often characterized by hasty decisionmaking. Failure on the part of the defense to prepare a strong case and call appropriate witnesses, pressure on the prosecution to bring the alleged perpetrator to justice, media coverage of the alleged incident, and other factors tend to increase the chance of a false conviction. The role that each of these will play in the trial is a function of many things, including the financial resources of the defendant, the venue, the credibility of the witnesses, and the defendant's prior background. In the criminal justice literature, the role of victim race has been extensively investigated. Scholarship that examines the role of race in criminal justice processing has consistently documented the importance of victim race in sentencing outcomes. Investigations of rape, sexual assault, and murder demonstrate that offenders who victimize whites are more likely than those who victimize African Americans to receive severe sanctions (Acker et al., 1998; Baldus and Woodworth, 2003; Free, 1996; Paternoster, 1991; Paternoster, et al., 2007; Phillips, 2012; Spohn and Spears, 1996; Walsh, 1987; Williams et al., 2007).[6] Because the race of the victim and the alleged offender are typically identical in child abuse incidents, this disparity poses an intriguing, albeit unanswered, question: Do the racial differences observed in child abuse cases reflect a greater importance attached to white children by the judicial system? If so, this may account for the greater presence of wrongful child abuse convictions among white women as the criminal justice system attempts to quickly sanction the alleged violators of white victims.

Notes

1. The McMartin preschool child sex abuse investigation represents the quintessential case of coercive and suggestive manipulation of children's memories during the epidemic of child sex abuse cases. At a cost of $15 million and seven years of investigation and prosecution, the McMartin preschool child sex abuse trial is the longest and most expensive criminal trial in the history of this country.

It all began with a phone call to the Manhattan Beach (California) Police Department to report sexual abuse involving a two-and-a-half-year-old boy at the McMartin preschool facility. His mother, Judy Johnson, who was a paranoid schizophrenic and an alcoholic, claimed that a school aide, twenty-five-year-old Ray Buckey, had molested her son. Despite no physical signs of sexual abuse and the inability of the child to pick out his alleged perpetrator from photographs, Ray was arrested on September 3, 1983. The day after his arrest, the police chief mailed letters to all of the parents who had children attending the preschool to inform them of the accusations and to request any additional information they might possess.

Meanwhile the accusations being made against the preschool began to get more unusual. The little boy's mother was now contending that Peggy McMartin Buckey, Ray's mother, was involved in satanic practices and had taken her son to a church in which a baby was beheaded and her son was forced to drink the blood. She also insisted that Ray could fly and implicated other teachers, stating that they were mutilating rabbits. Although it had become apparent that the original complainant was delusional, suspicions had been swirling since the letter was sent.

Parents were encouraged to take their children to Children's Institute International (CII) to be evaluated. At CII the children were paraded through a series of leading questions with the possibility of rewards if they reported abuse at the preschool facility. Although many initially denied witnessing any abuse at the preschool, they eventually acquiesced and told their interviewers what they wanted to hear. By March 1984 the number of allegedly sexually abused children stood at 384. Some of the children also received medical examinations from Dr. Astrid Heppenstall Heger, an employee of CII. She determined that 80 percent of the children she had examined had been sexually abused based on minute scarring, which she attributed to anal penetration.

By March 22, 1984, seven individuals had been indicted by a grand jury. In addition to Ray and Peggy, the indictment included Ray's sister, the founder of the preschool, and three other teachers. The "McMartin Seven" were eventually indicted on over 200 counts of child sex abuse.

The preliminary hearing, which lasted more than a year, revealed little support for the allegations. Stories about "secret tunnels" and "secret rooms" where many of the rituals occurred failed to be corroborated. No nude photographs of children were found at the preschool or the homes of defendants. The children's testimony continued to be inconsistent and contradictory. Their stories included sexual assaults on farms, in circuses, and in car washes, among others. Some of the claims included children being flushed down toilets to a secret room where they would be sodomized. An equally outrageous account involved a trip to the cemetery where children were required to excavate coffins. Once removed, they were opened, whereupon the teachers would begin savagely destroying the remains with knives.

The tales were so strange and the manner in which the children had been interviewed so questionable that even during the preliminary hearing some members of the prosecution team became concerned about the legitimacy of the accusations. Nevertheless, the chief prosecutor believed all of the defendants should be prosecuted. It was only after a meeting in December 1985 that the district attorney's office decided to drop charges against all but Ray and Peggy Buckey.

The McMartin trial began on July 14, 1987, and included over sixty witnesses for the prosecution, a jailhouse snitch, parents whose children attended the preschool, medical specialists, therapists, as well as one of Ray's former lovers. Despite an absence of evidence to support the existence of secret tunnels, pornographic pictures, and sacrificed animals, the prosecution attempted to characterize the trial as one about the betrayal of trust. The snitch, who later admitted that he committed perjury, was a nine-time felon. At the trial, however, he testified that his cell mate, Ray Buckey, had confessed to molesting the children.

After almost thirty months of testimony, the jury began deliberation. Two and a half months elapsed before the jury acquitted Peggy of all charges against her and all but thirteen of the charges against Ray. The jury eventually conceded that it was deadlocked on the remaining charges. As the foreperson of the jury explained, "The interview tapes were too biased; too leading" (Linder, 2003). Although Peggy was not convicted of any wrongdoing, she served two years in jail.

Public pressure resulted in a decision to retry Ray. Two new prosecutors joined a new judge and a scaled-down trial. Charged with only eight counts of child sex abuse, the trial proceeded more quickly. The three-month long trial, nevertheless, resulted in the same outcome: a mistrial when the jurors became deadlocked. The District Attorney decided against a third trial and all charges were subsequently dismissed. Although no defendant was ever convicted of any of these wild accusations, Ray served five years in jail prior to gaining his freedom (Linder, 2003; "McMartin preschool trial" 2014; Talbot, 2001).

2. Prior to the start of the first trial involving Bob Kelly, PBS aired a documentary titled "Innocence Lost" as part of its *Frontline* series. The documentary was extremely critical of the handling of the individuals charged in this case and suggested that many of the alleged events could not have conceivably happened.

3. Over a seven-year period, three episodes of PBS *Frontline* were devoted to the Little Rascals day care center scandal: "Innocence Lost" (aired on May 7, 1991), "Innocence Lost: The Verdict" (aired on July 21, 1993), and "Innocence Lost: The Plea" (aired on May 27, 1997). For further information, consult the PBS website.

4. Apparently there is some confusion regarding which girl drove around with Bob Perez that day. The National Registry of Exonerations indicates that Donna Everett accompanied Perez on that trip. Yet a book written about the hysteria that prevailed in Wenatchee identifies Ann Everett as the individual. We elected to use the name of "Ann" rather than "Donna" since the book was written by a former prosecutor from Wenatchee, Washington.

5. It was later learned that his diagnosis of Yvonne's mental state preceded his interview of her. He later devoted a chapter in a book about MSBP about her case.

6. The importance attached to victim race is especially pronounced in capital trials. According to Martha Myers (2000, p. 460), the race of the victim "may reflect not only the devalued status of Black victims" but also greater societal outrage over the victimization of a member of the dominant white group.

3

When Women Kill

Eighty-five-year-old Cecilia Cadigan and her ninety-year-old sister, Ann, were retired schoolteachers living together in their rural home near Casco, Wisconsin. Apparently wealthy by some standards, they were stabbed and beaten to death sometime during the afternoon of November 16, 1991. Their bodies were discovered by a neighbor that evening. On that same day, a light-colored, four-door sedan was seen with a white male in the driver's seat. There was no evidence of forced entry into the home, although the downstairs telephone line cord had been disconnected. In addition, the women's purses and wallets, usually kept on a small living room table, were missing. With no substantive leads in the case, it became a cold case file for nearly four years.

A parole violation resulted in Beth LaBatte's arrest on July 25, 1995. Beth, who had issues with alcohol and drugs, had a prior criminal record. She had robbed an elderly woman approximately ten months prior to the murders in Casco. She was charged with two attempted robberies (including one that involved an elderly man) only a few months after the Cadigans were killed. Consequently, she became a suspect in the unsolved crime.

After six hours of intensive interrogation by the police, Beth made incriminating remarks, which were interpreted as a confession. Intimating that she was probably drunk on the day of the crime and that she may have blacked out, she spoke about a "Bad Beth" side to her personality. According to the police, she said, "I think Bad Beth would have known what happened to the old ladies in Casco" (Possley, n.d. a). Nevertheless, she remained adamant that she was not involved in the murders.

Late the following year, an ex-boyfriend of one of her sisters came forward with the revelation that Beth had admitted to the murders.

According to him, she also implicated her then-boyfriend, Charles Benoit. With this information, the county prosecutor charged Beth with two counts of first-degree intentional homicide and two counts of armed robbery in December 1996. In February 1997 Charles was charged with being her accomplice since he had allegedly driven her to the murder site.

Media publicity led to the trial being moved to another county. The case against Beth was largely circumstantial because there was no physical evidence linking her to the murders, nor were there any witnesses to the crime. Three jail informants testified that she had admitted to the murders. Within nine days the jurors returned a verdict of guilty on all counts. At the age of thirty Beth faced two consecutive life terms for the murders plus twenty years for the armed robbery. During the sentencing, the circuit court judge made her ineligible for parole until she turned eighty-five for the first life term and ninety for the second life term, to coincide with the ages of the dead women. Interestingly, her former boyfriend was acquitted one month after her conviction.

Before her sentencing in 1998, Beth told the court that despite her numerous shortcomings, "taking the life of another human being is not one of them." She went on to say, "God knows that I'm innocent. . . . I'm not guilty, and I know that the Cadigan sisters and Kewaunee County will not be able to rest until the real killer is found" (Silvers, 2008).

The Wisconsin Innocence Project at the University of Wisconsin became interested in Beth's case when it learned that several of the crime scene items contained DNA evidence. In May 2004, a judge consented to have the items examined to determine if Beth's DNA matched that found on evidence. The results of the tests were released in June 2005: the DNA found at the crime scene did not match that of Beth. Based on this discovery, a new trial was ordered. On January 15, 2006, Beth was released from prison while awaiting a new trial after having spent almost ten years behind bars for a crime she didn't commit. Finally, on August 1, 2006, the district attorney announced that the charges were being dismissed.

With this segment of her life over, Beth attempted to carve out a new existence. She now had an adult son who had grown up without his mother and a grandson. She moved to a new town to start her new life with a new boyfriend. But as her mother stated, "She [Beth] didn't have that kind of willpower. And there were still people who remembered [the murder case] and didn't let her forget" (Silvers, 2008). Unfortunately, trouble was never very far removed from Beth. She still had a drinking problem, which was her eventual undoing. On September 1, 2007, after just a little more than one year of freedom, she lost control of her pickup truck and was killed when she was thrown from the vehicle. Her boyfriend survived the crash. At the time of her death she had a blood alcohol level of 0.21, well over the legal limit of 0.08 (Nelesen, 2006; Piaskowski, 2007; Possley, n.d. a; Silvers, 2008; *State of Wisconsin v. Beth LaBatte*, Court of Appeals, District III, 98-3677-CR, 1999; Wisconsin Innocence Project, n.d.).

Beth LaBatte's wrongful conviction is atypical of many wrongful murder convictions involving women in that the victims were not people with whom she had an acquaintance. Many of the false murder convictions discussed in this chapter include victims that the women knew. Boyfriends, ex-boyfriends, husbands, ex-husbands, sons, daughters, parents, and children being babysat are among the most common victims in these cases. Indeed, this is one of the distinguishing gender differences in wrongful murder convictions. In false murder convictions involving men, the victim is much more likely to be a stranger.

In the sections that follow, the reader is exposed to a variety of false murder convictions designed to reveal the scope of this problem. It may be recalled from Chapter 1 that wrongful murder convictions accounted for approximately 37 percent of the total number of female wrongful convictions in the sample. When these convictions were disaggregated by race, it was further discovered that white women were somewhat more likely than black women to be falsely convicted for this offense. Almost 40 percent of the white false convictions were for murder, compared with one third of the black false convictions.

Shaken Baby Syndrome and Wrongful Murder Convictions

In Chapter 2 several cases involving shaken baby syndrome (SBS) were examined. The cases discussed instances whereby a woman was charged with contributing to the infant's death but was not formally charged with murder. This section examines five cases in which the prosecutor brought charges of murder for the baby's demise.

Before reviewing these cases, it is prudent to examine SBS more thoroughly. As Chapter 2 noted, during the 1980s through the 1990s, SBS became an accepted diagnosis for infants showing evidence of subdural and retinal hemorrhaging as well as swelling of the brain. Because the neck muscles of infants tend to be undeveloped and their brain tissue is fragile, it is believed that violent shaking can cause permanent damage and even death. Controversy currently surrounds the extent to which shaking alone can result in irreparable damage and death. The previously mentioned symptoms, once thought to be exclusive to SBS, can be attributed to a number of maladies including blood disorders and vitamin deficiencies. Moreover, during an autopsy a small amount of blood may be dislodged into the skull during the removal of the skull cap. The difficulty associated with properly diagnosing SBS is so acute that an editorial appearing in 1998 in *Lancet*, a prestigious British medical journal, implored those given the responsibility for diagnosing it to approach it with great care:

> With such an uncertain definition, it is not surprising that the syndrome has been misdiagnosed. . . . The consequences of such an error are appalling. . . . If 26 years after Caffey's description, doctors are still undecided about the "shaken baby syndrome," the difficulties faced by experts in presenting medical evidence in court, and by the judge and jury in making sense of it, are readily imaginable. . . . Let us hope that increased awareness is tempered with caution against overdiagnosis. (cited in Siegel, 1999)

Teresa Engberg-Lehmer

Teresa Engberg-Lehmer lived with her significant other, Joel, and their three-month-old son, Jonathan. Jonathan was a blue-eyed, blond infant who weighed fifteen pounds and appeared to be healthy. The evening of April 4, 1997, was much like every other weekday evening. Jonathan was fed between 7 and 7:30 p.m. that night and put on a blanket (the couple could not afford a crib) on the floor in the back bedroom to sleep. Teresa and Joel then went to their bedroom until 11:15 p.m., when Teresa got up to make coffee for Joel while he prepared himself for his job delivering bundled newspapers. After Joel left, Teresa went to the back bedroom to check on Jonathan. To her shock, she found him cold and unresponsive. Because they did not have a telephone, she went to a neighbor to call 911. Jonathan was taken by ambulance to a hospital. Although the infant showed no outward signs of physical injury he was pronounced dead just after midnight.

Thirty-nine-year-old attorney Rick Crowl requested that Dr. Thomas Bennett autopsy the deceased infant in Des Moines, Iowa. The pathologist was frequently used by prosecutors in cases like this one. He was known for having a tendency to overdiagnose a victim, and his charm and self-confidence in the courtroom made him an excellent expert witness for the prosecution. He concluded that Jonathan's death was a homicide resulting from "slammed baby syndrome," although he listed "shaken-slammed baby syndrome" as the immediate cause of death on the death certificate. Bennett based his conclusion on four small blotches of blood inside the skull, and one cubic centimeter of blood in the brain, trace amounts of which could have leaked during the opening of the skull. Nevertheless, he was convinced that Jonathan had died at the hands of either or both his parents.

Hesitant to go to trial with such flimsy evidence, Crowl waited until July 1997 to charge Teresa and Joel with first-degree murder. Even then he felt that he had a weak case but was reassured by the medical examiner's autopsy report. Neither defendant was able to pay for an attorney, so they received two court-appointed attorneys. Both attorneys accepted the findings of the medical examiner and did not try to refute the conclusions of his report. Teresa's and Joel's cases were further weakened by their backgrounds. They were known to use drugs and they were not married at the time of Jonathan's death, although they married after Jonathan died. Joel had assaulted a previous girlfriend and on two occasions his parental rights to babies he had fathered were terminated. It was also well known that the two often had disagreements over Jonathan. Joel wanted to give him up for adoption. Perhaps even more damaging to his case was a statement he made to a relative while agitated in which he indicated that he had been "mean" to Jonathan.

Given the perceived weakness of this case, Crowl attempted to get them to implicate each other by offering plea bargains. His most generous offer was to dismiss the charges against one of them in return for testifying against the other. This strategy was unsuccessful as Teresa and Joel adamantly defended each other. Teresa repeatedly told detectives, "I never shook Jonathan. I never personally saw Joel do it . . . I never saw Joel shake him." When Joel was asked about the alleged incident he replied, "No! No sir, no sir. I didn't shake the baby. Teresa didn't shake the baby. I know Teresa better than she knows herself, and she didn't do this" (Siegel, 1999). Despite their protestations, they could see the writing on the wall. Even if the charge was reduced to second-degree murder, they would receive a period of incarceration of at least forty-two years. Reluctantly, they agreed to an "Alford plea," in which they avoided admitting guilt while admitting that the prosecutor had sufficient evidence to win the case. As a result they pleaded guilty to involuntary manslaughter at the recommendation of their defense counsel. They were subsequently sentenced to fifteen years in prison.

Two weeks later, the medical examiner who had concluded that their child's death was a homicide abruptly resigned during an ongoing investigation of his office. Bennett had become the state medical examiner in Iowa in 1986. Unlike his predecessors, he was quite content to cooperate fully with law enforcement and diagnose potential cases of child abuse. Between 1989 and 1997 he diagnosed seventeen cases of SBS and served as an expert witness in other cases. Although Bennett's resignation was officially due to misuse of state resources when he conducted autopsies for private corporate clients, several of his previous autopsies in which he concluded that child abuse was responsible for the child's death were being seriously questioned.

On November 14, 1997, while serving time in prison, Teresa penned a letter to attorney Stephen Brennecke, whom she had read about in a newspaper. He had successfully defended another woman who had been wrongly accused of killing her infant by shaking. Her letter began,

> To Mr. S. Brennecke, My name is Teresa Lehmer . . . We, my husband and myself, both feel that we are a victim of circumstances, probably due to Dr. Bennett. . . . We want to thank you for your article in the newspaper. We believe it was inspired by God. . . . If there is any information that you may have that can help us . . . we would greatly appreciate anything. . . . May God bless you. (Siegel, 1999)

Teresa's letter caught Brennecke's attention and in March 1998 he requested her case file from the state medical examiner's office. Dr. Peter Stephens, a pathologist, consented to review the file. After a two-week delay and several follow-up phone calls, Brennecke was informed that the slides and tissue samples from the case had been destroyed by accident several months earlier. Indeed, someone at the state crime lab had, contrary to policy, destroyed evidence from 356 autopsies involving Bennett, including 4 SBS cases. As a result Brennecke received only fourteen color photographs from the autopsy. By June the report on Jonathan's autopsy was complete. Stephens concluded that no "responsible pathologist would certify death as being due to trauma based on the evidence that I have seen to date" (Siegel, 1999).

Because Stephens had been a vocal critic of Bennett's work, a decision was made to send the file to a neutral expert. Dr. Jerry Jones, who had conducted approximately 5,000 autopsies and diagnosed 8 SBS cases, concurred with the earlier conclusion: there was no evidence of any trauma, nor was there any evidence that Jonathan had died as a result of severe shaking. Instead, Jones determined that Jonathan died of sudden infant death syndrome (SIDS). He called Crowl to inform him that Teresa and Joel were innocent and "should not spend another day in jail" (Siegel, 1999). Upon receiving this information, Crowl immediately called a district court judge to request a hearing based on the new evidence. At the hearing, Crowl moved to vacate the convictions and dis-

Box 3.1 Spotlight on Audrey Edmunds

Audrey Edmunds consented to respond to queries regarding her wrongful conviction via email. The following story is based on those answers and other documents obtained during the data collection phase of this research.

Fall in Wisconsin is a particularly beautiful season. The air is getting crisper, a reminder that winter is drawing near. Leaves are changing from green to various hues of yellow, gold, and red in a kaleidoscope of colors. The Mid-Continent Railway offers autumn color train rides on restored vintage passenger cars through the rural countryside of Sauk County. For many people, October is one of the more enjoyable months in the state, but October 16, 1995, is forever etched in the mind of Audrey Edmunds, for that is the date that forever changed her life.

Audrey Edmunds was a wife, mother, and neighborhood child care provider. She had previously worked as a secretary before deciding to stay home and take care of her two young daughters. Carrie was four and Allison was eighteen months. Audrey was five months pregnant with her next child. To supplement her husband's salary, she provided child care for a few of their neighbors. Each morning she would see her husband off to work and help Carrie get ready for preschool.

One of the children that Audrey babysat was seven-month-old Natalie Beard. When Natalie's mother, Cindy Beard, walked into Audrey's house on that Monday morning, she said that Natalie had been fussy. Because Natalie had just gotten over an ear infection the previous week, Audrey did not think her behavior was unusual. She tried to get her to eat something, but the child refused any food or bottle. By 8:00 a.m. Audrey wanted to give Natalie some time away from the other children and noise, so she put her in her car seat in the master bedroom. In case she was hungry, she gave her a bottle and left the door ajar so that she could hear her. She then proceeded to check on the other children to make sure that they were okay and that Carrie was ready for preschool. The first time she checked on Natalie, the child appeared to be fine. Audrey then went to see if all of the children were ready for their walk to preschool before checking on Natalie again. At 8:35 a.m. Audrey returned and found Natalie limp and barely responsive. Frantic, Audrey rushed to call 911, believing the child had choked on something.

Six minutes elapsed between her phone call and the arrival of the paramedics. Natalie's pupils were dilated and she was taking short breaths. She was airlifted to the University of Wisconsin–Madison hospital, where she died later that evening. Dr. Gregory Holmgren, a physician in the emergency room, saw a subdural hematoma and bleeding in Natalie's eyes. Typically a subdural hematoma occurs as a result of a serious head injury. The bleeding on the brain compresses the brain tissue, which leads to brain injury and frequently death. These two symptoms are commonly associated with shaken baby syndrome (SBS). After Holmgren learned that Natalie had "seemed normal" when she arrived at Audrey's house, he deduced that the injury occurred after her arrival. He further believed that Natalie was the victim of SBS even though she had no external signs of having been shaken. Although the symptoms that the little girl had were consistent with this type of diagnosis, the physicians neglected to look at other medical symptoms or Natalie's prior medical history.

Audrey waited anxiously that night to find out Natalie's condition. When she discovered that Natalie had died, she was heartbroken. She attended the child's funeral and expressed her willingness to cooperate with authorities to ascertain the cause of death.

Over the next few months, Audrey and her family were busy preparing for their move to Lakeville, Minnesota. Four months after Natalie's death, Audrey gave birth to the couple's third daughter, Jeni. On March 19, 1996, she was charged with first-degree reckless homicide in the death of Natalie Beard. Though she was afraid of the possibility of going to prison for a crime that she didn't commit, she also did not believe that she would be convicted on circumstantial evidence.

SBS, a common diagnosis in 1995, is often difficult to diagnose with certainty. There has also been considerable disagreement about what to call the syndrome. At different times it has been called shaken baby syndrome, shaken-impact syndrome, and abusive head trauma. In 1997 the first well-known case that brought to light this problem occurred in Massachusetts, when a nanny was convicted of involuntary manslaughter. Back then it was still generally assumed that the last person who had been with the child had caused the injuries.

Holding on to the hope that the trial would reveal her innocence, Audrey discovered that her expectations would not be realized. Her attorney, Steven Hurley, had been highly recommended as a good defense attorney. He based his defense on her years as a "good and patient" child care provider. To counter the defense's claim, Assistant District Attorney Gretchen Hayward painted a different picture. The prosecution presented a witness who testified that Audrey hit a child on the head with a book while at the library and did not console the crying child. The testimony was questionable at best since the witness did not actually see Audrey commit the act. The most damaging evidence was the extensive medical testimony that Natalie had experienced extreme trauma as the result of severe force. The medical experts maintained this stance despite the fact that the deceased girl did not have any external injuries, which usually accompany SBS cases. It was also asserted that Natalie could not have sustained her injuries as the result of an accident. Hayward portrayed Audrey as someone who snapped while caring for a sick baby, which resulted in Natalie's injuries.

Meanwhile, Hurley was unable to locate an expert who did not think that the victim's injuries were the result of violent shaking. He did find one, a pediatric neurologist named Dr. Mary Dominski, who testified that Natalie's injuries could have preceded her arrival at Audrey's house. Her defense counsel further suggested that Natalie's injuries could have been caused by choking on her bottle formula or by something her parents did. Neighbors who knew Audrey additionally testified that she was very patient and very good with children and that she would never do anything to harm a child.

In an attempt to persuade the jury of her innocence, Audrey took the stand in her own defense. For three and a half hours she answered questions to the best of her knowledge, but she sometimes came across as hesitant during the cross-examination, which weakened her credibility with the jury. Hurley later admitted that this testimony may have hurt their chances of winning the case. She was found guilty on November 26, 1996, and sentenced to eighteen years in prison.

After Audrey's conviction, she was sent to the state's maximum security prison for women, a place she called home for the next eight years. She had never been in trouble with the law, and she found herself experiencing difficulty adjusting to the prison routine. She missed her family and knew that while she was incarcerated she would miss the many milestones in her daughters' lives. Audrey appealed her conviction and filed two petitions for new trials, all of which were denied by the courts. In 2003 she was further denied parole, although she was considered a model prisoner. She continued to hold on to the hope that one day she would be exonerated and returned to her family.

After all of her appeals had been exhausted, Keith Findley of the Wisconsin Innocence Project took on Audrey's cause in 2003. Findley and his team of law students began to assemble the evidence that eventually freed her from prison. By the end of 2004, Audrey was transferred to a minimum security prison. Although she was still in prison, it was not as rigid, and she was allowed to participate in a work-release program.

By 2006 the medical community had started to question its earlier assumptions about SBS. It was now recognized that other causes such as accidents, illnesses, and infections could result in similar types of conditions. Findley filed a motion for a new trial, using the new evidence as additional proof of Audrey's innocence. His first motion was denied, but after an appeal, the Wisconsin Fourth District Court of Appeals ordered a new trial on January 31, 2008. On July 11, 2008, the district attorney's office dismissed the case, and Audrey was finally exonerated.

Since leaving prison, Audrey has been trying to reconstruct the pieces of her former life. Her husband divorced her while she was imprisoned. To financially support herself, Audrey worked for nearly five years at a convenience store before moving to northern Wisconsin to be with her boyfriend. There she found a job at a dairy. Her three girls are grown now; two are in college and the oldest recently moved to Cleveland, Ohio to accept a job promotion. In addition to actively trying to assist others who have been convicted, Audrey coauthored a book about her experiences while speaking at conferences about her wrongful conviction. Her book, *It Happened to Audrey: A Terrifying Journey from Loving Mom to Accused Baby Killer*, was released in 2012.

miss the charges against Teresa and Joel. In a little over one hour the judge granted the motion and the two were given their freedom on September 28, 1998 (Possley, n.d. q; Siegel, 1999).

Mary Weaver

Forty-one-year-old Mary Weaver was a part-time babysitter in Marshalltown, Iowa, when she met Tessia Mathes for the first time. Tessia was pregnant with her daughter, Melissa. After Melissa was born, Tessia and her husband, Brad, began experiencing problems finding a suitable babysitter. At first reluctant to become a full-time babysitter, Mary agreed to take the infant into her care in August 1992. Little did she know that in six months Melissa would die while under her care and that she would become the prime suspect in the infant's death.

Mary was well liked in her community and a devout Christian. Those who knew her considered her to be a gentle woman who sincerely cared about others. As a result, when she was charged with first-degree murder on May 26, 1993, the town was split into factions. According to Captain Mike Hanken of the Marshalltown Police Department, the Weaver case was one of the most divisive cases in his approximately thirty-year tenure with the department: "It is a case you will always remember. They don't get any easier as time goes on" (Alexander, 2013).

The incident leading up to Melissa's death began on the morning of January 22, 1993. Mary had just picked up eleven-month-old Melissa from the Mathes' home to take her back to her house to babysit. Shortly after arriving at her house, Mary noticed that Melissa was not breathing. After a call to 911, paramedics were successful in reviving the infant, and she was flown to a hospital in Iowa City, where she died the next day. An autopsy conducted by Dr. Thomas Bennett—the same state medical examiner who incorrectly diagnosed Jonathan's cause of death in Teresa Engberg-Lehmer's case—concluded that the cause of Melissa's death was SBS.

During Mary's first trial in 1993, the evidence was circumstantial and hotly contested. None of the town's citizens came forward to testify against Mary, and apparently the police had no other suspects in the case. The autopsy had revealed that Melissa had incurred a two-inch skull fracture sometime before her death. Tessia testified that the morning of January 22, 1993, Melissa had hit her head on the padded footrest of a recliner before Mary arrived but appeared to be unaffected by the incident. Experts for the prosecutor contended that the earlier accident was unrelated to the baby's death and that the death was caused by violent shaking or slamming of the infant. The defense countered with the argument that there was no physical evidence linking Mary to Melissa's death and that the infant had already suffered life-threatening injuries prior to the time Mary arrived. A cemetery employee testified that before Melissa's death Tessia had asked about the cost of burying an infant and whether the ground could be excavated during the winter, a statement Tessia vehemently denied. On December 28, 1993, the jury was hopelessly deadlocked and a mistrial was declared.

Figuring that a bench trial would be a more effective forum in which to argue her innocence, Mary's second trial was tried by Marshall County District Judge Carl Peterson, the same judge who presided over her first trial. She retained her attorney from the first trial, Stephen Brennecke. Unfortunately, the outcome was not what she had anticipated. Mary was sentenced to life without parole on May 3, 1994. Although the Iowa Court of Appeals upheld the conviction on September 22, 1995, the Iowa Supreme Court later remanded her case for a hearing on a motion for a new trial.

New evidence was presented at the hearing that buttressed Mary's argument that she was not responsible for Melissa's death. While meeting at Hardee's restaurant where Tessia worked, three women heard her say that Melissa had hit her head on a coffee table, not on a padded recliner, prior to Mary's arrival that day. Moreover, the defense presented testimony from an expert witness questioning the findings of the autopsy. A district judge granted the motion for a new trial on January 31, 1996, and Mary was released on bond after having been wrongfully incarcerated for two years.

Mary's third trial began in February 1997. Brennecke was allowed to present the new evidence in support of his client. Finally, on March 5, 1997, a jury acquitted Mary of the charges, closing this chapter in her life.

Having since moved to another town, Mary continues to remember the little girl. She visits her grave frequently and regrets that her trials overshadowed the tragedy of the child's death. Tessia moved to Nebraska shortly after Mary was exonerated. She divorced Brad after having a son and has been diagnosed with multiple sclerosis, an autoimmune disease that affects the central nervous system (Alexander, 2013; Possley, n.d. j).

Trenda Kemmerer

Trenda Kemmerer lived in the Houston area with her second husband. She had two children from her first husband, a Houston police officer, and another child from her second husband. In 1995 she decided to babysit some of the neighbors' children. One year later she began babysitting a toddler named Danielle Mazzu, whose parents lived several streets away. During the fall of that year, the child was injured when she attempted to climb on two white plastic stackable chairs while in Trenda's care. Though the injuries were not life-threatening, she took the little girl to the emergency room and called the mother, Debbie Mazzu. She offered to pay all the medical bills and notified her insurance agent. Although Danielle's father dismissed the incident as an accident, the Mazzus sued Trenda's insurance company for their daughter's injury. The insurance company refused to pay since Danielle was okay and suffered no ill effects. There was never any investigation of the accident by either the police or Child Protective Services (CPS).

In 1997 Trenda began babysitting eight-week-old Christina Dew and two of her brothers, ages six and eight. On September 2 their mother, Laura Dew, quickly dropped off Christina and her young brothers. She explained that her sixteen-year-old son, Nicholas, had been expelled from high school for drug use and she needed to take him to the Alternate Learning Center. Laura had been experiencing problems with depression as her husband had an affair when she was pregnant with Christina and eventually divorced her. After taking ten-month-old Christina from her, Trenda noticed that she was particularly fussy. The infant was still crying when she took her to the bathroom to change a dirty diaper. Then she stopped crying and had problems breathing. Trenda rushed her to a neighbor's house where she called 911 and then phoned Laura. Both the medics and the police inspected Christina and could not find any evidence of an injury. The medics dismissed the possibility that this was an abuse case and the infant was air lifted to Memorial Hermann Children's Hospital. On September 3, Christina died.[1]

Trenda met with two detectives to discuss the particulars of the incident. At that time she learned that Laura had twice failed a polygraph test and had modified her statements regarding the events of that day. The police began to suspect that either Laura or Nicholas was responsible for Christina's death. Later CPS conducted a full investigation of the incident and cleared Trenda of child neglect or abuse. At the request of the police, Trenda also took and passed two polygraph tests.

Sometime during 1998, the Kemmerers were informed that Laura was bringing a civil suit against them for the wrongful death of Christina. Laura encouraged the Mazzu family to join her in this litigation. Trenda contacted her attorney, Jimmy Phillips, Jr., about the impending civil action and he told her that during the deposition to answer the questions to the best of her knowledge but exhibit no emotion.

By 1999 Trenda learned that she was being charged with injury to a child for the accident involving Danielle Mazzu. When she appeared in court, she was immediately handcuffed and informed that she was now being charged with injury to a child for the death of Christina Dew. After paying the bail bondsman, Trenda was released pending her trial. Realizing her dilemma, she employed the services of Richard "Racehorse" Haynes, a well-known attorney. She additionally retained the services of Phillips, who was handling the civil suit.

Trenda's first trial began in July 2000. The charge was first-degree murder, weapon unknown/or hand. David Dew testified that his ex-wife Laura had failed her polygraph tests. His new wife testified that Laura had been violent at the hospital and had hit the carrier with David's new baby inside. She further informed the jury that Nicholas, who shared a bedroom with Christina, threw an object at Christina's crib one night when she refused to stop crying. The defense inquired why the medical examiner, Dr. Patricia Moore, had changed her autopsy report three times before concluding that Trenda was responsible for the infant's death. It was also learned that Harris County District Attorney Charles Rosenthal had written a letter to Moore expressing his disagreement with her earlier findings and expressing his belief that Trenda was not at fault in the death. Unfortunately, the judge would not allow this letter to be admitted into evidence. Although Moore was later released from her position as medical examiner for her willingness to slant autopsies in favor of the prosecution, the only negative comments presented at the trial were from Joy Carter, her supervisor, who testified as to Moore's sloppy work and overdiagnosis of the results of her autopsies.

A detective from the police department also testified that Trenda was not initially a suspect as the evidence suggested that it was either Laura or Nicholas. The paramedics who arrived the day Christina was airlifted to a hospital further testified that the infant exhibited no outward signs of abuse. The paramedics and a nurse at the hospital additionally testified that they heard the little girl cry, something that according to the prosecution experts could not have happened if Christina had been the victim of SBS.

The second day of the trial proved to be more damaging to Trenda's case. Rosenthal was permitted to play the taped deposition from the civil case. As the jury watched the television screen, they saw a stoic Trenda merely answering "yes" or "no" to a series of questions as she had been requested to do by her attorney. The prosecution was quick to point out how "emotionless" she was throughout the deposition. One prosecuting attorney told the jury that Christina's injuries suggested she had died from "shaken impact syndrome." After seven and a half weeks, the jury was unable to reach a verdict and a mistrial was declared.

On September 10, 2001, the second trial began. Attorney Haynes requested a postponement as his wife was in the hospital, but this was denied. The trial was briefly delayed, however, as a result of the terrorist attacks of September 11, 2001. When the trial began in earnest the next week, the prosecutors were successful in eliminating most of the damaging evidence to their case. Laura's failed polygraph tests, the testimony from David's wife, which suggested that Laura had hit her and her baby at the hospital, and the testimony about Nicholas throwing an object at Christina's baby crib were noticeably absent. Also conspicuously missing were the favorable reports from the paramedics who first saw Christina after the accident. Reprimands of the medical examiner were disallowed, and her supervisor was unexpectedly called out of the country, thereby eliminating her testimony. The detective who interrogated her was allowed to testify but could not mention that he was suspicious of Laura or that he had recommended that murder charges be brought against her. Jurors were exposed again to the deposition tape and photographs of the infant showing her after her death and after the autopsy. On October 24, 2001, the jury pronounced her guilty. Five days later the judge sentenced her to fifty-five years in prison. Shortly after her trial concluded, Patricia Moore was removed as the medical examiner because of numerous improprieties in her work. In 2008 Charles Rosenthal was dismissed from his position as district attorney for a history of corruption in his department.

Trenda is currently serving time at a women's prison in Texas. She is divorced from her second husband. About four months after her arrival she was notified that her insurance company had paid the Dews $100,000 in compensation for the wrongful death of Christina and an additional $2,500 to the Mazzus for the injury sustained by Danielle. After coming to terms with her predicament, Trenda began a positive program to improve herself as an individual. She has earned a certificate in computer software and hardware and has also been certified as a paralegal in the state of Texas. Trenda became an ordained minister on December 30, 2009, and remains hopeful that one day she will be exonerated and the world will know her story (Christian, 2001; Kemmerer, 2010a, 2010b; *Kemmerer v. State of Texas*, 113 S.W.3d 513, 2003; Tilghman, 2004; "Trenda Loue Kemmerer," 2011).

Shirley Ree Smith

Whereas the first three cases of wrongful conviction for SBS involved white women, the last two cases involved women of color. Shirley Ree

Smith was a thirty-seven-year-old grandmother at the time of her conviction. She had moved from Illinois to Van Nuys, California, to be
closer to her daughter and grandchildren. On the night of November 30,
1996, she was accused of killing her seven-week-old grandson, Etzel
Dean Glass, III, by violently shaking him. Yet the infant exhibited none
of the signs of SBS. There was no swelling of the brain, no blood behind
the retinas, and no bruises on his body. Shirley contended that Etzel had
fallen off the couch and hit his head on the carpet earlier, but he
appeared to be unaffected by his fall. An autopsy revealed a small
amount of blood in his brain, although some could have spilled into this
cavity during the procedure.

At the trial prosecutors theorized that the infant had been shaken so
severely that death was instantaneous and therefore there were no other
signs of SBS, a proposition that could neither be confirmed nor denied.
The prosecution did not present any evidence to support the accusation
that Shirley had a sudden rage that caused her to violently shake Etzel.
Nor could the prosecution explain how the infant's mother would be
unaware of this behavior, sleeping just a few feet away from the little
boy. Three medical experts testified that no definitive cause of death
could be established and SIDS, which had been suspected as the cause
of death by the doctor in the emergency room, could not be ruled out.
Shirley's daughter, Tomeka, testified during the trial that her mother
never physically abused her or any of her siblings. Nonetheless, based
largely on the results of the autopsy, Shirley was convicted of second-
degree murder in December 1997 and received a sentence of fifteen
years to life.

For ten years Shirley sought to prove her innocence. On three different occasions the Ninth Circuit Court of Appeals overturned her conviction, ruling that the evidence used to convict her "is simply not the stuff
from which reasonable doubt can be established" (Williams, 2012).
Citing the case as a likely miscarriage of justice, a circuit court judge
wrote in 2006 that it was "extremely unlikely" that Shirley could have
shaken Etzel so violently as to instantaneously kill him while his mother
lay sleeping only a few feet away. Undeterred by the earlier appellate
decisions, the US Supreme Court reinstated her conviction in 2011. In a
six-to-three decision, the unsigned majority opined that "Doubts about
whether Smith is in fact guilty are understandable. But it is not the job
of this court, and was not that of the 9th Circuit, to decide whether the
state's theory was correct. The jury decided that question, and its decision is supported by the record."

In contrast, three dissenters referred to the decision to reinstate her
conviction as "a misuse of discretion." In particular, Justice Ruth Bader

Ginsburg was especially critical of the ruling. Using more recent medical findings, she demonstrated greater support for the defense's version of Etzel's death. Writing for the minority opinion, Justice Ginsburg went on to say, "In light of current information, it is unlikely that the prosecution's experts would today testify as adamantly as they did in 1997" (Williams, 2011).

Shirley finally received some positive news in April 2012 when California Governor Jerry Brown commuted her sentence to time served and acknowledged the problematic nature of her conviction. This was only the second sentence he had commuted during his time as governor from 1975 to 1980 and since taking office again in 2011. Talking to the *Los Angeles Times*, Shirley expressed her amazement that some closure had been reached. "I just can't believe this is finally over with," Shirley exclaimed. "Everybody's so excited, but I just can't believe it" (Williams, 2012). She is undecided as to whether she will pursue a new trial so she can legally clear her name. (Greene, 2012; Williams, 2011; Williams, 2012).

Melonie Ware

When you are wrongfully convicted, the cost of legally demonstrating your innocence can be prohibitive. For many, the expense may be too great, thus their exoneration must depend on organizations that provide free research and legal counsel necessary for such an endeavor. For those who can afford it, however, the financial and emotional costs can still be exorbitant. The case of Melonie Ware aptly illustrates these high legal and emotional costs.

On March 21, 2004, nine-month-old Jaden Paige died in a hospital in Decatur, Georgia. He had been under the care of Melonie Ware, his babysitter. In November 2005 she was convicted of murdering the infant by severely shaking him after an autopsy revealed a bruised scalp, blood in the brain and eyes, and a fractured leg. DeKalb County Medical Examiner Gerald Gowitt labeled the death a homicide caused by "craniocerebral trauma." He also justified his diagnosis by noting that the hospital had evaluated Jaden as a likely victim of child abuse. Although Gowitt later admitted that the leg fracture was the result of a hospital procedure designed to save the child's life, he dismissed the possibility that the boy had died from complications arising from his sickle cell anemia (SCA). His testimony was largely responsible for a jury finding of guilty of felony murder. Melonie was subsequently sentenced to life in prison.

In 2006 her conviction was overturned, and she was granted a new trial as a result of ineffective assistance of counsel. Although she was released on a $20,000 bond pending another trial, it wasn't until 2009—and many legal maneuvers later—that she was retried. Securing the services of expert witnesses and other legal fees had proven to be quite expensive for Melonie and her husband, Reginald. They sold over $700,000 in assets to pay for the right to defend her from a false conviction. Among the real estate they sold, it was most difficult to part with the house in which Melonie's grandmother had lived. As Reginald later acknowledged, "We had to move in with my parents. It just messed us up totally" (Smith, 2011a).

During the second trial, two prominent physicians testified that Jaden's death could be attributed to complications arising from SCA. Because SCA can result in infections and blood-clotting issues, the symptoms can mimic those of SBS. They additionally provided slides from the autopsy that revealed the presence of numerous sickle cells, a finding the medical examiner had disputed. Moreover, the bruises observed on the infant's scalp were probably a result of the emergency procedures employed by the hospital when the staff had tried on several occasions to insert a probe into his skull. With new information to process, the jury acquitted Melonie of the murder on October 6, 2009.

But once you're labeled a felon, it is difficult to remove its shackles. When she received her freedom, Melonie immediately sought employment but her applications were rejected. As she observed, "I even tried McDonald's" (Smith, 2011a). Further complicating her attempt to return to a life of normalcy was her mugshot, which continued to remain on the Georgia Department of Corrections website after her exoneration. Even today a cursory examination of websites discloses a mugshot of her along with personal information, a constant reminder that it is difficult to overcome the stigma attached to a wrongful conviction even after an acquittal (Gross, n.d. e; Shapiro, 2011; Smith, 2011a, 2011b).

When the Decedent Is a Husband or Ex-Husband

As observed earlier, women are more likely than their male counterparts to murder someone to whom they are emotionally attached. For instance, although women commit only about 10 percent of the homicides in the United States, they account for almost 35 percent of murders involving intimate partners and almost 30 percent of murders involving another family member. Nevertheless, they are less likely than their male counterparts to engage in premeditated murder, and they are less likely to use a gun. According to the Department of Justice, women are responsible for 36 percent of the poisonings in this country (Michels et al., 2009).

In this section we review two cases—Tanya Harden and Marie La Pinta—in which the wives were the victims of abusive husbands. Then we examine the case of Virginia Larzelere, who was falsely accused of having her husband killed to inherent his wealth and collect on his life insurance policy. Similarly, the fourth case involves Cynthia Sommer, who was accused of poisoning her husband for his life insurance money and survivor benefits. The section concludes with a woman falsely convicted of killing her ex-husband.

Tanya Harden

Married at the age of sixteen, Tanya Harden lived with her abusive husband, Danuel, for years in their trailer in West Virginia. Her case is not unlike that of many battered wives, particularly those living in more rural regions. Danuel would not allow her to get a driver's license or work outside the home. He carefully monitored the friends she was allowed to have visit, keeping her isolated from the outside world. Her entire life was controlled by Danuel.

At the time of his death in 2004 the couple had two children, a nine-year-old son and a ten-year-old daughter. During a "night of domestic terror," that even the *prosecution* admitted to at trial, Tanya's life and that of her children were repeatedly threatened by her husband. Danuel was drinking excessively that night and had a blood-alcohol level of 0.22 at the time of death. He brutally beat Tanya using the butt and barrel of his shotgun and his fists. He violently raped her as well. When Tanya was admitted to the emergency room, the attending physician noted that she "had contusions of both orbital areas, the right upper arm, a puncture wound with a foreign body of the right forearm, contusions of her chest, left facial cheek, the left upper lip" and that "X-rays done at the time demonstrated a nasal fracture" (*State of West Virginia v. Tanya D. Harden*, 679 S.E. 2d 628, 2009).

The violence was so extreme that the state did not even attempt to refute the brutal nature of the encounter. Instead, prosecutors argued that Tanya's argument of self-defense was untenable as she had made no attempt to retreat from her husband. Therefore, when she shot her husband as he was lying down on the couch, the use of deadly force was unreasonable. Conveniently overlooked was the fact that on previous occasions when she left, she was forcibly brought back and severely battered by Danuel. Prosecutors further contended that Danuel may have been "asleep" or "passed out" at the time she killed him since the violence had been ongoing for several hours and he had been drinking.

Tanya appealed her life sentence for murder. In 2009 the West Virginia Supreme Court of Appeals overturned her murder conviction

Box 3.2 Spotlight on Ginny LeFever

Ginny LeFever was interviewed by Mitch Ruesink on May 28, 2014. The following story is based on that interview and other documents obtained during the data collection phase of this research.

William and Virginia "Ginny" LeFever were married in September 1977. They had four children together (one died after birth). For the most part, Ginny's life was not unlike that of many other mothers who worked at the time. "I lived in Newark, Ohio, about thirty minutes maybe east of Columbus. . . . I worked at the local hospital, initially in labor and delivery; then I went to coronary care. I took the kids to T-ball, Brownies, help drive the Brownie troop for field trips."

By September 1988, William and Ginny were in the middle of a messy divorce. The couple had separated earlier, and final proceedings were scheduled for later in the month. Ginny had grown tired of living with an addict and supporting her husband's drug habit. When he became abusive to her and the children, she filed for divorce and temporarily moved with her children to a battered women's shelter. Despondent over the divorce, William began writing messages on the mirrors telling Ginny that he could not live without her. He was also fearful that he would lose his job because of his poor attendance and the possible relocation of his employer.

On September 20, 1988, William returned to their house to retrieve the remainder of his belongings. While Ginny was away, William apparently took a variety of substances, including some household poisons and a prescription antidepressant. When Ginny returned about twenty minutes later, she had no idea he had consumed any drugs. After watching some videos with the rest of the family, William fell asleep on the couch. Later that night, he began making noises and woke up his son. The boy informed his mother that his dad was drunk and acting strange. When Ginny went downstairs to check on William, she saw him on his back and bruised as the bathroom was filling with water from a broken shower door and an overflowing toilet. Then she suspected he was overdosing on drugs. Although she knew that she should call the paramedics, she hesitated. William had threatened violence if she called the paramedics once before. Ginny did not want people to know about the overdose as the couple was about to divorce. It was not until the following day, after she discovered that her bottle of antidepressants was nearly empty, that paramedics were called. On September 22, 1988, at 11:37 a.m. William died, one day after being admitted to the hospital.

The coroner's report (nearly two months later) determined that William died from an overdose of amitriptyline, an antidepressant. The toxicology reports from the autopsy revealed that he had consumed other drugs, including alcohol, marijuana, and opiates. Within a week, Ginny was indicted and arrested for the murder of her husband.

While waiting in jail for her trial to begin, the bank foreclosed on her house, and her children were placed in foster care. Ginny hired a private attorney to represent her, but in so doing exhausted her funds. During the trial, prosecutors speculated that Ginny, a registered nurse, gave William the shot of amitriptyline and, when that did not work, she shut her semi-conscious husband in a room with pesticide fumigants. James Ferguson, a toxicologist and the main witness for the prosecution, testified at the trial that only an injection of the medication would have killed William. It was also brought out at the trial that the injection could not have been self-inflicted. It was conveniently ignored that William was much larger than Ginny (and therefore capable of violence) and nothing was found in the house that would support this theory. Ferguson's theory was not based on solid evidence and turned what was originally ruled as a suicide into a homicide. When he presented his findings at Ginny's trial, she could hardly believe what she was hearing. Ginny was not the only person affected by Ferguson's erroneous testimony. He had appeared in hundreds of trials as an expert witness while he was with the coroner's office. Eventually, it was discovered that he had lied before in court and most likely had influenced the outcome of other cases. On February 22, 1990, Ginny was found guilty and sentenced to life in prison.

Bothered by the testimony of the coroner, Ginny was running out of options to prove that Ferguson's science did not add up. In a last-ditch effort, she reached out to a former inmate. This person had been paroled and had access to resources that Ginny did not. Since Ferguson had attended Ohio State University, her plan was to have the alumni association check him out. Ginny's friend sent off an e-mail and it didn't take long to find out that Ferguson did not graduate in 1972, as he had claimed during the trial. Further research confirmed that he did attend the university between 1964 and 1967 but was put on probation for low grades.

At this point, Ginny was wondering what else Ferguson had lied about at her trial. She contacted Marty Yant, a private investigator, and gave him the updated report on Ferguson. Yant came back with some very interesting information. According to Ginny, "The conclusion was that he [Ferguson] did tell the truth about his name and date of birth and that is pretty much it. The rest is all smoke and mirrors."

Armed with this information, Ginny sought a new trial. The prosecutor offered her all sorts of deals to withdraw the motion, so they would not have to examine Ferguson's perjured testimony. Ginny could have pleaded guilty to a lesser charge and been released based on time already served, but she said that she was not going to be an accomplice to the people who stole her life. In November 2010 Judge Mark Wiest, the same judge Ginny faced twenty years before when she was convicted, granted her a new trial. Based on the new evidence that had been discovered, her wrongful conviction was vacated and she was immediately released from prison.

Since being exonerated, Ginny's life has changed in many ways.

[When] I got out . . . I was like a kid in a candy store. I was just crazy and I have been on this whirlwind of trying to figure out what to do. I have not done well with some of my relationships. I think that I have finally come to understand that I do suffer from PTSD [post-traumatic stress disorder]. I think that many of the exonerees do suffer from PTSD to a greater or lesser degree. Initially, I was sort of manic. I . . . was able to do a little traveling [and] I was able to buy . . . [a] Jeep.

When asked if she planned to pursue a nursing position, which she held before being convicted, Ginny replied:

I thought that I could go back to nursing and have. That took a Herculean effort. The state board, in the interest of safety, put a lot of conditions on reactivating my nursing license after the twenty-two-year gap. My criminal conviction failed, Judge Wiest did that for me. That allows me to pass background checks, as it should, [as] I am not guilty of anything. I did not do anything, other than be a victim of the system. There are those who would argue that I am guilty anyways, but I assure you that I am not. Nurses, as a rule, that is just not what we do. That is not how we are wired.

Ginny has also experienced problems reconnecting with her children who are now grown. As she explains,

My older daughter . . . I thought she was the same twenty-year-old I knew and she's not. Flash forward, living in the Bible belt, raising her kids in a good way, different than I did. We just got a rift in our relationship and I don't know how to fix it.

Two of my younger kids went into foster care because there was nobody to take care of them. I've tried to have a relationship with my younger daughter. The only constant I have is with my baby, Alex, who was only four when I was arrested. He's read through the transcripts, he actually has an associate degree in law enforcement and looked at it with fresh eyes and said that he believed me. He has been incredibly supportive and loving. We communicate daily.

Ginny is further contemplating assisting with the Women's Project at Northwestern University. As she acknowledged near the end of the interview, "I just love and appreciate every one of my fellow exonerees. It is really an honor to be among their company."

and ordered her immediate release. Justice Menis Ketchum, II, in delivering the majority opinion, noted that the state failed to prove its contention that this wasn't an act of self-defense. He further observed that West Virginia was among a minority of states that required a co-occupant of a dwelling to retreat if in danger, drawing a distinction between this situation and one involving an intruder. Ketchum additionally questioned the assumption that Danuel might have been asleep or passed out when he was shot. More to the point, he wrote: "Reviewing the record, there is just no evidence, only conjecture, that the defendant's 'night of terror' had ended or that the defendant and the children in her care were safe from death or serious bodily injury" (Anderson, 2009).

Hence, the state Supreme Court decision established a precedent for battered women in West Virginia since the duty to retreat was no longer incumbent in cases of abuse such as this one. Finally, after four years and nine months of wrongful incarceration for murder, Tanya was exonerated (Anderson, 2009; Rosser, 2009; *State of West Virginia v. Tanya D. Harden*, 2009).

Marie La Pinta

Marie La Pinta was married to her husband, Michael, for twenty-seven turbulent years, enduring physical and emotional abuse during much of that time. On the night of March 27, 1983, her time of torment came to an end. As their disagreement escalated, in a fit of anger, Marie hit her husband with a baseball bat and her brother, Leonardo Crociata, shot and killed him. Marie apparently helped Leonardo dispose of the body at a landfill. When her trial began in 1984, there was no battered wife defense, so she was convicted of second-degree murder and sentenced to twenty-five years to life. She began serving her sentence at the age of forty-seven.

For twenty-two years she languished in prison. Her conviction inspired one of her sons (Anthony) to become an attorney, in part to pursue a legal remedy for his mother. Another son (Lenny) unsuccessfully lobbied the governor of New York for a pardon while developing a website to expedite her freedom. Persistence paid off, and Anthony was eventually successful in having the New York Supreme Court overturn his mother's conviction because of ineffective assistance of counsel. During her trial the jury had never been informed of the many years of domestic abuse that Marie had suffered. District Attorney Thomas Spota agreed with the decision and sought to find a remedy to the dilemma. To avoid admitting that Marie should never have been tried for second-degree murder under the circumstances, Spota permitted her to plead guilty to first-degree manslaughter, which carries a sentence of eight and one-third years to twenty-five years in prison. Since she had already been incarcerated for twenty-two years, she was eligible for release based on time served.

As the sixty-nine-year-old Marie walked out of the courtroom—free at last—she was greeted by her sons and a bouquet of roses from her three grandchildren. Lenny best expressed his emotions after seeing his mother being released: "It's been so long that we've learned to live without her around. And now that she's going to have the opportunity to be home with us and to see her grandchildren's bedroom and to go into my backyard and do simple things like that, (it) is the greatest joy that we can ever feel" ("N.Y. woman released after 2 decades in prison," 2005).

After exiting the courtroom, Marie insisted that they stop at St. Lawrence the Martyr Church to give thanks to God for making it possible for her to endure years in prison and watching over her loved ones in her absence. (Castillo, 2005; "N.Y. woman released after 2 decades in prison," 2005).

Virginia Larzelere

A common denominator among wrongful convictions is the socioeconomic status of the defendants. Virtually all of the falsely convicted individuals are people of limited financial means. The same is true of cases involving wrongfully convicted women. This case departs from that scenario in that Virginia Larzelere enjoyed considerable wealth and had few financial issues with which to endure. Yet her case reveals the extent to which the police and prosecutors can become preoccupied with a single person once they have decided that she is the perpetrator. Failure to examine other possible suspects has undoubtedly led to many wrongful convictions since alternative explanations are given short shrift.

Virginia Larzelere was accused of arranging to have her husband, Norman, killed for approximately $2 million in insurance money and $1 million in assets on March 8, 1991, in Edgewater, Florida. Police suspected her almost immediately. The alleged assassin, Jason Larzelere, the couple's eighteen-year-old adopted son, was supposedly lured into this crime by Virginia with promises of receiving financial remuneration. Never considered by the police was the possibility that this could have been a botched robbery, as the safe had been opened and some of its contents had spilled onto the floor. Virginia informed the police that their safe contained a gold collection, money, and narcotics. (Norman was a dentist and could legally have certain drugs.) She also mentioned that during the incident, which occurred in his office, she observed the offender and had some of his DNA under her nails as he pushed her aside to exit the office after the shots were fired. She had written down a partial license plate number from his car before he sped off. An additional witness at the scene noted that the license plate was from New Jersey. Neither the DNA nor the license plate number were deemed important by the police. The police even neglected to dust for fingerprints. From their perspective, they already had their perpetrator and they didn't need any physical evidence.

Virginia hired Gary McDaniel, a private investigator, to pursue the perpetrator. He provides a full account of his findings in an online article outlining his extensive investigation. McDaniel concludes that Virginia was not involved in the murder and the two informants used at trial repeatedly perjured themselves in return for special treatment by the prosecutor. The informants had their own criminal charges dropped by the prosecutor and were given immunity in return for testifying. Moreover, her defense attorney, Jack Wilkins, provided little assistance for his client. As one juror noted, the attorney appeared to be "pompous" and offered no alternative explanation for the crime. In fact, the juror concluded, if a feasible alternative theory could have been provided, the jury would have been inclined to acquit Virginia of the charges. There is also some suspicion that Wilkins was under the influence of drugs during the brief trial (he presented only four hours of defense testimony). Virginia additionally contends that he tampered with her finances.

In contrast, the defense attorney at Jason's trial, which occurred one year after Virginia's conviction, summoned more than twenty witnesses, and he was acquitted of all charges. Furthermore, two former boyfriends of Virginia, who had testified at her trial that she had solicited them to kill her husband, were cross-examined during Jason's trial and admitted that she made the remarks flippantly, and neither considered them to be serious. Jason's acquittal posed an interesting dilemma: if Virginia was guilty of first-degree murder for allegedly hiring him to kill her husband and he was acquitted, then how could she be guilty of being a coconspirator if there was no other conspirator?

Admittedly, Virginia was not a model wife. She violated many of the gender role expectations that society has for women. She acknowledged having had three affairs, all of which Norman knew about. By her own admission she "worked hard and played harder." A video showed Virginia confessing that she was a bad mother, a bad sister, and a bad wife. Thus, at the trial newspapers portrayed her as an undesirable woman who was greedy and promiscuous. Indeed, Virginia had spent the night before the crime at the home of her lover.

On May 11, 1993, Virginia was sentenced to die by electrocution for the death of her husband. Later investigations revealed that the prosecution failed to disclose exculpatory evidence to the defense. Additionally, her defense counsel was convicted of criminal activities from 1989 through 1994 and sentenced to fifty-four months in a federal prison. Aerial photographs corroborate Virginia's statement regarding the car that sped away from the dental office. One of the informants has since committed suicide, and his testimony cannot be recanted. The weapons produced at the trial were not the actual murder weapons. Now impoverished, Virginia cannot afford to seek more legal remedies. After numerous unsuccessful attempts to win her freedom, she was resentenced on August 1, 2008, to life with the possibility of parole in twenty-five years. She remains incarcerated (Carter, 1998; Commission on Capital Cases, 2008; Cressy, 1991; Lancaster, 1993; McDaniel, n.d.; Somerville, 1992; "What happened?," 2007).

Cynthiaï Sommer

Todd Sommer, a twenty-three-year-old marine who appeared to be healthy, became very ill in February 2002. He had a high temperature and complained of gastrointestinal discomfort a few days prior to his death. Apparently, he felt well enough to consume alcohol during a family visit to an amusement park the weekend before he died on February 18. His widow, twenty-eight-year-old Cynthia Sommer, a mother of four, stood to gain monetarily from his premature death, including over a quarter of a million dollars from life insurance and almost $2,000 a month in survivor benefits.

The initial cause of death was listed as heart failure after the military analyzed tissue samples from his body. An autopsy revealed that there were unusually high levels of arsenic in tissue taken from his liver and kidneys. Specifically, laboratory results indicated that the level of arsenic was over 1,000 times above a normal amount in his liver and over 250 times above a normal amount in his kidneys. Cynthia, who had moved from San Diego and was living in Florida, became the number one suspect. She was arrested in Florida in November 2005 and extradited to California the following year.

Cynthia's demeanor was called into question during her trial when her attorney attempted to portray her as a grieving widow. Indeed, she was anything but a grieving widow after Todd's death. Instead of going into quiet seclusion and grieving over her loss, she used some of the insurance money to get breast implants and witnesses claimed that they saw her at wet T-shirt contests. She was allegedly involved in several casual sexual encounters with other men in the military before moving to Florida with her new boyfriend. As her second lawyer explained, "They labeled Cindy with a big red 'S' [slut] on her back because she didn't grieve the way they wanted her to" (Hoffman, 2008). Thus, the deputy district attorney, using largely circumstantial evidence since there was no link between Cynthia and the arsenic found in her husband's body, attempted to depict her as an immoral woman who wanted a more luxurious lifestyle than Todd could provide, so she poisoned him for financial reasons. On January 30, 2007, a jury found her guilty of first-degree murder with "special circumstances," which referred to the murder by poison for financial gain. This distinction is important because it qualified the case for a possible sentence of life without parole.

Cynthia's new attorney, Allen Bloom, filed a motion for a new trial after her conviction but before sentencing. After the superior court judge ruled that she received ineffective assistance of counsel, her conviction was vacated in November 2007 and a new trial was ordered for May 2008. While preparing her defense, Bloom repeated a request that other tissue samples from the autopsy be examined given the fact that high concentrations of arsenic had not been found in other parts of his body. In fact, an expert retained by Bloom had reported that the initial results were "physiologically improbable." Repeatedly prosecutors claimed that there were no remaining tissue samples available to autopsy. Only after the defense made a formal discovery demand were tissue samples mysteriously located. A reexamination disclosed no arsenic in Todd's liver or kidneys. Consequently, in April 2008 the prosecution agreed to dismiss the charges and release Cynthia. When she heard the news, Cynthia exclaimed, "I'm in shock. I haven't even processed being outside yet, and wearing normal clothes." She continued, "I knew all along that the testing was wrong and I was just waiting for that to come out. That's what I said since the day I was arrested" (Hoffman, 2008).

The cost of proving her innocence was steep. She spent over $500,000 on defense attorneys alone. Additional funds were required to purchase airline tickets and make hotel reservations so that her family could be present during her anticipated retrial. Nevertheless, Cynthia never lost faith that she would eventually be found innocent of the charges and reunited with her children, who had been living with her brother in Michigan. She was wrongfully incarcerated in California for two years and four months. She has since filed a $20 million lawsuit against the state of California. The results of that case are unknown (Denzel, n.d. a; Hoffman, 2008; Littlefield, 2008).

Patricia Wright

Patricia Wright and her husband, Willie Jerome Scott, had what appeared to be a happy marriage. Everything seemed to be fine until 1978, when Jerome informed Patricia that he was gay and wanted a divorce. The next year they divorced, although they remained good friends and Jerome continued to see his children.

Unfortunately, Jerome's gay lifestyle, his love of expensive jewelry, his tendency to keep large sums of money at his disposal, and his use of illegal drugs put him at constant risk for harm. In September 1981 he was found dead in his motor home, which was parked in a high-crime area of downtown Los Angeles. His decomposed body had a knife protruding from his chest and his head had been covered with a plastic bag. He had been stabbed multiple times and appeared to have had anal sex shortly before he was killed. Although he had recently withdrawn $10,000 from the bank, there was less than $4 remaining, and his expensive jewelry was missing. When the police examined the physical evidence at the crime scene, neither the blood nor the fingerprints matched that of Patricia.

For years the case went unsolved. Then, in 1995, the case was reopened when the Los Angeles Police Department (LAPD) began a "cold case" task force. The police were stymied by the absence of possible suspects to investigate. One of Jerome's nephews, whose fingerprints were found in the motor home, was already incarcerated for a violent crime so the police didn't question him. Herman Cross, one of Jerome's ex-lovers, another possible suspect, had died of AIDS shortly after the murder. The last known person to have been with him could not be found. Then the police received a tip that Patricia's brother, Larry, was willing to talk to them about the incident. Angry with his sister, he implicated her and a man named Larry Slaughter in Jerome's murder.

In 1997 Patricia was arrested and charged with the murder of her former husband. When the case was brought before Judge Lance Ito (known best for the O.J. Simpson trial), he threw it out due to lack of evidence and ordered her immediate release. Undeterred, the detectives found a more sympathetic judge two weeks later. Now the police were alleging that they possessed a taped confession from Slaughter, the supposed killer hired by Patricia. Without making them disclose the tape, the judge concluded that there was sufficient evidence to detain her for trial. When Patricia's public defender requested the tape, the LAPD said that the tape had been lost. Realizing that they had no provable case against Patricia, the detectives flew to Connecticut, where her brother was now incarcerated for child abuse. Two detectives offered to get his sentence downgraded to eight months for a misdemeanor and strike the felony convictions from his criminal record. Facing the prospect of spending twelve years in prison, Larry readily conceded to their demands and made a videotaped statement in which he declared that Patricia had Slaughter kill Jerome.

Patricia's trial started in 1998. By then, Larry had time to consider the consequences of his lies and recanted his earlier statement. An LAPD officer testified in court that Slaughter had confessed (on the missing tape) that Patricia paid him $25,000 to murder Jerome. The prosecutor played a videotape of an eighty-three-year-old insurance agent in the final stages of Alzheimer's disease and lacking coherence. The elderly man claimed to remember that Jerome had taken out some large life insurance policies prior to his murder. Because this was on videotape, there was no opportunity to cross-examine the witness. Although the blood and fingerprints on the murder weapon excluded both Patricia and Slaughter, the evidence had been misplaced by the LAPD and was unavailable for use in her defense. Forensic examination of Jerome's heart and brain was not possible because the coroner had lost the organs. The prosecution's assertion that Jerome was straight and therefore his death could not be attributed to a gay lifestyle was not refuted by Patricia's public defender, who failed to call witnesses who could corroborate Jerome's sexual preference. Notwithstanding the absence of physical or forensic evidence and any eyewitnesses to the murder, Patricia was convicted of first-degree murder and conspiracy to commit murder and received a sentence of life without parole.

Since the conviction, Patricia has been able to accumulate exculpatory evidence. The New York Life Insurance Company provided documentation that the smaller of the two life insurance policies (valued at approximately $30,000) was secured over a year before Jerome's murder, and the larger policy had been canceled by Patricia prior to the commission of the crime. This information runs counter to the prosecutor's argument that she had Jerome killed for financial gain. A letter sent by the coroner to Jerome's mother verified that at the time of his murder Jerome was critically ill and was months removed from dying. Again, this refutes the argument that Patricia had him killed for financial gain since she would receive payments from his insurance shortly anyway. Fortuitously, while talking to fellow inmates, Patricia learned the name of the gay prostitute that Jerome frequently used. The inmate provided an affidavit in which she described the gay lifestyle that contributed to Jerome's demise. She also acknowledged that the word on the street after his murder was that a gay man known as "Ms. Ross" was responsible for the crime. A neighbor later recanted her testimony that Patricia and Slaughter were responsible for the murder. She asserted that the LAPD had intimidated her and had her rehearse and record a false statement. Moreover, Slaughter, who was also wrongfully convicted of first-degree murder, swore in an affidavit that in his tape to the LAPD he never suggested that either Patricia or he were involved in the murder. Finally, on three separate occasions Larry admitted in affidavits that Patricia was innocent and that he only implicated her to avoid a long prison sentence.

In 2011 Patricia sought release from prison to be able to die in the presence of family members. Then sixty years old and legally blind since the age of sixteen, she had stage four cancer in her breasts and brain. In November that year, three tumors were removed from her brainstem. Because her conviction for murder represented a "third strike," the governor rescinded his grant of clemency. The two earlier strikes involved an incident in which her then seven-year-old son stole two cheap toys and a hand towel from an open house that they were visiting. Although the items were valued under $400, these criminal events were both classified as felonies, thus qualifying as two strikes under the legislation enacted in California. A request to change the two offenses to misdemeanors failed when a judge refused to do so. As of March 2012, Patricia remained incarcerated (Carter, 2011a, 2011b; Juarez, 2011; Law, 2012; Muhammad, 2011; Ramdhan-Wright, 2007; "Release Patricia Wright," 2013).

When the Decedent Is a Boyfriend or Ex-Boyfriend

Because women who kill are more likely than their male counterparts to kill someone with whom they share an intimate relationship, it should come as no surprise to learn that some of the wrongful convictions include cases in which women were falsely convicted of killing their boyfriends or ex-boyfriends. The narratives below reveal some of the diversity that exists among this genre of false convictions.

Teresa Thomas

Twenty-nine-year-old Teresa Thomas, a woman of color, lived in her mobile home in a rural area of Athens County, Ohio, with her boyfriend, Jerry "Jake" Flowers. She had known Jake for a long time but didn't date the forty-year-old man until 1991. On September 15, 1993, after an extended argument, Teresa fatally shot Jake. She argued that it was self-defense as he had brutally attacked her for months prior to the terminal event. Nonetheless, she was arrested and convicted of murder in 1993.

She received a sentence of eighteen years to life imprisonment for her actions.

The back story of this wrongful conviction is similar to that of many battered women. Jake monitored and controlled Teresa's every movement. To minimize contact with the outside world, she was not usually allowed to do the grocery shopping. On those rare occasions he permitted it, she was expected to bring back exact change and the receipt to document where she had been. Jake further controlled the finances and regularly threatened to kill her if she did not do what he demanded. Rape was another strategy he used to induce powerlessness and lower her self-concept. Violence was a regular occurrence, and some of it was extreme. Once, after he pushed her into a wall, Teresa had to be treated at an emergency room. Another time Jake punched her in the abdomen with such force that it caused an ovarian cyst to rupture. He also withheld food as punishment, with Teresa sometimes not having any food for three to four days.

The violence had become increasingly intense in the three weeks preceding the shooting. Jake would wake Teresa in the middle of the night and place his hands over her mouth and nose to make her feel as if she was suffocating. He would remind her how easy it would be for him to kill her during the night. Just two days prior to the shooting, he had forced anal intercourse with her, and on the night before, he had thrown food on the floor as they bitterly argued. When Jake left for work that morning, he told Teresa to clean up the mess before he returned home or he would kill her. Although she had begun cleaning, Jake arrived home early, before she had finished. Seeing the mess, he became enraged. Fearful for her life, Teresa fled to the bathroom, but the small window precluded her exit. She then proceeded to the bedroom, where Jake kept his pistol, and ran back to the kitchen. After she fired two warning shots, he continued to move toward her. Teresa then shot him in the arm twice, with one of the bullets piercing his chest. When Jake fell and then began to get up, she fired the fatal shots.

During the trial the prosecution portrayed Jake as a peaceful man who refrained from violence. In contrast, the defense called a psychologist who testified that Teresa suffered from battered woman syndrome (BWS). The prosecutor countered with the argument that a four-hour interview is not long enough to accurately draw this conclusion. On December 20, 1993, the jury sided with the prosecution and found Teresa guilty of murder.

When the case reached the Ohio Supreme Court on January 22, 1997, the conviction was vacated. The court ruled that the instructions to the jury regarding BWS were inadequate and that the judge failed to note that Teresa had no duty to retreat from a cohabitant in their home.

A retrial began in August 1997. This time the defense had two new witnesses to testify on Teresa's behalf. One had been treating Teresa since she was charged with murder. Donna Mabry, a psychologist, testified that shortly after the shooting Teresa had regressed to the age of twelve and had no recollection of the shooting. She noted that this type of behavior is symptomatic of someone undergoing acute traumatic stress syndrome (TSS). The second witness, a forensic psychologist, testified that Teresa's profile fit that of a victim of BWS. Perhaps more important was the discovery that the prosecution had withheld exculpatory evidence from the defense in the first trial. Rather than the peace-loving man that Jake had been portrayed to be, it was found that he had a previous criminal conviction for assaulting his ex-wife. On August 21, 1997, Teresa was acquitted of murder.

Unfortunately, the story doesn't end here. Teresa, it seems, continues to make poor choices for mates. Shortly thereafter she remarried, but was involved in a domestic dispute. Her new husband had hit her and choked her, resulting in injuries that required medical attention. He pleaded guilty to the charges and was fined $50 and jailed for three months (Possley, n.d. r; "Teresa Thomas, the Athens County women [*sic*] who was convicted, then acquitted," n.d.).

Beverly Monroe

This tragic miscarriage of justice involving Beverly Monroe in Windsor, Virginia, began on March 5, 1992, when Beverly discovered her boyfriend, sixty-year-old Roger de la Burde, lying dead on his couch. A bullet through his forehead had ended his life. Although investigators first concluded that the incident was a suicide, Detective David Riley thought otherwise. He quickly dismissed other possible suspects and began focusing exclusively on Beverly. On numerous occasions he interrogated her, attempting to convince her that she was present during her boyfriend's "suicide" but was blocking the memory because of the trauma. On one occasion he questioned Beverly for eight hours until she reluctantly said that she might have fallen asleep after dinner at her boyfriend's house the night of his death and not be cognizant of it. He recorded at least one conversation with her without her permission. Furthermore, he presented her with an outline of the case that indicated her guilt and offered her a fictitious plea bargain. This ploy proved to be successful: Beverly agreed to sign a statement that she had been asleep in the house when the incident took place.

Once Riley had this signed statement, Beverly was arrested for Roger's murder.

The trial was fraught with legally questionable behaviors. Over ten pieces of exculpatory evidence was withheld from the defense. For instance, the prosecution failed to mention that Zelma Smith, who testified that Beverly had tried to purchase a gun earlier that year, was offered a deal by the prosecution in exchange for her testimony, thereby raising questions regarding the veracity of her statement. The defense was also not informed that witnesses had seen a dark vehicle leave Roger's house the night of his death. Of particular interest was a statement from the groundskeeper that he had moved the gun when he discovered the body—a fact that was not made available to defense counsel. This information could have been used to potentially defuse the prosecution's argument that based on the position of the decedent when the police arrived, he could not have killed himself. Also excluded from the trial were medical documents ruling Roger's death a suicide.

Throughout the trial the prosecution attempted to portray Beverly as a jealous girlfriend who was angry that Roger had impregnated another woman. It seemed to matter little that her relationship with Roger had survived twelve years, so she probably had learned to accept various aspects of his behavior that she didn't like. Despite the fact that prosecution experts could not rule out the possibility of suicide and that at the time of his death Beverly was at a grocery store fifteen miles from his house, she was convicted of first-degree murder and the use of a firearm in the commission of a felony and sentenced to twenty-two years in prison.

While incarcerated, Beverly adjusted to her new role as inmate. She taught others how to use a computer and assisted inmates with their cases, many of which were similar to her situation. She also relied heavily on her religious faith and support from friends and family to help her pass the time. Nevertheless, she admits the adversity that she had to overcome. "I lost several friends and a brother while I was in there." Also while she was incarcerated, her first grandson was born. Her mother was too sick to travel, so Beverly did not see her for three and a half years. According to Beverly, "I worried a lot about her. I worried that she would die when I was in there. . . the worst part, I think, was the pressure I felt I was putting on my children. Not knowing if we would get the decision we were looking for. The frustration . . . it was awful" (Decker, 2002).

Beverly's daughter, Katie, became an attorney with the US Commission on Civil Rights and began to actively pursue her mother's case. Katie assembled a team of lawyers and filed a writ of habeas corpus. On March 28, 2002, the US District Court vacated Beverly's conviction. The judge who presided over the proceedings was highly critical of the handling of her trial. He referred to the case as a "monument to prosecutorial indiscretions and mishandling" and questioned the "manipulative tactics" employed by the police during their interrogations. He further noted the overall weakness of the case, especially in the area of forensics.

"When the judge's decision came it was like sunshine pushing all the clouds and the rocks away," Beverly observed when learning about the decision. "I was given the phone and Katie was on the other line and we just cried. We could barely talk" (Decker, 2002). Despite her joy, Beverly knew her freedom could be short-lived as the prosecutor might still retry her case. It wasn't until the US Fourth Circuit Court of Appeals in June 2003 unanimously upheld the district court's decision that the state announced its intention to not retry her case (Decker, 2002; Dickerson and Kulstad, 2002; Mid-Atlantic Innocence Project, 2010).

Lerlene Evonne Roever

Pahrump, Nevada, is a city with a fascinating history. Located about one hour west from Las Vegas, this unincorporated city grew from 2,000 residents in 1980 to over 36,000 residents in 2010. Inhabitants did not receive telephone service until the 1960s and the first paved road from Las Vegas to the city was not constructed until the late 1960s.

On January 16, 1993, five-foot, blue-eyed, blond Lerlene Evonne Roever (also known as Shasta or Peanut) was watching television with her live-in boyfriend, Ian Wilhite, and her three children in Pahrump. About 9 p.m. the younger children went to bed. Shortly thereafter Ian retired to the master bedroom of the trailer home to go to sleep. Lerlene turned off the television and joined him in bed. They had both had a few rum and colas earlier, and Ian didn't want to be disturbed so Lerlene decided to return to the living room to watch more television before falling asleep on the sofa. Sometime that night Raymond, her five-year-old son, awakened her to ask about the back door, which was ajar. Assuming that a storm had blown it open, Lerlene asked the boy to shut the door. After briefly joining her on the sofa, Raymond returned to his bedroom. The following morning she found Ian unresponsive and became panicked. When she was unable to revive him, she called the sheriff's department. It was then discovered that Ian had been shot in the base of his skull with a .22 caliber pistol.

When the deputies arrived, they made Lerlene stay in the living room for approximately twelve hours while they repeatedly questioned her. They questioned her again the next day. Lerlene, who owned a .22 caliber gun, was arrested on January 18 and charged with Ian's murder. Though ballistic tests later disclosed that her gun was not the one used to kill Ian, she remained the prime suspect. She was not unknown to law enforcement as she had two prior infractions: one in 1988 and another in 1990, both of which were for driving under the influence. Throughout her life she failed to live up to society's expectation of motherhood as she struggled financially and had a drinking problem, which contributed to her spotty employment record. Nevertheless, there was no direct evidence that she committed the murder, and Ian's death came at a considerable cost to her and her children. They had been living in his trailer, and he had provided the children with a father figure. Because they were not married, she was not eligible to receive funds from his life insurance policy. The fact that Lerlene claimed to not have heard shots being fired that night may be attributed to the thunder that accompanied the storms.

During her first trial, the district attorney withheld exculpatory evidence from the court-appointed defense attorney. The trial judge called this "the most egregious discovery violation I've seen in 21 years on the bench," yet did not sanction the prosecutors and permitted the trial to proceed after a two-hour recess. Moreover, the primary investigator for the case regularly socialized with the jurors when he took smoke breaks during the trial. While the police focused on Lerlene from the beginning, she surmised that an unknown assailant had broken into the trailer and killed Ian, noting that he had moved from Las Vegas to Pahrump to avoid some unsavory people whom he had encountered when he was involved with drugs. Unimpressed with the defense's presentation and despite any evidence linking Lerlene to the murder, the jury deliberated for less than four hours before finding her guilty of murdering Ian and possession of marijuana in August 1993.[2]

Lerlene never wavered from her contention that she was innocent. In an interview while in jail she commented, "I did not commit this crime. I did not kill Ian." While professing her love for him, she reminisced about how she met him:

> We met in Pahrump at the Laundromat across from the Moose Lodge in 1990. It was three days after his fortieth birthday. It was sort of a laundry party, and there was a barbecue, and I ended up doing most of everyone's laundry. Well, Ian was the only one who thanked me and gave me a kiss. (Shemeligian, 1996)

She further noted that "There were ups and downs, but for the most part we got along wonderfully. He had just given me an engagement ring, and he was good to the kids. But I didn't know Ian was doing some of the things that people have told me he was doing" (Shemeligian, 1996).

In August 1995 the Supreme Court of Nevada unanimously reversed her conviction and remanded her case back to the same court for retrial. Before Lerlene's second trial she experienced difficulty conversing with her counsel. Her public defender did not return her phone calls and refused to answer her letters. It was not until the first day of jury selection that she was able to meet with him personally. Preoccupied with seeking a plea bargain, he refused to subpoena any witnesses on a two-page list Lerlene had compiled for him and insulted the only witness on her behalf, her uncle. When she testified in court, her attorney refrained from inquiring about Ian's past and some of his questionable associates in Las Vegas. Because the district attorney admitted that he had no actual evidence, he resorted to testimony from individuals who disliked Lerlene to defame her character and make her appear to be a dangerous woman. For instance, her neighbor, Marlene Chidester, "testified that Roever had described in detail how she murdered her mother in a bathtub and watched her mother's teeth float in the water, that she had snapped her newborn baby's neck, and that she had scalped an African American schoolgirl and cut out her teeth while Roever was experiencing a blackout" (*Roever v. State of Nevada*, 114 Nev. 867, 963 P.2d 503, 1998). This perversion of the truth served only to prejudice the jury even more. Indeed, her mother did drown, but an investigation determined that occlusive arteriosclerosis of the coronary arteries contributed to her death. Although she did have an infant die at childbirth, the child died during delivery at the hospital of asphyxiation as a result of the umbilical cord being wrapped around his neck.

Lerlene's ex-husband, Craig Bruske, who was still married to her when she met Ian, additionally testified that Lerlene had killed one of her classmates and tried to slash him with a knife. He further claimed that she has a personality disorder in which she speaks using different voices and experiences blackouts. Two of her acquaintances—Gloria and William Lambert—told the jury that Lerlene had "gutted an ex-beau." Some of the accusations were more ambiguous. Her former employer, Carole Phillips, for example, testified that Lerlene was a "thief" and a "liar."

After six days of jury selection and trial, Lerlene was again found guilty and was sentenced to two consecutive life sentences for murder and one year for possession of a controlled substance. Again, her case was unanimously overturned by the Nevada Supreme Court. Regarding the false and ambiguous testimonies, the court was insistent that its use was inappropriate and in violation of her fundamental right to a fair trial. The justices concluded, "Much of the bad act evidence admitted was so inflammatory, speculative, and utterly fantastic as to bear practically no probative value" (*Roever v. State of Nevada*, 1998).[3] As a result, the court remanded the case for a new trial on September 2, 1998.

Lerlene has now been involved in three trials and as of 2012 remains incarcerated with little hope of being exonerated. She has resigned herself to her fate. In a letter to a friend, she explains

> My children's lives were so torn up through the three trials I went through to try to get truth heard, and be freed. The "State" insisted (no matter how I begged for them to leave my children alone) each trial to subpoena them, question them and repeatedly destroy their lives. Since I refused to plead guilty the ADA [Assistant District Attorney] would do anything he could to "convince" me to give up. (Nevada Innocence Network, 2012)

While imprisoned, Lerlene has reassessed her life and attempted to work through many of her problems. As she states in another letter to a friend,

> I worked through years of self-esteem issues, taught classes in life skills, English, Humanities, Greek Mythology and its behavioral applications, keys to loving relationships, and many more. I became Born Again and learned much through in-depth studies of the Word. I have a 4-year diploma from Rhema, and Assoc. from Cypress and am currently doing Moody courses for CEU's. I have been ministering to others here as He leads me. (Nevada Innocence Network, 2012)

Even after extensive searches with metal detectors on the property, the weapon used in Ian's murder was never found. There was no physical evidence linking Lerlene to her boyfriend's death. If she killed Ian and hid the gun, as suggested by the prosecution, why were there no footprints in the soft ground left by the storm, and no wet clothes from the alleged event (they did not have a clothes dryer in the trailer, so her clothes would still be saturated from the storm)? If the police were convinced that she was the perpetrator, why didn't they do a test for paraffin residue to determine if she was in proximity to the gun that was used to kill Ian? Many questions remain unanswered in this false conviction that will never be exonerated (Boggs, 2000; Nevada Innocence Network, 2005, 2012; Roever, 1999; *Roever v. State of Nevada*, 111 Nev. 1052, 901 P.2d 145, 1995, 1998; Shemeligian, 1996).

Sandy Murphy

Sandy Murphy's childhood was relatively unremarkable. Her father worked and her mother was a homemaker at their modest home in Downey, California, a suburb of Los Angeles. According to Sandy, "My parents were the epitome of what good parents should be. My mom was home every day after school; she was always involving me in extracurricular activities; she was on the PTA. . . . My dad went to work every day. Everything is about family" (Heller, 2010).

An attractive young woman, Sandy was runner-up in a beauty contest at the age of seventeen. Her desire to make money from an early business venture with a friend, however, cost her a high school diploma as she acquired excessive absences and never graduated. After several minor incidents with the law (including driving while intoxicated) she moved to Las Vegas in February 1994 to seek her fortune.

Sandy quickly learned an important lesson: the house always wins. After losing at least $12,000 of her savings at casinos, she needed a job. She began working as a topless dancer when she met casino mogul Ted Binion, a man twenty-eight years her senior. Ted, a millionaire, had problems of his own. A former casino executive, his heroin addiction had led to his removal from that position, although his family still owned the business. Sandy took residence in Ted's Las Vegas mansion as his live-in girlfriend. With imported white marble floors, this 8,500-square-foot home had a 1,000-square-foot master bedroom. Ted gave her access to a Mercedes and a credit card with a $10,000 limit. They commonly dined at the finest restaurants in the area.

But all was not well with their relationship. According to their gardener, Tom Loveday, Sandy was frequently physically abused. One day he remembered seeing her with a bruised face and a section of her hair missing after having had an argument with Ted. "She took a lot of crap from him," Tom told author Jeff German. After Ted lost his gaming license in March 1998, he began using heroin even more frequently. Over his lifetime Ted estimated that he had spent $1 million on heroin.

On September 17, 1998, Sandy found fifty-five-year-old Ted dead on his den floor. When the paramedics arrived, they found him on a yoga mat with an empty Xanax bottle next to him in what appeared to be an apparent drug overdose. Believing this was a routine drug overdose, the police did not immediately secure potential evidence. But this view changed within a few days.

Ted had befriended Rick Tabish, a contractor from Montana who had a criminal record, prior to his death. He hired him to haul sand from his property in Pahrump, Nevada, where he was constructing an underground vault in which to keep his silver bullion and coins worth an estimated $7 million. Rick was arrested two days after Ted's death when he was found with two other men using heavy equipment to excavate the lot where the vault had been built. Rick argued that he had received instructions from Ted that in the event of his demise he was to remove the contents of the vault and give them to Ted's daughter, Bonnie. When Sandy heard that Rick and his helpers had been arrested, she assisted them with their bail. Police now surmised that Sandy, who had become Rick's lover while they lived together in Ted's spacious home, had plotted with Rick to kill Ted and retrieve his buried wealth.

The joint trial of Sandy Murphy and Rick Tabish began in 2000 with much fanfare and Court TV broadcasting the trial. Since that trial there have been at least four books written about the events, a made-for-television movie ("Sex and Lies in Sin City") in 2008, a documentary on the Discovery Channel in 2009, and a discussion of the case on CBS's *48 Hours Mystery* in 2010. With largely circumstantial evidence, the prosecution relied heavily on the testimony of former Las Vegas homicide detective Tom Dillard. He contended that red marks found on the victim's chest were from shirt buttons from the killers, who sat on him while suffocating him. More potentially damaging evidence came from the estate's attorney, James Brown, who testified that Ted Binion informed him the night before he died to "Take Sandy out of the will if she doesn't kill me tonight. If I'm dead you'll know what happened." During the trial several experts testified that the victim's death was the result of a drug overdose. Only one expert, pathologist Michael Baden, testified that the death was due to burking.[4]

After seven weeks of testimony and almost sixty-eight hours of deliberation by the jury, the trial concluded on May 19, 2000. Sandy was convicted on charges of first-degree murder, robbery, and conspiracy to commit burglary and/or larceny. Rick was also convicted of these charges. Before pronouncing her sentence, the judge said, "Ms. Murphy, your involvement in these crimes is horrific and strikes at the very core of trust between significant others." He went on to characterize what she did as the "ultimate betrayal" (Heller, 2010). Both received life sentences for their alleged involvement. At the age of twenty-eight, Sandy faced a possible lifetime in prison for crimes for which only circumstantial evidence existed.

On July 14, 2003, the Nevada Supreme Court reversed the murder convictions of Sandy and Rick. Stating that a separate trial should have been convened for Rick's alleged kidnapping, beating, and extortion of his business partner, Leo Casey, the court determined that Sandy's case was prejudiced by these allegations. The court further concluded that the statement by the estate attorney should have been accompanied with instructions to the jury regarding the possible absence of impartiality of the testimony. In the majority opinion the court stated, "The prejudicial impact was great: the statement strongly implied Murphy killed Binion" ("Murder convictions in Binion case overturned," 2003).

The second trial, which was televised on Court TV and carried live by local television stations, resulted in a different outcome. Two medical experts for the prosecution testified that Ted was killed but only one of them testified that he was suffocated. In contrast, the defense called nine medical experts who attributed Ted's death to an overdose of heroin and the prescription drug Xanax, which were found in large quantities during his autopsy. The prejudicial remark previously made in the first trial by James Brown was now more muted and qualified. Jurors now viewed with greater skepticism some of the statements made by prosecution witnesses, who received thousands of dollars of reward money from the victim's estate in return for their testimonies. On November 23, 2004, Sandy and Rick were acquitted of murder, robbery, and conspiracy to commit murder, but were convicted of burglary, grand larceny, and conspiracy to commit burglary and/or larceny. Both received five-year prison sentences for their involvement in the theft of Ted's valuables.

Because Sandy had already completed over four years of the earlier sentence, she was eligible for release in August 2005. When she was released, she immediately hugged her attorney. Rick was released on parole in May 2010.[5] Sandy has been unsuccessful in overturning her burglary and related charges. In March 2008 a three-justice panel of the Nevada Supreme Court upheld her conviction. Her appeal to have the full court rule on her case was denied in November 2008.

Sandy's legal expenses were paid by a wealthy businessman, Bill Fuller, who had followed her case and believed she was innocent. Upon her release from prison, he gave her a job with his company and helped her with financing a home in suburban Las Vegas. Sandy frequently traveled back to southern California to see her family, where in September 2006 she was introduced to Kevin Pieropan, the owner of a Laguna Beach art gallery. They began dating, and in February 2007 she moved in with him in his Monarch Beach house. Sandy married Kevin in April 2009. Now a full partner in the art gallery, Sandy has left behind her life in the fast lane. She has gained an appreciation for art and during her spare time plays golf, surfs, and goes boating. According to her, "I go to work every day. I have a very happy life, and I love my husband" (Heller, 2010). She remains committed to one day being fully exonerated for the remaining crimes (Associated Press, 2012; Cesare, 2005; Heller, 2010; Lagos, 2003; "Murder convictions in Binion case overturned," 2003; Ryan, 2008; Thevenot, 2010; Thevenot and Geary, 2004).

When the Decedent Is a Stranger

Considerably less common among the wrongfully convicted women in this investigation are cases in which the deceased victim was a stranger. In this section, the reader will again be exposed to a diversity of cases, the first of which involved six individuals (three women and three men) who were falsely convicted of the death of a sixty-eight-year-old widow. Two African American women—Ella Mae Ellison and Paula Gray—are profiled next. Ella Mae was allegedly involved in a botched robbery in which an off-duty police officer was killed. Seventeen-year-old Paula Gray was charged with murder, rape, and perjury in an abduction of a white couple. In yet another case from Nevada, Kirstin Lobato was wrongly convicted of first-degree murder and the mutilation of a corpse. The section concludes with the case of an abused woman, Laverne Pavlinac, who falsely implicated her boyfriend in the murder of a twenty-three-year-old woman. Laverne's attempt to have the police arrest the boyfriend backfired, however, and resulted in both of them being charged and convicted of the murder.

The Beatrice Six

Sixty-eight-year-old widow Helen Wilson lived alone in her downtown apartment in Beatrice, Nebraska. On February 6, 1985, she was found by her sister, having been stabbed, raped, and suffocated. Although this case precedes the advent of DNA testing, the Beatrice Police Department (BPD) carefully collected biological evidence—including semen and blood—from the victim and fingerprints from a knife and a door frame. This crime was preceded by three similar but unsuccessful sexual assaults on elderly women in the same neighborhood. In each incident the perpetrator was described as a tall, thin white man. Police initially suspected Bruce Allen Smith, but he moved and was unavailable for forensic testing. Nevertheless, the Oklahoma authorities cooperated with the BPD and conducted serology tests to determine if he could have been the perpetrator. The woman who conducted the tests incorrectly interpreted the results and excluded Smith as a possible suspect.

Four years elapsed before the police found another suspect. In jail on an unrelated charge, Thomas Winslow was charged with the murder and rape of the elderly woman. When the investigation was finished, six persons were charged with the crime: Thomas Winslow, Joseph White, James Dean, Ada JoAnn Taylor, Kathy Gonzalez, and Debra Shelden. Police surmised that these six had engaged in a night of drinking and drug use prior to the sexual assault and murder. After their arrests, blood and semen samples from the crime scene were tested, but the mixture of fluids from the victim and perpetrator resulted in biological evidence that was inconclusive. Additionally, fingerprints found in the apartment did not match those of the defendants. With no physical evidence or witnesses to the crime, authorities worked diligently to obtain confessions. The Gage County Attorney and sheriff deputies threatened the Beatrice Six with the death penalty if they went to trial and were found guilty. Consequently, the only defendant to go to trial was Joseph White. Three of the others testified against him to receive more favorable sentences. After deliberating for two and a half hours, the jury found White guilty of first-degree felony murder and sentenced him to life in prison in February 1990. Although he had no memory of what occurred that night, Winslow pleaded no contest to his charge of aiding and abetting second-degree murder and was sentenced to a prison term of up to fifty years. Taylor pleaded guilty to second-degree murder and received a sentence of ten to forty years. The three remaining defendants received sentences of ten years for aiding and abetting second-degree murder. Collectively, the Beatrice Six were wrongfully incarcerated for over seventy-five years for a crime that was committed by a single perpetrator, Bruce Allen Smith.

Ada JoAnn Taylor was twenty-six years old at the time of her conviction. An abuser of alcohol and drugs, her background made her a viable suspect. To avoid the electric chair, she falsely testified that White and Winslow raped the victim while she held a pillow over the elderly woman's face. On November 10, 2008, at the age of forty-five, JoAnn was released on parole after it was determined through DNA testing that Smith was the lone offender. From the time of her arrest until her release, she spent almost twenty years in prison for a crime in which she did not participate. She was formally pardoned by the state of Nebraska on January 26, 2009.

JoAnn used her period of wrongful incarceration to put her life back together. She earned her GED and took off-campus courses from a community college while in prison. Realizing the futility of drug and alcohol use, she dealt with her addiction and got counseling for her personal problems that led to the alcohol and drug consumption. Based on the latest information available, she was continuing her pursuit of a four-year college degree and expressed an interest in the fields of psychology and social work. To assist with her transition to the general population, JoAnn participated in Compassion in Action, an Omaha program designed to assist with the development of life skills while offering temporary housing. In September 2012 she received $500,000 from the state of Nebraska for her wrongful conviction (Duggan, 2008; Hansen, 2008; Innocence Project, n.d. a; National Registry of Exonerations, n.d. a; Sherrer, 2008a).

Kathy Gonzalez was twenty-nine at the time of her conviction. To receive a less severe sentence, she testified that White had broached the notion of burglarizing the victim's apartment when she lived in the same apartment building as the victim. For her cooperation and false confession, she was allowed to plead guilty to a lesser charge and received a ten-year sentence in 1990. When she was released in 1994 at the age of thirty-four, she had been wrongly incarcerated for almost five years. Kathy was formally pardoned by the state of Nebraska on January 26, 2009 (Innocence Project, n.d. i; National Registry of Exonerations, n.d. d; Sherrer, 2008a).

Debra Shelden, the third woman of the Beatrice Six defendants, was thirty-one when she was incarcerated for the 1985 murder/rape. She confessed to being at the victim's apartment along with the other defendants but claimed that she tried to prevent the crime until White hit her. Convicted in 1989, she received a ten-year prison sentence for aiding and abetting second-degree murder. She was incarcerated in jail and prison for almost five and a half years prior to gaining her release in August 1994. On January 29, 2009, she was officially pardoned by the state of Nebraska. The Beatrice Six defendants represent the first innocents in Nebraska to be exonerated through DNA testing (Innocence Project, n.d. c; National Registry of Exonerations, n.d. c).

Ella Mae Ellison

At approximately noon on November 30, 1973, three young, armed African American men held up a pawn shop in Roxbury, Massachusetts. The three men involved in the robbery were later identified as twenty-year-old Nathaniel Williams, seventeen-year-old Anthony Irving, and twenty-three-year-old Terrell Walker. While the robbery was in progress, Detective John Schroeder, an off-duty Boston police officer, attempted to subdue the robbers but was shot and killed by Walker.[6] About $900 in cash and 250 rings and watches were taken.

Box 3.3 Spotlight on Gloria Killian

Gloria Killian was interviewed by Mitch Ruesink on July 14, 2014. The following story is based on that interview and other documents obtained during the data collection phase of this research.

On August 8, 2002, Gloria Killian walked through the doors of the California Institute for Women as a free woman. She said goodbye to all the inmates who had befriended her during her incarceration. For a long time she dreamed about this day, and it seemed as though she would never be released from prison. Throughout her ordeal she maintained her innocence to anyone who would listen—the problem was that nobody would listen. Escorted to the main gate in a golf cart, Gloria met Joyce Ride, the mother of astronaut Sally Ride, who was waiting on a bench. As she approached the main gate, she was informed that her paperwork was incorrect—a not uncommon occurrence—and she could not be released. The mistake was quickly remedied and Gloria finally passed the main gate where Joyce waited to take her home.

The circuitous path that led to her wrongful conviction and eventual exoneration began in Rosemont, California, on December 9, 1981, when Stephen DeSantis and Gary Masse, disguised as telephone repair men, entered the home of Ed and Grace Davies. According to Gloria, "Mr. Davies was a heavy investor in coins, gold, silver, anything like that. He didn't keep it in the bank, he kept it at home." After entering the house, DeSantis tied up the couple and demanded to know where the gold and silver was hidden. Not wanting to part with his bullion, Ed told him that he kept his collection at his coin store. DeSantis knew he was lying and put a knife to Grace's throat. Ed then told him that the valuables were stored in the garage, hoping that he would take them and leave. DeSantis had other ideas. After recovering six suitcases full of silver, jewelry, coins, and guns, he wanted to make sure that the couple would not be able to identify him and send him to prison. He and Masse reentered the house and shot Ed and Grace.

Detective Stan Reed was the first person to arrive on the scene. He saw Ed, who had been shot twice in the head, lying dead on the kitchen floor. Grace was also shot in the head, but miraculously survived by crawling out to the sidewalk before being discovered by a neighbor. Five days after the incident, the Sacramento County Sheriff's Department received an anonymous phone call saying that two cousins, DeSantis and Masse, had committed the home invasion. This crime was part of a larger series of home robberies in the Sacramento area. Sergeant Harry Machen and Detective Joseph Dean had been assigned to this high-profile case and were under intense pressure to apprehend the suspects. It was not long before the two officers had another break in the case when Joanne Masse, Gary's wife, walked into the sheriff's office, ready to tell everything she knew about the robbery. She claimed that the two men were mere pawns for a woman named Gloria who had masterminded the entire robbery.

At the time Gloria Killian was working for Virgil Fletcher, co-owner of Allied Coins, doing some private investigation work. She had nearly completed her law degree and was taking some time off to enjoy life before finishing law school. She was also doing some bookkeeping for her boyfriend, Brian, who had an automobile repair business. Fletcher, who allegedly had a heart condition, told Gloria that the police had questioned him about the robbery since he was a coin collector. He appeared visibly upset and asked Gloria and Brian to come out to his house to stay with him.

The following day Gloria stopped by to see her boyfriend over the lunch hour. Just as they had locked up the shop to be together, three men knocked on the door. They said that they were looking for Gloria Killian. At the time she thought that they just wanted her to tell them about Fletcher. Instead, she was taken downtown and left in an interrogation room for an hour.

> Then they came in and they asked me if they could waive my rights. You are a law student and you know what that means. I just looked at them and I thought, sure, why not? I don't have anything to hide. I really did not have anything to say as far as that goes, so I waived my rights, and I talked to them for about three hours and the very first question was an attack. . . . They just pounded at me for three hours. They said, "We know you did this, we have all of this information. Blah, blah, blah."

The police found a notebook that she had used in her investigative work for Fletcher that contained an address just two doors away from the Davies house and a list that could have been used in the robbery. Despite their inability to secure a confession, at the conclusion of the interrogation the officers stood up and told her, "You're under arrest for murder."

Gloria was shocked that she was being arrested. This was the last thing that she had expected since she was innocent. According to her, the police warned her that "you are going someplace a nice little white girl like you has never been and you are going to get death. You are not going to believe what is going to happen to you." As they exited the building, Detective Joseph Dean told Gloria that they were going to cover her face since there would probably be some media people outside. Since she was wearing a long sweater coat, "he takes my sweater and puts it over my head and there is nothing that I can do because my hands are cuffed behind my back." Even though her face was covered Gloria could see that every media outlet from Sacramento to the Bay Area was there waiting for her, wanting to record this moment.

By the time she reached the jail, everyone was glaring at her. The unkind treatment was intended to get her to talk, but instead had the opposite effect. She was processed and put in a tank with a group of other women.

> They put me in what is known as the iron tomb and it seems to have people who are crazy. That is where they stuck me and then they left the speaker on all night long and all day long. I guess they thought that I was going to write out my confession and then read it aloud for errors. I have no idea what they thought. Eventually, they took me out of there. But mainly, we went to court several times and that was the first time actually that I saw Gary Masse, who had turned himself in or his wife had turned him in, as the case may be. I stared at him. I didn't know him.

Gloria sat in jail for four and a half months, waiting for a trial. She was released due to lack of evidence as abruptly as she had been arrested.

> They literally took me back from court and they took me to a little room in the back of the courthouse and they gave me my clothes. I asked for my purse and they said that it had been booked into evidence and I couldn't have it. So I was dressed but I had nothing, literally nothing. And they told me to go down the stairway and out the door at the bottom of the stairs and I was sure that they were going to shoot me in the back.

Career criminal Gary Masse had surrendered to police on December 17, 1981, the same day they arrested Gloria. He did not go to trial until May 1983. Having already confessed to the crime, he was found guilty and convicted of first-degree murder and sentenced to life without parole. Knowing that he needed to do something fast or spend the rest of his life in prison, Masse contacted the Sacramento County Sheriff's Department to try to make a deal to have his sentence reduced. After the district attorney's office expressed an interest in his offer, he told them that Stephen DeSantis had committed the murder and Gloria Killian had masterminded the entire incident. As a result, Masse had his sentence recalled and remained without a sentence for the next three years. In the meantime Gloria had been keeping a low profile since being released, not wanting to be in the spotlight. She was no longer working for Fletcher, but was still doing the books for Brian's car repair business. In fact, she was working in Brian's office in June 1983 when the police returned to arrest her and charge her with murder again.

DeSantis had been living in Texas under an alias and, after searching for a year, the FBI found him and arrested him. He and Gloria went to trial in connection with the robbery and murder. DeSantis went first and, while testifying in his own defense, denied ever knowing anyone named Gloria Killian and stated that she did not have anything to do with the crime. He also testified that Joanne Masse had previously tried to gain access to the Davies' home to use their telephone, not Gloria Killian as Masse had asserted.

Gloria's trial began in February 1986. The star witness against her was none other than Masse, who testified that Gloria orchestrated the crime. He further contended that she had entered the Davies' home previously and demanded her share of the loot. Masse additionally testified that he did not have a deal with the prosecution that would reduce his sentence. Grace also testified that a woman had earlier come to the door of their house but was unable to identify Gloria as that individual. Largely due to Masse's testimony, the jury found Gloria guilty on February 26, 1986, and she was subsequently sentenced to thirty-two years to life in prison. Contrary to Masse's statement, his sentence was reduced from life without parole to twenty-five years in prison.

For Gloria's automatic appeals, the court appointed Julian Macias, who was the lead attorney in the case involving DeSantis. The obvious conflict of interest was contested by the Public Defender's Office, but a judge determined that Macias could continue to represent Gloria. Macias briefly considered filing a claim of ineffective assistance of counsel to justify a new trial but later declined to do so when he realized that he would need to give incriminating evidence against his former client.

Within about five years all of Gloria's appeals had been exhausted and she was still in prison. She began to lose hope, something that happens to many sentenced to life in prison, usually around the five- to seven-year mark. At times she believed that she would spend the rest of her life in prison and that nobody cared what happened to her. In 1992 she became acquainted with Joyce Ride, who had been a volunteer visitor at women's prisons for several years. Over time Joyce came to believe that Gloria was innocent. During the next ten years she spent $100,000 of her own money to help Gloria gain her freedom.

Joyce hired Bill Genego, an attorney who works with clients who have postconviction appeals. She also had Darryl Carson, a private investigator, assist with the case. Although Genego agreed to take the case, he was not optimistic about Gloria's chances. He knew how difficult it was to challenge a case after a ruling was in place. However, as he started examining the case, he became convinced that Masse had cut a deal for his testimony against Gloria. He even had a letter written by Masse to the prosecutor's office that discussed a verbal agreement regarding a lighter sentence for testifying. About the same time, DeSantis's appellate lawyers contacted Gloria saying that they wanted to meet with her. As Gloria observed,

> At the time I had been instrumental in the creation of the CIW [California Institute for Women] law project. I didn't know if I wanted to talk to these people or not. Before I decided, I got another letter from DeSantis's lawyers that was kind of pressuring me and I thought, screw you guys. I don't remember if they called Darryl or he called them but anyhow my investigator arranged that we were all going to get together. They turned out to be absolutely fabulous. They were so nice. They spent the whole day there and

they told me about all of the evidence that they had uncovered. This included all of the letters that Masse had written, all of the stuff that had been done, everything that had gone on, the evidence that the cops had found; it was just a bunch of stuff.

When Gloria's case finally made it to the California Supreme Court in about five and a half years, the court made every finding and fact in her favor and then ruled against her. In a sixty-three-page opinion, the court admitted that it is exceedingly rare to see cases where actual innocence is an issue and this case was one of those. Then it ended by denying her appeal. Not to be deterred, her case finally made it to the US Court of Appeals for the Ninth Circuit in March 2002. As Gloria explains

So we went to the Ninth Circuit and the decision, again favorable, came out March 8th. The only problem was that I could not get out of prison. I sat in prison for another four months because Kit Cleland [the prosecutor in Gloria's original trial] did every possible thing he could think of to keep me in prison. It went around and around and around. It really impacted my sunny attitude. When I finally did find out that I was going to be released, it was a great night because we all celebrated.

In September 2002 the charges were finally dismissed. The California State Bar later censured Cleland for his role in this miscarriage of justice.

As Gloria passed through the gates of the prison, her good friend Joyce rose from the bench that she was sitting on and gave her a hug. It was at this point that she realized that she was free at last.

Two of the assailants—Williams and Irving—used a portion of their proceeds to buy heroin. Fearful of being caught, they fled to Atlanta on a bus later that day. The third assailant chose to remain in the Boston area and was arrested. On December 1, Williams and Irving were arrested by the Danville, Virginia, police while en route to Atlanta. When arrested they had heroin, weapons (including the detective's revolver), and jewelry from the pawn shop. They were questioned separately by the police and signed statements regarding their involvement in the robbery. The following day police officers from the Boston Police Department arrived and interviewed them as well. The two gave conflicting statements about the robbery. Whereas Irving alluded to only three people being involved in the heist, Williams contended that a young African American woman had driven them to and from the crime scene. He described the woman as young (about eighteen) with a complexion that was "lighter-skinned" or "medium."

While confined together in a Boston jail, they inquired about a possible plea bargain. Irving's attorney informed them that to be considered for a plea bargain, a complete description of the events surrounding the crime must be forthcoming, including the name of the female driver. In exchange for their cooperation, the charge would be reduced to second-degree murder, which would make the men eligible for parole after fifteen years. With this offer in the balance, the accounts of the crime by Williams and Irving began to converge. Whereas only three participants were mentioned in the statements to the Danville police, after sharing a cell in Boston, Williams and Irving identified a woman known as "Sue" as the driver of the getaway vehicle. Because none of the customers or employees in the pawn shop had seen the robbers' vehicle, they were unable to corroborate the assailants' accounts regarding a fourth perpetrator. Ella Mae Ellison, a twenty-seven-year-old dark-skinned African American mother of four, who had moved to Rochester, New York, was arrested in May 1974 and indicted on charges of first-degree murder and armed robbery.

During Ella Mae's trial, Williams and Irving testified that she drove them to and from the pawn shop and shared in the proceeds of the robbery. Their previous contradictory statements regarding the events of that day were not made available to her defense counsel. It was not until Williams was cross-examined that he confessed that he did not mention Ella Mae in his statements to the police in Virginia. Other inconsistencies in the two men's stories raised questions regarding Ella Mae's involvement in the botched robbery. Apart from the questionable testimony by informants with incentives to lie, only the testimony provided by Boston police officer Lewis McConkey implicated her in the robbery. According to McConkey, who interviewed Ella Mae in Rochester, she asked how the police had acquired her name. McConkey allegedly responded, "You're no dope. What do you think?" She then allegedly replied, "It could only come from the three people involved in the hold-up" (*Commonwealth of Massachusetts v. Ella Mae Ellison*, 376 Mass. 1, 1978). Nevertheless, upon cross-examination it was disclosed that no mention of this discussion appeared in either the handwritten or typed report of the visit.

Ella Mae testified on her behalf during the trial and admitted that she knew the three assailants but was shopping on the day of the crime and was driving home when she heard that a police officer had been fatally wounded. Her father also testified that between April 1973 and February 1974 he sent his daughter seventeen money orders because she had little money to support herself and her family. If she had been involved in the robbery, as suggested by Williams and Irving, then she

Box 3.4 Spotlight on Joyce Brown

Joyce Brown was interviewed by Mitch Ruesink on October 22, 2014. The following story is based on that interview and other documents obtained during the data collection phase of this research.

When Joyce Brown woke up on Friday, May 9, 1980, she had no reason to believe that day would be any different than any other. She would get up and go to work as she had in the past. By the time her mother, Ruby Kelly, called, she realized the day would be anything but ordinary. She tried to make sense out of what her mother was saying. It had something to do with a robbery and a murder that appeared in the newspaper and the fact that the police were looking for a woman named Joyce Brown who supposedly was involved in the incident. How could that be? Joyce was at work the day before, and she could prove it. Ruby thought this must be some sort of joke or misunderstanding, so Joyce called a friend. A short time later Ruby called back and told Joyce that she had been contacted by Miss Nanny, a respected elder, who confirmed that the police wanted to talk to her. Although she knew that her mother was telling the truth, Joyce wanted to talk directly to Miss Nanny. When she called, Miss Nanny verified that the police were searching for her. Joyce then heard something even stranger: the individual being sought by the police had fled to Denver, Colorado, to avoid prosecution. Shocked, Joyce responded, "But I'm here."

The article appearing in the *Dallas Morning News* stated that on Tuesday, May 6, 1980, Ruben Danziger, the owner of Fine Furs by Rubin, had been shot and killed by two armed black women. Rubin's wife, Ala, was also shot at, but not hit. Thinking quickly, she had lied to the shooters about dying of cancer and was spared. The two women fled the scene in a brown 1980 Datsun. A day later, the vehicle was found by the police. It was discovered that the Datsun had been rented by a woman whose name was Joyce Ann Brown. Assisted by Ala, the police learned that the trigger woman was wearing pink pants and dark glasses and her accomplice was wearing a navy blue jogging suit. Ala was also asked to look at a photograph lineup to see if any of the individuals resembled the offenders. A Dallas vice officer remembered a Joyce Brown from previous prostitution arrests, and her photograph was added to the lineup. Unaware that her previous indiscretions would eventually lead to her being arrested and convicted of a crime that she didn't commit, Joyce had quit being a call girl when she became concerned that her children might find out about her occupation. Instead, she now worked full-time at Koslow's Furs, and although she didn't make as much money as before, it was honest money. When Ala picked out Joyce's photograph and the police learned that she worked at another fur store in Dallas, the stage was set for a miscarriage of justice.

Even after reading the newspaper account of the robbery and murder,

Joyce could hardly believe that the police thought she could have had anything to do with the crime. She talked to a detective on the telephone who informed her that his reaction was "That is not Joyce's M.O." She believed it had to be a case of mistaken identity and a trip to the police station would straighten things out.

During the early 1980s the city of Dallas was in the middle of an oil boom and the district attorney's office was known for hardly ever losing a case. Their mantra appeared to be, "Anybody can convict a guilty man; it takes a real prosecutor to convict an innocent one." This office milieu eventually led to Joyce's wrongful conviction.

Before Joyce went to trial, the police had determined the automobile had been rented by a different Joyce Brown who lived in Denver, Colorado. When the Denver woman was questioned by the police, she told them that she had loaned the car to a friend and that she had not seen her friend or the car since that time. The "friend" was identified as Renee Michelle Taylor of Denver. Although Taylor escaped detection, authorities found several items connected to the crime. They found the furs that had been taken, the pink pants worn by the assailant, and a .22 caliber pistol that had not been cleaned after the robbery.

Meanwhile back in Dallas, Joyce, accompanied by her attorney, Robert Rose, met with the police for questioning. Joyce was certain that the police would realize that they had the wrong person and release her. They questioned her, and she told the officers that she did not know what they were talking about and that she definitely hadn't seen a man being shot. "They gave me seven and a half minutes to go and commit this robbery and get back to work without being missed. Totally impossible," she said. Still, the officers believed that Joyce was hiding something and that she wasn't telling the truth. She finally had enough of their accusations. After being called a liar, Joyce calmly told the detectives that the interview was over. The officers informed her that they had more questions and that she was not free to leave. At that juncture Joyce responded by saying, "I'm sorry, no white boy looks me in my face and calls me a liar when I know I'm not." A few minutes later she was charged with capital murder.

With an additional charge of fleeing arrest, Joyce was placed in jail and a $1 million bond was issued for her case. When the police searched her home they failed to find any evidence linking her to the crime. Her attorney requested a physical lineup, but the police refused since she had previously been identified during a photograph lineup. Joyce knew that she needed a good defense lawyer and that it would be better if someone else represented her. A court-appointed attorney, Kerry Fitzgerald, consented to take her case. While Joyce was in jail, Fitzgerald managed to get her bond reduced to $500,000 and eventually $25,000. After six weeks, her family was able to post her bond. Her temporary freedom came at a price, though. Since her family was able to afford the bond, Joyce was no longer entitled to a court-appointed attorney. Nevertheless, she liked Fitzgerald and asked him to represent her at trial as her personal lawyer.

When Joyce's trial began in October 1980, Taylor was still at large. Joyce believed that if Taylor were located, then she would be cleared of the charges. Although Taylor was captured by authorities six months later after giving birth to a baby in a Dallas hospital, she slipped out of the leg chain while a guard was in the restroom and left the hospital. Using a salary check she found in the guard's purse, she was later arrested in a department store when she attempted to cash it. Taylor later pleaded guilty to the crime to avoid a possible death sentence and testified that Joyce Brown had nothing to do with the robbery.

Taylor's statements did little to dissuade the prosecution from trying Joyce for the robbery and death of the store owner. At her trial, the primary evidence used against her was the eyewitness testimony of the victim's wife and a jailhouse snitch. Ala pointed to Joyce when she was asked in court if the person who committed the crime was in the courtroom. Perjured testimony from Martha Jean Bruce, a jailhouse informant with an incentive to lie, was also used against her. The prosecution further contended that Joyce had sufficient time to complete the crime and return to work during her thirty-six-minute lunch break.

Fitzgerald wanted to know who Bruce was as she was introduced to the court. After Joyce explained the connection, the attorney told her that her testimony was probably not going to be truthful. Bruce contended that Joyce had confessed to the crime while in jail with her. What she did not tell the court was that she had been convicted of lying to police several months earlier or that recently she had been sentenced to five years for attempted murder. She denied that any leniency was discussed in exchange for her testimony.

To counter the charges, Joyce had eyewitnesses who testified that she was at work when the crime occurred. A timecard showed that she had spent the day at work, with the exception of a thirty-six-minute lunch break. The prosecution's contention was that during that brief time span Joyce had driven the three miles between Koslow's Furs and Fine Furs by Rubin, committed the crime, and then returned to work. Fitzgerald noted that there was no physical evidence tying Joyce to the crime and called into question the credibility of the prosecution's timeline of events. During the eight-day trial, several people expressed their views that her case would be dropped due to a lack of evidence. Joyce believed the jury would quickly reach a verdict of not guilty after weighing the evidence. Instead, however, the all-white jury voted to convict her on charges of murder and aggravated robbery. She received a sentence of twenty-five years to life.

A month after Joyce was convicted, Dallas District Attorney Henry Wade contacted the Texas Board of Pardons and Paroles, recommending a reduction in Bruce's sentence. The board approved the request and the governor ordered officials to release Bruce immediately. For Joyce, however, it was nine years, five months, and twenty-four days before she was freed.

Unsuccessful in her appeal, Joyce had to learn how to survive in prison. She was ill-prepared for the dehumanizing effects of incarceration. All of the things she took for granted were denied to her. She had been reduced to little more than a number and a prison uniform for a crime she did not commit. She became bitter and filled with anger about her situation. She turned to God and asked Him to replace her bitterness with compassion.

Joyce continued to maintain her innocence, stating that during her first trial she had been railroaded by Norman Kinne, an assistant district attorney for Dallas County. She contacted James McCloskey at Centurion Ministries (CM), who discovered that Kinne and his associates knew that Bruce had been convicted of lying before and that they never told the defense about it. Kinne thus agreed that Joyce should receive a new trial. CM's investigation also disclosed that Taylor was wanted in New Mexico for a 1978 armed robbery of a fur store.

Joyce's case was not the first one in the Dallas area that came under scrutiny. Three years before she went on trial, Randall Dale Adams was sentenced to death for murdering Dallas police officer Robert Wood. Despite the fact that Adams was innocent, he spent twelve years in prison, including time on death row. The same appeals court that eventually heard Joyce's case overturned his conviction after evidence was presented that the Dallas district attorney's office had withheld evidence and used perjured testimony to affect the outcome of the trial. The Adams story was made into the movie, *A Thin Blue Line*. The evidence ultimately helped Adam win his freedom.

In October 1989 Joyce's conviction was reversed. She was released from prison on November 3, 1989, and three months later all charges were dropped. While in prison Joyce vowed that she would dedicate herself to helping young people once she gained her freedom. Since her release she has talked to several youth groups about her experiences. She also formed a nonprofit foundation known as MASS (Mothers [Fathers] for the Advancement of Social Systems). Initially, her vision was to provide support for those who were wrongfully convicted. The organization later expanded its mission and began to provide support to the children and families of offenders who may experience substance abuse, physical or psychological disorders, and poverty. It also promotes educational advancement and job opportunities, as well as providing assistance to innocence programs.

Joyce has always maintained that since she is innocent she doesn't need to apply for a pardon for something she didn't do. Since the state of Texas requires a pardon before compensation is awarded, she has not received any remuneration for the years of her life spent behind bars.

should not have required any financial assistance during this time. After deliberating for only three hours, a jury found Ella Mae guilty of first-degree murder and four counts of armed robbery. She received two concurrent life sentences.

In May 1976 Williams and Irving signed sworn affidavits recanting their accusations regarding the involvement of Ella Mae in the crime. Williams acknowledged that he fabricated the story of a female driver to lessen Irving's culpability in the crime. Both admitted that they continued to include a female driver in their accounts to be eligible for a plea bargain. What motivated them to recant their testimony remains somewhat of a mystery. They were both informed that an admission of perjury could result in a sentence of life in prison. Even if they were not sentenced to life in prison, perjury during the murder trial could adversely affect their chances for parole. Thus, it appears that their recantations were not self-serving and probably genuine. When the Massachusetts Supreme Judicial Court heard Ella Mae's case in 1978, the court overturned her conviction due to the withholding of exculpatory evidence during the trial and the recantations. The indictments against her were also dismissed. This mother of four, who had no previous criminal history, received her freedom after four years of false imprisonment (Center for Public Integrity, n.d.; *Commonwealth of Massachusetts v. Ella Mae Ellison*, 1978; "Ella Mae Ellison—Massachusetts," 1980).

Paula Gray

Homewood, Illinois, is a thriving Chicago suburb that is one of the three most "livable" suburbs in the Chicago vicinity, according to *Forbes* magazine. In 2010 it had a population of almost 20,000 inhabitants. This predominantly white community in 2000 had a median family income of $70,941. On May 11, 1978, Homewood was shocked to learn that a recently engaged white couple had been abducted and murdered during the early morning hours and the woman had been repeatedly raped. Their bodies were found in an abandoned townhouse in the Ford Heights area, a predominantly black community with a declining population base and a median family income of only $16,706 in 2000.

Charles McCraney, who lived in Ford Heights, mistakenly identified four black men as the perpetrators: Verneal Jimerson, Dennis Williams, Kenneth Adams, and Willie Rainge. In addition to the four men, a seventeen-year-old woman was questioned. Paula Gray, who has an IQ of 64, can neither read nor write and is unable to tell time correctly. After repeatedly being questioned over two nights in motels without benefit of counsel, she falsely confessed to the grand jury on May 16 regarding her involvement in the crime and identified Jimerson, Williams, Adams, and Rainge as the perpetrators. On June 19, however, she recanted her testimony during a preliminary hearing in which she claimed that the police had fed her the information that she needed to implicate the men. Her confession, which contained only two new pieces of information not already known to the police, was ultimately found to be baseless. Because the only evidence linking Jimerson to the crime was Paula's recanted testimony, charges against him were dropped. In turn, Paula was charged with rape, murder, and perjury.

Based primarily on the testimony of McCraney and faulty forensic evidence, the jury found Paula guilty and sentenced her to fifty years in prison for the murders of the couple and ten years, concurrently, for perjury. Williams received the death penalty, Rainge received a life sentence, and Adams received a seventy-five-year prison sentence. Williams and Rainge were awarded retrials in 1982 based on ineffective assistance of counsel. In exchange for early release, Paula agreed to testify against Williams, Rainge, and Jimerson. As a result of Paula's false testimony and that of McCraney, Williams was again sentenced to death while Rainge was again sentenced to life imprisonment. Jimerson was also convicted and sentenced to death although his conviction was overturned in 1995 based on prosecutorial misconduct. In 1996 DNA testing revealed that none of the defendants matched the DNA evidence found at the crime scene. The DNA analysis further resulted in the identification and arrest of three of the four offenders (the fourth offender had died), each of whom later confessed to the crime. The actual murderers had killed other individuals during the time Williams, Rainge, Adams, and Jimerson were incarcerated.

In March 1999 the wrongfully convicted men, now referred to as the Ford Heights Four, were awarded $36 million in civil rights damages. Williams was most insistent that the money would not replace his eighteen years on death row. According to Williams, "If they could give me back the entire 18 years they took out of my life, then that would be compensation" (CBS News, 1999). In his early twenties when arrested, Williams recalls that sheriff deputies placed a gun to his forehead and threatened him that "If I didn't confess . . . they would splatter my brains all over the wall" (CBS News, 1999). Paula was awarded $4 million in the last of the civil lawsuits in 2008 (CBS News, 1999; Center on Wrongful Convictions, n.d. b; Innocence Project, n.d. j; National Registry of Exonerations, n.d. e).

Kirstin Lobato

By any standard one might employ, Kirstin Lobato's childhood was horrendous. When she left her biological father to live with her biological mother, her nightmare was just beginning. At the young age of six, she was repeatedly raped by her mother's boyfriend with her mother's knowledge. After a year of abuse, Kirstin moved back with her father, who had remarried. While living with her drug-addicted father, she began experimenting with methamphetamine, which she used to compensate for her suicidal thoughts and melancholy. Kirstin was also sexually violated at the age of thirteen and again at the age of seventeen after the father of her best friend forced himself on her. Because of these assaults, Kirstin's father gave her a knife to use for protection. In her car she carried a baseball bat. Upon receiving her high school diploma, she moved to Las Vegas to begin a new life.

But moving failed to improve her life. On May 25, 2001, eighteen-year-old Kirstin left her car during the early morning hours only to discover an imposing African American man, who began to molest her. Although there were some people in the vicinity, no one offered assistance. At five foot, six inches in height and only one hundred pounds, she was no match for her attacker. Since her father had given her a knife for such occasions, she stabbed the assailant's exposed genitals to get free. As she quickly drove away, she could see her perpetrator lying in the parking lot in obvious pain. She hesitated to notify authorities because previous sexual assaults had gone unacted on by the police. Her memory of the event was somewhat cloudy because at the time she had just ended a three-day methamphetamine binge. When she reported the crime seven weeks later, she described her assailant as a "really big" older black man. Though she had stabbed him in his genitals, there had been no police reports of a deceased black man who fit her description during the latter part of May and early part of June, so apparently her assailant did not die as a result of the encounter.

Two weeks after the attack, a forty-four-year-old homeless black man was found behind a dumpster. Duran Bailey, who was a drug seller and user, had been stabbed, beaten, and sexually mutilated. The medical examiner determined that the man died on July 8, 2001. At five foot, ten inches in stature and weighing only 135 pounds, the dead man did not seem to fit the description of Kirstin's attacker. The extreme violence with which the victim had died suggested that his assailant was a male. When the police arrived, they found that the victim's penis had been severed sometime after his death and his anus had been repeatedly stabbed and sliced. Given the extent of the victim's injuries, any woman the size of Kirstin would have experienced visible physical reminders of the encounter, yet Kirstin had no such abrasions and had not visited a doctor or emergency room between July 8 and July 20. Moreover, a man's size ten shoe print was discovered in the blood around Bailey's body, although this lead was never pursued by the police.

Because Kirstin's earlier attack had gone unreported to the police until after this murder was uncovered, the police became interested in her as a possible suspect since she had attacked her assailant with a knife in the groin area and both her attacker and the murder victim were black men. When detectives Thomas Thowsen and Jim LaRochelle from the Las Vegas Metropolitan Police Department arrived where Kirstin was living on July 20, 2001, she thought that they were referring to the incident of May 25, 2001. As a result, her comments to the police did not match the circumstances surrounding the murder that they were investigating. Nevertheless, after their interrogation, the detectives arrested her and drove her to the Clark County Detention Center (CCDC) in Las Vegas.

Although Kirstin knew that she faced a possible life sentence if found guilty, she believed that she would be found innocent, so she refused the prosecutor's plea bargain to manslaughter and a possible three-year sentence. At the trial an informant with an apparent incentive to lie testified that Kirstin had loudly bragged about the murder while awaiting trial. Korinda Martin, who claimed to have kept a log of these encounters, never produced the log in court and the "facts" she asserted were later proven to be false. Perhaps most peculiar was the inability of the prosecutor to locate any other inmates who had overheard Kirstin boasting about the murder. When Martin's perjured testimony came to the attention of the prosecutors after the trial, there was no effort made to prosecute her. Prosecutors were also unable to explain why the skull fractures on the victim were not depressed as they would be if Kirstin had used a baseball bat to inflict the injuries. In fact, the skull fractures were more consistent with the victim's head striking the concrete as he descended to the ground. Kirstin's bat, moreover, contained no blood, hairs, or tissue, which should be present if it had been used in the commission of the crime. Evidence of her innocence was so compelling that George Schiro, a nationally recognized forensic scientist who had testified for the prosecution in over one hundred cases but only testified for the defense on four occasions, stated that Kirstin could not have been the perpetrator. The prosecution was also at a loss to reconcile the size ten man's shoeprint found at the crime scene, which did not match the size seven shoe that Kirstin wears. Instead, the prosecution attempted to portray the incident as a drug transaction gone awry when Bailey demanded sex.

With Kirstin's previous sexual assault history, and her own admission that she had been awake for three days after using meth, the jury bought the prosecution's scenario and found her guilty after deliberating for only about five hours. She was convicted of first-degree murder and the sexual penetration of a corpse. Kirstin, who had been free on $50,000 bail, was immediately taken into custody. She was sentenced to a minimum of forty years, thereby making her eligible for parole at the earliest at age fifty-nine.

The Nevada Supreme Court heard Kirstin's case and reversed her conviction on September 3, 2004. Because the judge did not permit the defense to cross-examine Martin and other prejudicial errors, the court remanded her case for retrial. This time, however, her bail was set at $500,000, so she was forced to remain in custody while awaiting the second trial.

Now twenty-three years old, Kirstin's second trial was in the same courtroom as her earlier one. Her defense counsel was now composed of two female attorneys from San Francisco who were working pro bono and Special Public Defender David Scheck from the Innocence Project (IP). The IP, which had become interested in her case, was pursuing a DNA analysis of the evidence. Unfortunately, this request was denied, and Kirstin was found guilty of one count of voluntary manslaughter with a deadly weapon and one count of sexual penetration of a corpse. Oral arguments before the Nevada Supreme Court were scheduled for September 9, 2014, in Carson City, Nevada ("Key points regarding Kirstin Lobato's Las Vegas wrongful conviction," n.d.; Longobardy, 2006; Sherrer, 2004).

Laverne Pavlinac

Perhaps the idiom, "Be careful what you wish for," best characterizes this wrongful conviction. Our story examines the misadventures of fifty-seven-year-old Laverne Pavlinac, who was involved in a ten-year-long abusive relationship with John Sosnovske, a man who was eighteen years her junior. As she struggled for ways to end their relationship, she became intrigued by a recent murder involving a twenty-three-year-old woman in a remote area outside of Portland, Oregon. The unsolved murder represented a possible solution to her dilemma. If she could convince the police that her boyfriend was responsible for the crime, she would be free of him at last.

Laverne began leaving anonymous tips for the police stating that John had been boasting about the crime. When this tactic failed, she proceeded to call the detectives who were assigned to the case. She explained that she was a battered woman who lived with the man who committed the rape/murder. To make her story more cogent, she began to embellish by informing the police that after meeting the crime victim at a local bar, John forced her to participate in the rape and assist in the disposal of the body. To corroborate her new story, Laverne planted fake evidence in her car in an attempt to steer the police toward her boyfriend. While the police remained skeptical, they continued to interview her. After taking her to the vicinity where the victim's body was recovered, she was able to identify the actual location of the body, although she was unable to identify the locations of the victim's personal belongings. Nonetheless, the police had heard and seen enough and turned over their case to the local district attorney's office.

In February 1990, John and Laverne were arrested and charged with the murder of Taunja Bennett. The main evidence used to support the charges included Laverne's false confession (which she later retracted) and her ability to correctly identify where the body had been found. Tried first, Laverne was convicted by a jury of felony murder and was sentenced to ten years to life in January 1991. Fearful of the death penalty, John pleaded no contest to murder and kidnapping charges and received a life sentence for his alleged involvement in March 1991.

Three years later anonymous letters began to appear in newspapers from an individual claiming to be the actual killer. At the same time authorities began receiving anonymous letters to that effect. In 1995 the police obtained a confession from Keith Hunter Jesperson (a.k.a. the Happy Face Killer), who provided information about the case that only the police and the actual perpetrator would know.[7] Polygraph tests administered by the FBI indicated that he was telling the truth about the crime. After Jesperson was convicted of the murder in November 1995, Circuit Court Judge Paul Lipscomb ordered Laverne and John to be released. The judge commented, "There's no longer any doubt that these two individuals are innocent. The evidence is compelling." John had his conviction vacated, but Laverne, because of her abuse of the legal system, did not. They were incarcerated for four years each for a crime that neither committed (*Laverne Pavlinac*, n.d.; Perry, n.d.).

Crimes in Which the Murder Was Facilitated Through Arson

To conclude our discussion of wrongful murder convictions, we turn to three cases in which falsely convicted women were alleged to have killed their victims through the use of arson. In each case the victim was a relative. Although arson murders are atypical of this genre of wrongful conviction, they are included to reveal the diversity that exists within female wrongful convictions.

Sheila Bryan

Sheila Bryan lived in Omega, Georgia, with her husband and two daughters, Kari and Karla. She helped take care of her elderly mother, eighty-two-year-old Freda Weeks. On August 18, 1996, while taking her mother for an outing in the country, something went terribly wrong. "We just went riding around for a little bit, just reminiscing, which we've done for years," Sheila later told CBS News's *48 Hours* (2000). While driving she became temporarily distracted and her car careened off the road and ended up at the bottom of an eighteen-foot embankment. Unable to free her unresponsive mother from the car, she climbed back up to the road to seek help. As she looked back, Sheila detected smoke coming from the vehicle. When she reached the top of the hill she saw her cousin, Danny Weeks, and his wife driving down the road. By that time, the car was engulfed in flames.

The Georgia Bureau of Investigation (GBI) proceeded to investigate the incident since a death had occurred. GBI agent John Heinen considered the case suspicious. According to him, there had been "No damage to the vehicle, no personal items in the car, the gas cap of the car was missing, and the fuel door was open" (CBS News, 2000). The state medical examiner was unable to determine if Freda had died of a heart attack before or after the fire. State fire investigators incorrectly concluded that the fire had been deliberately set when they found what they believed was a "pour pattern" caused by an accelerant.

Sheila was indicted on December 18, 1997, and charged with arson and murder. Prosecutors surmised that she had become tired of taking care of her aging mother and saw this as an opportunity to kill her and collect on her vehicle's liability insurance policy. On August 28, 1998, her case went to trial. After a week, the jury began deliberating. At the conclusion of eight hours they arrived at a guilty verdict and Sheila was sentenced to life for murder plus twenty years for arson. Her husband recalls his emotions at the time: "I just went numb. I had resigned to the fact that our life would be four or five hours together once a week at the prison." As would be expected, Sheila was also upset with the verdict. "You think because you're innocent that things won't go wrong. You're mistaken" (CBS News, 2000). After sentencing she was temporarily placed in jail before being transferred to a state prison.

Although the Georgia Supreme Court overturned her conviction on June 14, 1999, the state decided to retry her. While awaiting her new trial, Sheila enjoyed her temporary freedom. Using the time to get reacquainted with her husband and children, she also took on a part-time job in which she delivered meals to the elderly.

The new trial began in January 2000, only this time her defense counsel retained the services of an arson expert from Austin, Texas. Dr. Gerald Hurst testified that the fire could have been the product of a faulty ignition switch given the age of the car (it was a 1987 model) and the fact that from 1984 to 1993 Ford and Mercury ignition switches have been linked to some automobile fires. He also provided documentation for his statement from experiments he conducted with burning plastic from a 1987 Mercury Cougar, the same make and model Shelia had been driving. Hurst additionally refuted the state's contention that the door must have been open to achieve a burn pattern such as that found in this case. Explaining that the door seal still permitted the free passage of air into the passenger compartment because it was not air tight, there was sufficient oxygen for the fire to start. It was further revealed at the second trial that one of the prosecution's expert witnesses had ties to the Ford Motor Company and had received approximately $150,000 in consulting fees from Ford. On cross-examination, fire expert Ronnie Dobbins admitted that he did not even know what an ignition switch looked like, despite his argument that this device could not have caused the fire. The trial concluded after four days and three hours of deliberation by the jury. On January 28, 2000, Sheila was exonerated when the jury found her not guilty on all counts (CBS News, 2000; Possley, n.d. n).

Kristine Bunch

Living in a trailer in Decatur County, Indiana in 1995, single, unemployed mom Kristine Bunch, pregnant with another child, struggled financially to provide for her three-year-old son, Anthony. On June 30, 1995, her struggle took on a new dimension when the trailer caught fire. When she awoke she tried in vain to extinguish the fire. Unable to reach her son because of the flames, she ran to get assistance. Fire investigators later found Anthony's body between his bed and a wall.

When asked to recall those events years after the incident, Kristine replied, "A lot of it is like a fog. You kind of remember, kind of don't, are confused. I had some burns on my face. My hair was singed off. So were my eyebrows and eyelashes. I had cuts on the bottom of my feet from running out" (Chapman, 2012). When she inquired if Anthony had been found in the rubble, her requests were interpreted as evidence of her involvement in the crime. Kristine explains that her interest in locating her child was seen as proof "that I had hidden him or tried to keep him from being found" (Chapman, 2012).

During the trial the prosecution argued that investigators found a chair blocking the door to Anthony's bedroom. (It was eventually determined that the "chair" was actually a charred wall.) At the trial Brian Frank, a state arson investigator, testified that

> There were two separate fires. One was in the south bedroom, along the south wall. That was caused by the liquid accelerant being present. The second fire originated at the doorway, the area of the doorway of the south bedroom into the living room. And there was a liquid accelerant poured across the floor of the living room that went to the front door of the mobile home. (Warden, n.d.)

William Kinard, a forensic analyst with the Bureau of Alcohol, Tobacco, and Firearms (ATF) corroborated Frank's testimony. Kinard testified that flooring samples taken from the living room and Anthony's bedroom evidenced "a heavy petroleum distillate."

Despite no prior criminal or arrest record, no history of psychiatric issues, no motive, no flammable liquid present on her clothes, and no witnesses, Kristine was found guilty of arson and murder on March 4, 1996. On April 1, she was sentenced to fifty years in prison for arson and sixty years in prison for murder with the terms to be served concurrently. At the age of twenty-two, Kristine's worst nightmare had begun. She remembers vividly the thoughts that went through her mind when she learned of her fate: "I remember thinking, I'm six months pregnant and they just sentenced me to 110 years. And I just kept on saying that 'I didn't'" (Chapman, 2012).

Shortly after she was incarcerated, she gave birth to a healthy baby boy whom she named Trenton. The day after delivering her son at a local hospital, she was whisked back to the prison to continue serving her sentence. At this juncture, Kristine had an epiphany. While analyzing a Texas arson case in the prison law library, she discovered similarities between their cases. The outdated fire investigation techniques used to prove that she initiated the fire with an accelerant were now known to be faulty. In 2006 one of Kristine's supporters wrote to the Center on Wrongful Convictions (CWC) to request assistance with her appeal. After being referred to attorney Jane Raley at the CWC, the evidence used to convict her was examined by three fire forensic experts. All three concurred that by current standards the arson testimony in her trial was flawed and that she was probably innocent. Files from the ATF that were not disclosed to the defense revealed that no heavy petroleum distillate had been found in the flooring from the victim's bedroom. Although there was some evidence of kerosene on the living room floor, during the winter Kristine used a kerosene heater and occasionally some would inevitably spill onto the floor.

Although an amended petition for postconviction relief was unsuccessful, a three-member panel of the Indiana Court of Appeals agreed to hear her case on July 13, 2011. On March 21, 2012, the court finally vacated her conviction and stated that Kristine was eligible for a new trial because the improved fire technology now available constituted new evidence and the ATF documents "directly contradict Kinard's trial testimony supporting fires originating in two places" (Warden, n.d.). When the Indiana Supreme Court left the decision by the Indiana Court of Appeals intact on August 8, 2012, the possibility of freedom now existed. On August 22, Kristine left the jail where she had been temporarily staying. She was released on a $5,000 cash bond to her mother, Susan Hubbard, and her sixteen-year-old son, Trenton. Upon seeing her daughter, Hubbard said, "I haven't been able to cry all these years, and it's been very emotional. I probably won't really cry until I get her home. That will be the moment that we share" (Hopkins, 2012). While in prison, Kristine earned undergraduate degrees in English and anthropology from Ball State University. Before her life could assume any measure of normality, she had to await a possible retrial.

For months prosecutors toyed with the notion of retrying Kristine for arson and the murder of her child. On December 17, 2012, the charges against her were formally dropped (Chapman, 2012; Hopkins, 2012; Koonse, 2012; Schadler and Berman, 2010; Vanderborg, 2012; Warden, n.d.; Worldwide Women's Criminal Justice Network, 2012).

Sonia Cacy

As the two previous cases suggest, the determination of the origin of a fire is an inexact science. Much of what was regarded as unassailable in the recent past is considered "junk science" today. The wrongful conviction of Sonia Cacy in 1993 raises serious questions regarding the determination of guilt based on some of these tests.

In 1991, Sonia Cacy shared a home near Fort Stockton, Texas, with her seventy-six-year-old uncle, Bill Richardson. She had a very strong relationship with her elderly uncle, who was a father figure. "We were like soul mates. If I needed anyone to go talk to, it was going to be Uncle Bill," Sonia said when interviewed by the *Texas Tribune* in 2010 (Grissom, 2010). The feeling was mutual. In a handwritten will composed shortly before his death, her uncle wrote: "I love my Sonia she has helped me out for many years" (Grissom, 2010).

During the early morning hours of November 10, 1991, however, everything changed. That is when Sonia awoke to the smell of smoke and the sight of flames. She unsuccessfully tried to awaken her uncle, who was sleeping in another room, but the fire forced her to exit the home. When firefighters arrived they found Sonia attempting to get back into the burning building through a broken window. While she was in the hospital being treated for smoke inhalation, the police took scrapings of her fingernails and blood samples.

Bill Richardson's charred body was moved to the Bexar County Forensic Science Center where Robert Bux, a medical examiner, performed the autopsy. Results of that autopsy suggest that Richardson died of a probable heart attack. His lungs were not filled with smoke and soot, and the amount of carbon monoxide in his blood was consistent with his heavy smoking. There was no soot in his trachea or larynx. Furthermore, there was approximately 80 percent blockage of the left descending artery, symptomatic of heart failure. In short, the autopsy seemed to suggest that he was dead before the fire began.

Her uncle, who suffered from dementia, was well known among the local residents as a careless chain smoker. With numerous cigarette burn marks on his furniture, it was apparent that he frequently tempted fate. Fire Marshal Frank Salvato had, in fact, been called to Richardson's house on three occasions the month before his death. Salvato testified that he observed Richardson lighting his furnace with a blowtorch. But this dangerous behavior represented the tip of the iceberg. According to Sonia, "if you're talking about my Uncle Bill you could mention fifty. He torched his own lease house about three years prior to that—burnt it to the ground" (Daecher, 1998). Yet only three fires were brought to the attention of the jury during the trial.

When Sonia's case came to trial in 1993, there were no eyewitnesses to the event. During the five-day trial, her court-appointed attorney, Tony Chavez, did little to defend his client. He failed to challenge damaging testimony presented at the trial, ignored inconsistencies in the prosecution's case, and presented no experts to testify on Sonia's behalf. Although he informed her that there was no money available for expert witnesses, he never attempted to secure any funding. Yet he billed the county for $15,000 for his services. Perhaps most telling of the quality of her legal counsel was the fact that five years later, Chavez pleaded guilty to drug trafficking charges involving several tons of marijuana.

The prosecution portrayed Sonia as a drunk who deliberately started the fire to collect money from her uncle's will. She then allegedly tried to distract the firefighters and the police by walking around in a short nightgown. (She was actually wearing a red Mexican house dress that a neighbor had given her to use.) Pecos County District Attorney Albert Valadez, who prosecuted her case, had only one crucial bit of evidence to corroborate his story: the presence of gasoline on her uncle's clothing. Using a process known as gas chromatography-mass spectrometry (GC-MS), toxicologist Joe Castorena testified that a Class II accelerant was detected on Richardson's clothing. His findings were based on a graph that resembles an EKG printout. In other words, the information must be interpreted to be of any value, and other forensic scientists might have come to a different conclusion. When Richard Henderson, a chemist with twenty-five years of experience in the field, later examined the information obtained from the GC-MS, he noted, "I've shown those charts to hundreds of students around the country as part of a training exercise. No one, including those at the FBI academy, has ever found gasoline in that sample" (Daecher, 1998). Nevertheless, based on this evidence alone, Sonia was sentenced to ninety-nine years in prison for the arson murder of her uncle in February 1993 after only two hours of jury deliberation.

When later interviewed in prison, Sonia shared these thoughts regarding her legal ordeal:

> I'm scared to death, because the system is a lot less than what I thought before all this began. Juries in this country, when they hear a D.A. talk, they believe it. They hear an expert witness on the stand, they believe it. They don't even consider them being corrupt. I didn't, and I was right in the middle of it. I didn't think they were corrupt until it was proven to me. Juries aren't educated to listen to all that complicated testimony. (Daecher, 1998)

Despite nationwide attention from such sources as the *Wall Street Journal*, ABC News, and NBC's *Dateline*—all of which determined that Sonia was innocent of the charges—she has not been exonerated. Quite telling of the confidence with which even the criminal justice system in Texas views her conviction, Sonia was released on parole in November 1998 after serving almost six years of her sentence. Early parole releases are uncommon in general and largely unheard of in Texas in particular. During the parole hearing, several relatives of the victim spoke on behalf of Sonia. It is their belief that Richardson inadvertently initiated the fire when he had heart failure and his lit cigarette ignited a blaze.

When released Sonia said, "I'm so excited, I can't calm down. I've got so much to be thankful for this Thanksgiving" (Smith, 1998).

Although she obtained her freedom, there was still a cost. Sonia was put on parole and therefore has restrictions on her movement. For instance, she must receive permission from her parole officer to go to Colorado to visit her daughter and grandchildren. Now sixty-six years old, Sonia is disabled from a stroke but is making one last attempt to clear her name. With the assistance of the Innocence Project of Texas, she was able to secure a hearing. The hearing concluded on July 1, 2014, without any immediate decision regarding her fate. When asked what she thought the eventual outcome would be, Sonia appeared to be cautiously optimistic. "I don't know exactly what the result will be. The judge, it appeared to me like he was on our side." Even if the decision is favorable, the Texas Court of Criminal Appeals has final jurisdiction over her case ("The case of Sonia Cacy," 2010; Daecher, 1998; Grissom, 2010; Innocence Project of Texas, n.d.; MacCormack, 1998; Merchant, 2014; Smith, 1998; Victims of the State, n.d.).

Summary

As evidenced from the sample of wrongful murder and manslaughter convictions presented in this chapter, there is considerable diversity. There are substantial differences between this group of false convictions and those of child abuse. Prosecutorial misconduct, for instance, was present to a greater degree among wrongful murder and manslaughter convictions. This factor contributed to the miscarriage of justice in almost 48 percent of these cases compared with only 36 percent of the child abuse cases. Forensic errors, a minor factor in child abuse wrongful convictions, were present in 43 percent of the murder and manslaughter wrongful convictions. Moreover, factors other than those typically delineated in the wrongful conviction scholarship were found in nearly one third of these cases, suggesting the importance of expanding our paradigm when false convictions of women are the primary focus.

Although the social class of the defendant is seldom specifically mentioned in data on wrongful convictions, it can sometimes be teased out by examining the neighborhood in which the defendant lives or descriptions of her surroundings. Alternatively, social class can be deduced through the analysis of the type of defender representing the defendant. The use of a public defender or court-appointed attorney, for instance, indicates that the defendant has few financial resources at her disposal. Again, however, data pertaining to wrongful convictions is inconsistent in its inclusion of this valuable piece of information. Therefore, since legal representation by public defenders and court-appointed attorneys is frequently less successful, ineffective assistance of counsel can be used as a rough proxy for social class.[8] Despite the fact that ineffective assistance of counsel is a factor that tends to be understated in the scholarship on wrongful convictions, it was still present in almost three out of every ten cases involving murder and manslaughter. This finding would seem to suggest that poverty plays an important role in many of these wrongful convictions. In fact, incompetent lawyering was responsible for a greater percentage of these false convictions than those in which the defendant was erroneously convicted for child abuse.

Three other factors were found in at least one fifth of the murder and manslaughter convictions. False confessions (23 percent), the use of an informant (22 percent), and perjury by criminal justice officials (20 percent) played some role in the false conviction process. It appears, therefore, that a greater variety of factors contributed to wrongful murder and manslaughter convictions than to wrongful child abuse convictions.

Nevertheless, one variable appeared in about equal percentages of wrongful convictions of murder/manslaughter and child abuse. Police misconduct was a factor in 36 percent of the child abuse cases and 32 percent of the murder and manslaughter cases. Hence, police misconduct is an important recurring factor leading to the erroneous conviction of women in cases involving both child abuse and the death of an individual.

One finding that particularly reveals the relative importance of these factors by type of offense involves eyewitness error. Recall that this factor played a very significant role in child abuse cases. Approximately seven of every ten wrongful child abuse convictions were influenced by this factor. The strong impact of eyewitness error in child abuse cases is probably best understood by the circumstances leading to these wrongful convictions: many of the eyewitness errors involved impressionable, young children who had been unduly influenced by therapists, parents, and authorities. Nonetheless, one would expect eyewitness error to play some role in the misidentification of murder and manslaughter suspects as well. Yet this factor played a minimal role in the false conviction of women for this offense. Slightly over 6 percent of the wrongful murder and manslaughter convictions were affected by eyewitness error.

When these factors are separated by race, some interesting results emerge. In particular, it becomes apparent that wrongful convictions of blacks typically involve a greater number of factors than they do for whites. More to the point, for seven of the nine factors (excluding "other") the percentage of cases involving wrongfully convicted black women exceeded that of their white counterparts. Furthermore, for six factors this black/white differential was in excess of 10 percent. The largest racial disparity was found among cases in which police misconduct was at least partially responsible for the false conviction. Police misconduct was found in over half of the black wrongful convictions but in only 30 percent of the white wrongful convictions. Perhaps most intriguing is eyewitness error, which was present in almost one of every five cases involving black women but was conspicuously absent from any of the cases involving white women. Black women were also more adversely affected by ineffective assistance of counsel than their white counterparts. Approximately 44 percent of the black false convictions included this factor as at least partially responsible for the miscarriage of justice. By comparison, 25 percent of the white false convictions included ineffective assistance of counsel as a factor.

Three additional factors were more common in black than white wrongful convictions. False confessions were found among 38 percent of the black cases versus 21 percent of the white cases. Prosecutorial misconduct, which was present in 63 percent of the black cases, was a factor in 46 percent of the white cases. Insufficient evidence to support a conviction, a factor that should not be present in trials involving such serious charges as murder and manslaughter, was present to a greater degree in cases involving black women. This factor was found in nearly one of every five black cases but in only one of every twenty white cases.

Conversely, forensic errors were more prevalent among white women than black women. In half of the cases in which white women had been wrongfully convicted of murder or manslaughter, forensic errors were present. In contrast, this figure was 31 percent for black women. Moreover, two of the factors were about equally important for white and black women: use of informants and perjury by criminal justice officials. The former was present in about one fourth of the cases for both racial groups, whereas the latter was only marginally higher for black women (25 percent for black women versus 21 percent for white women).

An analysis of the miscellaneous category ("other") disclosed that this factor was equally prevalent among wrongful convictions of black and white women. This catchall category was present in approximately 31 percent of the cases for both racial groups. Thus, a substantial number of false murder and manslaughter convictions appear to be influenced by factors not typically examined in the male-dominated literature on wrongful convictions.

An additional breakdown of the data by race reveals that both black and white women are much more likely to be falsely convicted for victimizing a family member or relative than a fiancé/boyfriend, acquaintance, or stranger. Family members and relatives constituted 44 percent of the cases involving black women and 51 percent of the cases involving white women. However, black women are considerably more likely than their white counterparts to be wrongly convicted for murder/manslaughter when the victim is a stranger. Whereas 38 percent of the black cases involved a stranger, only 15 percent of the white cases did. Moreover, in all but one of the six cases involving a stranger among the black wrongful convictions, the victim was white. Although the circumstances surrounding these cases varied, the results suggest the possibility that victim race may have played some role in the miscarriage of justice for black women. Nevertheless, this finding remains speculative since the proposition cannot be directly tested through the data collected in this sample.

Notes

1. Immediately after Christina's autopsy, Laura Dew had her daughter cremated, thereby eliminating any possibility of further examination of the cause of the death.

2. According to *Roever v. State of Nevada* (114 Nev. 867, 963 P.2d 503, 1998) Lerlene had been convicted of one count of first-degree murder and one count of possession of marijuana. The incidental drug offense apparently resulted from a search that the police conducted and may have been Ian's since he allegedly used drugs. It is not mentioned in any of the other articles and materials about this case.

3. In fact, the prosecution later admitted that it did not take seriously many of the statements made by their own witnesses.

4. *Burking* refers to a process whereby one individual sits on the victim's chest while another individual obstructs the victim's mouth and nose, thereby leading to suffocation. The term is attributed to William Burke, who in nineteenth-century Scotland killed women in this manner. In the trial, pathologist Michael Baden suggested that the defendants had forced the victim to take an overdose of heroin and other drugs before suffocating him.

5. After being released on parole, Rick Tabish, now forty-five years old, was allowed to return to his home state of Montana subject to some provisions. On April 7, 2012, while traveling on I-84 through Idaho, Rick was pulled over

for speeding and failing to stay in his lane. He had a blood-alcohol level of 0.087, just slightly over the legal limit of 0.08.

6. Coincidentally, the deceased police officer's brother, Patrolman Walter Schroeder, was also shot to death while attempting to intercede in a bank holdup three years earlier.

7. Keith Jesperson was known as the Happy Face Killer because he would draw smiley faces on the letters that he wrote acknowledging his involvement in the crime.

8. This is not meant to imply that private attorneys are never ineffective in their legal representation of a case and public defenders and court-appointed attorneys are always ineffective. Nevertheless, the latter are more likely to encounter financial limitations for hiring expert witnesses and conducting more in-depth investigations of the facts of their cases. Frequently they suffer from large caseloads that reduce the amount of time they can devote to each client. Additionally, their legal training may not have properly prepared them for murder or manslaughter trials. Collectively, this may result in a recommendation to the client to accept a plea even when a case has merit. While each of these issues may also affect the outcome of cases in which the individual has employed private counsel, they are generally less likely to appear.

4

The War on Drugs

According to prosecutors, Ryan Logsdon, an informant, called thirty-two-year-old Larita Barnes of Tulsa, Oklahoma, to inquire about purchasing some methamphetamine. Larita told him that her father, Larry Barnes, would have to be included in the transaction. In a later phone conversation, Larita and Ryan discussed the quantity and price of the drug. When Ryan went to their house in April 2007 to examine the illicit drug he saw Larita, Larry, and Larita's sister, Kelie. To illustrate the high quality of the meth, Larita broke off a piece and smoked it, claiming it was "good shit." A price was again discussed, although Ryan left without buying anything.

Several days later, Ryan talked to Jeff Henderson of the Tulsa Police Department and Special Agent Brandon McFadden of the Bureau of Alcohol, Tobacco, and Firearms (ATF) about the incident. A meeting was arranged to purchase three ounces of meth from Larita and Larry. On May 8, 2007, Ryan purchased the drug as planned, while Henderson and McFadden observed the transaction from outside the house. Larita and her father were arrested, and each was charged with one count of possession of methamphetamine with intent to distribute and one count of maintaining a location to distribute a controlled substance. They were found guilty in 2008, and Larita was sentenced to two concurrent ten-year terms, whereas Larry was sentenced to five and a half years in prison.

There is only one problem with this drug trafficking scenario: it never happened! Ryan, who began working as a drug informant for Henderson and McFadden after they found a large quantity of meth in his house in January 2007, later admitted that he had lied. Moreover, Kelie, who supposedly was at the Barnes's home when the transaction occurred, was working at a restaurant at the time of the alleged crime, a fact discounted by the jurors in their haste to convict. Jurors also over-looked the fact that the two officers never produced records of the money used for the drug purchase. There were no written records of the alleged phone calls used to arrange the drug sale.

While imprisoned, Larita's nine-year-old son, Hershel Clark, was struck by a drunk driver and killed. She was denied a furlough to attend his funeral. However, on July 2, 2009, Larita and Larry were released from prison and charges were dismissed as a result of a probe into police corruption at the Tulsa Police Department. In 2010 Henderson was charged with fifty-eight counts of drug conspiracy, perjury, witness tampering, and civil rights violations. Three other police officers were indicted in June of that year. Since that time almost fifty individuals have been released from prison or had their charges dropped because of legal issues surrounding their cases resulting from police corruption in Tulsa. At least seventeen lawsuits related to this scandal have been filed. Former ATF agent McFadden pleaded guilty in US District Court to drug conspiracy.

In December 2013 the city of Tulsa agreed to reimburse Larita $300,000 for her wrongful conviction. She is also suing the US government for McFadden's involvement in her false conviction. Her father was awarded $425,000 in January 2014 for his wrongful incarceration (Gillham, 2010a; "Grand jury investigation results," 2010; Harper, 2013; Off and Gillham, 2010; "Tulsa, Oklahoma, settles police corruption case for $425K," 2014; "Tulsa police officers subject of photo lineup, sources say," n.d.; *United States v. Larry Wayne Barnes* [07-CR-0135-CVE (N.D. Okla. April 15, 2008)]; "Woman wrongfully imprisoned in Tulsa police corruption case files lawsuit," 2010).

This wrongful drug conviction is in many ways typical of the twenty similar cases identified in our sample. A common characteristic of this genre is the extent to which perjury is involved. Frequently the individuals committing the perjury are the informants and one or more officers assigned to the case. Larita Barnes's case is not isolated but is part of a larger problem in the enforcement of drug legislation. Although the individuals in the previous narrative were white, a majority (85 percent) of the cases analyzed here involved nonwhite women. As is true of wrongful convictions in general, the persons most likely to come to the attention of the authorities are people with limited financial resources. Before proceeding to a discussion of the remaining cases, a succinct overview of drug prohibition in the United States is warranted.

A Brief History of Drug Legislation in the United States

Prior to the passage of the Harrison Narcotics Tax Act (HNTA) of 1914, many medicines, drinks, and foods possessed what are now called controlled substances. For instance, cough elixirs had morphine, whereas wines, Coca-Cola, liquors, and cigarettes contained cocaine. Cocaine was used to treat fatigue and morphine addiction and was once an official remedy of the Hay Fever Association. Marijuana, available in cigarette form and fluid extracts, was used to alleviate migraine headaches, asthma, and other diseases. Opium was the drug of choice for women with gynecological and nervous disorders. So frequently were these drugs prescribed to women that the typical drug user during the nineteenth century was a Southern white, middle-aged woman from the middle or upper class. (Because disease-carrying insects were more prominent in the South, individuals living in the Southern states were more likely than other regions to be prescribed medication containing addictive drugs.) Perhaps most revealing of the acceptance of these drugs is the fact that some employers provided opium to their workers because it was thought to enhance their physical and mental capacities and thereby increase their productivity. Opium-based derivatives were viewed as cures for "pain, colds, fevers, athlete's foot, alcoholism, diarrhea, hiccups, and other ailments" (Parsons, 2014, p. 27). For forty-five cents, a person could have Sears Roebuck deliver a bottle of triple-strength opium to their door as late as the early twentieth century (Brecher, 1972; Kennedy, 2003; Musto, 1999; Parsons, 2014).

The earliest attempt to control drug use in the United States appeared during the latter part of the nineteenth century. Opium, which was used mostly by the Chinese, was outlawed by some cities that had ordinances prohibiting opium-smoking dens. These attempts to restrict drug use were predicated on racism, xenophobia, and a fear that the Chinese would displace whites in employment because opium use was thought to enhance one's productivity. In 1887 a federal law prohibited the Chinese from importing opium, although it remained legal for other groups. It wasn't until 1909 that this legislation was expanded to include all racial groups (Helmer, 1975; Musto, 1999; Parsons, 2014).

As the United States entered the twentieth century, a number of factors coalesced that led to the emergence of national drug legislation. Financial concerns of the pharmaceutical industry, law enforcement's desire to expand its authority, the increased professionalization of medicine, and international treaties provided the impetus for the change (Fang, 2014; Levine, 2013; Musto, 1999; Parsons, 2014). These forces culminated in the passage of the HNTA, which regulated and taxed the importation, production, and distribution of opiates and cocaine.

During the early part of the twentieth century, many white Americans were growing increasingly concerned about the perceived use of cocaine among African Americans. The drug was thought to be used primarily by impoverished African Americans to alleviate symptoms associated with bronchitis and tuberculosis. Despite a perception to the contrary, African Americans probably did not use the drug to a greater extent than their white counterparts since they were less likely to see a physician who could write them a prescription for it. Nonetheless, media attention from such sources as the *New York Tribune* and the *Literary Digest* portrayed blacks as dangerous people who were capable of violence, in particular inflicting violence on innocent white women in the South (see Regoli and Hewitt, 1997, pp. 379–380). One scholar has suggested that this fear of superhuman strength resulted in the change from .32 caliber to .38 caliber pistols by Southern police departments (Musto, 1999). Although the impact of the HNTA was less pronounced on blacks than was the crack cocaine legislation of the mid-1980s, it nevertheless disproportionately led to their arrest and conviction. While making up approximately 9 percent of the US population during the latter part of the 1920s, blacks accounted for 23 percent of all incarcerated drug offenders (Kennedy, 2003).

Although marijuana was not included among the controlled substances under the jurisdiction of the HNTA, it was only a matter of time before it was federally regulated. In the minds of many Americans, marijuana use was associated with Mexican immigrants in the Southwest who had immigrated seeking employment to support their families. While tolerance prevailed during the prosperity of the 1920s, this turned to intolerance during the 1930s as the immigrants were seen as taking jobs from Americans as the Great Depression deepened. Their willingness to work for lower wages (like the Chinese before them) exacerbated these fears. As they began to seek better wages and organize, however, employers saw them as an economic threat and began to side with those seeking their deportation. Further stimulating legislation that eventually led to the regulation of marijuana was the belief that it could lead to outbursts of violence and even insanity. The movie *Reefer Madness*, for instance, suggests that marijuana is more dangerous than any other drug, including heroin.

During this time, the Federal Bureau of Narcotics (FBN) began experiencing declining funding as a result of the Great Depression. Harry Anslinger, who presided over the FBN, in an attempt to expand his organization's jurisdiction and therefore increase its level of funding, began an aggressive campaign to have marijuana declared a controlled substance. In 1937 his efforts proved to be successful, as the Marijuana Tax Act (MTA) was enacted. By 1938 one fourth of all federal drug convictions were for violations of the MTA. Deportation of Mexican workers to their home country also accompanied the passage of this legislation (Helmer, 1975; Musto, 1999; Parsons, 2014).

The Crack Cocaine Panic of the 1980s

The hyperbole associated with the marijuana fears of the 1930s pales in comparison to the crack cocaine panic of the mid-1980s. Although this encompassed a different drug and a different target population, there were many similarities. The individuals associated most with crack cocaine use and trafficking were African Americans. The end result was the same: Drug legislation disproportionately affected a powerless minority despite the fact that various racial and ethnic groups self-report similar amounts of cocaine use (Maguire and Pastore, 2001, tables 3.97–3.101).

The Anti-Drug Abuse Act of 1986 was significant because it made crack cocaine and powder cocaine separate drugs for sentencing purposes. Since crack, which was less expensive and therefore used more commonly by people of limited financial resources, was thought to be an instantly addicting substance that incited violence among its users, the penalties for its use and distribution were greater than that for powder cocaine. Prior to this legislation, both types of cocaine were sanctioned the same way. In 1988 federal legislation made even modest crack cocaine use a major felony. The Anti-Drug Abuse Act of 1988 specified a mandatory minimum prison sentence of five years for five grams for first-time offenders. Previously, a first-time offender with only five grams typically received probation. In contrast, five grams of powder cocaine was only a misdemeanor. To receive a five-year mandatory minimum sentence, a person with powder cocaine had to possess 500 grams, or 100 times the quantity of crack cocaine (Wallace, 1993).

As state legislatures began to adjust their drug laws to reflect the greater concern for crack cocaine, the racial composition of prison inmates incarcerated on drug charges began to change dramatically. From 1980 through the early 1990s, arrests for African Americans increased from 21 percent to approximately 35 percent of all drug arrests. Even more striking was the impact the new legislation had on African American juveniles. Black juvenile arrests for drugs went from 13 percent to approximately 40 percent. The significance of this legislation and subsequent law enforcement on black youths is revealed by the fact that in 1980, prior to the crack cocaine epidemic, white youths were actually more likely than nonwhite youths to be arrested for possession of illegal substances (Blumstein, 1993; Mauer, 1999; Tollet and Close, 1991). Attempts to remedy this disparity were met with political outrage until the Fair Sentencing Act of 2010 was passed; it reduced the disparity from a 100-to-1 weight rate to an 18-to-1 ratio. A first-time offender now had to have at least twenty-eight grams of crack to receive a five-year mandatory sentence. This act additionally removed the mandatory minimum sentence for simple possession of crack cocaine ("The Fair Sentencing Act corrects a long-time wrong in cocaine cases," 2010).

Since the 1990s a major focus of the war on drugs has been on marijuana. In recent years, marijuana arrests have accounted for over half of all drug arrests in the United States. African Americans particularly appear to be singled out by law enforcement. Although African Americans and whites are about equally likely to use marijuana, African Americans are more likely to be arrested for it. Stop-and-search tactics employed in low-income neighborhoods where blacks reside often disclose "a small amount hidden in their clothing, vehicle, or personal effects" (Levine, 2013, p. 19). In more affluent neighborhoods police typically refrain from such intrusive measures. As a result the black arrest rate is six times that of whites (Levine, 2013). Nor is this disparity limited to any one geographic area. For instance, in Madison, Wisconsin, a city known for its liberal proclivities, blacks make up over half of all marijuana arrests and citations although they represent only 7.3 percent of that city's population. Even more disturbing are the results of a 2007 study from the Justice Policy Institute (JPI). The JPI reported that black defendants in Dane County (which includes Madison) were ninety-seven times more likely than their white counterparts to be imprisoned on drug charges (Savidge, 2014). Given this racial disparity, it should come as no surprise to learn that black men and women are also overrepresented among wrongful drug convictions.

The Tulia Drug Scandal

Early in the morning of July 23, 1999, a drug sting occurred in the town of Tulia, Texas, that put this small town on the map. As part of this sting operation, police raided homes and arrested citizens, most of whom had no idea what was happening, why they were being arrested, or what crime they had committed. Almost fifty people were targeted in this mass arrest, the vast majority of which were African American. The others had strong ties to the African American community in Tulia (Gumbel, 2007).

It is hardly a coincidence that Tulia's law enforcement officials targeted the town's small (approximately 10 percent) African American population in this drug bust. Many African Americans there were unemployed or lived on relatively meager incomes. There was concern about drug trafficking among their citizens, and in an effort to clean up this town, the city hired Tom Coleman to work undercover as a narcotics agent to seek out drug dealers. Coleman was hired for this position despite a questionable past and no experience in the area of undercover narcotics. During the course of his assignment, he claimed to have made over one hundred drug buys (Gumbel, 2007). This number would have been a major accomplishment for someone who had several years of experience as a narcotics agent. In the case of Coleman, an inexperienced agent, it seemed a nearly impossible task. Despite the scope of the bust, searches failed to disclose any evidence related to drug dealing. According to author Jennifer Gonnerman (2001), "There were no wiretaps, no surveillance photos, and virtually no secondary witnesses. The morning that cops barged into the suspects' homes they found no weapons, money, or drugs."

While Coleman was working undercover, he claimed that he wrote down important information on his leg when nobody was watching. Nonetheless, he was unable to identify many of the people he arrested when in court (Gonnerman, 2001). The assumption seemed to be that if someone was arrested, then they must have committed the crime—in total contradiction to the lack of evidence in this case. Those who were arrested were tried, convicted, and sent to prison, all on the word of Coleman. Because the accused citizens also had insufficient funds to hire competent lawyers, they were represented by court-appointed attorneys with limited legal expertise. As a consequence, nearly all of those arrested were falsely accused and charged. The legal system that was supposed to guarantee each and every citizen a fair trial failed the citizens of Tulia.

As the suspected drug dealers started going to trial, they were quickly convicted by all-white juries. In almost all trials, nothing was mentioned about Coleman's checkered career in law enforcement or his lack of evidence in the drug cases. The juries believed they were convicting drug dealers. Indeed, after the arrests were made, it was widely believed by the local citizens that law enforcement personnel had cleaned up the town and virtually eliminated the city's drug problem.

Even those who escaped without being caught up in the drug bust suffered in numerous ways. Tonya White was one of the fortunate few who managed to avoid being convicted when she was able to document that she was in Oklahoma City making a withdrawal at a local bank when she was allegedly selling cocaine. Then there was the case of Mattie White, a fifty-year-old mother of six who was never accused of drug trafficking but endured the arrest of her two sons, one daughter, one brother-in-law, two nephews, one son-in-law, one niece, and two cousins. To raise her daughter's two children, Mattie had to work at two jobs, including one as a correctional officer. When asked how the drug sting operation affected her, she replied, "It has made my life miserable. My whole world seems like it fell down on me" (cited in Gonnerman, 2001).

Nearly all of the people arrested were charged with dealing cocaine, resulting in lengthy jail terms or probation in some cases. Even though a few of the accused admitted that they had sold drugs to Coleman when he was working undercover, many more did not recognize him when they saw him. One of the accused, Joe Moore, a farmer, received an especially long sentence of ninety years and was, according to Coleman, one of the leaders of the drug operation (CBS News, 2003). Another arrested resident was Cash Love, accused by Coleman of selling drugs. Love, a white man, had strong ties to the African American community and was sentenced to more than 300 years in prison. It was generally believed that he was set up so that the drug sting did not appear racist (CNN, 2000).

In a very short time, Coleman went from an inexperienced narcotics officer to the most celebrated lawman in Texas. He was viewed as a hero who had rescued Tulia from the problem of drug dealers. The sentences of those convicted were frequently enhanced because Coleman testified that the drugs were sold within a short distance of a nearby school. This charge was made despite the fact that most of the defendants lived in a trailer park, several miles from the school where the drugs were allegedly sold (Gonnerman, 2001).

Eventually a group of lawyers from around the country, working pro bono, secured new trials for the Tulia residents found guilty of drug trafficking. Unfortunately, many of those who had been wrongly convicted were already incarcerated. On August 22, 2003—four years after the drug raid—Texas Governor Rick Perry issued a formal pardon for thirty-five defendants. A settlement of $5 million was agreed on as compensation for this scandal. Coleman was ultimately charged with perjury and received a sentence of ten years of probation, thereby ending his law enforcement career (Blakeslee, 2005).

Twelve of the women in our sample were part of this coterie of wrongfully convicted Tulia inhabitants. Eleven were African American, and one was Hispanic. Although the men in the drug bust typically received longer sentences than did their female counterparts, some of the women received substantial sentences. Kizzie White received the longest sentence for women: twenty-five years in prison. The second longest sentence belonged to Alberta Williams, who received ten years for her alleged involvement. Others receiving prison sentences included Yolanda Smith (six years), Laura Ann Mata (five years), Michelle Williams (two years), and Denise Kelly (one year). Etta Kelly and Lawanda Smith each received a three-year deferred sentence, and Vickie Fry and Finaye Shelton each received five years of probation. Marilyn Joyce Cooper was sentenced to three days in jail and given a $2,000 fine. She was also required to reimburse for court costs and attorney fees. Finally, Ramona Strickland was fined $2,000 for her alleged part in the drug scandal. In 2003 Governor Perry formally pardoned ten of the twelve wrongfully convicted women. Only Etta Kelly and Lawanda Smith, who had received three-year deferred sentences, were excluded.

The Hearne Drug Scandal

The Tulia drug scandal was not an isolated instance of overzealous drug enforcement. In 2000 in south Texas, some 468 miles from Tulia, another drug bust involving an African American community occurred, and it resembled the earlier drug bust. Hearne, Texas, is a city of approximately 4,500 inhabitants of which whites represent only 38 percent of the population. Here again, the bust was based predominantly on a single informant of questionable integrity. The informant, Derrick Megress, had two prior convictions for theft, frequently used marijuana and cocaine, and was mentally unstable and suicidal. He consented to incriminate the list of African Americans that Robertson County District Attorney John Paschall had designated as drug traffickers only to avoid incarceration on burglary charges (Levy, 2005).

On November 2, 2000, the Columbus Village Apartments, a public housing project, was the location of a mass drug arrest employing thirty to forty armed law enforcement officials. According to the American Civil Liberties Union:

> The officers detained almost the entire African American community in Hearne, without provocation or cause, and demanded identification from the residents regardless of whether they remotely matched the gender, age, or physical description of those named by Megress.

Young children playing on the street, individuals sitting in their cars, and elderly residents relaxing on their porches were all directed to remain still by defendants wielding guns. Each of the individual defendants possessed the names and addresses of the individuals whom they sought to arrest. Nonetheless, after demanding identification, the officers continued to detain many individuals who did not appear on their arrest list (US District Court for the Western District of Texas, 2002, pp. 40-41).

Although the sting focused on black men, two women were arrested during that raid. Neither appears in our sample because Regina Kelly's case was dismissed prior to conviction and there was insufficient documentation to include Erma Faye Stewart among our sample of wrongfully convicted women. Nevertheless, their stories represent a significant chapter in the false arrest of women of color and are therefore included in this section.

Regina Kelly

A single mother of four, Regina Kelly was working a double shift as a waitress when she was arrested. She believed the reason for her arrest was related to unpaid parking tickets. For nearly two days she remained in custody, believing that her most serious problem was finding a way to reimburse the city for her parking fines. When she was finally informed that she was being held on felony drug distribution charges and that her bail had been set at $70,000, Regina was shocked. Unable to post bail, she remained in jail. The charges against her were based on an audio tape in which she was allegedly selling drugs to Megress. However, none of the sounds on the tape appeared to be female voices. Moreover, her name was misspelled on the indictment, and her address was incorrect. Regina's court-appointed attorney provided little legal assistance, instead recommending that she plead guilty to receive leniency, an unacceptable alternative since it would make her ineligible to remain in government-subsidized housing. Regina's bail was eventually reduced to $10,000 as the weakness of her case became evident. Around Thanksgiving her parents were able to raise sufficient funds to post her bail and get her released. Although Regina's case was ultimately dismissed, the accusations against her resulted in her loss of employment. Her acceptance at a local college was also rescinded when the school learned that she had been arrested on drug charges. Similarly, the arrest precluded her being a teacher's aide at the local high school. Her daughters were harassed by their schoolmates, who claimed that their mother was a "dope dealer." Five years after the arrest, she was dismissed from her job when the Hearne district attorney had a discussion with her manager. In 2008 a movie based on Regina's life was released. The movie, *American Violet*, revealed the unscrupulous practices employed by law enforcement during the drug raid. Unable to escape her past, Regina reluctantly moved from Hearne in 2009 to begin a new life elsewhere ("'American Violet' tells story of ill-fated Hearne drug raids," 2009; Levy, 2005, "Stories of ACLU clients swept up in the Hearne drug bust of November 2000," 2002).

Erma Faye Stewart

Another single black mother, Erma Faye Stewart, was arrested for selling crack cocaine. Erma, who briefly shared a jail cell with Regina, was also provided a court-appointed attorney who recommended that she accept a plea bargain in return for probation. With no one to supervise her two young children, she consented to plead guilty to a charge of delivery of a controlled substance of over four grams in a drug-free zone. In return, she was put on probation for ten years and required to pay $1,800 in fines. Because she had pleaded guilty, she was not eligible for food stamps or federal money for education. Her right to vote was revoked until successful completion of her probation. Unable to pay her rent and now a convicted drug dealer, Erma was evicted from the government-subsidized housing project. In 2004, when *Frontline* reported on her case, she was making only $5.25 an hour as a cook. She still owed $1,000 of her fine plus court costs and late probation fees (PBS *Frontline*, 2004).

The Mansfield Drug Scandal

It would be a mistake to assume that racially motivated drug busts are limited to the South. Mansfield, Ohio, approximately seventy miles southwest of Cleveland, became the site of yet another drug raid in which an impoverished African American community was the primary focus. In typical fashion, it involved an informant with an incentive to lie. Of the individuals arrested during Operation Turnaround on November 10, 2005, Geneva France was apparently the only falsely convicted woman.

The Mansfield drug raid occurred as a result of the murder of Timothy Harris, a career criminal, on December 31, 2004. After discovering his bloody body in the snow, authorities surmised that it was the work of drug traffickers, so they began questioning known drug dealers around Mansfield. When the investigation in Richland County failed to turn up any leads, they turned to the Drug Enforcement Administration (DEA) in Cleveland for assistance. Veteran DEA agent Lee Lucas became the primary investigator. Lucas was considered a top agent despite the fact that some of his practices in previous cases were not by the book. He knew Jerrell Bray, a convicted felon who had been diagnosed as schizophrenic, from the collaborative work they did on previous cases in Cleveland. Two months after Operation Turnaround began, Bray had set up drug transactions that led to the arrest of twenty-six people.

Geneva France, a twenty-two-year-old mother with three small children, first met Bray, a stocky man who liked to talk, prior to the drug sting. Unimpressed with him, it is likely that she knew that something was awry. She met Bray while he was dating one of her friends. On one occasion as they were talking, he told Geneva that he could make her disappear and that she would never be heard from again. After threatening her, in another strange twist, he asked her out on a date. She turned him down immediately, afraid of what he might do.

Although Geneva had never been in trouble with the law, she was one of the people Bray identified as dealing drugs in Mansfield. She will never forget the day federal narcotics agents came to her door. The agents knocked on her door, demanded to be let in, and stormed the house, searching everywhere for evidence of drugs. According to Geneva, "I was getting my children ready for school when all of a sudden people started screaming, 'Where are the drugs.' There were no drugs" (Caniglia, 2008b). Unable to find any contraband, the agents cuffed Geneva and told her that she was being taken into custody. They also threatened to take her children to child welfare if she didn't accommodate their requests. Fortunately, her eighteen-year-old sister, Natasha, was living with her and was eligible to be a guardian for the children. Geneva was hurried to a sheriff's squad car and driven to Cleveland, about ninety minutes away. Nobody told her what she was being charged with despite the fact that she was taken to a holding cell and booked as a criminal. While she was trying to deal with the reality of the situation, she continued to hold out hope that someone would realize that this was all a big mistake. Yet her problems were only beginning.

Because she had done nothing wrong, Geneva refused to accept a plea bargain. Like the others who had been arrested, her plea of innocence quickly became a case of her word against the authorities. Arrested for selling fifty grams of crack cocaine, she was sentenced to ten years in prison after a four-day trial in which Bray had identified her from a sixth-grade photograph. Bray charged Ronald Davis as Geneva's drug supplier, although they were unacquainted. When his home was searched, two handguns were discovered but no drugs were found. Nevertheless, Davis was convicted of firearm and drug charges and sentenced to eleven years behind bars. Another Mansfield resident, Robert Harris, was actually a stand-in for Bray. Eventually Bray turned on Harris and accused him of selling cocaine in a drug-free school zone. Harris was also convicted and sentenced to five years. After Dwight Nabors, the alleged kingpin of the Mansfield drug connection, was acquitted on drug charges, the entire operation started to unravel and questions were raised about the raid.

By May 2007, Bray was facing charges for shooting a man while making a drug deal in Cleveland. While under arrest, he admitted that he had lied about the drug transactions in Mansfield. As the investigation into Bray continued, it was also determined that he had used buys to steal money and drugs. Geneva, who was one of the first individuals to be convicted, was released after spending sixteen months in prison. Other defendants were released sometime around February 1, 2008, after more than two years in prison. People such as Dwayne Nabors tried to return to the life they left behind before being arrested. Prior to his arrest, he ran a successful car detailing business that now stands empty. Many of those convicted have since left Mansfield, looking for a new start.

Lee Lucas also engaged in illegitimate activities during Operation Turnaround. He was indicted for obstruction of justice, making false statements, perjury, and deprivation of civil rights. In 2007 Bray was sentenced to fifteen years in prison for perjury and civil rights violations. He died in prison in 2012 (Caniglia, 2008a, 2008b, 2012; Kroll, 2008a, 2008b, 2008c, 2008d, 2008e; Love, 2009, Turner, 2007).

The Manatee Drug Scandal

Manatee County, Florida, has a population of over 300,000 people and covers nearly 900 square miles. Its largest city, Bradenton, has approximately 50,000 inhabitants and is the county seat. The county was named after the manatee, which is on the list of endangered species. However, during the late 1990s this county became known for its corruption in the Delta Division of the Manatee County Sheriff's Office. An FBI investigation revealed that it was common for officers to plant drugs on suspects and perjure themselves about the drug bust during trial. Prosecutors dropped over seventy cases against sixty-seven defendants in the summer of 1998 after these allegations began to surface. Ultimately, five persons assigned to this unit were charged and convicted of these offenses. The following cases involve two white women who were wrongfully convicted during the culmination of this corruption (Barrouquere, 2000).

Sarah Smith

On November 14, 1997, nineteen-year-old Sarah Smith of Bradenton was startled when she saw men with black masks breaking down the door to her home. The masked men were officers from the Delta Division of the Sheriff's Office, who began rummaging through her personal belongings. One of the officers produced a small bottle which he claimed contained crack cocaine. Sarah was immediately arrested and charged with possession of a controlled substance. Scarcely a day removed from the drug seizure her fourteen-month-old daughter was placed in foster care by social services.

Her jury trial began in February 1998, and despite her protestations of innocence she was convicted of drug possession largely on the testimony of the sheriff's officers, who claimed that she confessed to owning the crack cocaine. In lieu of house arrest for one year, Sarah agreed to serve thirty days in jail. She was also fined $400 and placed on probation for six months following her incarceration. In October 1999 when she heard that one of the officers in her case had admitted to planting the crack in her medicine bottle, she sought dismissal of her conviction. In February 2000 she successfully had her conviction vacated and the charge dismissed. The following year she sued the county and the officers for $5 million for malicious prosecution and false arrest. In 2004 the lawsuit was finally settled for an undisclosed amount (Barrouquere, 2000; Possley, n.d. m).

Karen O'Dell

While driving home, thirty-seven-year-old Karen O'Dell, who was employed as a construction worker, was stopped by officers from the Sheriff's Office. After they failed to find any illicit drugs in her vehicle, she was allowed to leave. A short while after arriving home in Bradenton, the officers again approached her. As two of the men kept Karen preoccupied at her door, other officers began searching her garage. They exited the garage with a container of cocaine, which they allegedly found in her truck. Karen was arrested and charged with possession of a controlled substance and destruction of evidence in November 1997. She was also charged with battery when one of the officers contended that she struck him with her truck during the earlier stop. Her truck was seized by the sheriff's department for almost a year.

Although Karen had no prior record of criminal activities, she chose to plead no contest to the charges in March 1998. According to her defense counsel, "At the time, it was just Karen's word that she had been framed against three or four healthy, upstanding young police officers. We didn't think . . . that she would be believed" (Barrouquere, 2000). She was sentenced to one year of probation and fifty hours of community service. Had she chosen to go to trial and lost, she probably would have received a prison sentence.

On February 15, 2000, Karen again found herself in a courtroom. The situation was quite different. In less than two minutes the judge, citing perjured testimony and planted evidence, overturned Karen's convictions. After she was cleared of the charges, Karen acknowledged, "It's been two years, and it's still affecting me. You don't trust anybody." She further observed, "It makes me sick thinking about it. I'm a nervous person anyway" (Barrouquere, 2000).

Although Karen avoided jail, she was affected by the wrongful conviction in numerous ways. Because her truck had been seized by authorities for allegedly being used in drug activity, she had to impose on friends to give her rides to and from her construction job for almost a year until it was finally returned. Furthermore, it was only at the insistence of some of her friends that her employer was convinced to retain her services. Despite having her conviction struck down, a public record of her false arrest remains, an issue she plans to address at a later date (Barrouquere, 2000; Possley, n.d. d).

Cheryle Beridon

A self-admitted drug addict and prostitute, twenty-two-year-old Cheryle Beridon was a woman with a checkered past. She had a seven-year-old son, Leroy, with whom she had limited interaction given her lifestyle. Cheryle had recently broken up with Norval Rhodes, the Terrebonne Parish, Louisiana, district attorney. Offended by her rejection, Rhodes threatened to have her incarcerated. Against this backdrop, our story begins.

During the evening of August 8, 1977, Rhodes learned from an informant, Lynn Blanchard, that Cheryle had heroin she was willing to sell. Along with his chief investigator, A. J. Dagate, Rhodes gave Blanchard money to consummate the deal. Blanchard met Cheryle at the Sugar Bowl Motel before they both left to go to the Paradise Lounge.

Approximately fifteen minutes later they returned to the motel. Shortly thereafter, Blanchard gave Rhodes and Dagate two small packets of heroin that she claimed she purchased from Cheryle. The heroin had an estimated street value of $125.

Charged with unlawful distribution of heroin by a grand jury, Cheryle pleaded not guilty to the charge. During the voir dire process, the prosecution used five of its eight peremptory challenges to strike African Americans from jury participation. Although Cheryle was also African American, only one person of color was ultimately chosen to be on the jury. Testimony from Rhodes, Dagate, and Blanchard was used to convict her, and in 1979 Cheryle received a mandatory life sentence. If she had been convicted in federal court she would have received only a fifteen-year prison sentence.

For twenty years Cheryle was incarcerated in a tiny cell at the Louisiana Correctional Institute for Women in St. Gabriel. Her pleas for assistance were finally answered when the local chapter of the National Association for the Advancement of Colored People (NAACP) became actively involved in seeking her release. After the NAACP was successful in having the governor commute her sentence to forty-five years, Cheryle was eligible for parole. However, because she had been cited for several infractions while in prison, the parole board insisted that she spend six months at a halfway house prior to gaining her freedom. In November 2000, Cheryle was finally paroled. Conditions of her parole required her to report to a parole officer for twenty-one additional years. Furthermore, she was required to pay $53 a month for those monthly visits.

Cheryle willingly admits that she made poor life choices growing up, although she adamantly contends that she never offered to sell heroin to the informant. In July 2003 she learned that she had received a pardon that would restore all her civil rights except the right to bear arms. When she heard the good news, she was elated. "I can't put my feelings into words," she exclaimed. "I feel so relieved. It feels so good to be a citizen again, to not be an outcast anymore" (Thurston, 2003b).

Many things have changed for the better in Cheryle's life since receiving her freedom and the restoration of her rights. She has been reunited with her now-grown son, Leroy, who moved from California to be with his mom. "When he needs help, he calls me. That means so much . . . it makes me feel so good to know that I am someone he can call for help," she recently said. The feeling apparently is mutual. When asked what he thought about his mother, Leroy replied, "I'm really proud of her and what she's done and accomplished" (Thurston, 2003a).

While in prison Cheryle became a devoted Christian who now does volunteer work for churches and adolescents. She is additionally actively involved in the NAACP. Of course, her life is frequently kept busy with her five grandchildren (Innocence Project of New Orleans, n.d.; National Registry of Exonerations, n.d. b; *State of Louisiana v. Cheryl Beridon*, 449 SO. 2d 2 [1984]; Thurston 2003a, 2003b).

Mary Ann Colomb

For a decade, Mary Ann Colomb, her husband, James Colomb, and their sons, Edward Colomb, Danny Davis, and Sammy Davis, Jr., were harassed by the local police. On four separate occasions her sons had been accused by law enforcement of illegal drug activities, although three of those incidents were eventually dismissed. The fourth involved a 1993 conviction for a felony drug possession that resulted from Edward and Sammy being in an automobile with two other men who were transporting marijuana and cocaine when they were pulled over by the police.

Convinced of the family's involvement in illicit drugs, the police conducted a raid on the Colomb residence on October 22, 2001. Armed with assault weapons and a battering ram, the Acadia Parish Sheriff's Office task force found seventy-two grams of crack cocaine and a loaded pistol in the guest bedroom being occupied by Mary Ann's daughter, Jennifer, and her future husband, Timothy Price. Mary Ann was handcuffed at gunpoint while the officers ransacked her house. During the raid, Price drove Mary Ann's husband to the emergency room when he began experiencing a severe panic attack and an abnormal heart beat. Although Price later informed the police that the drugs were his and that the gun belonged to his mother, who was a police officer, his testimony was immediately dismissed by the officers.

On May 15, 2002, after the federal government became involved, Mary Ann and her sons were indicted on charges of purchasing cocaine with a street value in excess of $70 million over a period of ten years. Although one of the sons drove a car that did not have a functioning reverse gear and they worked at multiple jobs to support a modest lifestyle, federal officials remained adamant that they had discovered one of the largest cocaine drug rings in south Louisiana.

After receiving numerous phone calls and letters from incarcerated inmates offering to testify against the defendants in return for leniency, the prosecuting attorney began preparing for the trial. Although Mary Ann, Edward, Danny, and Sammy had allegedly purchased large quantities of cocaine for resale over a ten-year span, no individuals testified that they had bought drugs from them. Despite a dearth of evidence, on March 31, 2006, all four defendants were convicted of various drug-related crimes based largely on the testimony of jailhouse informants with an incentive to lie.

A curious letter received earlier in March 2006 began the process that ultimately unraveled the case. An assistant US attorney received a letter from Quinn Alex, an inmate in a federal penitentiary. Alex noted that his cellmate, Charles Anderson, had promised to provide pictures of the Colomb family and key documents relevant to their case in return for $2,200 so that he could also testify against them to receive a shorter sentence. However, Alex was not agitated because of the injustice being done to the Colombs. Rather, he was upset that he paid the money and never received anything when Anderson was transferred to another facility. After verifying the contents of the letter, the information was turned over to US District Judge Tucker Melancon, who denied the request from the defense counsel to declare a mistrial. Melancon later admitted that he erred in denying this request.

While awaiting sentencing at the Lafayette Parish Correctional Center, Sammy became acquainted with an inmate who had previously resided at a federal prison in south Texas in which several of the witnesses from the trial had been housed. The inmate wrote a letter to the court explaining how the witnesses had been privy to information that allowed them to falsely implicate members of the Colomb family in return for sentence reductions. Five months after the Colombs had been wrongly convicted, they were released when Melancon set aside the jury's verdict on August 31, 2006. In making this unusual move, he noted "Had the facts . . . been known to the jury when it began its deliberations . . . some, and possibly all of the defendants would have been acquitted. The defendants were adversely impacted and denied their basic right to a fair trial, not a perfect trial, but a fair trial" (Miller, 2011).

Melancon additionally noted his skepticism regarding the veracity of the drug allegations.

> Now, I'm not saying drug dealers are all flashy and drive big cars . . . but when you tell me . . . over whatever period of time . . . this drug conspiracy in a little bitty house in Church Point, Louisiana, there were $4 million worth of drugs going through there. I'll tell you that defies any kind of credibility at all based on my 61-plus years on the planet. (Miller, 2011)

Although Melancon did not disallow retrying the defendants, he stipulated that it was incumbent on the government to investigate the allegations involving the sharing of information among inmate snitches and report back on the impact of this system on the criminal justice system before going forward. The US Attorney's Office chose not to retry the Colombs, and their charges were dismissed with prejudice on December 14, 2006 (Miller, 2011; Possley, n.d. h; *United States v. Mary Ann Colomb*, 419 F, 3d 292, Court of Appeals, 5th Circuit, 2005).

Sherri Frederick

What do you do if the police falsely accuse you of possessing a small quantity of a controlled substance when you have a criminal record that includes convictions for drugs and prostitution and you fulfill the racial stereotype of a drug offender? That quandary was undoubtedly on the mind of thirty-three-year-old Sherri Frederick when she was arrested on September 12, 2010, for dropping a packet allegedly containing 0.27 gram of crack cocaine as officers approached her while she was walking on the street. Before the substance in the packet was analyzed by the Houston Police Department crime laboratory, Sherri accepted a plea bargain and was sentenced to six months in jail on October 1, 2010.

On February 23, 2011, the crime laboratory finally completed its testing of the alleged crack cocaine. The laboratory concluded that the substance was not narcotic. Then into her fifth month of a six-month sentence, Sherri was given her freedom on March 10, 2011. On September 28, 2011, the Texas Court of Criminal Appeals overturned her conviction, and on February 24, 2012, the charge against her was dismissed. Although rare among drug-related exonerations in Harris County, Sherrie was awarded $40,000 in March 2012 as compensation for her wrongful incarceration (*Ex Parte Sherri Frederick*, Texas Court of Criminal Appeals, 339th Judicial District Ct., No. AP-76,646, 2011; Possley 2012; West 2014).

Paula M. Reeves

In the opening vignette for this chapter, the reader was introduced to Larita Barnes who, along with her father, was wrongly convicted of attempting to sell methamphetamine. After an investigation into police corruption in the Tulsa Police Department (TPD), Larita and her father were released and their charges were dropped. The following case, involving a forty-three-year-old African American woman, also occurred in Tulsa during the era of police corruption.

When Paula Reeves was charged with drug trafficking and other related charges on June 14, 2004, her immediate future looked bleak. When the charges were later reduced to unlawful possession of a controlled substance with intent to distribute, she agreed to plead no contest on March 14, 2005. As a result of her plea, Paula received an eight-year suspended sentence for the reduced charge plus a one-year suspended sentence for possession of drug paraphernalia. Her former boyfriend, Bobby Wayne Haley, was convicted of drug-related charges in September 2005 and received a twenty-two-year prison sentence.

On September 10, 2010, Paula's suspended sentences were overturned as a result of a federal grand jury inquiry into police practices in Tulsa. Fabricated evidence had been used to arrest and convict Paula according to the forejustice.org wrongly convicted database. She was the nineteenth person to have a case dismissed or be released from prison because of the police corruption investigation. Paula's former boyfriend was also exonerated in 2010 after an informant in his case admitted to providing false testimony at the request of two Tulsa police officers. He had been incarcerated for four years before being released on May 21, 2010 (Gilham, 2010b; "Tulsa judge overturns conviction," 2010).

Summary

The wrongful drug convictions discussed in this chapter have several distinguishing features that make this group stand apart from other categories of crimes. First, the drug cases are almost exclusively from Southern states. Nineteen of the twenty wrongful drug convictions are from Louisiana, Texas, Florida, and Oklahoma. Only one case from Ohio prevents the sample from being exclusively from the South. One should, nevertheless, avoid the temptation to conclude that the problem of false drug convictions is primarily confined to a single geographic area. The Southern influence evident in this sample is largely the result of a heavy concentration of cases from the Tulia drug bust in Texas during the summer of 1999. More precisely, 60 percent of the wrongly convicted women in this study were a product of that particular drug raid.

A second distinctive feature of this genre of false convictions is the racial identity of the defendants. Sixteen were African American, whereas only three defendants were white. One defendant was Hispanic. This racial composition is in direct contrast to self-reported drug use, which consistently discloses similar rates of drug usage for African Americans and whites. Again, contributing to this disparity were the twelve Tulia drug raid defendants, of which eleven were African American and one was Hispanic. Since the war on drugs has been largely confined to inner-city areas where minorities are disproportionately found, their overrepresentation among drug arrests is axiomatic. Furthermore, to the extent that some police and other criminal justice personnel engage in questionable practices to obtain a conviction, it is more likely to result in the wrongful conviction of people of color than of whites.

When factors contributing to the wrongful drug convictions are examined, several additional characteristics become apparent. Compared to earlier analyses, perjury and prosecutorial misconduct are more pronounced. Indeed, in 85 percent of the cases, perjury by criminal justice officials was a major contributor to this miscarriage of justice. Furthermore, prosecutorial misconduct was present in 70 percent of this subsample. Other factors associated with these false convictions include the use of informants during the trial and police misconduct. Each was a factor contributing to false convictions in a fourth of the cases. It thus appears that at least among the wrongful drug convictions examined here, there were major violations of the law that preceded the wrongful convictions.

Although one should be cautious in generalizing these findings, the racial disparity found among these wrongful drug convictions tends to mirror the racial disparity found in drug arrest data for the United States. Though it may be argued that in this sample the racial disparity is largely a function of the Tulia drug bust, the disproportionality found in drug arrests is not limited to any one geographic region within the United States. To be certain, the racial influence of the Tulia drug raid is quite evident in these data. Nonetheless, the enforcement of drug legislation, which has been primarily concentrated in the central city where drug transactions are more visible than in the more affluent parts of the city, has resulted in a disproportionate number of minority citizens being arrested. Given the limited financial resources for legal counsel available to many of these defendants, it is highly unlikely that these cases will receive the adequate legal representation required to ensure that innocent defendants are found not guilty. Since a number of these individuals may have spotty criminal records, it is doubtful that these wrongful convictions are likely to lead to a public outcry and, for that reason, less likely to come to the attention of organizations that provide legal assistance for those who have been falsely convicted. Consequently, many erroneous drug convictions never appear in the literature. For that reason caution should be exercised when analyzing exonerations involving drug offenses.

5

Property Crimes
and Beyond

The city of Gilbert, Arizona, is located approximately twenty-two miles from Phoenix and eleven miles from Tempe. About 15 percent of its residents are Hispanic. On September 20, 2000, a five-foot Hispanic woman with acne slipped a note to a teller at a bank indicating that she had a gun and would use it if she didn't give her the money. The teller complied with the request and the robber left with more than $5,000 without having said anything. Several weeks later, two other banks in nearby cities were robbed using the same approach. In each case the perpetrator was a short Hispanic woman in her thirties with facial acne.

While the FBI was investigating the bank robbery it was concomitantly investigating possible postage stamp thefts at a nearby post office. One of the agents observed that Rachel Jernigan, who was a suspect of the theft from the post office, physically resembled the description of the bank robber.[1] A comparison of a photograph of Rachel to the grainy surveillance tape resulted in her arrest on November 10, 2000. Rachel, who had had run-ins with the law since the age of eleven, had a previous record and thereby qualified as a legitimate suspect. Although most of the charges against her were minor (e.g., stolen groceries or shoes), she also had two convictions while in her twenties for trying to sell $20 worth of cocaine to undercover officers. Charged with three separate bank robberies, Rachel proclaimed her innocence from the outset. "From the beginning, I told the FBI man it wasn't me." She added that "there was going to continue to be bank robberies after they locked me up" (Associated Press, 2008). Indeed, three banks were robbed after her trial started. In each case the perpetrator was apparently the same woman whose description matched that of Rachel.

Five bank eyewitnesses testified at the trial for the prosecution, and a surveillance videotape was entered into evidence. The eyewitness misidentifications of Rachel as the offender were preceded by a faulty photograph lineup in which a picture of Rachel appeared with five other women, none of whom looked like her. Nor was there physical evidence linking her to the crime. The one fingerprint on the teller's window failed to provide a match. Moreover, the money was never recovered, no weapon was ever found, and no clothing worn by the perpetrator was ever located. Her defense attorney argued that she had been incorrectly identified by the eyewitnesses. Rachel was convinced that she would be found not guilty as she later admitted, "I knew I was going to walk away from that court, because I knew I did not commit that crime" (Martin, 2011). Unfortunately, the jury was not convinced of her innocence. Convicted of bank robbery and use of a firearm during one heist, the thirty-one-year-old mother of four was sentenced to fourteen years in prison plus five years of supervised release on March 23, 2001. Because her felony was a federal offense, she was assigned to a federal prison in California, where she was allowed to talk to her children and family only five hours every month. Her children, ages five through eleven at the time of her sentence, were dispersed to various relatives, making regular communication with them difficult.

After serving seven years and three months of her sentence, the charges were dismissed after the US Court of Appeals for the Ninth Circuit overturned her conviction and granted a new trial on July 9, 2007. The actual perpetrator, Juanita Rodriquez-Gallegos, who bore a strong resemblance to Rachel, had been captured in December 2001 after robbing the same bank allegedly robbed by Rachel. Although FBI investigators were apparently aware of a woman of similar appearance involved in bank heists at the time of Rachel's trial, this exculpatory information was not shared with either the prosecution or the defense.

Upon being released in February 2008 Rachel immediately reunited with her family. Although she was free, she continued to bemoan the loss of time with her children. "Those are seven years that they can never give me back. They robbed my kids of their childhood" (Martin, 2011). "I was so overwhelmed, and I wanted to continually keep holding my daughter" (Hensley and Collom, 2008).

Looking to the future, Rachel recognized the importance of moving forward. "What matters is what I do from this point on to get me a job, to do right, to restore my motherhood. That's all that matters" (Martin, 2011). She added, "I'll work at McDonald's, I'll work at Jack in the Box, Circle K, whatever. I'll do whatever they'll let me do" (Associated Press, 2008; Hensley and Collom, 2008; *Jernigan v. Richard*, No. CV-08-2332-PHX-GMS, 2010; Martin, 2011; Possley, n.d. k).

This chapter examines wrongful convictions that fall outside the more typical range of offenses such as child abuse and neglect, murder and manslaughter, and drugs. The offenses are many and varied as are the innocents who were falsely convicted. Of the thirty-three miscellaneous cases examined in the study, a majority were property crimes. Among the offenses included in this category were money laundering, burglary, arson, embezzlement, fraud, larceny and theft, and criminal mischief. Personal (or violent) crimes, which constituted 18 percent of the wrongful convictions, were composed of robbery, extortion, assault, harassment, and second-degree menacing offenses. The remaining offenses included a potpourri of crimes that ran the gamut from risk of injury to a minor (pornographic computer pop-ups by a substitute teacher) to filing a false police report. Other miscellaneous offenses included prostitution, rendering criminal assistance, computer fraud (creating a fake account on MySpace), customs violation, criminal contempt, felony nonpayment of child support, perjury, and obstruction of justice. Because many of these offenses are relatively minor, they frequently received little publicity and consequently much less is known about these false convictions than the cases discussed in previous chapters. That limitation notwithstanding, this chapter offers the reader a sample of cases indicative of the variety of miscellaneous wrongful convictions found in this investigation.

Two Cases Involving Crimes Allegedly Committed While Working

The first wrongful conviction discussed in this section involves twenty-five-year-old Lisa Hansen from Grand Rapids, Michigan, who was falsely convicted of embezzlement in 2006. In contrast, fifty-two-year-old Debbie Hennen of Elizabeth, West Virginia, was wrongfully pronounced guilty of fraud in 2010 when she allegedly falsified an employee's timesheet. Although neither innocent was incarcerated for these nonexistent crimes, both cases involve the wrongful conviction of women who had done nothing illegal during the course of their employment. Their cases appear below.

Lisa Hansen
On September 3, 2005, Lisa Hansen left her receptionist position at Panopoulos Salon to make a night deposit of $80 in cash and $345 in checks at a Huntington National Bank branch, as she had been instructed to do. Two days later her manager found out that the deposit was

never received by the bank. Furthermore, none of the bank's fifteen surveillance cameras contained a visual image of her depositing the money during the time she said she arrived at the bank. Although her employer informed her that no charges would be filed if she repaid the money and checks, Lisa remained adamant about her innocence and refused to reimburse the salon. In October 2005, she was fired.

To attempt to document her innocence, she agreed to take a polygraph test in December 2005. The test, administered by the Michigan State Police, was particularly stressful because the officer directly accused her of stealing the money and being deceptive when responding to his questions. Consequently, she failed the test and was arrested the following month and charged with misdemeanor embezzlement.

She was unable to afford her own counsel, so an attorney was appointed to represent her. His legal advice consisted of a recommendation to plead guilty to avoid a trial and possible jail sentence. The district court judge, after listening to Lisa's explanation, refused to accept her plea. In lieu of incarceration, she was required to pay $400 for a diversion program that required her to provide forty hours of community service. After successfully completing the program, her charges were dropped in April 2006.

On August 9, 2006, an employee of the bank found the night deposit, which had become lodged somewhere in the depository's mechanism. The bank refused to comment on why the security cameras failed to detect Lisa's presence on the night of September 3, or why the deposit remained undetected for almost a year. When Lisa learned about the discovery, she was elated. "I cried. It was all that emotional buildup for a year that I just let go," she explained. "I was hurt more than anything. It was embarrassing. I hid it from my family and most of my friends." She went on to say, "This has been a huge burden to bear for a year. It feels wonderful that it doesn't need to be my burden anymore" ("Grand Rapids, Michigan woman punished and humiliated, and now exonerated," 2006).

To compensate for her wrongful conviction, the county prosecutor agreed to reimburse Lisa for the diversion program and pay her $10 an hour for her hours of community service. Lisa's new attorney put the bank on notice that he expects the financial institution to pay his client for lost wages since the incident. Lisa and her lawyer do not anticipate taking any action against either the police or her previous employer for this incident (Denzel, n.d. d; "Grand Rapids, Michigan woman punished and humiliated, and now exonerated," 2006; "Michigan state police polygrapher who wrongly accused innocent woman named," 2006).

Debbie Hennen

Longtime Wirt County (West Virginia) Assessor Debbie Hennen had no reservations when she signed a time card for a part-time salaried deputy assessor, as the timesheet was merely a formality for him to receive his salary. He did not have a typical five-day work week but instead was required to complete all assigned work by January 1 of each year to qualify for an annual salary of $9,000. "This was not designed to be an eight-to-four job," Debbie explained in defense of the flexible hours her colleague was allowed to work. "I can't offer my employees benefits, but I can give them a good working environment" (Dunlap, 2010a). For reimbursement purposes Debbie broke down his total salary into twelve monthly installments, which meant that each month's timesheet did not necessarily accurately reflect the actual amount of time spent working that month. Moreover, Debbie had returned to her office during her vacation to complete the timesheet so that he would receive his check on time. She had no intention of deliberately misleading the state since the deputy assessor had a year in which to complete his required workload.

Yet at her hearing on February 17, 2010, a special magistrate pronounced her guilty of fraudulent falsification of a record. A special prosecutor contended that the timesheets constituted official records of the actual amount of work an employee engaged in and that Debbie knowingly submitted falsified information when she filed them for reimbursement. Her defense attorney argued that since Hennen did not receive any benefit from her act, the behavior did not constitute fraud. Nevertheless, Debbie was fined $100 for her behavior and required to pay the court costs. On September 29, 2010, however, a circuit judge overturned her conviction, stating that there was no evidence of fraud since neither party had received any benefit from the incident (Associated Press, 2010; Dunlap, 2010a, 2010b).

Wrongful Conviction for Arson: A Tale of Two Women

Forensics has had a major impact on wrongful convictions. Although still in its infancy in the determination of false convictions, DNA testing provides an instrument to be used in the correction of judicial errors. Perhaps nowhere has forensics dramatically changed the landscape as it has in cases involving arson. Improvements in the forensics of arson testing have questioned previous assumptions about factors associated with accelerant-aided fires. Yet some false arson convictions are the result of sloppy investigative work or falsified evidence by the police. The first wrongful conviction analyzed in this section resulted from an inadequate investigation of the crime scene, whereas false evidence provided by the police led to the wrongful conviction in the second example.

Jennifer Hall

In 2001 twenty-year-old Jennifer Hall worked as a respiratory therapist in Harrison, Missouri, a town of fewer than 10,000 inhabitants. Jennifer suffered from occasional epileptic seizures but was generally able to minimize the problem with proper medication. She had experienced sexual harassment from a colleague, although the coworker responsible for the problem had recently died of a cardiac condition. Although Jennifer usually wore her hair straight, she decided to curl her hair for a change of pace on the night of the alleged arson. Who could imagine that something as insignificant as curly hair would soon be used by the prosecution as a reason she was a suspect?

The story begins on January 24, 2001, while Jennifer was working. She had exited the medical center to retrieve a soda from her truck because she would soon be unable to leave the building, as she would be with a patient who required her constant attention. Sometime after 7 p.m. a fire alarm went off and Jennifer and two coworkers responded to the alarm. While attempting to shut off a valve releasing highly explosive oxygen, she sustained a burn on her hand by coming into contact with a hot metal door frame. Although she was successful in shutting off the flow of oxygen, the fire did an estimated $23,000 in damage to a desk, computer, and wall in the room. The Harrison fire investigator and the Missouri State Fire Marshal's Office later found no obvious cause for the blaze. An inordinate amount of charred paper near the fire was noted, however, suggesting that the fire may have been intentional. The burn on Jennifer's hand made her a likely suspect. What went unobserved at the time was a bead of copper on a wire to the clock, which indicated that a short-circuit was to blame for the fire.

Three weeks after the fire Jennifer was arrested and charged with arson. Her parents, people of modest means, hired Gary Cover to represent her. The defense mainly focused on the fact that Jennifer was not present in the room when the fire originated and was therefore innocent. Unfortunately, her defense counsel repeatedly confused the jury when he mixed up facts, dates, and names. Cover also failed to hire a fire expert to assist with the case. Prosecutors contended that Jennifer's burn occurred while she was setting the fire and that she had curled her hair that day so that she would look especially nice when she was interviewed for her heroics. They further argued that she had been discontented with the way the medical center had handled her sexual harassment case and that was her way of paying back her employer. In September 2001 a jury concurred with the prosecution and found her guilty of second-degree arson.

On the day of the sentencing, Cover advised Jennifer to admit to starting the fire because the court might look more favorably on her if she confessed. According to Jennifer, "He said that I needed to go with their theory that I was doing it for attention. And I said, 'I don't want to say that, because it is going to make me look even worse'" (Pflaum, 2005). Nevertheless, she eventually acquiesced and said that she had accidentally dropped a lit cigarette, even though she didn't smoke. After the probation officer informed the judge, Jennifer's parents were billed for $10,000 for damage incurred due to her negligence and she was sentenced to three years in prison.

Dissatisfied with the outcome from her trial, her parents hired another attorney, Matt O'Connor, to handle Jennifer's appeals. Immediately recognizing the need for a forensics specialist, O'Connor acquired the services of Carl Martin. Martin concluded that the fire inspectors had overlooked a very important piece of evidence. Not mincing any words, Martin was very critical of the lack of attention to detail that his predecessors had devoted to the fire.

> I don't know what the heck went on in that case, but I've never seen anything like it before. There wasn't any doubt that there had been an electrical short circuit. Everything was very consistent with it being a long-term short circuit in a very old power cord on an old clock very near the fire's origin. It was black-and-white after we tested it. (Pflaum, 2005)

Despite this new evidence, Jennifer's appeals were rejected. The first motion for a hearing based on new evidence was denied, as was a second appeal on July 22, 2003, in the Missouri Court of Appeals. Three days after her unsuccessful second appeal, Jennifer began serving her sentence at a women's maximum-security facility.

During Jennifer's incarceration, stress increased the frequency of her seizures despite the medication. Typically she would have a seizure once every eight to ten months; she now had them two to three times weekly. Because the prison was known for its laxity in administering medicine (the previous summer twelve inmates had to be hospitalized for being given the wrong medications), O'Connor faxed information on Jennifer's medication to the prison daily. Contributing to her seizures was the strain resulting from living with a cellmate who was serving time for murder. Jennifer informed O'Connor that if she was killed while imprisoned that she knew who did it. She further said, "I flat-out told him, I think I'm going to die in here. Bad things can happen there. You wouldn't believe what people can make into a weapon. Anything" (Pflaum, 2005).

As Jennifer struggled with her daily existence in prison, her parents struggled with mounting legal bills. They began working at second jobs. By the time a judge overturned Jennifer's sentence because of ineffective assistance of counsel on June 29, 2004, and remanded the case, the Halls were $80,000 in debt. When Jennifer was finally exonerated by a jury in February 2005, the Halls' debt for legal services had risen to $100,000.

Jennifer ultimately served one year of her three-year sentence. In July 2004 she was paroled. The impact of her time in prison is still evident. Her parents had a security camera installed in their home with a monitor located in Jennifer's bedroom. "I'm constantly worried, even now that it's over, that they're going to come back with something else," Jennifer explained to *The Pitch* in 2005. She also struggles to get licensed to work since her false conviction. "People still don't believe you totally, even if you've been exonerated" (Associated Press, 2005b; Denzel, n.d. c; Pflaum, 2005).

Shirley Kinge

A black single mother of two, Shirley had no prior criminal record before her wrongful conviction. Her employers described her as a hard worker and conscientious individual who was dependable and honest. But one day she succumbed to the temptation to use another person's credit cards to make some purchases. Although she knew the cards were stolen, at the time she did not realize the cards had previously belonged to a family that had been murdered and set on fire by her son. That incident proved to be an event that forever scarred her.

On December 22, 1989, the charred bodies of the Harris family were discovered by the police in a suburb of Ithaca, New York. The perpetrator had tied them up, covered their heads with pillowcases, and shot them each in the back of the head before igniting a fire in an attempt to conceal the murders. Thirty-nine-year-old Warren Harris, his forty-one-year-old wife, Dolores, and their two children (ages eleven and fifteen) were executed gangster-style in their home. The next month the police received a tip from an informant that thirty-three-year-old Michael Kinge was responsible for the crime. Using a battering ram, police stormed his apartment on February 7, 1990. An exchange of bullets left him dead. His fifty-four-year-old mother, Shirley, who lived in the apartment next door, was immediately arrested and charged with being an accomplice to the arson and using stolen credit cards from the victims.

During the trial, New York State Police Trooper David Harding testified that Shirley's fingerprints had been found on a gasoline can inside the victims' house. With this incontrovertible evidence, the jury found Shirley guilty of arson, burglary, hindering prosecution, criminal possession of stolen property, and forgery in November 1990. During sentencing she read from a prepared statement in which she admitted to using a stolen credit card but nothing more. She was sentenced to seventeen to forty-four years in prison for her alleged involvement in the crime.

In 1992 an investigation by the US Department of Justice disclosed the existence of improprieties in the New York State Police department. Numerous cases involving troopers from Troops C and F, which includes the Ithaca region, had been contaminated by evidence tampering. Harding, who had testified against Shirley, confessed to lying about the presence of her fingerprints on the gasoline can. Her case represented the first of more than thirty defendants whose criminal cases were tried using evidence fabricated by the state police. Harding was eventually found guilty and received a four- to twelve-year sentence.

As a result of the investigation, Shirley was granted a new trial and released on bond in 1992 after having been incarcerated for over two and a half years. With no evidence to document any involvement by her in the arson and murder, the prosecution dropped all but one charge. In November 1992 Shirley pleaded guilty to misdemeanor forgery for using stolen credit cards. Although she was now exonerated of the arson/murder, the time spent in prison had forever changed her.

Two years prior to her arrest, Shirley had worked at a bed and breakfast in Ithaca. She became good friends with Nancy Falconer, the owner, who was also a trained psychiatric social worker. Nancy noticed marked differences in Shirley after she had spent a short time in the Tompkins County Jail. According to Nancy, "When she came to work for me, she was immaculate. She was very personable, and quite animated in our conversations. And, of course, that diminished. I mean, it changed quite completely when she went first to Tompkins [County Jail] and then to Bedford [Hills Correctional Facility]" (*Kinge v. State of New York*, 2009). Through correspondence while at Bedford Hills, Nancy noticed the effects of depression on Shirley, which continued after her release and relocation to New Jersey.

When she went to New Jersey, she just fell apart. I talked to her on the phone fairly often and . . . that's when I observed, as a friend and social worker, a lot of depression. I mean a deep depression that seemed to immobilize her, and I was trying to get her to a psychiatrist or a counselor. (*Kinge v. State of New York*, 2009)

Shirley and her mother moved to Georgia for ten years beginning in 1998. While there she worked part-time as a nurse's aide before moving to North Carolina. Finally, at the age of seventy-three, Shirley was awarded a quarter of a million dollars for malicious prosecution in July 2009 (Kenyon, 2009; *Kinge v. State of New York*, 2009; O'Hara, 2009; Pasnik, 1993; Possley, n.d. o).

Witness Misidentification and Race

Although less apparent in wrongful convictions involving black women than those with black men, witness error is still an issue in some false convictions. This problem is more evident in miscarriages of justice involving women of color than those involving white women. In many instances the misidentification occurs when the witness and the alleged perpetrator are of different races. The following cases illustrate the problematic nature of witness error in wrongful convictions. Although there was no deliberate attempt to misidentify the perpetrator in either example, the effect was the same: the individual was convicted of a crime for which she was innocent.

Malenne Joseph

Peter Spaziano was a contractor in central Florida in fall 2007 whose overextended work commitments necessitated hiring part-time help. In December he received a $2,000 down payment from Kittsie Simmons to have her house painted and tile installed. He hired a female subcontractor whom he had met only a few times to paint the house. After the woman completed the assignment, she became enmeshed in a payment dispute with Spaziano. Angered by this, she vandalized the home, doing approximately $10,000 worth of damage.

Officer Jose Varela of the Orlando Police Department responded to the crime by calling the cell phone number Spaziano said belonged to the woman he hired to do the painting. A woman who identified herself as Marlene confessed to the destruction of property but then hung up on the officer.[2] No immediate action was taken at this point. However, the homeowner noticed a suspicious-looking black man driving a green pickup truck past the residence sometime later and got the license number, which was passed on to the police. Varela followed up on the complaint and discovered that the truck was registered to a man whose last name was Joseph.[3] While perusing driver's license records, the officer found the name of Malenne Joseph. He proceeded to show her photograph to Kittsie Simmons and her sister, who identified the person in the picture as the individual who had painted the house. In January 2008 Varela arrested Malenne for felony criminal mischief, but she was released on bond. The following month the state decided not to proceed with the case. Nonetheless, in April 2009 Malenne was again arrested and charged with the crime. Her trial was eventually set for June 2010.

Unable to afford a lawyer, twenty-nine-year-old Haitian-born Malenne, a mother of three, was represented by a court-appointed attorney, Robert Wesley. A public defender since 2000, Wesley boasted on his website that his office is able "to professionally and competently represent citizens for less than an hourly consultation in a local law firm" ("Malenne Joseph files lawsuit for mistaken identity wrongful conviction," 2012). In monetary terms, the public defender's office spends an average of $196 per case. Malenne's legal representation exhibited this no-frills legal counsel.

At the trial Malenne testified that she had never painted and was not responsible for the damage. The contractor, who had not seen the woman he had hired for nearly three years, identified Malenne as the woman who performed the work, as did Simmons and her sister. Based primarily on the witness identifications, she was convicted of felony criminal mischief. While awaiting sentencing, she began receiving legal assistance from two new lawyers, Paula Coffman and Nicole Benjamin. They discovered that she was employed at two jobs and was working during the times that the Simmons's home was being painted. Coffman and Benjamin also discovered that the perpetrator was a woman over 5'6" tall, yet Malenne was barely 5'2". The contractor later admitted his mistake in identifying her, adding that he would have known that she was the wrong person if her public defender had asked Malenne to stand up. Based on the new information, her attorneys filed a motion for a new trial in August 2010. As a result, Malenne was released on bail on September 15, 2010. She had been in jail awaiting sentencing for three months. On October 7, 2010, the charges against her were finally dismissed. Because the statute of limitations had expired, no one was held legally responsible for the damage.

Alleging ineffective assistance of counsel from her public defender, Malenne sued the city of Orlando for her wrongful conviction in 2011. Because she also had allegations of civil rights violations, the lawsuit was subsequently moved to the federal court system on January 27, 2012, and her state lawsuit was dismissed (Colarossi, 2010a, 2010b, 2010c, 2011; Innocence Project of Florida, 2011; "Malenne Joseph files lawsuit for mistaken identity wrongful conviction," 2012; "Orlando woman too short to be criminal exonerated," 2010; Possley, n.d. f; "Woman jailed for vandalism may not be guilty," 2010).

Reshenda Strickland

On February 13, 2004, twenty-four-year-old Reshenda Strickland was convicted of third-degree theft and fourth-degree assault for allegedly struggling with Dawn Porter, a loss prevention officer at a store in Vancouver, Washington. Her court-appointed attorney chose to focus on differences between his client and the individual on the store's surveillance video. No witnesses were called to testify on Reshenda's behalf, although two other women were present when the items were taken from the store on March 21, 2003. With a surveillance camera videotape and positive identifications from the store manager and Porter, an all-white jury convicted her of the charges in less than one hour. Because she had previous convictions for theft, Reshenda was sentenced to six months in jail. In a typical case like this with a short jail sentence, there would be no postconviction review of the evidence and the defendant (guilty or innocent) would usually serve the sentence without benefit of new counsel. But Reshenda's mother, Juanita Strickland, contacted the Vancouver branch of the National Association for the Advancement of Colored People (NAACP) and was successful in securing the services of another attorney to represent her daughter.

On May 19, 2004, the case was reopened. After closer scrutiny of the videotape, it was determined that the woman involved in the incident was Reshenda's twenty-one-year-old sister, Starlisha Strickland. Starlisha immediately confessed to the crime and was released after posting $1,500 bail. Reshenda was released after a district court judge overturned the conviction. She had served over half of her sentence at the time. The fact that both witnesses were "100 percent" certain of their identifications, yet Starlisha is visibly lighter skinned than her sister and does not have a mole above the right side of her mouth raised issues of racial overtones. Earl Ford, president of the Vancouver chapter of the NAACP, believes that the conviction resulted from the inability of the white witnesses to ascertain differences among blacks. "Folks say we all look alike. I think that happened in this case," Ford suggested. Reshenda's NAACP attorney echoed that sentiment: "We don't all look the same. That girl is at least two shades lighter than the defendant" (Mize, 2004).

The prosecutor, however, has a different take on the false conviction. "If two people closely resemble each other, there is a chance that people are going to confuse them. I don't think it comes down to race. I do think it comes down to looking at what evidence was and was not presented" ("Woman freed from jail after sister confesses to crime," 2004).

Whatever role race played in this case, one thing is certain. Justice comes at a cost. Both the family and the NAACP had to pay for an attorney to get the case reexamined, and it was only after the city prosecutor consented to review the videotape that the mistaken identity was detected. A more thorough review of the video the first time or a more robust defense by Reshenda's court-appointed attorney could have prevented this miscarriage of justice. According to Ford, "All this victory says today is if you can pay for it, you can still get justice. And that's something fundamentally wrong about our system" (Mize, 2004; Possley, n.d. 1; "Woman freed from jail after sister confesses to crime," 2004; Vancouver Branch NAACP newsletter, 2004).

The Case of the Amorous Prosecutor

In May 2003 when thirty-three-year-old Tamara McAnally and her husband, Jon, were indicted by a San Diego grand jury, they owned JDM Enterprises, a construction contracting business. They were charged with conspiring to defraud the California State Compensation Insurance Fund (CSCIF). According to CSCIF, their company had underpaid the fund by $375,000. Jon and Tamara argued that a bookkeeping error was responsible for the underpayment and that there was no intent to defraud the agency.

Prior to the indictment, Ernest Marugg, a deputy district attorney, and an investigator from the fund had met with Tamara to discuss the investigation while Jon was in Hawaii on business. Instead, however, Marugg discussed Tamara's personal life with her and gave her his cell phone number should she wish to contact him later. At no point did Marugg identify himself as a prosecutor.

Although the authenticity of the evidence heard by the grand jury was questioned by Tamara and Jon, on April 19, 2004, on advice from their counsel, the couple agreed to plead guilty to a single count of conspiring to commit insurance fraud to avoid prison. They were required to pay restitution of $412,096 to the state in $400 monthly increments. Jon was allowed to retain his contracting license as a part of the plea offer. Yet despite their payments, the McAnallys began receiving delinquency notices. Shortly thereafter a collection agency was assigned to their case, and Jon's contracting license was suspended in August 2004.

At that point Tamara made the mistake of contacting Marugg for assistance. She provided him with documentation of payments to the state. He assured her that he would look into the problem but did nothing. Instead, he again began to inquire about her personal life. Faced with financial ruin, Tamara and Jon started experiencing marital problems. Tamara, feeling depressed, began to confide in Marugg since she believed that he was genuinely trying to assist them. In January 2005 she was relieved to learn that he would reduce their convictions to a misdemeanor. He later offered to expunge their convictions to demonstrate his affection for her.

In 2006 Jon was still without his contracting license. Tamara agreed to meet Marugg in his office for coffee to discuss the contracting license. At this time he became more assertive. While driving back from a coffee shop, he placed his hand on her thigh and tried to kiss her. Although Tamara resisted his sexual overtures, Marugg later sent her an email that said, "I can't stop thinking about you" (Possley, n.d. p). He continued to pursue her through telephone calls and emails for several years thereafter.[4]

On November 2, 2009, Tamara became acquainted with Kim Alvarez, another woman who had been prosecuted by Marugg.[5] She learned that he had admitted to having had numerous sexual relationships with women he had prosecuted. A further investigation by Tamara and Jon revealed that Marugg had previously had an affair with Kathey Bradley, a woman who was responsible for investigating possible cases of insurance fraud involving the CSCIF and who conducted their audit. Moreover, the district attorney's office was aware of their colleague's indiscretions because others had filed complaints regarding his inappropriate relationships with female defendants. Finally, it was learned that the CSCIF awarded grants to prosecutorial offices based on successful convictions. Perhaps most alarming was the fact that San Diego County had almost twice the amount of grant money as Los Angeles County, despite having about half the population.

On September 23, 2010, at the age of seventy, Marugg retired in the midst of an internal investigation without any disciplinary action being taken. Tamara pursued her quest to have her conviction vacated. Her persistence paid off when on May 16, 2011, she was declared factually innocent. In deciding in favor of Tamara, the superior court judge noted "substantial irregularities" in the case, concluding that

Marugg "obtained her conviction as the result of his failure to discharge ethical obligations" (Moran, 2011). The signed order further stipulated that all arrest and conviction records were to be sealed for three years and then destroyed. The next year Jon sought to have his conviction dismissed but was unsuccessful.

On November 4, 2011, a federal civil rights lawsuit was filed on behalf of Tamara McAnally naming San Diego County, the district attorney's office, and Marugg as defendants. Although Marugg died in 2013, the lawsuit was scheduled to be revised to include Marugg's estate as a defendant. The lawsuit alleges that "Marugg's supervisors failed to discipline him for his relationships with female former defendants because they didn't want to jeopardize the insurance company grants" (Repard, 2013). No further information on the lawsuit was available (Moran, 2011; Possley, n.d. p; Repard, 2013; Warmerdam, 2013).

Georgia Thompson: Political Pawn

In 2008 Georgia Thompson earned an honorable mention for the Virginia Hart Special Recognition Award from the Office of State Employee Relations in Wisconsin. The award is given "for exemplary performance and contributions to the citizens of the state." That recognition stands in distinct contrast to the events that occurred earlier when she became enmeshed in a politically inspired prosecution for fraud and was forced to resign her state job.

In 2001 Georgia Thompson began working for the state of Wisconsin as a purchasing officer, after working in the travel industry for many years. When she awarded a $750,000 contract to the Wisconsin-based Adelman Travel Group in 2006, some politicians accused her of manipulating the bidding process in favor of a company in which two executives had given money to the governor's campaign for reelection, despite the fact that the company's bid was the lowest and preference was typically given to in-state companies. Georgia later resigned from her position, cashed in her state pension, and sold her condominium to cover her legal expenses of approximately $300,000. She was virtually penniless and facing possible incarceration in federal court.

Before filing charges and before and after the trial, the prosecuting attorney and his colleagues began discussing offers of leniency if she would come forward with the names of those higher up who pressured her to award the contract. Her lawyer later observed that "I began to get the impression that the indictment was being used to squeeze her. It was the only time in my career that, after the person was sentenced, the prosecutor called to renew the discussion" (Lueders, 2007).[6] Offers from the prosecutors to change the two felonies to misdemeanors and thus avoid imprisonment were also broached. Georgia refused to accede to their requests because she had not been pressured into awarding the contract to the Adelman Travel Group. She had been convinced that their bid was the best available and worthy of a contract.

Georgia was found guilty and was sentenced to eighteen months in federal prison. Although already convicted of two felonies, the offers of leniency continued. On September 25, 2006, another attorney reiterated his office's willingness to "give her appropriate protections and considerations in exchange for her assistance" (Lueders, 2007). More specifically, they were willing to reduce her sentence for cooperating with the prosecution. The offer was again extended on September 27, and one or two days later. To further enhance the probability that Georgia would accept their offer, she was retained in jail while appealing her conviction even though she was neither a flight risk nor did she pose any danger to herself or others. In November 2006 Georgia was sent to a federal prison to begin her sentence.

Her appeal was based on two claims: (1) there was insufficient evidence to convict and (2) the indictment had failed to reveal the presence of criminal behavior. The appeal was heard by a three-person panel in the Seventh Circuit Court of Appeals in Chicago in April 2007. In a stunning reversal, the federal court of appeals dismissed her conviction during oral arguments and ordered that she be immediately released from prison. One of the federal judges admonished the prosecutors and said, "I have to say it strikes me that your evidence is beyond thin. I'm not sure what your actual theory in this case is" (Stein, 2007). It is especially noteworthy that the federal appeals court, rather than remanding her case back to a trial court, chose to acquit her immediately and order her freedom. Georgia's defense attorney noted, "It's extraordinary for a US Court of Appeals to issue a decision on the day of oral arguments without a written opinion. What they're saying is, 'There's no evidence, she's acquitted.'" He went on to say, "The government charged Thompson with conduct that did not constitute a crime. It cost Georgia her job, her life savings, her home, and her liberty, and it cost Georgia her good name" (Stein, 2007).

Since this injustice Georgia has attempted to get her life back together. She got another job with the state of Wisconsin at her previous annual salary. She has also received back pay. In 2008, both houses of the Wisconsin state legislature approved reimbursement for her legal fees. In a rare moment of bipartisanship, the two houses reached a consensus on the matter (Lueders, 2007; Marley, 2008; Marley and Walters, 2007; Stein, 2007).

Wrongful Convictions Involving Minors

Extremely rare in the research on wrongful convictions are cases in which the falsely convicted individual is a juvenile. Because the juvenile court is viewed as salvaging wayward children and not an instrument of punishment, the problem of false convictions is largely ignored. The possibility of discovering judicial errors in the juvenile court is further diminished because the names of minors are typically not disclosed to the media to protect their identity. Consequently, false convictions infrequently come to light in cases tried in the juvenile justice system. Of the thirty-three cases involving miscellaneous crimes in this chapter, three included females under the age of eighteen. Two of those cases are discussed in this section.

The first involves a fifteen-year-old girl from Michigan. Eyewitness error resulted in her being erroneously convicted of felony assault and retail fraud. If her miscarriage of justice had not been discovered, she could have been held in custody for up to six years. The second involves a sixteen-year-old girl from Maryland who was repeatedly raped by her stepfather. When she came forward with allegations of his sexual advances, she wasn't believed and was found guilty of filing a false police report. Both cases reveal the potentially serious nature of wrongful convictions for underage females and demonstrate the need to provide greater illumination of erroneous judicial decisions within the juvenile court.

Wrongfully Convicted of
Felony Assault and Retail Fraud

Lincoln Park, Michigan, is a suburb of Detroit. On April 15, 2002, the local Sears was the site of a botched shoplifting incident. A young woman attempted to steal $1,300 in clothes from the store. When confronted by a security guard, the would-be thief severely bit the employee. When police arrived, the perpetrator was taken to the police station for questioning. She identified herself as Dominique Brim and provided the officers with a telephone number and home address. After their interview, the police released her without calling her parents or booking her. They made no attempt to verify her name prior to her release.

Two weeks after the incident, Dominique was charged with retail fraud and felony assault for her attack on the store's security guard. Her parents hired attorney Akbar Rasul to represent her at the juvenile court. During the hearing several Sears employees (including the security guard) testified that she was the individual responsible for the crime. Consequently, Rasul was unable to convince the judge that Dominique was not the actual culprit, and she was found guilty of both charges. Because the case was tried in juvenile court, she could have been incarcerated until turning twenty-one. Before sentencing, however, Sears consented to review their surveillance videotape of the event. When the tape revealed that the offender was a different person, the store immediately notified Dominique's attorney and the prosecutor. The charges were dismissed, and the judge vacated her conviction.

Police were later able to ascertain the correct identity of the offender. Her name was Chalaundra Latham, a twenty-five-year-old woman, who was friends with Dominique's sister and therefore knew personal information about Dominique. What remains an enigma about this case is how the police could mistake a twenty-five-year-old woman for a fifteen-year-old girl and not verify the identity that she had given them.[7]

A new attorney, Gary Blumberg, was hired by Dominique's family. In 2004, Sears settled for an undisclosed amount. One year later a lawsuit naming the city of Lincoln Park and several police officers was filed. The lawsuit alleged negligence on the part of the city and the police for failing to properly investigate the case and failing to ask for identification from the suspect in their custody. According to Blumberg, "You can't blame the police when someone says, 'I am so and so,' and you do everything you can do to confirm that's true. But the Lincoln Park Police Department didn't do that" (Alley, 2009). Blumberg was particularly critical of the handling of the suspect's release. "They don't turn her over to juvenile authorities or to her parents. They just let her go. Had they turned her over to juvenile authorities, they may have figured out she wasn't who she was saying she was. I don't know what they did or didn't do, but turning her loose wasn't right" (Alley, 2009).

Results of the lawsuit involving the city and four police officers were unavailable. The actual perpetrator was never charged with the crime because the Sears employees had positively identified Dominique (Alley, 2009; Denzel, n.d. b; Tepfer et al., 2010; "Woman wrongly convicted by mistaken identity sues police," 2005).

Sexually Abused and No One Would Believe Her

In 2000 when Emily Rogers[8] was thirteen, she complained to her mother, Laura, that her stepfather, Walter, had placed his hand on her breasts. At the time the family was living in Mississippi. A subsequent police investigation resulted in Walter being charged with a crime, but the case was eventually dismissed. Although Laura suffered emotional and physical abuse from Walter, she couldn't conceive of her husband harming Emily. In May 2003, Emily again came forward with disturbing news. She now claimed that he was abusing her sexually. When police and social services investigated, Walter portrayed himself as the victim of a false accusation. He was so convincing that Emily was convicted of filing a false police report in juvenile court.

In April 2004, Emily, who was seven months pregnant, told her mother that her stepfather had made videotapes of the rapes and kept them in his armoire behind his collection of *Playboy* magazines. Laura retrieved the tapes and watched what she could tolerate before turning off the machine. She later confessed, "He was never going to harm my daughter again. At that point I knew that he was doing it and there was no way for him to convince me otherwise" (Rich, 2004b). After Walter went to bed, Laura stared aimlessly at the television in the living room. Sometime before sunrise she crept back into his bedroom and got the shotgun he left under the bed. She returned to the living room, where she loaded the weapon with a single shell before returning to the bedroom. She doesn't recall shooting him. "I remember hearing the gun go off, and running, saying, 'What the hell have I done?'" (Rich, 2004b).

When the police first arrived, they believed it might be a suicide. An autopsy soon revealed that his death was a homicide. Concerned that her mother would be charged with Walter's death, Emily confessed to the crime, a story the detectives disregarded because she did not know how to load the shotgun. After the detectives informed Laura about her daughter's admission of guilt, she immediately confessed to murdering Walter.

Originally charged with first-degree murder, Laura, a victim of battered spouse syndrome, was allowed to plea bargain to manslaughter to avoid having to make her teenage daughter testify. Although the circuit court judge sentenced her to ten years behind bars, he suspended all but the 198 days Laura had been in jail since her arrest. Now aware that Emily's accusations of sexual abuse by her stepfather were true, her juvenile court conviction was vacated on November 10, 2004. When Emily's baby was born in summer 2004, she put him up for adoption. DNA tests disclosed that Walter was the father of the infant (Kobell, 2004; Rich, 2004a, 2004b).

Asya Richardson: Guilty by Association

The war on drugs in the United States is frequently known for its excesses in an attempt to eradicate illicit substances. Very few of the many people arrested are drug kingpins; many are users or individuals who peddle a small quantity of the substance to other users. One exception to that involved a two-state raid on August 10, 2005, at the home of Alton "Ace Capone" Coles, who ran a $25 million cocaine distribution operation and a record company. Arrested during the raid was Asya Richardson, one of Cole's three girlfriends, and several others.

During the 2008 trial, Asya was convicted of two counts of money laundering for allegedly assisting Cole in funneling drug proceeds to purchase his $500,000 home in New Jersey.[9] Prosecutors portrayed her as his accomplice who helped him use money obtained illegally to buy a house. More specifically, Asya was accused of helping launder $114,000 in drug sales to make a down payment on the building. During the trial her attorney argued that her client believed the money was from his legitimate business. The prosecution never determined how much of the money used for the mortgage came directly from his drug operation. Although Asya had no prior criminal record, she was convicted and sentenced to two years in prison and two years of supervised release. The actual sentence reflected a favorable departure from federal sentencing guidelines, which called for an incarceration period of fifty-one to sixty-three months. The judge believed that the guidelines were too restrictive and imposed a shorter sentence. When Asya heard the sentence, she fell over backward, gasped, and clutched her neck and chest. Though she was all right, the stress of the sentencing hearing had brought on her symptoms. After Asya regained her composure, the judge instructed her to report to a federal women's penitentiary.

After spending eight months in prison, Asya was released when a federal appeals court vacated her conviction for lack of evidence. In a twenty-page opinion the three-judge panel observed that Coles was responsible for "funneling cash through the Take Down Records bank account" ("Philly drug kingpin Ace Capone's girlfriend released from prison on appeal," 2011). Indeed, Asya had only been involved in one cash deposit involving less than $10,000. The judges also reasoned that when she embellished her income when applying for the mortgage, it was because Coles was known to have bad credit and this was not an attempt to understate his role in the loan application. On September 23, 2011, Asya left prison and was free to begin a new life at the age of thirty-one (Anastasia, 2011; Dale, 2009; "Philly drug kingpin Ace Capone's girlfriend released from prison on appeal," 2011; Shaw, 2011).

Police Speculation and an Edited Surveillance Videotape

Tevya Urquhart worked at a mobile phone store in Detroit, along with Kimberly Sykes and Kimberly Holmes. On March 7, 2002, as they were opening the store, two armed men forcibly entered the building and demanded money. Tevya was the only employee with the combination to open the safe, so the intruders forced her to go to the room containing the safe and give them its contents. She withdrew a bag containing $27,762 and gave it to the robbers. Unknown to her assailants, Tevya had not given them a second bag, which contained approximately $14,000. Before they fled they warned the women that they would return and kill them if they did anything to prevent their escape. Tevya, who was three months pregnant and had been robbed three weeks earlier while working there, became hysterical and became increasingly agitated when police officers arrived to take witness statements.[10] The officer who interviewed Tevya became suspicious of her behavior and felt that the robbery was coordinated by the three women. A videotape taken from the store's surveillance camera was secured by the police and carefully edited to reveal only those images that could be construed as support for the supposition that the robbery was an inside job.

On May 11, 2002, Kimberly Sykes was arrested at her home. After learning of Kimberly's arrest, Tevya turned herself into the police. Both were charged with larceny by conversion and filing a false report of a felony. Released on bond while awaiting trail, Kimberly, who was believed to be less culpable, was sentenced in October 2002 to three months in jail, three years probation, and 120 days of community service. Tevya, who was also released pending her trial, was sentenced originally to up to ten years in prison. A subsequent resentencing hearing on December 20, 2002, resulted in a sentence of five months in jail and three years probation. She was released after being incarcerated for approximately two and a half months. On May 4, 2004, the Michigan Court of Appeals vacated their convictions based on lack of evidence and speculation. Kimberly Holmes—the third suspect—had been successful in having her felony charges dismissed in September 2003 when she pleaded guilty to a misdemeanor in return for probation.

The appellate court, in reviewing Tevya's conviction, was skeptical of the prosecution's premise about the heist.

> The detective admitted that he had no evidence that [the three women] conspired to take Sprint's money and there was no evidence that defendant ever came into possession of any of the missing money. The prosecution's assertion that defendant took the money is based on pure speculation. (cited in Sherrer, 2008b, pp. 8–9)

The court acknowledged, "The conclusion that defendant aided and abetted [the robbers] in taking the money was supported only by impermissible inferences and not by evidence" (cited in Sherrer, 2008b, p. 9). A similar rationale was used in vacating Sykes's conviction that same day. Finally, the charges against the women were dropped in the fall of 2004.

Tevya and Kimberly eventually brought lawsuits against the police officers responsible for their wrongful conviction and the city of Detroit. The lawsuit against the officers charged them with false imprisonment, malicious prosecution, and failure to provide due process. Similarly, the lawsuit against the city alleged "that the City failed to respond to citizen complaints and failed to train and supervise its employees" (*Sykes v. Anderson*, US Ct. of Appeals, 6th Circuit, Nos. 08-2088, 08-2090, 08-2118, 2010). Although the lawsuit against the city was dismissed by the district court prior to trial, the complaints against the officers went forward. The trial lasted over three weeks before a jury found in favor of the plaintiffs on February 25, 2008. Tevya was awarded $1.27 million and Kimberly Sykes was awarded $1.31 million. The surveillance video that was used to convict the two women has never been released to the public and remains the property of the Detroit Police Department (Bukowski, 2008; *People of the State of Michigan v. Tevya Urquhart*, Wayne Circuit Court, LC No. 02-009124-01, 2004; Sherrer, 2008b; *Sykes v. Anderson*; "Sykes, et. al. v. Anderson, et al.," n.d.).

Wrongful Conviction of Teachers

Notorious for its low pay, public school teaching is a profession where high moral standards are expected and strictly enforced. Any deviation from these expectations is likely to elicit strong overtones of resentment and a demand for action against the perpetrator. In the first case discussed in this section, a substitute teacher experienced pornographic pop-ups on her computer while she attempted to instruct her class. Without checking for malware on her computer, authorities convicted her of four counts of risk of injury to a minor. The second case involves a female teacher who had a sexual liaison with her sixteen-year-old student. Although the student was the aggressor in this situation, the court failed to recognize that the student was legally able to consent to the tryst and convicted the teacher of sexual assault. Both cases aptly illustrate the potential problems associated with emotional outrage associated with allegations of violations of teacher-student relationships.

Julie Amero

Julie Amero was a dedicated substitute teacher from Connecticut who enjoyed teaching and interacting with her students. Her husband, Wes Vello, worked seven days a week as a shipbuilder. Both were eagerly awaiting the birth of their first child.

On the fateful morning of October 19, 2004, Julie was teaching a seventh-grade language class at a middle school. After checking her e-mail, she briefly exited the classroom to use the restroom before class was to begin. While she was out of the room, the computer began flashing pornographic images on its screen. The computer had neither an up-to-date firewall nor antispyware software to prevent these unwanted pop-ups. Julie had been told to never turn off the computer, so she clumsily attempted to close the inappropriate images. Nevertheless, when one would close, another would open. "The pop-ups never went away. It was one after another," she later exclaimed. "Every time I clicked the box in the corner . . . more were generated" (Ibanga, 2009). She tried to turn the screen away from the class but several students saw the images before she could successfully block their view. During her break she informed the school's vice principal, who seemed relatively unconcerned. A newspaper journalist who followed this story observed, "At the time no big deal was made of it. Then kids went home, told their parents and it exploded from there" (Ibanga, 2009). Shortly after the school notified the police of the incident, Julie was arrested and charged with ten counts of risk of injury to a minor or impairing the morals of a child.

In an attempt to settle out of court, prosecutors offered a plea bargain deal that would efface the charges from her record if she exhibited good behavior for two years. Being innocent of the allegations, however, Julie refused the deal and her case proceeded to trial. On January 5, 2007, she was convicted of four felony counts of risk of injury to a minor, which carries a maximum sentence of forty years in prison. During the trial an expert witness for the prosecution testified unequivocally that Julie was responsible for the pop-ups on the classroom computer.[11] The defense was not allowed to present contradictory evidence that malware programs were responsible for the unwanted images. Refusal to allow Julie's attorney to present this defense made Alex Eckelberry, the president of Sunbelt Software, a manufacturer of antispyware products, irate. As Eckelberry later explained, "The fact that the machine was never scanned for spyware by the investigating authorities is outrageous. In fact, this alone should have resulted in the case being dismissed, as the defense found a major spyware infection by their expert forensic evidence" (Beyerstein, 2007).

As publicity of the events became disseminated, a number of computer science professors became incensed that a person could be convicted for uncontrollable pop-ups on a computer. Twenty-eight professors paid for an advertisement in the paper in which they expressed their opinion that Julie could not have controlled the images appearing on her screen. Given the questions raised about her conviction, sentencing was repeatedly delayed. A subsequent forensic investigation of the computer by the Connecticut State Patrol revealed that it had been infected with a malicious spyware program five days prior to Julie's class. Consequently, a superior court judge overturned the conviction and ordered a new trial on June 6, 2007. Unwilling to admit their mistake, the prosecution looked for a way to save face. Knowing that Julie was experiencing health issues after her miscarriage and was exhausted from being in court, the prosecution agreed to dismiss the felony charges if she would pay a $100 fine and plead guilty to a single count of disorderly conduct. She was also required to surrender her teaching credentials as part of the agreement. Wanting to bring a conclusion to the four-year ordeal, Julie acquiesced.

Well before Julie had been tried in a court of law, she had been tried and found guilty in the court of public opinion. A week after the incident, the school sent a notice to all parents that Julie would never be allowed to teach in their school district again. There was no attempt to defend her from public ridicule, even though an estimated four million computers are infected with some type of malware. The shocked parents didn't need anyone to tell them why this happened. Obviously they thought this substitute teacher had been watching pornographic websites. Thus a pregnant woman with no previous criminal background was found guilty of exposing youth to pornographic images. As Julie noted in 2009, "Everybody out there should be afraid. If it can happen to me, it can certainly happen to you" (Beyerstein, 2007; Carvin, 2007; Green, 2008; Horner, 2007; Ibanga, 2009; Willard, 2007).

Melissa Lee Chase

In November 2006, twenty-eight-year-old Melissa Lee Chase was a highly respected teacher in Georgia, and she was also the school's softball coach. Since August of that year she had been spending time with a former student, sixteen-year-old Christy Elaine Garcia. Their time together eventually evolved into a romantic relationship, which culminated in a sexual encounter. Christy's mother found out about their relationship and contacted the police. Melissa was subsequently arrested and charged with felony sexual assault since Christy was still a minor at the time.

During the ensuing bench trial, Melissa's attorney attempted to show that Christy was not only a willing participant but actually encouraged the development of the relationship. Since the age of consent in Georgia is sixteen, he argued that no crime had been committed. The prosecution contended that the question of consent was irrelevant because state law prohibited contact between people whose position of authority over others makes consent impossible. More specifically, the law refers to relationships between prison correctional officers and inmates and between psychiatrists and their clients. The consent status of teacher and student is not expressly spelled out under the law. Prosecutors were successful in convincing the judge to object to a consent defense and to concur that a broad interpretation of the statute was required to protect students from predatory teachers. Thus, Christy's testimony that she had been the aggressor and "had feelings for her [Melissa]" was no longer relevant. After finding Melissa guilty of sexual assault, the judge sentenced her to ten years in prison and five years of probation. She was required to register as a sex offender. The Georgia Court of Appeals subsequently upheld the ruling.

During the summer of 2009, the Georgia Supreme Court reviewed the case. In a five-to-two majority, the court overturned Melissa's conviction, stating,

> If consent is no defense to a charge of sexual assault of a person enrolled in school, then the age of the teacher and the student have no effect on whether a crime has been committed. Consequently, a 30-year-old law school professor who engaged in a fully consensual sexual encounter with a 50-year-old law school student embarking on a second career would be guilty of a felony and subject to punishment of 10-30 years in prison. That result—not the situation in this case—would be truly absurd and unjust. But that is precisely what the statute would mean were we to accept the reading adopted by the trial court and the Court of Appeals. (cited in "Georgia Supreme Court tosses teacher's conviction for sex with student," 2009)

When Melissa was officially released on July 31, 2009, she had been wrongfully incarcerated for almost two years ("Georgia Supreme Court tosses teacher's conviction for sex with student," 2009; Hodson, 2009; Rankin, 2009; United Press International, 2009).

Summary

This chapter examined a potpourri of offenses, the majority of which are property crimes. Although some of the offenses are common to wrongfully convicted men as well, others are more gender-specific. Consider, for instance, the prosecutor who falsely convicted Tamara McAnally, a married woman, while he was attempting to secure sexual favors from her. Or the teenage girl who was convicted of filing a false police report because she accused her stepfather of sexually abusing her, an accusation that later was confirmed and documented. Girlfriends of drug traffickers are especially vulnerable to wrongful convictions because of their association with men who are violating the law. In earlier chapters we learned about women who were convicted of felonies for essentially being sloppy housekeepers and women who were falsely accused of child abuse because they were evaluated using a double standard.[12] What these cases collectively suggest is that the greater variety of false convictions involving women requires essentially a new approach to the study of these miscarriages of justice. Certainly, the traditional factors associated with wrongful convictions should not be abandoned; however, the number of factors should be expanded to account for gender differences in this area.

Earlier in the book we discussed the impact of race. The potential significance of race and ethnicity should not be understated, whether the focus is wrongly convicted men or women. One of the more intriguing aspects of this group of miscellaneous offenses is the overrepresentation of nonwhites among those who were victims of false convictions. Although the race of the defendant could not be determined in about a fourth of the cases, nonwhites still made up 30 percent of those appearing in this group.[13] Only among wrongful drug convictions was the racial disparity more pronounced.[14] The most serious offenses resulting in a wrongful conviction for nonwhites in the miscellaneous category were second-degree menacing, rendering criminal assistance, robbery, criminal mischief, arson, burglary, felony nonpayment of child support, money laundering, third-degree theft, and larceny. Because many of these offenses fail to be included among the more common categories of wrongful convictions, a heavier concentration on these offenses might disclose an even greater racial disparity among erroneously convicted women.

Given the nature of these various offenses, fewer of the defendants came from the lower strata of society than in the previous chapters. Nonetheless, social class remains an issue in wrongful convictions. Most individuals whose miscarriage of justice has been documented have limited financial resources. Consequently, their legal representation is frequently inadequate, enhancing their likelihood of a wrongful conviction. For women this problem is perhaps more acute because women are more likely than men to be falsely convicted of less serious crimes, which are less likely to come to the attention of the public. Impoverished women who agree to plead guilty to a crime they didn't commit to receive probation or a shorter sentence are seldom found among the known wrongful conviction cases in the literature.

Given the small number of cases in this sample in which exoneration was accomplished through DNA testing, reliance on DNA appears to hold limited promise for enumerating wrongfully convicted women in the future. Although this statement applies to falsely convicted men as well, their greater presence among murder and sexual assault cases makes the successful use of DNA testing to prove innocence somewhat more likely. Thus, if greater recognition of miscarriages of justice involving women is going to occur, it is likely to happen without much assistance from this method.

A word of caution should be introduced at this point. The findings of this investigation are meant to be suggestive, not definitive. There is little basis for arguing that the 163 cases identified in this research constitute the actual universe of wrongful conviction cases for women from the 1970s through 2012. Future scholarship might benefit from more localized research in which all of the cases of one or two jurisdictions are extensively analyzed to ascertain potential wrongful convictions. This approach would enable the investigator to determine more accurately the underlying factors that make the study of wrongfully convicted women a necessity rather than an appendage to the more common study of wrongfully convicted men.

Notes

1. Rachel later confessed to stealing the stamps at the post office in 2000.

2. It should be noted that a TV station identified the woman responsible for the vandalism as Merline Keller. Since the name was ascertained through a telephone conversation, it is possible that the officer misheard the name. Alternatively, the woman may have attempted to deceive the officer by providing a similar-sounding but incorrect name.

3. The man, whose name was registered as the truck owner, was not Malenne Joseph's husband. Her longtime boyfriend, Geordany Francois, owned a truck but it was red, not green.

4. Sometimes he would call and e-mail as frequently as ten times a day.

5. Kim Alvarez and her then-husband, Joe, were also prosecuted by Marugg for workers' compensation fraud. In 2003 they pleaded guilty to misdemeanor fraud and after the conviction and her subsequent divorce from Joe, Kim began dating Marugg. They eventually married in 2010 and divorced the following year.

6. The Wisconsin Republican Party seized on the opportunity to portray Governor Jim Doyle's administration as corrupt. Doyle's Republican challenger, Mark Green, and others ran political advertisements painting his administration as corrupt. Other politicians issued the same message in an attempt to gain political advantage.

7. It is possible that this case illustrates the problem associated with cross-racial identifications. Although the forejustice.org website lists Dominique as black, the National Registry of Exonerations lists her race as unknown.

8. None of the information available on this case mentions the name of the daughter. On the forejustice.org website the case is merely referred to as "daughter of Laura Rogers." Emily is a pseudonym. The use of pseudonyms is somewhat common in discussions of sexual abuse involving juvenile victims.

9. Interestingly, the articles about Cole's drug empire repeatedly mention his "mansion" in New Jersey. Although the home, which was purchased for $500,000, is undoubtedly a large structure, it seems to be an exaggeration to refer to the building as a "mansion."

10. As if that weren't enough, this was Tevya's first day back at work after having a short leave of absence following a home invasion involving her and her boyfriend.

11. According to a forensic specialist who did not testify at the trial, it was physically impossible to have clicked on the pornographic websites as fast as the prosecution claimed Julie did.

12. The double standard argument primarily applies in cases in which child abuse is alleged for the mistreatment of one's own children. During the 1980s and 1990s men and women were regularly prosecuted for alleged crimes of sexual abuse of children who were staying at their child care facilities.

13. There were several more possible cases involving nonwhites, but it was impossible to conclusively document their race, so they were grouped with women whose race was unknown.

14. It should also be recalled that among wrongful child abuse convictions, white women were dramatically overrepresented. A better understanding is required of the racial dynamics involved in the various types of wrongful convictions in future research.

6

Looking Back, Moving Forward

The problem of wrongfully convicted women has not received the same public scrutiny as that of wrongfully convicted men. This omission is shortsighted and ignores the significance of false convictions among the female population. A major premise of this book is that wrongful convictions involving women are frequently qualitatively different from that of their male counterparts. One notable difference is their higher probability of being convicted of a crime that never happened. History is replete with examples, the most notorious of which was the Salem witch trials.[1] Child sexual abuse and satanic ritual cases that captured the attention of the media during the last two decades of the twentieth century stand out as more contemporary illustrations of this problem. Discovery of the now largely discredited shaken baby syndrome further resulted in misdiagnosed cases of child abuse and murder.

DNA evidence is also less prevalent in offenses committed by women. Although routinely gathered in male-dominated murder and sexual assault cases today, the collection of DNA is considerably less common in drug offenses and nonviolent crimes, which are commonly associated with women. Obviously, for nonexistent crimes there can be no DNA. Further complicating this situation is the adverse impact that lack of DNA evidence has on the likelihood of case selection by organizations devoted to investigating potential wrongful convictions. The Innocence Project, for instance, accepts only cases in which DNA evidence is available for proving innocence.

Another distinction between male and female wrongful convictions is the greater variety of offenses associated with false convictions involving women. Of the 163 wrongfully convicted women examined in this book, for example, fewer than 43 percent of their offenses were Part I (or Index) crimes as designated by the *Uniform Crime Reports*.[2] Instead, a majority of their offenses were among the less serious Part II offenses. Because women are more likely to commit property crimes than men are, their sentences are typically less harsh and evoke less public concern than those involving men.

While the number of wrongfully convicted women pales in comparison to that of men, this is partially a function of the greater focus on false convictions for murder and rape/sexual assault, which tend to involve men. As alluded to earlier, the higher probability of women being convicted of less serious crimes that result in probation, fines, or short sentences makes their cases less attractive to organizations focusing on potential miscarriages of justice. With their limited financial resources, organizations charged with exonerating the innocent are more likely to select cases that include long periods of incarceration or a possible death sentence.

Contributing Factors to Wrongful Convictions

Scholarship on wrongful convictions typically focuses on factors that enhance the probability of a false conviction after the individual has become enmeshed in the criminal justice system. Factors such as witness error, prosecutorial and police misconduct, false confessions, use of informants, perjury by criminal justice officials, forensic errors, ineffective assistance of counsel, and insufficient evidence to support a conviction are among the factors most commonly examined. Although witness error has been found to be a major contributor to wrongful convictions in cases exonerated through DNA testing, our results suggest that its importance varies with the type of offense and the race of the defendant. Wrongful convictions for child abuse, for instance, were frequently the result of witness error, in which young children had been unduly influenced through suggestive interviewing techniques to identify the defendant. Furthermore, the current study suggests that witness error is more likely to be present among erroneous convictions involving African American women than among their white counterparts.

Prosecutorial misconduct and police misconduct were evident in many of the cases discussed herein. The cases of women wrongfully convicted contained numerous instances in which prosecutors suppressed evidence to secure convictions and police obtained confessions through questionable means. For prosecutors this mode of operation is often fueled by ambition, pride, or expediency and is intended to win the case at any cost. This type of deceit can easily prejudice a jury at the expense of the facts of the case. As the examples in this book demonstrate all too clearly, this behavior can lead to errors in the administration of justice and, ultimately, a wrongful conviction. Among police officers, a code of silence inhibits the detection of police brutality and corruption, making it difficult to detect police misconduct unless it is uncovered after a conviction.

Obviously these behaviors should not be tolerated. Often those involved receive little more than a proverbial slap on the wrist for actions that may have sent an innocent individual to prison. A logical conclusion would be to assume that the criminal justice system does not work. To a certain extent that is true, especially when roadblocks preclude the release of an innocent person. Too frequently once a wrongful conviction has been perpetrated, it may take years to remedy the error and gain the release of the innocent, if indeed the falsely convicted individual is ever released.

Neglected in much of the current wrongful conviction research are those factors that preceded the involvement of the innocent with the criminal justice system. A societal double standard for women that imposes greater responsibility for the care and protection of children enhances the risk of a hasty conviction in alleged child abuse cases. To the extent that some legislation is not gender-blind, the enforcement of those laws may unduly result in the arrest of women. A dearth of female police officers may also contribute to the wrongful arrest of women, although the impact of this is largely unknown.

When the sample of wrongfully convicted women was analyzed, the impact of race became readily apparent. African American women were significantly more likely than their white counterparts to be falsely convicted of drug offenses. Conversely, white women were significantly more likely than African American women to be wrongly convicted of child abuse. Furthermore, like their male counterparts, black women were overrepresented in the data on wrongfully convicted women. Despite making up approximately 13 percent of the US population, black women represented nearly 26 percent of the wrongful conviction cases in our sample.

An analysis of the sample also disclosed that factors other than those typically examined in the literature were present in a significant numerical minority of the female wrongful convictions. Although prosecutorial misconduct (over 40 percent) and police misconduct (30 percent) were the two most common factors associated with the wrongful conviction of women, over 28 percent of the cases included factors that were not specifically examined in this study. Thus, the greater diversity of offenses found in female false convictions is reflected in the greater diversity of factors associated with those cases.

Child Abuse and Wrongful Convictions

Of all of the offenses resulting in false convictions for women, only murder was more common than child abuse. Over one-fourth of the wrongful conviction cases involved some form of alleged child abuse. Particularly interesting is the substantial role played by witness error. The witness, typically an impressionable child who had been exposed to suggestive interviews by police and other child care advocates, was largely unable to sort out fact from fiction and would frequently testify to being the victim of sexually abusive behavior despite no physical evidence to corroborate the story. Some of the narratives told by the young witnesses included incidents that could not have occurred, but during the late twentieth century it was felt that children couldn't lie and that they had actually experienced some type of abuse. So prominent was this factor that it accounted for nearly seven of every ten cases appearing in the sample. No other factor came close to explaining wrongful child abuse convictions.

Racial differences were most evident among this category of cases. White women were dramatically overrepresented among those wrongfully convicted. Indeed, there was only a single child abuse case involving an African American woman. Such racial disparity begs the question: What accounts for the preponderance of white women among the child abuse wrongful convictions? Although the data do not permit a thorough analysis of this issue, the authors speculate that some of this disparity may result from a greater importance attached to lives of white children. In the prosecutor's quest to expedite the punishment for the perpetrator of this heinous act, haste takes precedence over a more systematic search for the truth and a false conviction ensues. Because a number of the wrongful convictions occurred during the hysteria associated with the belief that many child care facilities were sexually abusing children, factors other than race may account for some of the racial differences. Yet one could also legitimately inquire: Why did the child sexual abuse cases of the late twentieth century concentrate on child care facilities in which the children were predominantly white?

Murder and Manslaughter

The most common offense for which women were wrongfully convicted in our sample was murder and manslaughter. Prosecutorial misconduct was found in almost half of the erroneous convictions for this crime. Forensic errors, a minor contributor to child abuse false convictions, were present in 43 percent of the murder/manslaughter cases. Ineffective assistance of counsel was also a factor in nearly three out of ten cases, making it more common in murder/manslaughter wrongful convictions than child abuse wrongful convictions. Police misconduct was about equally important for both types of miscarriages of justice. Whereas police misconduct was present in 32 percent of the murders/manslaughters, it was found in 36 percent of the child abuses. Perhaps most interesting was the fact that almost a third of these cases involved factors not traditionally examined in the literature, suggesting the need to expand the number of variables analyzed in wrongful murder convictions involving women.

The race of the defendant in wrongful murder and manslaughter cases appeared to play a role as well. In particular, cases involving African American women frequently included a larger number of factors than those involving white women. Moreover, the relative importance of many factors varied by race. For instance, forensic errors were more likely to contribute to white wrongful convictions than to black wrongful convictions. Forensic errors were present in over half of the white cases but only slightly over 30 percent of the black cases. In contrast, police misconduct was more important in black false convictions (over half) than white false convictions (over 30 percent). False confessions, ineffective assistance of counsel, insufficient evidence to support a conviction, and prosecutorial misconduct were all more likely to be found in cases involving African American women than white women. Of these, prosecutorial misconduct was particularly prominent in black wrongful convictions. Nearly two thirds of the cases of wrongfully convicted African American women had been influenced by this factor. In contrast, the use of informants and perjury by criminal justice officials were present in similar quantities in erroneous convictions of black and white women in these cases.

Drug Offenses

An analysis of wrongful convictions involving drug offenses reveals several interesting findings. First, perjury by criminal justice officials and prosecutorial misconduct is more pronounced in these cases than in the other offenses resulting in erroneous convictions. More specifically, perjury was present in 85 percent of these cases and prosecutorial misconduct was a factor in 70 percent of these cases. Second, these wrongful convictions were dominated by nonwhite defendants. Of the twenty cases examined, 85 percent involved nonwhite women despite the fact that African Americans and whites report similar rates of drug use. Third, wrongful convictions for drug offenses resided primarily in Southern states. One should be cautious, however, not to misconstrue this finding. It would be fallacious to assume that wrongful drug convictions are only a problem in one region of the country. The failed drug bust in Tulia, Texas, heavily skewed this category of false convictions. The Tulia bust also strongly influenced the race of the defendant because it focused on the African American community in that city. Nevertheless, since most drug raids occur in the inner city where minorities are concentrated, it is reasonable to conclude that the bulk of the wrongful convictions will also originate from this group.

Of special import among these false convictions is the extent to which major violations of the law preceded the miscarriage of justice. As noted already, the vast majority of the cases included perjury by criminal justice officials and prosecutorial misconduct. However, one fourth of the wrongful convictions occurred as a result of police misconduct and the use of an informant with an incentive to lie. Of the major drug busts included in the investigation, three-fourths exclusively focused on the African American community, suggesting that racial discrimination is part and parcel of the enforcement of drug legislation. Only the Manatee, Florida, drug scandal was not specifically aimed at the black community.

Miscellaneous Offenses

We examined thirty-three false convictions that included miscellaneous offenses. Although a majority of these wrongful convictions were for property crimes, 18 percent involved violent crimes. The remaining cases represented a potpourri of offense categories, including filing a false police report, risk of injury to a minor (pornographic computer pop-ups by a substitute teacher), prostitution, computer fraud (creating a fake account on MySpace), a customs violation, criminal contempt, felony nonpayment of child support, perjury, obstruction of justice, and rendering criminal assistance. As evidenced from this enumeration of offenses, female wrongful convictions tend to be more diverse than those commonly associated with male wrongful convictions. Consequently, scholars in this area should greatly expand the number of factors they research when examining falsely convicted women.

Racial disparity again became evident among this category of wrongful convictions. Only among false drug convictions were African

American women more overrepresented. It thus appears that in many instances race and gender interact in such a way as to put black women at a greater disadvantage than their white counterparts.

Suggestions for Future Research

The generic study of wrongful convictions is fraught with incomplete and contradictory data. Regardless of the race/ethnicity and sex of the falsely convicted individual, important information is frequently unavailable, or the veracity of the data cannot be directly ascertained. This problem is particularly acute when researching older case files. Often the quality of the information varies from case to case. With the advent of the National Registry of Exonerations (NRE), this problem has been mitigated somewhat. However, because the NRE begins data collection with cases since 1989, earlier wrongful convictions remain more problematic. Unfortunately, these issues are inherent in all wrongful conviction scholarship and are not confined to investigations of falsely convicted women.

These problems notwithstanding, research on wrongly convicted women contains its own set of issues, arguably the most serious of which results from the greater involvement of women in less serious offenses. As noted, much of the focus on wrongful convictions has been on murder and sexual assault/rape, two male-dominated crimes. The more severe sanctions attached to the violation of these laws make them more attractive to those organizations that examine potential miscarriages of justice. Since women are less likely to be tried and found guilty for these violent crimes, they represent a much smaller proportion of those exonerated for murder and sexual assault/rape.

Because women are more likely to be convicted of property crimes and less serious offenses, their wrongful convictions are more likely to be forthcoming from those categories of crimes than are those of men. With a greater probability of probation, fines, or short sentences, their wrongful convictions tend to generate little interest from organizations seeking victims of false convictions. Furthermore, most of the wrongfully convicted women have limited financial means and thus don't have the resources to contest their verdict.[3] Absent financial support from outside sources, innocent women are unlikely to be exonerated. Thus, the use of national databases to examine female wrongful convictions will substantially understate the extent of the problem.

Though there are no easy solutions to this dilemma, future research should strive to go beyond the national databases and examine specific jurisdictions in depth to ferret out possible wrongful convictions that would otherwise never come to light. This would entail a more condensed time period, which would allow the investigator to ascertain information on the judge, attorneys, and jurors involved in the cases. It would also provide the possibility of ascertaining the circumstances that led to the arrest of the innocent. Although this approach would not necessarily be generalizable to other jurisdictions, it would facilitate the development of parameters for future scholarship. This approach could further elaborate those factors associated with female wrongful convictions that are not typically examined in the current literature.

If research is to be generated in this area, the public needs to be better informed about the significance of wrongfully convicted women. The introduction of the Women's Project at the Center on Wrongful Convictions at Northwestern University in 2012 represents an initial attempt to publicize women's wrongful convictions. Yet dissemination of this information must go beyond a single organization. Falsely convicted women must be willing to come forward to tell their stories, and the media must be encouraged to cover these events. Both regional and national conferences devoted to this theme must be heavily publicized. In turn, scholars of wrongful convictions must be willing to turn their attention to some of the less spectacular cases of judicial injustice if our understanding of female wrongful convictions is to flourish. Professional organizations such as the American Society of Criminology, the Academy of Criminal Justice Sciences, and the American Sociological Association could facilitate this process by promoting research in this area and by publishing special journal issues devoted to this topic. At annual meetings of these and other professional organizations, workshops and sessions focusing on female wrongful convictions should be regularly offered to further stimulate interest.

Although racial differences in male wrongful convictions have been examined by some scholars, the emergence of racial differences in female wrongful convictions has yet to receive the same level of scrutiny. The huge racial disparity found in false convictions involving drugs and child abuse reveal the importance of race. While the disproportionate number of African American women found in wrongful drug convictions may be a function of the war on drugs and its preoccupation with activities in the inner city and minority neighborhoods, the overrepresentation of white women in wrongful child abuse convictions has yet to be adequately addressed. Is this the result of the greater importance attached to the lives of their white victims, or is there some other reason (or set of reasons) associated with this disparity?

Conclusion

If this book can open dialogue about and increase awareness of the topic of wrongfully convicted women, then it will be worth the effort that it took to write it. Unless one has experienced those circumstances, it is difficult to fully comprehend the devastating effect of a false conviction. The women in this book have overcome the nightmare of prison and have tried their best to put their lives back together despite all they have forfeited in the process. They have lost time, relationships, jobs, and often just about everything that was important to them. The women who came forward to tell their stories deserve our admiration for their efforts. Julie Baumer, Joyce Brown, Audrey Edmunds, Gloria Killian, and Ginny LeFever have taken their cause to heart and, no matter its level of difficulty, continue to share their narratives so that others can better comprehend how these miscarriages of justice arise and how to prevent others from suffering a similar fate.

The study of female wrongful convictions is both a challenging and rewarding field. Because so little has been written about this area, the field represents an excellent opportunity for conducting original research. That a double standard still exists for women is clearly evident from recent legislation attempting to limit the health choices of women by pre-dominantly conservative white male politicians. Future research needs to approach the study of wrongfully convicted women with the same rigor that other areas of criminal justice have received. The rewards are there for those who choose to investigate this fascinating subject.

Notes

1. During the Salem witch trials, some men were also accused of being warlocks.

2. Published annually by the Federal Bureau of Investigation, the *Uniform Crime Reports* include twenty-nine offenses dichotomized as Part I and Part II offenses. The Part I offenses are considered to be the more serious crimes. This group includes four violent crimes (murder and nonnegligent manslaughter, rape, aggravated assault, and robbery) and four property crimes (burglary, larceny-theft, motor vehicle theft, and arson). Part II offenses include simple assault, forgery and counterfeiting, fraud, embezzlement, stolen property, prostitution and commercialized vice, and offenses against the family and children, among others. Interestingly, despite a protracted war on drugs, drug crimes are listed under the rubric of Part II offenses.

3. Poverty is not unique to cases involving wrongfully convicted women. Regardless of gender or race/ethnicity, most defendants who have been falsely convicted are indigent.

Appendix A:
Methods

The purpose of this investigation was to identify factually innocent women who were wrongfully convicted in the United States since the 1970s. This decade was selected because it represents a contemporary period in which false convictions were beginning to receive some attention from scholars. Furthermore, the women's movement of the 1960s had made researchers more cognizant of women's issues, including that of wrongful convictions. From a pragmatic standpoint, there were few researchable cases of wrongful convictions available prior to this time. Because the case identification phase of the research was ended in 2013, the sample contains known wrongful convictions through 2012.

To maximize the probability of identifying only those cases in which convicted defendants were factually innocent, the authors used the same databases employed in an earlier study of wrongly convicted African American men. Consequently, five databases and one website were scrutinized for cases in which women were the victims of wrongful convictions. The databases used in this investigation include those from the Center on Wrongful Convictions, the Innocence Project, the Death Penalty Information Center, forejustice.org, and the National Registry of Exonerations. In addition, *Justice Denied*, an electronic and print magazine devoted to false convictions, was examined to supplement information obtained from the databases.

The Center on Wrongful Convictions (CWC), which is housed at Northwestern University, has tracked wrongful convictions since its inception in 1998. Its list of known exonerations from the United States is broken down by state and the District of Columbia. Unfortunately, with the exception of wrongful convictions in Illinois and a few other well-documented cases, little usable information about the innocent individuals is available from this website. Nevertheless, the large number of exonerations enumerated there provides a useful point of departure for the identification of false convictions of women. Of particular interest is the recent inclusion of the Women's Project (WP) at the CWC. Launched on November 29, 2012, the WP has an ambitious agenda that includes the legal representation of selected clients and "plans to monitor potential cases of wrongfully convicted women across the country, facilitate the sharing of information about these cases, and educate the public about relevant issues" (Center on Wrongful Convictions, n.d. a). The WP will initially focus on cases in which false confessions and circumstantial evidence contributed to the miscarriage of justice.

In 1992 Barry Scheck and Peter Neufeld founded the Innocence Project (IP) at the Benjamin N. Cardozo School of Law at Yeshiva University in New York. The IP became an independent nonprofit organization in 2004 while retaining its ties to the law school. Accepting only cases in which DNA evidence is present, the IP has played a major role in the over 300 exonerations to date. All DNA exonerations are cataloged by last name and contain case narratives. The IP's contribution to our research project is limited by its exclusive focus on DNA cases, which are less likely to include wrongly convicted women.

Because women are seldom sentenced to death, the Death Penalty Information Center (DPIC) proved to be the least useful database. Nonetheless, it is an excellent source of information on falsely convicted death row inmates. Founded in 1990, the DPIC is a national nonprofit organization that was ranked among the top criminal justice nonprofits in 2011 by *Philanthropedia*, which evaluates nonprofit organizations according to the quality of their work. The website also received a five-star rating from Multimedia Educational Resource for Learning and Online Teaching, a program at the California State University system that provides free peer-reviewed materials for teaching and learning. Enumerating 150 death row exonerations since 1973 in March 2015, the list contains limited amounts of information about each case.

Created by Hans Sherrer in 1997, the forejustice.org website disclosed over 5,400 wrongful convictions from 114 countries in March 2015. A majority of those cases are from the United States, with some dating back to the early seventeenth century. Although the cases are sorted by location (state and District of Columbia) and last name, the sheer volume of cases makes extracting the appropriate ones labor intensive. The older cases frequently contained links to other sources that are no longer operable. Although this source provided little specific data on each case, it proved to be a wealth of information for identifying potentially relevant cases.

The most recent entrant to the field of wrongful convictions is the National Registry of Exonerations (NRE), a joint venture of the law schools at Northwestern University and the University of Michigan. Launched in May 2012, the NRE includes all known exonerations in the United States since 1989. In excess of 1,500 individuals appeared on its list of wrongful convictions as of March 2015. Though each case includes a detailed narrative of the events, only about 8 percent of the exonerees are women. Nevertheless, the information for each case is among the most thoroughly researched data currently available. Because the database begins with exonerations in 1989, however, it neglects a number of earlier cases required for this investigation.

First published on February 8, 1999, *Justice Denied* magazine is devoted exclusively to the dissemination of information on potential and known false convictions. Available as an electronic and print magazine, the website has an index of every article published since its inception. The articles were used to supplement information obtained from previous websites and to identify potential references for follow-up.

Computer searches were conducted to locate additional materials not previously found. In particular, the authors found relevant magazine articles and newspaper stories as well as court cases. When feasible the authors contacted journalists and attorneys familiar with the cases to reconcile contradictory information and/or incomplete data. To identify potential wrongful convictions that were excluded from the six websites, the authors also conducted several computer searches using generic terms (e.g., wrongful conviction, false conviction, innocent) to discover individuals who were factually innocent though not formally cleared of their crimes.

When we first discussed the creation of this book, it was decided that interviews with women who had been wrongfully convicted would be central to the purpose of the book. At first, this seemed like a daunting task. It is one thing to find sources and write summaries of what happened in a case; it is something entirely different to locate women who are willing to relive what is often a very painful ordeal. We were fortunate that some women were willing to come forward and share their stories. They are the true heroes of this book. Without their narratives, the book would not be nearly as authentic as a source to raise awareness about the problem of wrongful convictions.

Coauthor Mitch Ruesink was assigned the task of coordinating and interviewing the individuals whose stories appear in the box inserts. We appreciate the assistance many provided during this data collection phase. In particular, we are indebted to Karen Daniels and Judy Royal from the Women's Center at the Center on Wrongful Convictions at Northwestern University. Their untiring efforts paved the way for us to interview some of the women who were wrongfully convicted. After hearing about our proposed book, Karen and Judy were kind enough to contact three women whom they believed would be willing to share their experiences. We are also thankful to the three women—Julie Baumer, Ginny LeFever, and Audrey Edmunds—who were willing to be interviewed for this book.

During the course of this research, Mitch also found two other women who agreed to discuss their false convictions. Through Mitch's conversation with Kimberly Jenkins-Snodgrass, cofounder and president of JAB Productions, he was able to secure an interview with Joyce Brown. Another interview came about in a fortuitous way. While telephoning the Action Committee for Women in Prison, he spoke to Gloria Killian on his first call; after learning about our project, she consented to be interviewed as well.

Data collected from each case included the following: (1) defendant race; (2) state of jurisdiction; (3) victim race (for violent crimes); (4) charge(s); (5) sentence; (6) year convicted; (7) year released (if appropriate); (8) year cleared (if appropriate); (9) time spent in jail/prison; (10) age when convicted; (11) age when released; (12) whether DNA evidence was used to clear the defendant; and (13) factors contributing to the false conviction. In addition, personal information on the defendant was actively sought to better comprehend the circumstances surrounding the wrongful conviction.

Race was dichotomized into white and back categories with remaining racial groups classified as "other." An "unknown" category was used for cases in which the racial identity of the defendant and victim could not be determined. There were nine charge categories and a miscellaneous category. Cases involving any type of child abuse (e.g., neglect, sexual abuse of a minor) were classified under the generic heading of "child abuse." This category occasionally included cases in which the injury was serious enough to culminate in the death of the child *if* the defendant was not charged with murder or manslaughter. After the charges had been ascertained, the cases were then classified according to the most serious charge.

Thirteen different classifications were employed to differentiate sentence severity. Sentences that fell outside these categories were placed under the heading of "other." There was also an "unknown" category for those cases in which the sentence could not be determined. Years in jail/prison included any time detained in jail while awaiting trial as well as time spent in prison after being convicted. This variable included eight categories and a category for those cases in which it was impossible to calculate the length of incarceration. The defendant's age when convicted and the age when released were based on the actual age of the wrongly convicted individual. These variables also contained a category for cases in which the age was unknown. Age released included three additional categories: not released, not applicable (for defendants who never were incarcerated), and executed.

Because the use of DNA testing to exonerate innocents has been steadily increasing since its debut in 1989, the sample was further analyzed to ascertain the extent to which this method of exoneration has been used in female wrongful convictions. The variable was dichotomized into yes or no categories for each case.

Finally, nine of the most common factors associated with wrongful convictions were examined: (1) prosecutorial misconduct, (2) police misconduct, (3) eyewitness errors, (4) forensic errors, (5) perjury by criminal justice officials, (6) false confessions, (7) use of informants/snitches, (8) ineffective assistance of counsel, and (9) insufficient evidence to support the conviction. In addition, a miscellaneous category ("other") was included for factors that fell outside of these categories. For examples illustrating the types of behavior encompassed by these categories the reader is referred to Chapter 1.

Some limitations of the sample should be noted. Because the sample was drawn from national wrongful conviction databases, it contains only those false convictions that have received public scrutiny. Many wrongful convictions undoubtedly never come to the attention of these databases. A lack of financial resources by the defendant may preclude a reinvestigation of the circumstances of suspicious cases. Similarly, plea bargains involving little or no imprisonment may seem attractive to an innocent woman with limited financial resources as well as an innocent woman with a checkered past. Thus, there is no incentive to pursue the case. Moreover, organizations such as the Innocence Project, which investigates only those cases in which DNA evidence is present, will tend to overlook wrongfully convicted women since women are less likely than their male counterparts to be incarcerated for crimes in which DNA evidence is available.

These limitations notwithstanding, the final usable sample of 163 represents the largest collection of cases involving wrongly convicted women currently available. As observed in Chapter 1, most research on wrongful convictions has concentrated on cases in which men were falsely convicted. Consequently, the occasional wrongfully convicted woman appeared to be an anomaly in this field. The 163 cases located in this research are considerably larger than the 42 cases examined by

Mitch Ruesink and Marvin Free in 2005. Moreover, the sample is larger than the 138 cases identified by Zieva Konvisser (2012) in her investigation of wrongful convictions since the beginning of the twentieth century. Furthermore, the sample includes wrongful convictions from thirty-two states and one military court. The cases are geographically dispersed among all regions of the country with the largest number appearing among two of the most populated states—Texas (twenty-six cases) and California (twenty-three cases). It should additionally be noted that the variety of offenses as well as the numerous factors leading to the miscarriage of justice suggest that the sample contains a stratified population of false convictions. Thus, the sample exhibits considerable diversity despite the inherent limitations of the data collection process.

Appendix B:
Case Narratives

Code for race/ethnicity
B = Black or African American
H = Hispanic or Latina
NA = Native American or American Indian
W = White or Caucasian
Blank = Race unknown

A.B. (Indiana) (Juvenile)

A juvenile female (identified only as A.B.) was accused of the equivalent of criminal harassment of her former school principal on MySpace.com. She had used expletives to criticize the former principal over the school policy on body piercings. In 2006 she was found guilty of the accusation and received nine months probation. A.B. was cleared of the charges in 2008. Very little information is available on this case since it involved a minor.

Adams, Sandra (New York) (B)

This case involved an off-duty police officer who allegedly brandished a gun at a motorist who stopped suddenly in front of her. The police lineup was "suggestive" since Sandra Adams was the only African American in the lineup and she was the only individual wearing a police uniform. In addition, the driver of the vehicle had used different names as he had nearly thirty traffic citations, including twenty-two license suspensions. Because Sandra's car had dark tinted glass, it is unlikely that the complainant could have seen what she was doing in her car. Moreover, because she had injured her right shoulder, it is improbable that she could have lifted a gun in a threatening matter even if she had one. After being convicted of the misdemeanor of second-degree menacing in 1998, Sandra was suspended from the police force and eventually fired. When acquitted after a bench trial the following year, she was reinstated.

Amero, Julie (Connecticut) (W)

Julie Amero was a thirty-seven-year-old pregnant substitute teacher who was charged with risk of injury to a child when pornographic pop-ups began appearing on her computer. Although not formally sentenced after being found guilty, she could have received up to forty years in prison for the four felony counts. During the trial an expert witness for the prosecution falsely testified that pop-ups had to be the result of Julie visiting pornographic websites. The expert witness later admitted that he had not checked for malware. An overzealous prosecutor refused to allow expert testimony during the trial that would have proved Julie was innocent. On June 6, 2007, a judge overturned her conviction and on November 21, 2008, Julie agreed to plead guilty to a lesser charge of disorderly conduct and pay a $100 fine to avoid any further litigation against her.

Amirault, Violet (Massachusetts) (W)

Convicted in 1987 at the age of sixty-one, Violet Amirault was part of the child sex scandal at Fells Acres Day School. She spent eight years of her twenty-year sentence incarcerated for child sex abuse, which never occurred. Officially cleared in 1998, three years after her release from prison, Violet was wrongly convicted based largely on child witnesses who had been coaxed through suggestive interviewing techniques. Prosecutorial misconduct also contributed to her false conviction.

Baker-Krofft, Nancy (Oregon)

One of the "sloppy housekeeper" cases discussed in Chapter 2. Nancy Baker-Krofft was wrongfully accused of second-degree criminal mistreatment of a child, a felony. The main issue in this case was whether her unkempt house constituted a withholding of "necessary and adequate physical care" from her eleven-year-old son. She was cleared in 2010 when the Oregon Supreme Court ruled that the trial judge had erroneously interpreted the criminal statute.

Bala, Susan (North Dakota) (W)

In 2005 fifty-year-old Susan Bala was convicted of a total of twelve counts of criminal activity, including money laundering, bribery, and conspiracy for allegedly running an illegal gambling operation. She was instructed to pay $19 million in restitution. In 2007 she was released after having served eighteen months of her twenty-seven-month sentence. She was officially cleared of all charges that same year.

Banks, Victoria Bell (Alabama) (B)

This is an especially interesting wrongful conviction involving a nonexistent infant. Initially indicted for capital murder, the charge was subsequently reduced to manslaughter. Victoria Banks was sentenced in 2000 to fifteen years in prison and was still in prison as of 2011, the last time information was made publicly available. A coerced false confession, police misconduct, prosecutorial misconduct, and insufficient evidence to support a conviction (there was no body and no one ever saw the alleged infant) contributed to her false conviction. *See also:* Dianne Bell Tucker.

Barnes, Larita (Oklahoma) (W)

Larita Barnes and her father, Larry Barnes, were wrongfully convicted in 2008 of selling methamphetamine. The drug informant lied about the transaction after being told what to say by a police officer and an ATF agent. Larry and Larita served about one year in prison before being released on July 2, 2009, when their convictions were overturned and their charges were dismissed as a result of a probe into police corruption in the Tulsa Police Department. Nearly fifty individuals have been released from prison or had their charges dropped because of legal issues surrounding police corruption in that police department.

Baumer, Julie (Michigan) (W)

Julie Baumer was taking care of her nephew for her sister, an incarcerated drug addict, when she was accused of violently shaking six-week-old Philipp, causing brain injuries and blindness. Her attorney failed to pursue any other possible causes of Philipp's injuries during the first trial, and Julie was convicted of child abuse by a jury in September 2005. She received a ten- to fifteen-year sentence. While in prison, Julie convinced some new attorneys to work on her case. Philipp's brain scans were reviewed by doctors who specialized in pediatric head injuries and they unanimously concluded that he had suffered from venous sinus thrombosis, a form of childhood stroke. The judge reversed Julie's conviction and in December 2009, after four years in prison, she was released. Twice the prosecution tried to appeal this ruling, and both times the courts denied the appeals. After the prosecution decided to try Julie again, her lawyers presented evidence that proved the injuries were caused by a medical condition. Julie was found not guilty and exonerated on October 15, 2010.

Beridon, Cheryle (Louisiana) (B)

Wrongfully incarcerated for the unlawful distribution of $125 of heroin in 1979, Cheryle Beridon was given a life sentence based on the false testimony of an informant, the district attorney (a former lover who threatened to incarcerate her when they broke up), and an investigator. At the time of her conviction the penalty for this crime in a federal court was only fifteen years, but at the state level, she received a life sentence. Through efforts by the NAACP, the governor commuted her sentence to forty-five years, making her eligible for parole after having served twenty years of her sentence. She was paroled in November 2000 after serving six months at a halfway house. Conditions of her parole included a monthly visitation fee of $53 for her parole officer for the next twenty-one years. In July 2003 Cheryle was finally exonerated when she received a full pardon from the governor, which restored her civil rights sans the right to bear arms.

Briggs, Brandy (Texas) (W)

Brandy Briggs was wrongly accused of shaking her infant son so severely that he eventually died. The prosecution's forensics expert, Patricia Moore, was later criticized for her "defective and improper work" and had on numerous occasions interpreted her work to help police and prosecutors secure their cases. Her defense attorney failed to present expert and personal witnesses during the trial and did not realize that when Brandy's son arrived at the hospital, he had a breathing tube inadvertently inserted into his stomach instead of his lung for over 40 minutes. It was later determined that Brandy's son died of complications related to a urinary infection contracted shortly after birth. She served six years of a 17-year prison sentence before being released in 2005. Brandy was exonerated the following year.

Brim, Dominique (Michigan) (Juvenile)

Dominique Brim was falsely convicted of stealing $1,300 in clothes and assaulting a security guard on April 15, 2002, when an older woman used her identity after being captured and questioned by the police. Because Dominique was fifteen years old at the time of the conviction, she was tried in a juvenile court. She was convicted based on erroneous eyewitness testimony. The woman responsible for the crime was a twenty-five-year-old friend of her sister. Prior to sentencing, a review of the store's surveillance tape revealed that Dominique was not the perpetrator. When the store notified the prosecutor and the defense attorney, the juvenile judge vacated her conviction and immediately released her. Prosecutors never charged the actual perpetrator with the crime since the eyewitnesses had identified Dominique as the shoplifter/assailant.

Brown, Joyce Ann (Texas) (B)

Mistakenly identified as one of two armed women who robbed a fur store and killed the owner, thirty-three-year-old Joyce Ann Brown turned herself in when she read in the local newspaper that she was identified by the wife of the deceased as one of the perpetrators. When her trial began in October 1980, the wife of the owner and an informant with a history of lying identified Joyce as an accomplice of the woman who killed the owner. The defense presented evidence in the form of a time card and witnesses who documented that Joyce was at work the day of the crime with the exception of thirty-six minutes when she was at lunch. Prosecutors argued that thirty-six minutes was sufficient time for her to commit the lethal robbery. On October 23, 1980, Joyce was convicted of murder and aggravated robbery and sentenced to twenty-five years to life in prison. The following year one of the actual perpetrators, Renee Michelle Taylor, was arrested and provided an affidavit that Joyce was not her accomplice. A subsequent investigation revealed that the prosecution knew the informant had a previous conviction for lying to a police officer but had not disclosed that fact to the defense. Later Taylor revealed that another woman who physically resembled Joyce was her partner in the crime. On November 1, 1989, Joyce's conviction and sentence were overturned by the Texas Criminal Court of Appeals and she was released two days later. Charges against her were dismissed in February 1990.

Bryan, Sheila (Georgia) (W)
Wrongfully convicted in September 1998 of murdering her eighty-two-year-old mother when her automobile became engulfed in flames after crashing down an embankment, Sheila Bryan was found guilty on the basis of outdated forensic evidence regarding arson. Although the Georgia Supreme Court overturned her conviction in June 1999, the state retried her case. Armed with additional information on faulty ignition switches and the testimony of an arson expert, the defense was able to show that the vehicle was not deliberately set on fire using an accelerant. In January 2000, after three hours of deliberation, a jury found Sheila not guilty on all charges.

Bullington, Mashelle (California) (W)
Mashelle Bullington, a mother of two and drug user, was convicted of second-degree burglary with personal use of gun enhancement in 1995 and sentenced to four years and four months in prison. The actual perpetrator of the crime had paid her for the use of her automobile, and she was asleep inside the vehicle when the incident occurred. Mashelle completed her sentence in 1999. In 2008 her conviction was overturned and the charge was reduced to a misdemeanor.

Bunch, Kristine (Indiana) (W)
On March 4, 1996, a jury found Kristine Bunch guilty of arson and murder for a trailer fire in which her three-year-old son, Anthony, died. She received concurrent sentences of sixty years for murder and fifty years for arson. Exculpatory evidence from the Bureau of Alcohol, Tobacco, and Firearms was withheld from her defense counsel during her trial. The evidence used to convict her of deliberately setting a fire using an accelerant was later shown to be faulty. Assisted by the Center on Wrongful Convictions, Kristine had her conviction reversed by the Indiana Court of

Appeals on March 21, 2012. After the Indiana Supreme Court declined to reverse that decision, prosecutors finally dropped the charges in December 2012. Kristine spent sixteen years in prison for a crime that she did not commit.

Butler, Sabrina (Mississippi) (B)
Teenage Sabrina Butler arrived at a Columbus, Mississippi, hospital during the early morning hours of April 12, 1989, with her nine-month-old infant, Walter, whom she had been unable to resuscitate. After giving several conflicting accounts of the events preceding Walter's death, she eventually signed a statement in which she admitted to hitting him in the stomach when he refused to stop crying. Referring to an autopsy that disclosed internal injuries and peritonitis, the prosecution used her statement to accuse her of murder when the trial began on March 8, 1990. Sabrina's defense, who called no witnesses on her behalf, attempted to refute the prosecution's claim by arguing that the injuries were the result of her futile attempts to revive Walter. After six days of testimony and deliberation, the jury convicted Sabrina of murder, and she was subsequently sentenced to death, making her the only woman on death row in Mississippi. On August 25, 1992, the Mississippi Supreme Court vacated the verdict, and in December 1995 Sabrina went on trial again. This time the defense presented testimony from neighbors who observed Sabrina's clumsy attempt to resuscitate her infant son. One of her neighbors also unsuccessfully attempted to perform CPR on Walter. A medical expert additionally testified that the injuries disclosed by the autopsy could have been the result of these attempts to revive the victim. The physician who had performed the autopsy later admitted that his examination of the body was not as complete as it could have been. On December 17, 1995, after a succinct deliberation, the jury acquitted Sabrina.

Cacy, Sonia (Texas) (W)
When her 76-year-old uncle, with whom she shared a dwelling, died as a result of a house fire, Sonia Cacy was charged with arson murder and sentenced to ninety-nine years in prison in 1993. The only evidence that suggested that the fire was deliberately set was testimony from a toxicologist that clothing fragments from the victim contained gasoline. Yet an autopsy indicated that Sonia's elderly uncle died of a probable heart attack and was responsible for the fire when his lit cigarette ignited a blaze. He had on fifty previous occasions set small fires due to his careless behavior, important information not mentioned to the jury. Later examinations of the evidence failed to reveal the presence of an accelerant. Released on parole after almost six years, Sonia has yet to be exonerated of this crime as of mid-2014.

Cagle, Deon Kay (Nevada)

In March 1997, twenty-nine-year-old Deon Cagle was accused of soliciting sex from an undercover police officer in Reno, Nevada. She was sentenced to four to ten years in prison but was not incarcerated so that she could receive treatment for HIV. In September 1998 the Nevada Supreme Court overturned her conviction based on the finding of insufficient evidence. Deputy District Attorney Mary Petty later admitted that the evidence used to convict her was circumstantial. She was scheduled to go to trial again on October 26, 1998, in Washoe County District Court on another prostitution charge although no information was available on that case.

Canen, Lana (Indiana) (W)

In November 2002 ninety-four-year-old Helen Sailor, who lived in an apartment complex for the elderly, disabled, and handicapped, was found strangled to death. For almost a year the case was unsolved until a twenty-eight-year-old mentally challenged resident, Andrew Royer, was questioned by the police and admitted to the murder and robbery. The following year police, acting on a tip, interrogated another resident, forty-four-year-old Lana Canen. Although she denied any wrongdoing, a nearby resident who frequently used drugs informed the police that Lana had confessed her involvement in the crime. A police officer with little training in fingerprint analysis later erroneously concluded that a fingerprint found in the victim's apartment matched that of Lana. Andrew and Lana were found guilty of murder and sentenced to fifty-five years behind bars. In 2010, after a new attorney was appointed to represent Lana, additional evidence was found to suggest her innocence. An independent fingerprint examiner and the Indiana State Police Crime Lab concluded that the fingerprint in the victim's apartment did not match Lana's. The detective who testified that the fingerprints matched recanted his statement after receiving additional training in fingerprint analysis. Finally, on November 2, 2012, her conviction was overturned, the charge was dismissed, and she was released from prison after serving eight years and two months for a crime she did not commit.

Carbone, Patricia (Pennsylvania)

Patricia Carbone was poor and lived in public housing. While walking home from a bar on June 9, 1984, she was accosted by a twenty-six-year-old stranger who forced her into his car, drove her to a secluded area, and raped her. In her struggle to get away, Patricia removed a knife she had in her purse and stabbed him. He later died of the wounds from their encounter. The following year she was convicted of first-degree murder for the death of her assailant, Jerome Lint. During the trial the murder victim was portrayed as a religious, churchgoing, family man who didn't drink (although an autopsy revealed alcohol in his blood). Although not permitted to testify during the trial, an off-duty policewoman had an altercation with Patricia's rapist several weeks earlier when he attempted to pick her up. Patricia, who had been forced to live in public housing since her divorce from an abusive spouse in 1981, declined a plea bargain for manslaughter, believing that she would be found innocent due to self-defense. When it became apparent that she would never be released from prison unless she confessed to some crime, she eventually pleaded guilty to third-degree murder and was released in 1998 after serving twelve years of her sentence. She was put on probation for seven years as a condition of her new conviction.

Cash, Cynthia (Texas)
In 1999 forty-six-year-old Cynthia Cash was wrongfully convicted of felony injury to a child (shaken baby) and sentenced to seven years in prison. Although the four-month-old infant exhibited swelling of the brain and retinal hemorrhaging that is associated with shaken baby syndrome, she had received three vaccinations a few hours earlier, which could have contributed to her death. The baby had no external injuries or bruises at the time of death. The assistant coroner of Harris County, Texas, at the time was Patricia Moore, who had been previously chastised for failing to follow procedures and presenting evidence in a light favorable to prosecutors in cases involving children. In 2008 her original autopsy was quietly changed from "homicide" to "cause of death undetermined." The original listing of "evidence of trauma" was also changed to "no evidence of trauma" after a neurologist testified that the infant died of a fatal reaction to the vaccinations (anaphylactic shock). Cynthia was incarcerated for all seven years of her sentence.

Chase, Melissa Lee (Georgia) (W)
This case involved a sexual liaison between a twenty-eight-year-old teacher, Melissa Lee Chase, and a sixteen-year-old former student. In 2007 Melissa was found guilty of sexual assault and given a sentence of ten years in prison and five years of probation. During the bench trial, the student admitted that she was the aggressor in the sexual encounter. The prosecutor objected to the testimony on the grounds that a sixteen-year-old girl could not give consent and so the testimony was invalid, and the judge concurred. The Georgia Supreme Court ruled that the trial judge was in error in not allowing consent as a defense against a charge of sexual assault, as sixteen is the minimum age at which one can give consent. In 2009 Melissa was released after having served twenty-two months of her sentence.

Christoph, Dayna (Washington) (Juvenile)
Dayna Christoph came from an extremely difficult family background. She had been physically and sexually abused at an early age by an uncle,

cousins, and her mother's boyfriends. In addition, she was mentally disabled and emotionally disturbed. While living with her adoptive mother, she was accused of sexually abusing her younger sister. Recalling memories from her own childhood and feeling pressure to admit to the crime, Dayna falsely confessed. Her defense attorney devoted a total of 105 minutes (including the court appearance) to her case and failed to review her medical records, talk to her caregivers, or talk to her sister. The police never bothered to interview Dayna's sister, either. She was convicted in 1995 at the age of seventeen of molesting her sister. In January 2000 a Superior Court judge dismissed the conviction and referred to the case as a "manifest injustice." A false confession, police misconduct, and ineffective assistance of counsel contributed to her wrongful conviction.

Clemmons, LaTanya (Washington) (B)

Thirty-four-year-old LaTanya Clemmons was sentenced to five years in prison in 2010 after being convicted of two counts of first-degree rendering criminal assistance. LaTanya was accused of driving her boyfriend, Darcus Allen, to a hotel to facilitate his escape from the police and paying for a bus ticket to Arkansas. Darcus was accused of being the getaway driver after the fatal shooting of four police officers by LaTanya's brother, Maurice Clemmons. LaTanya was eligible for early release for good behavior and a sentence reduction as she was a first-time, nonviolent offender. On June 22, 2012, the Washington Court of Appeals officially overturned her conviction, citing insufficient evidence. The majority opinion noted, "The evidence does not show that Allen ever told LaTanya or her relatives that he knew Maurice intended to kill the police officers and helped or offered help in committing the murders."

Colomb, Mary Ann (Louisiana) (B)

For ten years local police harassed Mary Ann Colomb and her family in Church Point, Louisiana. Characterized by bogus traffic stops and false accusations of drug trafficking, this harassment culminated in a drug raid on their residence on October 22, 2001. An Acadia Parish Sheriff's Office task force found seventy-two grams of crack cocaine and a loaded pistol on the premises. Both items belonged to her daughter's future husband, who was residing in the guest bedroom. Although he acknowledged ownership, his statement was rejected by the authorities. On May 15, 2002, the case was moved to the federal system and finally on March 31, 2006, Mary Ann and three of her sons were convicted of various drug-related crimes and were incarcerated while awaiting sentencing. When it was discovered that jailhouse informants had lied to receive sentence reductions, the jury verdict was set aside on August 31, 2006. Shortly thereafter the US Attorney's Office decided not to retry the case and the charges were dismissed.

Cooper, Marilyn Joyce (Texas) (B)

Marilyn Joyce Cooper was one of twelve women who were falsely convicted of drug-related crimes in a drug raid in Tulia, Texas, on July 23, 1999. She spent three days in jail and was fined $2,000 plus court costs and attorney fees when she agreed to plead guilty to secure a more lenient sentence. Undercover agent Tom Coleman provided perjured testimony that led to her 2000 conviction. Prosecutorial misconduct also contributed to this miscarriage of justice. In 2003 she was pardoned by the governor. *See also:* Vickie Fry, Denise Kelly, Etta Kelly, Laura Ann Mata, Finaye Shelton, Lawanda Smith, Yolanda Smith, Ramona Strickland, Kizzie White, Alberta Stell Williams, and Michelle Williams.

Cox, Teresa Lynne (California) (W)

This is a child sexual abuse case from Kern County, California, involving multiple defendants. In October 1984 twelve-year-old Teresa Modahl informed her father that she had been sexually abused by her uncles. Following this accusation, police and social workers interviewed Teresa, her brother, and two sisters using highly suggestive interview techniques that have been shown to produce false accusations. Within a short period of time the accusations spread to include Teresa Cox. In May 1985 she was convicted of three counts of lewd and lascivious conduct based on the testimony of one of the young girls and two jailhouse snitches. Despite any physical evidence to corroborate these accounts, Teresa received a ten-year sentence. After serving half of her sentence she was placed on probation and became a registered sex offender in 1990. Teresa was finally exonerated in 2000 when her attorney petitioned to have the charges dismissed and the prosecutor concurred.

Craig, Sandra (Maryland) (B)

In 1981 Sandra Craig, mother of three, opened the Clarksville day care facility. In 1985 her son, Jamal Craig, was accused of being sexually inappropriate with a five-year-old girl at his mother's day care center. Although the charges were eventually dropped, his mother and Jamal were accused the next year of physically and sexually abusing some of the children. As more children came forward, Sandra was ultimately charged with thirteen counts of child abuse and Jamal (whose case was later dismissed) was ultimately charged with eight counts of child abuse. She was sentenced to concurrent ten-year prison sentences in 1987. The main evidence against her were the unfounded and contradictory statements provided by young children from the day care facility who had been extensively interviewed using suggestive and inappropriate techniques. Two years after being sentenced, the Maryland Court of Appeals reversed her conviction. In 1991 prosecutors decided not to retry the case. Prosecutorial misconduct (withholding exculpatory evidence) and eyewitness error contributed to this miscarriage of justice.

Crosby, Karla (Oregon) (W)

When Karla Crosby's seventy-six-year-old mother arrived at the emergency room in 2001, she was suffering from dehydration, malnutrition, and dementia. She also suffered from bed sores and had trouble swallowing. Karla had been taking care of her mother in the family's dilapidated house and was trying to keep her from being sent to a nursing home as per her mother's wishes. She died a week later of complications from bacteria that had poisoned her bloodstream and adversely affected major organs. During the trial the defense portrayed Karla as a hard-working woman who came from a family that took care of their own kin. Even the prosecutor admitted that she never intended to kill her mother. As a result the jury acquitted her of murder-by-abuse charges. Nevertheless, Karla was convicted of two counts of first-degree manslaughter and sentenced to ten years in prison in 2002. In March 2007 the Oregon Supreme Court overturned the manslaughter conviction after she had served five years of her sentence.

Croy, Norma Jean (California) (NA)

This was a racially charged wrongful conviction case in northern California involving several Native American youth. On July 14, 1978, twenty-three-year-old Norma Jean Croy became enmeshed in a situation involving her brother, Patrick "Hooty" Croy, and several other young people. When an altercation broke out between Patrick and the owner of the Sports and Spirits Liquor Store in Yreka, California, Norma Jean drove off with her brother and three others while the police pursued their vehicle. When the youth sought refuge at her grandmother's cabin in the Rocky Gulch area, authorities fired shots, with one bullet hitting Norma Jean in the back. By the time the shooting subsided over 200 rounds had been fired by law enforcement but only 6 rounds had been fired by the youths. One police officer was killed during the standoff. For her alleged involvement in the incident, Norma Jean was found guilty by an all-white jury of conspiracy to commit murder and sentenced to life in 1979. Her conviction was overturned in 1996 by a federal court, although she was not released until February 7, 1997, when the prosecution decided not to retry her case and dismissed the charges. Norma Jean was incarcerated for nineteen years before receiving her freedom.

Cummings, Susan (Washington) (W)

In 1983 sixteen-year-old Susan Cummings was accused of letting two men into the apartment of her eighty-eight-year-old neighbor, Christine Zacharias, a Russian immigrant. Convicted in 1985 of being an accomplice to the two men who beat, sexually assaulted, and strangled the neighbor during a botched burglary, Susan's conviction was primarily based on the testimony of two informants who received reduced sentences in return for their statements. While continuing to maintain her innocence, she signed a false confession in an attempt to receive a more lenient sentence. Although the two informants later recanted their testimony, Susan remained in prison. After serving nineteen years, she was released when the governor granted her a pardon in 2004. Almost fifty current and former employees at Susan's prison wrote letters on her behalf.

Cunningham, Connie (Washington) (W)
Connie Cunningham was one of the Wenatchee 43 defendants convicted of child sex abuse during the zenith of the hysteria. She was falsely convicted of molesting her three children when her husband, Henry, who has a bipolar disorder, falsely confessed to the accusations and implicated both himself and his wife in sex acts with their children. Forty-three years old at the time of conviction, Connie was sentenced to forty-six years and six months in prison in 1994. After serving approximately three years, the Washington Court of Appeals overturned her conviction in May 1997 and a new trial was ordered. Prosecutors declined to retry her case and she was released. *See also:* Carol Doggett, Idella Everett, Susan Everett, Sharon Filbeck, Barb Garass, Doris Green, Donna Hidalgo, Laura Holt, Sadie Hughes, Linda Miller, and Cherie Town.

DeJac, Lynn (New York) (W)
Lynn DeJac was the first woman in the United States to be exonerated based on DNA evidence. She was charged with strangling her thirteen-year-old daughter, Crystallynn Girard, after a night of heavy alcohol consumption. The medical examiner incorrectly determined that the girl had died of strangulation and indicated the cause of death as a homicide. (It was later determined that Crystallynn had died of a cocaine overdose.) A twice-convicted felon, Wayne Hudson, testified at the trial that Lynn had confessed to the murder. (In return for his testimony, his third felony was reduced to a misdemeanor and he received probation instead of a mandatory heavy sentence under the state's three strikes law.) DNA from the victim's bedroom later revealed that one of Lynn's ex-boyfriends (Dennis Donohue) was present with Crystallynn when she died. Because he had been given immunity for his testimony against Lynn, he could not be tried for this crime. However, only seven months after Crystallynn's death, he was charged with killing another person and eventually sentenced to twenty-five years in prison. He is also suspected in another strangulation death.

Dill, Grace (California) (W)

Grace Dill was one of the so-called Pitts Seven who were falsely accused of running a child sex ring in Bakersfield, California, in the mid-1980s. This case represents one of a number of similar incidents that allegedly occurred in that county during the latter part of the twentieth century. Grace was convicted in 1985 and sentenced to 405 years in prison. She was incarcerated for six years prior to her release in 1990. In 1991 she was exonerated of any wrongdoing. Prosecutorial misconduct and false eyewitness testimony from the children contributed to this wrongful conviction. *See also:* Colleen Dill Forsythe, Gina Miller, and Marcella Pitts.

Doggett, Carol (Washington) (W)

Carol Doggett was accused of being part of the alleged child sex abuse ring in Wenatchee, Washington. She and her husband, Mark, were arrested in December 1994 and charged with 1,000 counts each of child rape. In May 1995 they were convicted and received identical sentences of ten years and ten months for their involvement. The Washington Court of Appeals overturned their convictions in December 1997. The court expressed concern over the use of hearsay evidence, the trial judge's denial of the use of an expert regarding recovered memories, and in particular the highly suggestive and coercive manner in which the children had been interrogated. Released on bail on June 11, 1998, the Doggetts were officially cleared on May 17, 2000, when all charges were dismissed. *See also:* Connie Cunningham, Idella Everett, Susan Everett, Sharon Filbeck, Barb Garass, Doris Green, Donna Hidalgo, Laura Holt, Sadie Hughes, Linda Miller, and Cherie Town.

Dove, Gayle (Texas) (W)

Forty-year-old Gayle Dove worked as a teacher at the East Valley YMCA day care center in El Paso, Texas, in June 1985 when a four-year-old attending the facility used an inappropriate word at home. Upset by this behavior, the parents looked toward the day care center as the source of this problem. Gayle and another teacher were later implicated in a child sex abuse investigation. Seven or eight children testified during the trial via videotape. The children, who had been interviewed using suggestive techniques, testified that they had been kissed and fondled by twelve-foot-tall monsters, were forced to eat body parts, had pencils inserted in their rectums, were forced to watch animal killings, were spanked with a plastic tennis racket, were threatened to be eaten if they told anyone what occurred, and so on. During her first trial in 1986 Gayle received three life sentences plus sixty years for her alleged involvement. She was convicted of six counts of child abuse. The verdict was overturned in March 1987 because the jury had reviewed evidence that was never admitted at trial. At her new trial that same year she was convicted on a single count of aggravated battery and sentenced to twenty years. In April 1990 the charges against her were formally dismissed. *See also:* Michelle Noble.

Drew, Lori (California) (W)

A fake account on MySpace was created by forty-six-year-old Lori Drew, her daughter, and a family friend in 2006. The name on the account was "Josh Evans," supposedly a teenage boy. After establishing the account, "Josh" contacted thirteen-year-old Megan Meier, a former friend of Lori's daughter. Pretending to befriend her, he later sent Megan a menacing message that read, "The world would be a better place without you." The emotionally disturbed girl subsequently committed suicide. Using the Computer Fraud and Abuse Act of 1986, a statute intended for computer hackers, federal prosecutors successfully convicted Lori on three counts of misdemeanor computer fraud in 2008. They sought a maximum sentence of three years in prison and a fine of $300,000. In contrast, probation officials recommended that Lori be given a one year probation and $5,000 fine. Prior to sentencing, federal judge George Wu vacated her conviction in 2009, citing that the federal statute was too vague and, if the conviction wasn't vacated, "one could literally prosecute anyone who violates a terms of service agreement."

Edmunds, Audrey (Wisconsin) (W)

Seven-month-old Natalie Beard was under the care of Audrey Edmunds, a stay-at-home mom who babysat children from the neighborhood. On October 16, 1995, Natalie was especially fussy and had little interest in her bottle. When she later became unresponsive, Audrey called 911. Natalie never recovered and died soon thereafter. When a subsequent autopsy disclosed extensive brain damage, Audrey was accused of shaking the infant. On March 19, 1996, she was charged with first-degree reckless homicide. Prosecutors had several medical experts at the trial testify that this was a prototypical case of shaken baby syndrome (SBS). On November 26, 1996, Audrey was convicted and sentenced to eighteen years behind bars. It was not until 2003 that the Wisconsin Innocence Project agreed to examine her case. Since her conviction, emerging medical research on SBS raised serious questions regarding the earlier diagnosis. Finally, on January 31, 2008, the Wisconsin Fourth District Court of Appeals overturned her conviction and ordered a new trial. Audrey received her freedom on February 6, 2008, and later that year charges against her were dismissed, bringing to an end over eleven years of wrongful incarceration.

Eklof, Karlyn (Oregon) (W)

Accused of murdering James Salmu, a man who had assisted her and her three children when she had become temporarily homeless, Karlyn Eklof was brought to trial in September 1995. One of her defense lawyers was later disbarred for drug use, alcohol abuse, and embezzlement. During the trial the prosecution was allowed by the judge to refer to her as a "biker bitch" despite objections from her counsel. Nine days of eight-to-ten-hour interrogations eventually resulted in a false confession based on a story concocted by the police in which she "admitted" to stabbing Salmu repeatedly with a plastic knife. Although trial testimony suggested that the victim had been stabbed as indicated in her "confession," the victim's body had been pierced with bullets. Two of the witnesses for the prosecution were previous suspects in Salmu's death, yet the prosecution failed to disclose this fact to the jury. Nor did the prosecution mention that both witnesses testified to avoid prosecution themselves. Karlyn was convicted of aggravated murder, aggravated felony murder, and abuse of a corpse by a jury and on December 12, 1995, received two consecutive life sentences plus 202 months, although the case involved a single murder. After exhausting her state appeals, she filed a habeas petition in federal court in Portland. Her petition was unsuccessful and she remains imprisoned at Coffee Creek Correctional Facility.

Eldridge, Yvonne (California) (W)

Yvonne Eldridge and her husband ran a foster home in Walnut Creek, California, and became one of the first to participate in a program for medically fragile infants (e.g., babies born with drug addictions or life-threatening conditions such as AIDS). In 1988 Nancy Reagan recognized them as one of the "Great American Families" for their work with foster children. But in 1993 Yvonne was accused of harming infants in her care and convicted in 1996 of two counts of felony child abuse. She was subsequently sentenced to forty months in prison. Incorrectly accused of having a psychological disorder known as Munchausen syndrome by proxy, her wrongful conviction was heavily influenced by ineffective assistance of counsel. After two new attorneys agreed to accept her case, they were successful in showing that the children's ailments could be best understood medically and were not the result of any harm inflicted by Yvonne. On January 8, 2003, prosecutors finally dismissed the charges against her.

Elizondo, Mary Ann (Texas)

Mary Ann Elizondo had two sons from her former marriage: ten-year-old Robert and eight-year-old Richard. When Robert, who lived with his father and his stepmother, got into trouble at school for sexually inappropriate behavior, he accused his mother and her husband (Joe) of sexual abuse while visiting them. His eight-year-old brother later alleged the same. In September 1983, the two were arrested and charged with sexual abuse of a child. Joe received a life sentence for aggravated sexual assault and was fined $10,000. Mary Ann received a twenty-year sentence for the sexual abuse of Robert and entered a plea of no contest to a second charge which resulted in a thirty-five-year concurrent sentence. After turning seventeen in 1988, Robert learned of the consequences of his allegations. He immediately recanted his story, saying that his biological father had threatened to physically punish him if he didn't testify against his mother and stepfather. Richard also recanted his testimony, although he denied any pressure from his father to testify. In 1991 Mary Ann was released on parole, and charges against her were officially dropped in November 2005. Joe received his freedom in 1997 after charges against him were dropped.

Ellison, Ella Mae (Massachusetts) (B)

Accused of driving the getaway vehicle in a robbery/murder in Roxbury, Massachusetts, in 1973, Ella Mae Ellison was convicted of first-degree murder and four counts of armed robbery in 1974. She received two concurrent life sentences for her alleged involvement. This false conviction resulted from the withholding of exculpatory evidence from her defense counsel and the perjury of two informants who were actual participants in the crime. A mother of four with no criminal background, Ella Mae was wrongfully incarcerated for four years.

Engberg-Lehmer, Teresa (Iowa) (W)

Although Teresa Engberg-Lehmer and her husband, Joel, were initially charged with first-degree murder of their three-month-old son, they pleaded guilty to involuntary manslaughter to avoid long sentences. The state medical examiner, Dr. Thomas Bennett, labeled the death a homicide and attributed the cause to shaken baby syndrome. Due to improprieties, he unexpectedly resigned from his position approximately two weeks after Teresa and Joel pleaded guilty to the lesser charge on October 2, 1997. Each received a sentence of fifteen years in prison. On September 28, 1998, they were released from custody when the state moved to vacate the convictions and dismiss the charges. The prosecutor reached this decision after reviewing new evidence suggesting that the infant died of sudden infant death syndrome and after two pathologists testified that there was no evidence to support a conclusion of shaken baby syndrome. False or misleading forensic evidence contributed to their wrongful conviction.

Everett, Idella (Washington) (W)

One of the Wenatchee 43 cases, Idella Everett was wrongfully accused and convicted of raping children and aiding and abetting her husband, Harold, in the sexual abuse of ten children. Child Protective Services removed their five children and concealed medical evidence that their children were not sexually abused. Idella was developmentally disabled and illiterate, and she was unable to provide aid in her own defense. Originally accused of 1,586 counts of rape and 4,836 counts of aiding and abetting sexual abuse, she was convicted of two counts of child molestation on November 30, 1994, and sentenced to four years and eight months in prison. Harold, who was also mentally disabled and illiterate, was convicted on December 5, 1994, of eight counts of rape and molestation and received a twenty-three-year sentence. Their convictions were overturned by an appeals court in September 1998. Charges were dismissed and they were released later the same year. *See also:* Connie Cunningham, Carol Doggett, Susan Everett, Sharon Filbeck, Barb Garass, Doris Green, Donna Hidalgo, Laura Holt, Sadie Hughes, Linda Miller, and Cherie Town.

Everett, Susan (Washington) (W)

This is another of the so-called Wenatchee 43 cases in which individuals were falsely convicted of child sex abuse. Susan Everett was initially charged with multiple counts of child rape and molestation. She agreed to plead guilty in 1995 to the charge of communicating with a minor for immoral purposes to avoid a possible long-term prison sentence. After spending a few months in prison she was released on October 16, 1995, when the reliability of her accuser was questioned. In 2001 Susan moved to a new town, where she began working in a hotel. Police misconduct, false confession, and inappropriate evidence gathering by police, state social workers, and therapists contributed to this wrongful conviction. *See also:* Connie Cunningham, Carol Doggett, Idella Everett, Sharon Filbeck, Barb Garass, Doris Green, Donna Hidalgo, Laura Holt, Sadie Hughes, Linda Miller, and Cherie Town.

Filbeck, Sharon Ann (Washington) (W)

Another case involving an individual who was falsely convicted of nonexistent sex crimes against children in Wenatchee, Washington. To avoid being charged with a more serious offense, Sharon Filbeck, who had a diminished level of intelligence, confessed to a charge of second-degree assault in 1995. Although she received probation, Sharon later recanted her story, stating that she was coerced by the police into providing a false confession. Inappropriate evidence gathering by police, state social workers, and therapists contributed to her wrongful conviction. Police misconduct and a false confession also played roles. *See also:* Connie Cunningham, Carol Doggett, Idella Everett, Susan Everett, Barb Garass, Doris Green, Donna Hidalgo, Laura Holt, Sadie Hughes, Linda Miller, and Cherie Town.

Forsythe, Colleen Dill (California) (W)

Colleen Dill Forsythe is another individual from the Pitts Seven case in Kern County, California. Accused of being involved in a child sex ring in Bakersfield, she was originally charged with conspiracy; forcible, lewd, and lascivious acts on children under fourteen years of age; use of children for purposes of pornography; child endangerment; and assault. With no physical evidence to corroborate the children's stories, Colleen was sentenced to 373 years in prison in 1985. During the trial, the prosecutor knowingly coerced children into making false accusations. She was released in 1990 at the age of thirty-two and cleared of all wrongdoing the following year. *See also:* Grace Dill, Gina Miller, and Marcella Pitts.

France, Geneva (Ohio) (B)

On November 10, 2005, a drug sting operation known as Operation Turnaround led to the arrest of twenty-six people in Mansfield, Ohio. One of those accused of selling illicit drugs was an African American woman named Geneva France. After refusing to accept a plea bargain, the twenty-two-year-old mother of three was convicted on drug charges largely based on the tainted testimony of an informant, Jerrell Bray, and a longtime agent from the Drug Enforcement Administration, Lee Lucas. Geneva served sixteen months of her ten-year sentence before being released after Bray confessed to lying about the drugs. She contends that the false accusations were in response to her earlier rejection of him as a suitor.

Frederick, Sherri (Texas) (B)

At the age of thirty-three years, Sherri Frederick already had a criminal record with convictions for drugs and prostitution, so when the police arrested her for allegedly dropping a packet containing 0.27 gram of crack cocaine on September 12, 2010, she accepted a negotiated plea for six months in jail. There was only one problem: the substance did not contain any narcotics. Sherri spent five months of her six-month sentence in jail until the Houston Police Department crime laboratory finally tested the substance and reported its findings on February 23, 2011. She was released on March 10, 2011. On September 28, 2011, the Texas Court of Criminal Appeals vacated her conviction and on February 24, 2012, her charge was dismissed. Sherrie received $40,000 in compensation for her wrongful conviction in March 2012.

Fritz, Judith (Pennsylvania) (W)

Thirty-five-year-old Judith Fritz was incorrectly identified as the driver of a vehicle in which a thirty-three-year-old man, Randy Schnyder, was killed as he was thrown from the car during a vehicular rollover. In addition, thirty-year-old Robert Pribila was riding in the car. All three individuals had consumed alcoholic beverages and used cocaine prior to the accident. Based on their positions in the car, a pathologist incorrectly testified that he believed Judith was the driver. After being convicted of vehicular homicide, DUI, and drug possession, she hired attorney Frederick Fanelli, who discovered a witness who saw Schnyder get into the driver's seat that night. During her second trial, Judith was acquitted of vehicular homicide and DUI since she wasn't the driver. Nevertheless, she was convicted of drug possession and sentenced to two years of probation and given a $2,000 fine.

Fry, Vickie (Texas) (B)

Wrongly convicted in 2000 when a drug raid in Tulia, Texas, went awry, twenty-seven-year-old Vickie Fry received five years of probation for her alleged wrongdoing. An undercover agent, Tom Coleman, provided perjured testimony during these trials. Prosecutorial misconduct also contributed to this false conviction. In 2003 Vickie was pardoned by the governor of Texas. *See also:* Marilyn Joyce Cooper, Denise Kelly, Etta Kelly, Laura Ann Mata, Finaye Shelton, Lawanda Smith, Yolanda Smith, Ramona Strickland, Kizzie White, Alberta Stell Williams, and Michelle Williams.

Garass, Barb (Washington) (W)

Another wrongful conviction stemming from alleged child sex abuses in Wenatchee, Washington. Barb Garass and her common-law husband, Ralph Gausvik, were both charged on July 9, 1995, of sexually abusing their three children, ages seven, eleven, and fourteen. Although innocent, she accepted an Alford plea to avoid a long prison sentence and was sentenced to twenty-six months. Ralph, who also maintained his innocence, was convicted on November 2, 1995, of three counts of child abuse. His conviction was overturned on November 6, 1998. Charges against him were dismissed and he was later released. Police misconduct and the use of suggestive and coerced interrogation techniques on child witnesses by police, state social workers, and others contributed to this miscarriage of justice. *See also:* Connie Cunningham, Carol Doggett, Idella Everett, Susan Everett, Sharon Filbeck, Doris Green, Donna Hidalgo, Laura Holt, Sadie Hughes, Linda Miller, and Cherie Town.

George, Cynthia (Ohio) (W)

Fifty-one-year-old Cynthia George was accused of complicity to commit aggravated murder. Prosecutors theorized that she conspired with her lover, John Zaffino, to kill her former lover, Jeff Zack, who was threatening to take his baby away from her. In 2005 she was convicted of murder and given a life sentence. Her conviction was based entirely on circumstantial evidence. On March 27, 2007, after serving sixteen months in prison, Cynthia was released when her conviction was overturned due to insufficient evidence.

Golebiewski, Elizabeth (Ohio) (W)
Accused of killing her nineteen-month-old daughter, Tennille, after sexually assaulting her using a toy gun, Elizabeth Golebiewski was convicted in 1983 of involuntary manslaughter and felonious sexual penetration. She was sentenced to life in prison at the age of twenty-three years and served twenty-seven years of her sentence before being released in 2010. Ethel Jones, a jailhouse snitch, testified that Elizabeth confessed while in county jail, although records suggest that the two were never alone together. In fact, there are sworn affidavits from seven inmates who knew Jones, testifying that she admitted to lying about Elizabeth's confession. The time of death of her child was also incorrectly estimated as the victim's body temperature was not recorded until almost half an hour after arriving at the emergency room. Her ex-husband, Terry, who was the first person arrested for the crime, was probably the actual perpetrator. Elizabeth has yet to be officially exonerated of this offense and was under supervision for five years after release.

Gonzalez, Kathy (Nebraska) (H)
Kathy Gonzalez is one of six individuals (three women and three men) who were falsely convicted of the murder and rape of an elderly widow in 1985 in Beatrice, Nebraska. To avoid a potential death sentence, she cooperated with the prosecutor and falsely implicated herself and one other in the crime. For her assistance she was allowed to plead guilty to a lesser offense and received a ten-year sentence in 1990. In 1994 Kathy was released from prison after serving almost five years. She was formally pardoned by the state of Nebraska in January 2009 after the lone perpetrator was identified through DNA testing. The six wrongly convicted individuals in this crime are sometimes referred to as the Beatrice Six. *See also:* Debra Shelden and Ada JoAnn Taylor.

Grafton, Margorie (California) (W)
This is one of many wrongful convictions from Kern County, California, in which innocent individuals were convicted of child sex abuse. Margorie Grafton was found guilty of child sex abuse in 1985. She was sentenced to sixteen years in prison. During the trial the defense was not permitted to have medical examinations performed on the young boys who accused her and her codefendants of child sex abuse. Moreover, the defense was not allowed to use the testimony of Dr. Roger Mitchell, a psychologist, who ran

tests on Margorie and one other defendant and concluded that they didn't fit the profile of a sexual predator. After serving five years of her sentence, she was released in 1990. Prosecutorial misconduct and eyewitness error (coerced by the prosecutor) contributed to this miscarriage of justice.

Granda, Araceli Cremata (Florida)
In 1976 Araceli Cremata Granda was falsely convicted of a customs violation in federal court in Florida. She was cleared in 1978 when a court ruled that the trial judge had erroneously interpreted the law regarding customs violations.

Gray, Paula (Illinois) (Juvenile) (B)
A seventeen-year-old mentally disabled woman named Paula Gray was questioned intensively by authorities investigating the brutal slaying and rape of a white couple from a Chicago suburb. During a grand jury investigation, Paula falsely confessed to the crime and implicated four African American men who were later convicted and falsely imprisoned. She recanted her testimony later at a preliminary hearing. Sentenced to fifty years in prison for murder and ten concurrent years for perjury, she was released after nine years in exchange for falsely testifying again against three of the male defendants. In 1996 Paula and the so-called Ford Heights Four were exonerated when DNA testing excluded them as the perpetrators. The DNA analysis also identified the actual perpetrators of the offense. In 2001 Paula's conviction was overturned, and the following year she received a pardon based on innocence from the governor of Illinois. She received $4 million in a civil lawsuit from Cook County for her wrongful conviction.

Green, Doris (Washington) (W)
This is another individual from the Wenatchee 43 who was caught up in the child sex abuse hysteria during the last two decades of the twentieth century. While babysitting, Doris Green found a card left by Bob Perez of the Wenatchee Police Department requesting an interview. Although she was told she was being called in as a witness, after several hours of police interrogation, Doris falsely confessed to having sex with one of Laura's children. She was ultimately charged with raping and molesting seven children and in 1995 was convicted of three counts of rape and molestation and sentenced to twenty-three years. Doris was released on bond on July 15, 1999, while awaiting the outcome of her appeal. Later that year an appeals court overturned her conviction, and charges against her were dismissed in January 2000. Contributing to her false conviction were police misconduct, false confession, and the use of manipulative and coercive interviewing

techniques when questioning the children. *See also:* Connie Cunningham, Carol Doggett, Idella Everett, Susan Everett, Sharon Filbeck, Barb Garass, Donna Hidalgo, Laura Holt, Sadie Hughes, Linda Miller, and Cherie Town.

Hall, Jennifer (Missouri) (W)

In 2001 Jennifer Hall was wrongly convicted of arson and sentenced to three years in prison. Although convicted in 2001 she did not spend any time in jail until 2003 when the Missouri Court of Appeals denied a second appeal. Jennifer, an epileptic, was eventually placed in a maximum security facility, which increased her number of seizures from once every eight to ten months to two to three times weekly. While incarcerated, she lived in proximity to an inmate who was in prison for murder. In 2004, at the age of twenty-three, Jennifer was released and the following year she was cleared of her conviction. A false confession (requested by her defense counsel), forensic errors (an electrical short-circuit was overlooked), and ineffective assistance of counsel contributed to this false conviction.

Hall, Phyllis Elaine (Florida) (W)

Sentenced to twenty-five years to life in 1985 for first-degree murder, Phyllis Hall was cleared of the charges by the Florida District Court of Appeal in 1986. According to the court, "The entire position of the State is based on stacking inference upon inference." Evidence revealed that Phyllis's lover, Albert Freer, committed the murder. Although she was with Freer before and after the murder, there is no evidence connecting her to the crime. Phyllis was released in 1986 after serving one year of her sentence.

Hansen, Lisa (Michigan) (W)

Twenty-five-year-old Lisa Hansen was fired from her job as a receptionist at a Grand Rapids, Michigan, salon in 2006. She was accused of stealing the company's deposit, an accusation she denied. She failed a polygraph test when the operator badgered her and accused her of lying while being examined. Her court-appointed attorney recommended that she plead guilty to the charge of embezzlement, although the judge refused to accept her plea and put her in a diversion program. For her alleged theft of the deposit, Lisa received a sentence of forty hours of community service plus a $400 fine to cover the cost associated with the required diversion program. Almost one year later, the bank found the missing deposit, which had become lodged in a depository mechanism, exactly where Lisa claimed to have put it.

Harden, Tanya (West Virginia) (W)

Tanya Harden was wrongly convicted of killing her abusive husband, Danuel Harden, in 2004 after a night of extreme violence in which she was severely beaten, sexually assaulted, and threatened with death. Her spouse also threatened the life of her son when he placed a shotgun to the boy's head. She was sentenced to life imprisonment in 2007. The state contended that this was not a case of self-defense since she could have exited the trailer when it appeared that Danuel may have passed out due to excessive alcohol consumption. In 2009 the Supreme Court of Appeals of West Virginia ruled that Danuel's death was, in fact, a case of self-defense and that she was under no obligation to flee her own home given the circumstances. Tanya was wrongfully incarcerated for four years and nine months.

Hennen, Debbie (West Virginia) (W)

Fifty-two-year-old Debbie Hennen was found guilty of fraud and fined $100 plus court costs in February 2010 for allegedly falsifying a part-time state employee's time card. During her trial she explained that the employee was actually a salaried worker and that the time sheet was merely a requirement for him to receive a check and did not necessarily correlate with the actual hours worked during that period. For practical reasons she had chosen to break down his total salary into twelve-month increments and there was no intent to deceive the state regarding his work record. In fact, Debbie stated that she had come into her office during her vacation to complete the time sheet to ensure that he would get paid on time. In September 2010 a circuit court judge ruled that there was no evidence to support a fraud conviction and overturned the case.

Hidalgo, Donna Carol (Washington) (H)

A Wenatchee 43 case involving a Hispanic woman named Donna Hidalgo who was a home health aide and orchard worker. Arrested by Bob Perez of the Wenatchee Police Department on 416 counts of child rape of four half-siblings, Donna pleaded guilty to a lesser charge of one count of incest in 1995 to avoid a more protracted sentence. She received a fourteen-month sentence as a result. Although she later recanted her confession, stating that she was coerced by the police to confess, she was not released until completing her sentence in 1996. Police misconduct, false confession, and the use of manipulative and coercive techniques while questioning child witnesses were responsible for this false conviction. *See also:* Connie Cunningham, Carol Doggett, Idella Everett, Susan Everett, Sharon Filbeck, Barb Garass, Doris Green, Laura Holt, Sadie Hughes, Linda Miller, and Cherie Town.

Hill, Christina (Massachusetts) (Juvenile)

Wrongly convicted of poisoning two-year-old Henry Gallop, a foster child who lived with her family, seventeen-year-old Christina Hill was found guilty of second-degree murder in 1990. The main evidence used against her during the first trial was an alleged confession made in 1987 to a friend, Leslie Limehouse, and subsequently published in a 1989 *Boston Herald* story by reporter Michelle Caruso. During the second trial it was disclosed that Caruso lied to Limehouse when she informed her that Christina accused her of the child's death and that if she didn't implicate Christina she was going to be blamed for the crime. Witnesses confirmed that Limehouse later admitted that she fabricated the account, although she was afraid to retract her story for fear of being charged with perjury. After less than thirty minutes of deliberation, the jury acquitted Christina of the murder in 1991.

Holt, Laura (Washington) (W)

This is another Wenatchee 43 case in which an innocent individual was falsely convicted of child sex abuse. Laura Holt pleaded guilty to sexually abusing her daughter and son after an intense police interrogation. Her confession, which was coerced by the police, resulted in a forty-year prison sentence in 1994 for child rape. Laura was released from prison in October 1999 after accepting a plea agreement. Police misconduct and a false confession contributed to this wrongful conviction, as did the use of manipulative and coercive interviewing techniques when questioning the child witnesses. *See also:* Connie Cunningham, Carol Doggett, Idella Everett, Susan Everett, Sharon Filbeck, Barb Garass, Doris Green, Donna Hidalgo, Sadie Hughes, Linda Miller, and Cherie Town.

Hubbard, Donna Sue (California) (W)

This is another case from the Kern County, California, child sex abuse scandals of the late twentieth century. Donna Sue Hubbard became a suspect when a paid informant stated that David Duncan (another suspect) had told him that she had received money for allowing others to molest her son, Richie. At the trial, two young boys (Richie and another boy identified as "Billie") accused Donna Sue of involvement in a child sex abuse ring. A third alleged victim (six-year-old James) could not identify her. An examination by Kern County's child abuse expert disclosed no signs that Richie had been molested. Investigators used coercive and highly suggestive interview techniques to secure the accusations against her. In March 1985 at the age of thirty, Donna Sue was convicted of twenty felony counts of child molestation and sentenced to one hundred years in prison. She was incarcerated for ten years before gaining her release after the California Supreme Court reviewed her case in 1995. That same year Donna Sue was exonerated when prosecutors dismissed the charges against her.

Hughes, Sadie (Washington)

Thirty-two-year-old Sadie Hughes, one of the Wenatchee 43, pleaded guilty to one count of first-degree child molestation and received a sentence of five years and eight months in 1995. Sadie, who is severely mentally challenged, was originally charged with multiple counts of rape and molestation of ten children. She later recanted her confession, stating that it was coerced. Sadie was eventually released from prison early based on time served. *See also:* Connie Cunningham, Carol Doggett, Idella Everett, Susan Everett, Sharon Filbeck, Barb Garass, Doris Green, Donna Hidalgo, Laura Holt, Linda Miller, and Cherie Town.

Jacobs, Sonia (Florida) (W)

Sonia ("Sunny") Jacobs was in the back of a green Camaro parked at an I-95 rest stop. Her two young children accompanied her in the back seat. In the front seat sat her boyfriend, Jesse Joseph Tafero, an ex-con and his prison pal, Walter Rhodes. When the automobile was approached by a Florida Highway Patrol trooper and another law enforcement official, gunshots were fired, and the two officers were killed. While attempting an escape, the suspects were eventually captured at a roadblock. Sonia was charged with first-degree murder even though she had no gunpowder residue on her hands and she had not been allowed to exit the car after the murders. The judge, a former Florida trooper who had a miniature electric chair on his desk, gave Sonia the death penalty despite the jury's recommendation for a life sentence. In return for his testimony, Rhodes, the actual shooter, was allowed to plead guilty to second-degree murder and receive a life sentence. Taferno, who also received the death penalty, was executed in 1990. In 1981, Sonia's sentence was commuted to life by the Florida Supreme Court and in 1992 she was released after accepting a plea of second-degree murder in which she was not required to admit guilt. The 1996 ABC movie of the week, *In the Blink of an Eye*, chronicled her wrongful conviction. Sonia was wrongfully incarcerated for sixteen years, eight months, and twenty-nine days. The jailhouse informant who testified that she had confessed to the shootings later recanted her story.

Jernigan, Rachel (Arizona) (H)

A short Hispanic woman with acne robbed the Bank of America in Gilbert, Arizona, in September 2000. Five eyewitnesses, including the bank teller whom she allegedly robbed, identified thirty-one-year-old Rachel Jernigan as the perpetrator. Before her trial commenced, there were at least two additional bank robberies in the area committed by a short, Hispanic-looking woman who matched the description of Rachel. FBI agents who investigated these incidents were aware of this but alerted neither the prosecution nor the defense of the similarity between the two women. In March 2001 Rachel was found guilty of armed robbery based on the eyewitness accounts and some grainy surveillance video provided by the bank. She was sentenced to fourteen years in prison plus five years of supervised release. In 2008 Juanita Rodriguez-Gallegos confessed to the bank heist for which Rachel had been convicted. Rachel was wrongfully incarcerated for seven years and three months.

Joseph, Malenne (Florida) (B)

Malenne Joseph was wrongly convicted of felony criminal mischief in 2010 after three witnesses identified her as the woman who had vandalized a house in 2007 after a dispute with her employer over payment. One of the witnesses to misidentify her had not seen the actual perpetrator, a woman whom he had subcontracted to do the painting, for nearly three years. Twenty-seven-year-old Haitian-born Malenne Joseph, a mother of three, was cleared when the actual perpetrator was located. Although never formally sentenced, she spent three months in jail. Because the statute of limitations had expired, the woman responsible for about $10,000 in damage was never prosecuted. In addition to eyewitness error, lax police work and ineffective assistance of counsel contributed to this avoidable miscarriage of justice.

Kelly, Betsy (North Carolina) (W)

Betsy Kelly and her husband, Bob, ran the Little Rascals day care center in Edenton, North Carolina. After initial complaints of child abuse naming Bob as the perpetrator, the police notified parents and suggested that they take their children to therapists to determine whether they had been abused. As the hysteria grew, so did the number of alleged incidents of child sexual abuse. Overall, ninety children accused twenty adults of 429 instances of child molestation and satanic abuse as false memories were implanted into the minds of the children by therapists who believed that the events actually occurred. Eventually seven individuals were arrested as a result of these allegations. While awaiting her trial, Betsy spent two years in jail. Recognizing the futility of going to trial, she pleaded no contest to thirty counts of child abuse and received a seven-year sentence. After serving approximately a year in prison, she was released on parole. Because she didn't contest her charges, she was never officially exonerated of the charges. *See also:* Kathryn Dawn Wilson.

Kelly, Denise (Texas) (B)

Twenty-nine-year-old Denise Kelly was one of twelve women wrongfully convicted of drug-related crimes resulting from the Tulia, Texas, drug sting on July 23, 1999, in which undercover agent Tom Coleman provided perjured testimony during the trial. Also contributing to this miscarriage of justice was prosecutorial misconduct. Incarcerated for one year, five months, and twenty-four days, Denise received a pardon from the governor of Texas in 2003. *See also:* Marilyn Joyce Cooper, Vickie Fry, Etta Kelly, Laura Ann Mata, Finaye Shelton, Lawanda Smith, Yolanda Smith, Ramona Strickland, Kizzie White, Alberta Stell Williams, and Michelle Williams.

Kelly, Etta (Texas) (B)

This case represents another miscarriage of justice resulting from the July 23, 1999, Tulia, Texas, drug raid. Twenty-three-year-old Etta Kelly, one of twelve women caught up in the scandal, received a three-year deferred sentence for her alleged involvement. To secure convictions, undercover agent Tom Coleman provided perjured testimony during these trials. Prosecutorial misconduct additionally contributed to Etta's false conviction. *See also:* Marilyn Joyce Cooper, Vickie Fry, Denise Kelly, Laura Ann Mata, Finaye Shelton, Lawanda Smith, Yolanda Smith, Ramona Strickland, Kizzie White, Alberta Stell Williams, and Michelle Williams.

Kemmerer, Trenda (Texas) (W)

After a hung jury during the first trial, Trenda Kemmerer was found guilty of felony murder on October 24, 2001, in the death of ten-month-old Christina Dew, whom she had been babysitting. She was accused of violently shaking the infant. The medical examiner, Patricia Moore, who was later released from her position for her dubious findings in other trials, had modified her report at the recommendation of the prosecutor to implicate Trenda in the death of the little girl. Until the medical examiner's report was changed, police had suspected Christina's mother or her sixteen-year-old son, who shared a room with Christina. An investigation by Child Protective Services had previously cleared Trenda of any neglect or abuse. Despite passing two polygraph tests, Trenda was found guilty of first-degree murder and sentenced to fifty-five years in prison during her retrial. Immediately after the autopsy, the child's mother had Christina cremated, thereby making it impossible to conduct additional examinations of the body. The district attorney who prosecuted her case was later released for corruption during his tenure in the department. Trenda remains in prison today.

Killian, Gloria (California) (W)

An elderly couple were robbed of their silver on December 9, 1981. The husband was killed, although his wife survived a shot in the head. An anonymous phone call to the police suggested that Stephen DeSantis and

Gary Masse were responsible for the crime. After Masse was convicted and sentenced to life without parole in May 1983, he offered to assist authorities with the case in return for a more favorable sentence. The prosecution concurred, and Masse implicated DeSantis and Gloria Killian, a former law student with no prior record. In 1986 during Gloria's trial, Masse testified that she was the mastermind of the operation and had "cased" the house before their arrival. During the trial the wife recalled a woman coming to the house but could not identify Gloria as that person. The main evidence used to convict Gloria was the testimony provided by the actual perpetrator, who lied to the jury when he said that he wasn't receiving anything in return for his statement. On February 26, 1986, Gloria was sentenced to thirty-two years to life for her alleged involvement. Massey's cooperation with authorities resulted in a twenty-five-year sentence in lieu of life without parole. Ten years later documents were discovered in which Masse admitted in a letter to the prosecutor that "I lied my ass off for you people." In March 2002 the 9th Circuit US Court of Appeals finally overturned Gloria's conviction, citing false testimony. She was released in August of that year and her charges were dismissed the following month.

Kinge, Shirley (New York) (B)
Wrongly convicted in November 1990 for burglary, arson, hindering prosecution, criminal possession of stolen property, and forgery, fifty-five-year-old Shirley Kinge had no prior criminal record and was seen by many as a hard-working, honest woman. Unbeknownst to Shirley, her son, Michael, had broken into a house in Dryden, New York earlier, killed its occupants (a family of four), set fire to the building, and stolen credit cards. Exhibiting poor judgment, she used the stolen credit cards to purchase some merchandise. Although she admitted to using the stolen cards, she adamantly argued that she was never made aware of the events that preceded this. Because Michael was killed in a shootout when the police attempted to arrest him, Shirley had no one to corroborate her story. Corrupt police officers planted her fingerprints on a gasoline can found at the crime scene to ensure her conviction. She was sentenced to eighteen to forty-four years in prison for her involvement in the criminal events. In November 1992 Shirley was granted a new trial and her conviction was overturned when evidence of the fabricated fingerprints became known. The prosecution dropped all charges except misdemeanor forgery, to which she agreed to plead guilty. Shirley spent just over two and a half years in jail and prison for a crime for which she was not responsible.

Kirby, Janine (Military)
A rare military case in which twenty-four-year-old Janine Kirby, while liv-

ing on a military base in Germany, was accused of killing her infant daughter. She was convicted in 1983 of manslaughter by a military court-martial because the infant had suffered a skull fracture. In 1994 the Military Court of Appeals set aside her conviction when a scan of the victim taken earlier revealed no skull fracture prior to entering the hospital.

Kniffen, Brenda (California) (W)
Brenda Kniffen was one of four defendants (two were men) who were wrongfully accused of being part of a child sex ring and engaging in ritualistic practices in Kern County, California, in the mid-1980s. With no physical evidence to support the charges, the prosecution relied heavily on the testimony of the children and the expert testimony of Dr. Bruce Woodling, who had conducted a physical examination of the children. On May 16, 1984, all four defendants were convicted of child sex abuse. Brenda was sentenced to 240 years for her involvement in the alleged scheme. The testimony of the physician was later impeached as newer studies refuted his original conclusion. Testimony from the two Kniffen sons was later recanted after it was revealed that they were cajoled and intimidated into testifying by police and prosecutors. On August 12, 1996, the California Court of Appeal dismissed their convictions and the four defendants were immediately released and all charges were dropped. *See also:* Debbie McCuan.

Kriho, Laura (Colorado) (W)
On February 10, 1997, Laura Kriho was found guilty of contempt of court for her alleged obstruction of justice while serving on a 1996 jury in which she was a holdout. She was fined $1,200 for her behavior, which resulted in a mistrial. Although Laura answered all of the questions honestly during voir dire, she was charged with not volunteering information that could have compromised her position as an impartial juror. In particular, she had a previous arrest for an illicit drug, she had negative feelings about current drug legislation, and she was involved in the Colorado Hemp Initiative Project, designed to change current drug laws. She had not been asked about her experience with drugs or opinion of drug laws during the jury selection process, so she had not lied to the court. She was acquitted of a perjury charge. Her objection to current drug laws only became evident during jury deliberation. Laura's conviction was overturned in April 1999 by the Colorado Court of Appeals. The court was concerned that using comments made during jury deliberation to prosecute a juror could have a dampening effect on future jury discussions. Furthermore, it was argued, even if those comments were disregarded, there was still insufficient evidence to convict her of the charge. Finally, on August 9, 2000, the contempt charge was dismissed.

La Pinta, Marie (New York) (W)

A victim of psychological and physical abuse from her husband of twenty-seven years, Marie La Pinta was convicted of second-degree murder for his death on the night of March 27, 1983. During a heated exchange between her husband, Michael La Pinta, and her brother, Leonardo Crociata, Marie admits to hitting her husband with a baseball bat. The victim eventually died from gun shots fired by Leonardo. During the ensuing trial, Marie was found guilty and sentenced to twenty-five years to life for her role in his death and subsequent disposal of the victim's body. After serving twenty-two years of her sentence, her conviction was overturned by the state supreme court and she was allowed on retrial to plead guilty to first-degree manslaughter so that she would be eligible for immediate release based on time served. During her first trial the jury was not allowed to know that she was a battered woman and that she had been beaten and imprisoned by her husband. Today Maria would be eligible to use a battered wife defense, which wasn't available in 1984.

Labastida, Kriseya (Nevada) (H)

Twenty-six-year-old Kriseya Labastida was an abused spouse who was found guilty of murder of her seven-week-old son at the hands of her husband. She was also found guilty of felony child neglect for failing to protect the boy from his violent father. In 1993 she received a life sentence for murder and twenty years for child neglect. After serving seven years in prison for a murder committed by her husband without her knowledge or consent, the Nevada Supreme Court in October 1999 finally reversed her conviction. Three years earlier that same court had affirmed her conviction. This was only the second time in the history of that court for a case that it reconsidered to have its decision reversed.

LaBatte, Beth (Wisconsin) (W)

On November 16, 1991, two retired schoolteachers were found murdered in their home outside of Casco, Wisconsin. A cold case for four years, the case was reopened when Beth LaBatte was arrested on July 25, 1995, on an unrelated charge and was immediately suspected of involvement in the murders. With a checkered past that included robberies of elderly victims, she was intensely interrogated by the police. Some incriminating remarks Beth made during the six-hour interrogation were interpreted by the police as a confession of guilt, though she denied any involvement in the crime. Beth was arrested for murder and armed robbery on December 23, 1996, and her boyfriend, Charles Benoit, was arrested for allegedly driving her to the crime scene. During Beth's trial, three jail informants claimed she had admitted killing the two women. On December 11, 1997, she was convicted and later sentenced to two life terms plus twenty years. Charles was acquitted the following month. In 2004 several items from the murder scene were examined using DNA testing. The results excluded Beth as the perpetrator, and her conviction was overturned in November 2005. She was released from prison two months later after having been wrongfully incarcerated for almost ten years. Charges against her were dismissed on August 1, 2006. A year after her exoneration she was killed in an automobile accident.

Larzelere, Virginia (Florida) (W)
On March 8, 1991, Norman Larzelere was shot and killed in his dental office where he worked. His wife, Virginia Larzelere, was alleged to be responsible for his death as prosecutors contended that she had hired a gunman to assassinate Norman to collect $3 million in assets and insurance. Originally sentenced to death for first-degree murder in May 1993, she was resentenced to life in August 2008 by the Circuit Court. There was no physical evidence linking her to the murder. Police failed to pursue other possible leads in the case, choosing to focus primarily on Virginia from the outset. Her defense counsel appeared to be on drugs during the trial and provided inadequate legal assistance. Informants, with known incentives to lie, were later found to be guilty of perjury. Perhaps most intriguing is the fact that the alleged assailant (Jason Larzelere, her eighteen-year-old son) was acquitted of first-degree murder in 1994 one year after Virginia was found guilty of hiring him to murder his father. Virginia remains incarcerated today. She is eligible for parole after serving twenty-five years of her sentence.

LeFave, Cheryl Amirault (Massachusetts) (W)
This is another of the wrongful convictions resulting from the child sex scandal at the Fells Acres Day School in Malden, Massachusetts. Cheryl LeFave was sentenced in 1987 to eight to twenty years for alleged child sex abuse that never occurred. She was released in 1995 after spending eight years in prison. Convicted based largely on the statements of children who had been the recipients of suggestive interviewing techniques used to plant false memories of events that never transpired, Cheryl was thirty-seven years of age when released. Both police misconduct and prosecutorial misconduct contributed to her miscarriage of justice.

LeFever, Virginia (Ginny) (Ohio) (W)
Thirty-nine-year-old Ginny LeFever was accused of killing her husband, whom she was divorcing. William LeFever died of an apparent drug overdose, which Ginny claimed was a suicide. She was suspected in part because she was a registered nurse and would know how to administer

drugs to achieve death. Convicted of aggravated murder in 1990, she was sentenced to twenty years to life in prison. In 2010 she was released after having been imprisoned for over twenty years. The following year the prosecutor reluctantly dismissed the case without prejudice, which means that he can refile charges against her if either new admissible evidence is discovered or scientific advances permit the testing of old evidence in the case. Should the case ever be reinstated, however, Ginny has affidavits from three experts that the medical evidence was misrepresented during the trial and that she could not have played a role in her husband's death. Forensic errors and perjury by the toxicologist who lied about his credentials contributed to this wrongful conviction.

Likine, Selesa (Michigan) (B)

Selesa Likine divorced Elive Likine in 2003 and was required to pay $54 a month in child support for their three children, to whom he had been awarded custody. That amount was later raised to $181 a month before finally being raised to $1,131 in 2005. Selesa, who had been unemployed since September 2005, suffered from a mental disorder that eventually resulted in her inability to hold a job. Her incapacitation resulted in Social Security disability payments of approximately $600 a month beginning in early 2006. In 2006 she did not pay any child support and only $488.85 in 2007. In March 2008, after having paid only $100, forty-two-year-old Selesa was charged by the Oakland County Michigan Prosecutor's Office with failure to pay child support. During her trial the judge refused to allow her to present evidence regarding her financial status. Failure to pay child support was interpreted by the judge as a "strict liability" crime, and thus ability to pay is legally irrelevant. Consequently, Selesa was found guilty of failure to pay child support and was put on probation for one year and given credit for the forty-eight days she had spent in jail. In January 2010 a family court determined that the monthly payments had been calculated incorrectly and reduced her payments to $25 a month. Although the Michigan Court of Appeals in April 2010 upheld her conviction, in July 2012 Selesa's conviction was overturned by the Michigan Supreme Court, citing that due process had been violated when she was refused the right to show evidence of inability to pay. Later that year the case was dismissed by the prosecution.

Linehan, Mechele (Alaska) (W)

Falsely accused of murdering thirty-six-year-old Kent Leppink in May 1996, Mechele Linehan was arrested in fall 2006 after the Alaska State Police reopened their cold case on the incident. According to authorities, Mechele had convinced John Carlin III to kill Leppink after Mechele had lured him to Hope, Alaska. During the 2007 trial in Anchorage Superior

Court, prosecutors surmised that Mechele anticipated collecting on Leppink's $1 million life insurance policy. However, five days prior to his death Leppink had changed the beneficiary to his father, who was awarded the insurance money. Using circumstantial evidence, the prosecution was successful in getting a guilty verdict on October 22, 2007. She was sentenced to ninety-nine years in prison for first-degree murder. The conviction was overturned by the Court of Appeals on February 5, 2010, citing the use of inadmissible and prejudicial evidence. In May 2010 Mechele, who was now married to a physician and had children, was released on bond. Late the following year her indictment was dismissed. In the meantime her lawyers uncovered exculpatory evidence that the prosecution had withheld during the first trial. Prosecutors had been informed that some family members believed that Leppink's father had killed him, as he was in the vicinity and the victim had embezzled money from his father's business. The victim had additionally borrowed a substantial amount of money from his family. It was further discovered that the lead detective was writing a book about the case and had a financial incentive to obtain a conviction. On August 6, 2012, the prosecution declined to seek a new indictment.

Lobato, Kirstin (Nevada) (W)
Wrongly convicted for the murder and sexual penetration of the corpse of a homeless black man, Kirstin Lobato was 170 miles away from the crime scene at the time the crime was committed. Police mistook her confession involving an earlier attempted sexual assault by a black male as an admission of guilt and arrested her. Despite no physical evidence linking her to the murder, no witnesses to the crime, and the failure of the police to investigate other potential suspects, Kirstin was convicted and sentenced to a minimum of forty years in prison on July 2, 2002. After the Nevada Supreme Court reversed her conviction on September 3, 2004, she was retried and again found guilty, this time of voluntary manslaughter and sexual penetration of a corpse on October 6, 2006, despite futile efforts by the Innocence Project to have the evidence examined for DNA. The Nevada Supreme Court scheduled oral arguments on her case in Carson City, Nevada for September 9, 2014.

Lockett, Denise (Georgia) (Juvenile) (B)
Denise Lockett was a sixteen-year-old girl with an IQ of 61 when she delivered a baby boy in September 1997. It is unclear whether the baby was stillborn or if he lived a short while before dying. It is believed that Denise was unaware she was pregnant. On the night of September 21, 1997, she awoke and went to the bathroom thinking she needed to defecate in the toilet. Instead, however, she expelled a full-term infant. Unaware of what had tran-

spired, she returned to her bed. She was later charged with first-degree murder after a Mitchell County grand jury indicted her. Although the autopsy report could not establish a cause of death and the infant exhibited no marks or wounds, her court-appointed attorney, Billy Grantham, persuaded Denise to accept a plea of voluntary manslaughter. Grantham spent less than one hour on her case despite recommendations that because his client suffered from "impaired judgment and limited insight" he needed to spend more time explaining the options and consequences of her actions. Judge Wallace Cato immediately gave her the maximum sentence for voluntary manslaughter, twenty years in prison. In 2002 the Georgia Supreme Court refused to overturn her conviction.

Loveless, Debbie (Texas) (W)

The four-year-old daughter of thirty-one-year-old Debbie Loveless and forty-two-year-old common-law husband, John Harvey Miller, was mauled by wild dogs on January 4, 1989, outside their rural home near Emory, Texas. Despite airlifting the injured girl to a hospital in Tyler, she died during surgery. An autopsy the following day suggested that the victim's injuries were due to a sharp knife and a curling iron. A subsequent search of the couple's home found a curling iron and a sharp knife. Shortly thereafter the two were arrested and ultimately charged with murder. Although no blood was found on the knife, Debbie and John were convicted on November 5, 1989. Each received a life sentence. A 1992 investigation by attorneys representing the couple revealed photographs that were not disclosed to the defense. One of the photographs clearly showed the presence of a paw print on the back of the victim. The origin of the wound from a sharp knife was caused by a scalpel used at the hospital when doctors attempted to remove severed skin. On December 23, 1993, Debbie and John finally received their freedom and on May 2, 1994, their charges were formally dismissed.

Mata, Laura Ann (Texas) (H)

On July 23, 1999, drug agents raided a largely African American area of Tulia, Texas, on suspicion of drug trafficking and drug use. An undercover agent, Tom Coleman, falsely testified at these trials that he witnessed the selling and use of illicit drugs. In 2000 Laura Ann Mata, a Hispanic woman, was sentenced to five years in prison as a result of this perjured testimony and prosecutorial misconduct. In 2003 she, along with thirty-four other Tulia residents, were pardoned by the governor of Texas. *See also:* Marilyn Joyce Cooper, Vickie Fry, Denise Kelly, Etta Kelly, Finaye Shelton, Lawanda Smith, Yolanda Smith, Ramona Strickland, Kizzie White, Alberta Stell Williams, and Michelle Williams.

Matney, Donna (California)

A former Riverside County Regional Medical Center administrator, Donna Matney was found guilty of falsely accounting for public monies in 2007. She was convicted of preparing and signing time sheets for a contract employee for times in which he didn't work. In actuality, the employee in question worked more hours than required even though the exact dates on the time sheets did not correspondent to his work schedule. The jury found her not guilty of grand theft or altering public records. Donna, who was undergoing chemotherapy and radiation for cancer, was given three years of probation for her alleged wrongdoing. In summer 2009 the Fourth District Court of Appeal reversed her conviction, citing insufficient evidence that she had acted negligently or with criminal intent in her preparation of the time sheets.

McAnally, Tamara (California) (W)

Tamara McAnally and her husband, Jon, were accused of conspiring to commit insurance fraud. Assistant District Attorney Ernie Marugg presented information on the couple that made it appear that they conspired to defraud the California State Compensation Insurance Fund. To avoid prison time they pleaded guilty to one count of conspiring to commit insurance fraud. They admitted that they owed $30,000 due to a bookkeeping error, but their case was built around owing much more money than that. The couple was sentenced to probation plus $422,000 restitution. Marugg befriended Tamara and sought to use his position of power to gain sexual favors from her. It was later discovered that he had been doing this for some time but was allowed to retire rather than face any disciplinary action from the district attorney's office or the California State Bar. Marugg had sexually pursued more than half a dozen women whom he had prosecuted, according to the internal investigation of the DA's office. The conviction against Tamara was vacated on May 16, 2011, and she was declared factually innocent of the charges. San Diego County Superior Court Judge David Danielson ordered that records of her arrest and subsequent prosecution be sealed for three years and then destroyed. Her husband was unsuccessful in having his conviction vacated in 2012.

McCuan, Debbie (California) (W)

One of four defendants (two were men) who were wrongly accused by their sons and daughters of bizarre forms of child abuse and ritualistic behavior. As with similar cases, the children were interviewed on multiple occasions using highly suggestive techniques. Debbie and her codefendants were convicted based on the testimony of the children and questionable forensic evidence that has subsequently been disputed. Police and prosecutorial misconduct as well as perjury by criminal justice officials also contributed to this wrongful conviction. Convicted in 1983, Debbie was sentenced to 250 years behind bars. She did not gain her freedom for fourteen years. In 1996 she was finally cleared of the charges. *See also:* Brenda Kniffen.

Michaels, Margaret Kelly (New Jersey) (W)

Three boys accused twenty-two-year-old Margaret Kelly Michaels of sexually abusing them when she briefly worked for the Wee Care Nursery in Maplewood, New Jersey. Although she passed a polygraph test, she was indicted in June 1985 after an investigation concluded that she abused all fifty-one children under her care. Kelly's trial lasted approximately eleven months and cost the state $3 million. The children were permitted to testify via closed-circuit television in the judge's chambers. Despite an absence of evidence to corroborate the sensational stories being told by the children, Kelly was found guilty of 115 of 163 counts of child sexual abuse. After serving five years of her forty-seven-year sentence, the New Jersey Superior Appellate Court reversed her conviction in March 1993. The court was particularly critical of the expert testimony called by the prosecution. On June 1994 the state Supreme Court unanimously upheld the decision of the appellate court, stating, "We find that the interrogations in this case were improper and there is a substantial likelihood that the evidence derived from them is unreliable." The charges against Kelly were finally dismissed in December of that year.

Milke, Debra Jean (Arizona) (W)

In 1989 Debra Jean Milke's four-year-old son, Christopher, thinking he was going to go see Santa Claus, was driven to the desert where he was shot three times in the head. During her 1990 trial the prosecution accused her of hiring her boyfriend and another man to kill Christopher. Prosecutors speculated that the trio planned to share money from the boy's life insurance policy, worth about $5,000. Phoenix detective Armando Saldate testified at the trial that Debra had confessed to the crime, although she vehemently disputed that claim. The prosecution did not reveal that Saldate had a history of lying and was currently being investigated for perjury and corruption. There was never any physical evidence linking Debra to the murder. She also passed a polygraph test, which cannot be used in a court of law. Upon her conviction and death sentence, Debra proceeded to clear her name. After she spent twenty-two years on death row, the Ninth US Circuit Court of Appeals overturned her conviction in March 2013. Not content with the decision, the state petitioned the court to reconsider the case. In May 2013 the court denied the petition from the Arizona State Attorney General's Office and in December 2014 the Court of Appeals ordered dismissal of the charges and prohibited a retrial since it would constitute double jeopardy. Although the prosecution appealed her case to the Arizona Supreme Court, the court refused to hear the appeal. On March 23, 2015, all charges against her were dismissed. Debra was the first woman to be sentenced to death in Arizona since 1932.

Miller, Gina (California) (W)
Gina Miller was part of the so-called Pitts Seven who were accused of operating a child sex ring in Bakersfield, California, during the mid-1980s. With no physical evidence to support the children's outrageous claims, Gina was offered a lighter sentence if she would testify against the other defendants. She refused, and although only two children were able to identify her in a lineup, she was sentenced to 405 years in prison in 1985. After serving six years in prison, she was released and subsequently exonerated. Prosecutorial misconduct and false eyewitness testimony from the children were responsible for this false conviction. *See also:* Grace Dill, Colleen Dill Forsythe, and Marcella Pitts.

Miller, Linda (Washington) (W)
A welfare mother of four, Linda Miller was charged with 3,200 counts of child rape during the Wenatchee child sex ring hysteria. In 1995 she was convicted of eight counts of child molestation and sentenced to thirty-three years in prison. Her false confession included bizarre stories of orgies with children in two homes and a church and led to the additional persons being charged for sex crimes. After almost three years in prison, Linda agreed to a plea bargain in which she plead "no contest" to three counts of communicating with a minor for immoral purposes in return for her immediate release. Forty-three persons were wrongly arrested during the two-year investigation and charged with almost 30,000 counts of rape or molestation of sixty children. *See also:* Connie Cunningham, Carol Doggett, Idella Everett, Susan Everett, Sharon Filbeck, Barb Garass, Doris Green, Donna Hidalgo, Laura Holt, Sadie Hughes, and Cherie Town.

Monroe, Beverly (Virginia) (W)
Wrongly accused of killing her sixty-year-old boyfriend of twelve years on March 5, 1992, Beverly Monroe was sentenced to twenty-two years in prison on November 22, 1992. She confessed to having been in the same house with the victim during the night of his death only after extensive and manipulative interrogations by the police, though she never actually confessed to his murder. The prosecutor withheld exculpatory evidence during Beverly's trial and hid the fact that a witness for the prosecution had been given a deal in exchange for her damaging testimony. Medical documents that ruled the

death a suicide were discovered post-trial. Questionable forensics also contributed to this miscarriage of justice. Her conviction was overturned on March 28, 2002, by a US District Court and the decision was upheld by the US Fourth Circuit Court of Appeals. In June 2003 the state announced that it would not retry Beverly's case. She was wrongly incarcerated for ten years.

Mowbray, Susie (Texas) (W)

In the border town of Brownsville, Texas, on September 16, 1987, Bill Mowbray was shot while lying in bed. His wife, Susie, told police that he had been despondent over financial problems and had threatened suicide. An examination of gunshot residue and blood spatters at the crime scene was conducted by the police. When Susie's gown was examined, a blood spatter not visible to the naked eye was detected. A reanalysis of the blood spatter by a nationally known expert, however, failed to reveal anything on her gown. Although the prosecution was aware of the latter report discrediting the evidence against Susie for months prior to the trial, the defense was not given this report until two weeks before the start of the trial. Moreover, the prosecution failed to call the expert to testify at the trial. However, two police officers testified that their examination of the evidence suggested that Susie had murdered her husband. In June 1988 a jury convicted her of first-degree murder and she was sentenced to life. In 1995 the two officers admitted that there was no scientific evidence to support their positions. Susie was granted a new trial in December 1996 by the Texas Court of Criminal Appeals. She was not released from prison until May 1997 when she posted bond while awaiting an appeal by the prosecution. In 1998, after an unsuccessful attempt by the prosecution to get the US Supreme Court to review the decision, the prosecution retried Susie and on January 24, 1998, a jury acquitted her of the crime.

Murphy, Sandy (Nevada) (W)

Twenty-eight-year-old Sandy Murphy was convicted in 2000 of killing her boyfriend, fifty-five-year-old Ted Binion, a casino mogul and heroin addict, to obtain his wealth. Rick Tabish, her codefendant and lover, was alleged to have assisted in the murder and theft and was also convicted. Both received life sentences. In 2003 the Nevada Supreme Court ruled that statements made during their joint trial were prejudicial to Sandy's case and overturned her conviction. During their retrial in 2004, a jury acquitted both defendants of murder, conspiracy to commit murder, and robbery. However, they were convicted of burglary, grand larceny, and conspiracy to commit burglary and/or larceny. Sandy was released from prison in April 2005 after being given credit for time served. She has thus far been unsuccessful in overturning her remaining convictions. Prosecutorial misconduct and forensic errors are among the factors contributing to this false conviction for murder.

Murray, LaCresha (Texas) (Juvenile) (B)

Eleven-year-old LaCresha Murray was convicted of killing two-year-old Jayla Belton while babysitting. LaCresha, who has an IQ of 77, had not seen her grandparents in five days when she was threatened with incarceration by the police during extended interrogations. Police were able to cajole her into confessing that she dropped and kicked the child. LaCresha was the youngest person in Texas to ever face the death penalty. During her first trial in August 1996, the main evidence against her was her confession. At the suggestion of Assistant District Attorney Gary Cobb, the jury convicted her of criminally negligent homicide and injury to a child and she was sentenced to twenty years. When a retrial was ordered, the defense had a former Dallas County medical examiner testify that Jayla was a battered child and the injuries sustained may have occurred while trying to revive her. It was also noted that the victim had been lethargic when she arrived and that damage to her liver had probably occurred earlier. Nevertheless, LaCresha was again convicted and sentenced, this time to twenty-five years. After receiving national attention, the Texas Court of Appeals in 1999 overturned her conviction and she was released on April 21, 1999. Charges against LaCresha were not formally dismissed until August 13, 2001.

Newton, Frances (Texas) (B)

On September 14, 2005, Frances Newton became the third woman to be executed in the state of Texas and the first black woman to be executed since the Civil War. Imprisoned for eighteen years prior to her execution by lethal injection, twenty-three-year-old Frances was convicted in October 1988 of capital murder for allegedly murdering her husband and children to collect insurance money. Frances, who had a prior conviction for forgery and had been fired from a job for stealing money, maintained her innocence at the trial. Her court-appointed attorney, who was subsequently barred from capital murder cases, provided ineffective assistance of counsel. Frances claimed that the murders were a result of drug debts her husband had incurred. Prosecutors claimed that the nitrate found on her skirt was from gunpowder residue, yet a more probable source was garden fertilizer. Although there is controversy regarding whether ballistics tests of the bullets matched the gun Frances found and later hid, the life insurance policies that she purchased were the result of a recommendation made by a bank employee when she opened a savings account. It was also reported that someone sharing a cell with one of her relatives had admitted to the murders. At least three members of the jury later expressed reservations over the verdict given, the evidence that never appeared at the trial.

Noble, Michelle (Texas)

Thirty-four-year-old Michelle Noble was one of two teachers at the East Valley YMCA day care center in El Paso, Texas, who were accused of sexual misconduct with children. From videotaped testimony, Michelle was indicted on eighteen counts of child molestation. She was found guilty in 1986 and sentenced to life plus 311 years in prison. In November 1987 the verdict was overturned by an appellate court because videotaped confessions by the children violated her constitutional right to confront hostile witnesses. During her second trial in April 1988, she was acquitted after some of the witnesses withdrew from the case and an expert testified that the interviews and interrogations of the children had resulted in the internalization of false memories due to the suggestive and coercive nature of the technique. *See also:* Gayle Dove.

O'Dell, Karen (Florida) (W)

Thirty-seven-year-old Karen O'Dell was coming home from work in November 1997 when she was stopped by officers from the Manatee County Sheriff's Office. A search of her truck revealed no illicit drugs, so she proceeded home. Shortly after her arrival, several officers approached her. While two talked to her at the door of her house, the others conducted a search of her garage and vehicle. They claimed to find cocaine in her truck, and she was arrested and charged with possession of a controlled substance, destruction of evidence, and battery (for allegedly striking one of the officers when she was stopped). Although innocent of the charges, she pleaded no contest to avoid a prison sentence. In turn, Karen received a year of probation and fifty hours of community service in March 1998. An FBI investigation of the sheriff's office subsequently revealed that the cocaine had been planted by an officer. Eventually, five officers were charged and convicted of planting evidence on suspects. As a result, prosecutors dropped over seventy cases against sixty-seven defendants. In early 2000 a circuit court judge vacated her conviction and the charges were dismissed. *See also:* Sarah Smith.

Pavlinac, Laverne (Oregon) (W)

Suffering through a ten-year abusive relationship with her younger boyfriend, Laverne Pavlinac saw the unsolved murder of a twenty-three-year-old woman as a chance to rid herself of this problem. After repeated attempts to get the police to believe that her boyfriend, John Sosnovske, was responsible for the death of Taunja Bennett in a remote area outside of Portland, Oregon, she was successful in convincing the police and prosecution that both of them had participated in the crime. In January 1991 Laverne was sentenced to ten years to life for her alleged involvement in the rape and murder. Two months later John pleaded no contest to murder and kidnapping and received a life sentence. After the actual perpetrator was found and convicted, a circuit court judge ordered their release from prison on November 27, 1995. John's conviction was vacated, but Laverne's conviction was left intact as a result of her abuse of the legal system.

Peak, Carolyn June (Arizona)

Accused of shooting her husband of seventeen years in the head while the two slept in the same bed, forty-one-year-old Carolyn Peak was convicted of second-degree murder in 2000. Evidence suggested that his death may have been a suicide or their teenage daughter, who had been disciplined by him earlier, may have killed him. There were no fingerprints or other direct evidence linking Carolyn to his death. The original prosecutor, who was replaced because he was terminally ill, deliberately withheld exculpatory evidence from her defense counsel. When this was later disclosed, Superior Court Judge Virginia Kelly dismissed the charges against Carolyn and on September 12, 2003, she was cleared of murder. Carolyn was wrongfully incarcerated for approximately two months during this time.

Peterson, Linda C. (Georgia)

This is a federal case found in the forejustice.org database involving Linda Peterson, a state magistrate in Georgia, who was convicted on July 14, 2008 of perjury and making false statements to the FBI. In November 2008, before she was sentenced, the trial judge vacated her conviction and ordered an acquittal, citing insufficient evidence to support the charges. No additional information was found on this case.

Pitts, Marcella (California) (W)

Part of the so-called Pitts Seven, a group of Bakersfield citizens who were falsely accused of operating a child sex ring, Marcella Pitts was charged with conspiracy; forcible, lewd, and lascivious acts on children; use of children for pornography; child endangerment; and assault. In 1985 she was convicted and sentenced to 373 years in prison. With no adults witnessing the alleged crimes, and no videotapes to substantiate the accusations that the events were recorded, the prosecution and other investigators relied heavily on the testimony of children who had been extensively interviewed using coercive and manipulative techniques. One child later admitted that she was fed the information that she needed to say at the trial. In 1991 Marcella was cleared of the charges and by 1994 all the witnesses had recanted their stories and admitted that their testimony had been coerced. *See also:* Grace Dill, Colleen Dill Forsythe, and Gina Miller.

Pollock, Tabitha (Illinois) (W)

During the early morning hours of October 10, 1995, Scott English, Tabitha Pollock's boyfriend, killed her three-year-old daughter. In 1996 a jury found Tabitha guilty of first-degree murder and aggravated battery for failure to know that her boyfriend posed a threat to her daughter. The trial judge later admitted that she "did not commit the act of killing, nor did she intend to kill the child, nor was she present in the room when her boyfriend killed the child." Thus Tabitha was convicted based on what she should have known, not what she actually knew. Moreover, the prosecution could not locate any witnesses to testify that they suspected her boyfriend of prior abuse. Nevertheless, the judge sentenced her to thirty-six years in prison. In October 2002 the Illinois Supreme Court overturned her conviction when the court reasoned that an individual cannot be convicted for something that should be known. Tabitha was wrongfully incarcerated for six and a half years.

Porter, Sabrina (same as Sabrina Butler)

Ratzlaf, Loretta (Oregon) (W)

This federal case involved Loretta Ratzlaf and her husband, Waldemar. In 1991 they were convicted of currency structuring, and Loretta was sentenced to five years of probation, ten months of home detention, a $7,900 fine, and a $100 special assessment. In 1994 they were exonerated when it was determined that they had no knowledge of the law they violated and the government had failed to inform them of those laws. Consequently, there was no willful intent to violate the law, as required by the statute regarding currency structuring.

Rea-Harper, Julie (Illinois) (W)

Ten-year-old Joel Kirkpatrick, son of Julie Rea-Harper, was stabbed twelve times while sleeping in his bed on October 13, 1997. Julie claimed that after hearing her son's screams, she attempted to thwart the assailant, who eventually escaped. Three years later, after a special prosecutor was appointed when the state's attorney declined to press charges due to lack of evidence, a grand jury indicted her for murder and she was arrested in Indiana, where she was working on her doctoral degree. The trial began on February 21, 2002, and on March 4, 2002, a jury found her guilty despite the fact that her clothes, hands, arms, and legs exhibited no evidence of blood after the incident. A judge sentenced Julie to sixty-five years in prison. When Tommy Lynn Sells, a serial killer on death row, confessed to the crime, an appellate court overturned Julie's conviction and remanded the case for retrial. Released on bond, Julie received assistance from the Center on Wrongful

Convictions at Northwestern University. In 2006 the case was retried and forensic evidence was presented that supported Julie's contention that the injuries she received resulted from a struggle with the assailant and weren't self-inflicted. After her acquittal, she was awarded a Certificate of Innocence in 2010 and received $87,057 from the Illinois Court of Claims.

Reasonover, Ellen (Missouri) (B)

A nineteen-year-old gas station attendant was shot and killed on January 2, 1983, in Dellwood, Missouri. When twenty-four-year-old Ellen Reasonover called the police to report that she saw the murder and could identify the two men and the vehicle they were using, she became a suspect. On January 7, 1983, Ellen was charged with the murder of the attendant. Two jailhouse snitches testified at her trial that she had confessed to the crime. Both lied when they denied having received any favors from the prosecution in return for their statements. Her defense counsel chose not to cross-examine the informants, and an all-white jury found Ellen guilty on December 2, 1983. She was sentenced to life for her alleged wrongdoing. It was later discovered that one of the informants had lied about her criminal past and the prosecution had withheld exculpatory evidence. US District Court Judge Jean Hamilton overturned Ellen's conviction on August 2, 1999, and she was released from prison. In 2004 she was awarded $7.5 million from the town of Dellwood for her wrongful conviction. Ellen was falsely imprisoned for over sixteen years of her life.

Reeves, Paula M. (Oklahoma) (B)

On June 14, 2004, forty-eight-year-old Paula M. Reeves was charged with drug trafficking and other related offenses. A plea-negotiated offer on March 14, 2005, resulted in the charge being reduced to unlawful possession of a controlled drug with intent to distribute. Paula received an eight-year suspended sentence for the charge plus a one-year suspended sentence for possession of drug paraphernalia. Five years later Tulsa County District Judge William Kellough vacated her eight-year suspended sentence when it was discovered that the evidence had been fabricated. Paula was the nineteenth person to have a case dismissed or to be released from prison as a result of police corruption in the Tulsa Police Department. *See also:* Larita Barnes.

Reser, Pamela Sue (Oregon) (W)

Single mom Pamela Reser had a checkered past: she had a drug addiction, she sometimes stole to support her drug habit, she had multiple sex partners, and she wasn't a nurturing mother. In 1994 she took her four children, who were four to eight years of age, to visit a friend in Dallas, Texas, and returned to her McMinnville, Oregon, home without them. Her friend eventually became their foster mother. Five years later Pamela and her boyfriend, Jerry Littleton, were arrested in Oregon and charged with child sexual abuse. Her daughter and three sons alleged that Pamela had forced them to have sex with her, have sex with each other, and have sex with her boyfriends during a period from 1988 through 1994. They also claimed they had been physically abused. Charges against Jerry were later dropped for lack of evidence. Lacking physical evidence against Pamela, the prosecutor relied heavily on the testimony of her children. In August 1999 Pamela was convicted of seventeen counts of first-degree rape, eight counts of sodomy, and four counts of first-degree sex abuse. She received a 116-year prison sentence for her alleged wrongdoing. When it was discovered in 2002 that her children had recanted their stories and passed polygraph tests, her case was reinvestigated. This information led to her being released from prison on bail in May 2002. The following month all charges against her were dropped.

Richardson, Asya (Pennsylvania) (B)
Asya Richardson was wrongly convicted in 2008 of two counts of money laundering for allegedly assisting her boyfriend, drug kingpin Alton "Ace Capone" Coles, in securing a mortgage for a $500,000 house in New Jersey. In 2011 she was sentenced to two years in prison and two years of supervised release. After serving eight months in a federal women's prison, she received her freedom when an appeals court determined that there was insufficient evidence to convict her. Asya had no previous criminal history when she was charged with the offenses.

Roever, Lerlene Evonne (Nevada) (W)
On January 16, 1993, Ian Wilhite died of a single gunshot to the forehead. Lerlene (Shasta) Roever, who lived with Ian in his trailer in Pahrump, Nevada, was arrested and charged with his murder. There was no physical evidence linking Shasta to the murder, and the police questioned her relentlessly. Although she owned a rusty .22 caliber gun, ballistics tests ruled it out as the murder weapon. With a history of alcohol abuse and an alleged temper, Shasta was found guilty of first-degree murder and possession of marijuana, the latter of which probably belonged to Ian. Because she depended on Ian for a home in which to raise her children and as a father figure for them, his death adversely affected Shasta. Since they were unmarried, she did not benefit from any life insurance that he might have had. Her two consecutive life sentences for murder and one-year sentence for marijuana were never overturned despite two trials. Perjury by criminal officials, prosecutorial misconduct, and fraternizing by the primary investigator with

jurors during the trial resulted in this false conviction. Refusing to admit to a crime she didn't commit, Shasta has turned down plea bargains that would have resulted in her release. She remains incarcerated despite her apparent innocence.

Rogers (no first name) (Maryland) (Juvenile) (W)
A sixteen-year-old girl (whose first name was withheld) accused her stepfather of sexually abusing her and was found guilty by a juvenile court of filing a false police report. A year later the girl produced a video corroborating her story. After watching the videotape, her mother, Laura Rogers, a battered spouse, shot and killed her husband while he was asleep. At age seventeen, the girl had a baby as a result of her sexual liaison with her stepfather. The baby was immediately put up for adoption.

Routier, Darlie Lynn (Texas) (W)
In a case fraught with legal irregularities and media hype, Darlie Routier, a mother of three, was accused of killing two of her sons, Damon (age five) and Devon (age six). Darlie told police that someone entered the house and murdered her sons, but authorities believed her story to be contrived. Prosecutors suggested at trial that she arranged the crime scene to appear that an intruder had been there and that she was a materialistic woman who killed Damon because the family was having financial issues. (She was never formally charged with the death of Devon because a second murder weapon was never found.) Stories about "the mother from hell" pervaded the airwaves and print media. A video showed her frolicking at her sons' newly dug graves but neglected to mention that the silly string that Darlie was spraying was a favorite of Devon, who would have been seven years old if still alive. Pictures of the multiple injuries that Darlie sustained during the struggle were not shown to the jury, even though one of the cuts came to within two millimeters of severing her carotid artery. Nor were jurors permitted to view a video of a grieving mother at the graveside services. Two doctors who performed the autopsies on the boys failed to reveal to the court an absence of blood on the butcher knife, the alleged weapon used to kill Damon. The contamination of the crime scene was never an issue at the trial, although at least twenty paramedics and police entered the house before it was secured. Key evidence was moved during this time, and blood was trampled on. When her court-appointed attorney was dismissed, his replacement had represented Darlie's husband and therefore could not single him out as a likely perpetrator even though more recent evidence suggests that he may have been responsible for the crimes. Prosecutorial misconduct, police misconduct (a 911 call recording was altered), perjury by criminal justice officials, and forensic errors all contributed to her con-

viction on February 1, 1997. Darlie was sentenced to die by lethal injection. Since her conviction, discrepancies in the trial transcript have been uncovered. Sandra Halsey, the court reporter, took the Fifth Amendment rather than explain the errors. A neighbor has also come forward to say that she saw two men near the Routier home on the night of the murders. On January 29, 2014, further DNA testing of a bloody fingerprint, a bloody sock, and Darlie's nightgown were approved by Judge Fred Biery. As of January 17, 2015, Darlie remains on death row.

Scruggs, Judith (Connecticut) (W)
Judith Scruggs was a single mom in her fifties who worked sixty hours a week at two jobs. She had two children, one of whom was severely bullied at school and eventually committed suicide by hanging himself in his closet. Subsequently charged with contributing to his death because she kept a dirty, cluttered household and didn't pay attention to his personal hygiene (he had bad breath and body odor), Judith was convicted in 2003 and given an eighteen-month suspended sentence, five years of probation, 100 hours of community service, and required to undergo counseling. In 2006 she was exonerated when the court ruled there was no objective standard that could be applied to determine when poor housekeeping becomes a risk to the mental health of a child. Her son's death led to the founding of the Advocacy Group for Parents of Children Affected by Bullying and brought greater attention to this social concern.

Shelden, Debra (Nebraska) (W)
In February 1985 an elderly woman living in an apartment by herself was beaten, suffocated, and raped. Although there were no witnesses and no evidence, six people (a.k.a. the Beatrice Six) were arrested and charged with the crime. Debra Shelden was one of three women wrongfully convicted. She falsely confessed to involvement in the murder/rape and implicated others. For her assistance she was allowed to plead guilty to a lesser offense to avoid a long prison sentence or possible death sentence. In 1989 she was convicted and sentenced to ten years in prison. After serving approximately half of her sentence, she was released. In 2009 she was pardoned by the state of Nebraska when a DNA test revealed that an individual working alone had been identified as the perpetrator. *See also:* Kathy Gonzalez and Ada JoAnn Taylor.

Shelton, Finaye (Texas) (B)
During the predawn morning of July 23, 1999, drug agents awoke the residents of the predominantly African American section of Tulia, Texas, on suspicion of drug trafficking and drug use. Undercover agent Tom Coleman

supplied perjured testimony at the trials to secure convictions. As a result of this illicit drug operation, twenty-five-year-old Finaye Shelton received five years of probation for her alleged involvement. Prosecutorial misconduct also contributed to this miscarriage of justice. In 2003 Finaye received a pardon from the governor of Texas. *See also:* Marilyn Joyce Cooper, Vickie Fry, Denise Kelly, Etta Kelly, Laura Ann Mata, Lawanda Smith, Yolanda Smith, Ramona Strickland, Kizzie White, Alberta Stell Williams, and Michelle Williams.

Smith, Lawanda (Texas) (B)

Twenty-five-year-old Lawanda Smith received a three-year deferred sentence in 2000 as a result of the July 23, 1999, drug sting in Tulia, Texas. Tom Coleman, a white undercover agent, lied during the trials involving primarily African American residents. Prosecutorial misconduct also influenced the erroneous convictions. Although thirty-five residents were pardoned by the governor of Texas in 2003, Lawanda was not among them. *See also:* Marilyn Joyce Cooper, Vickie Fry, Denise Kelly, Etta Kelly, Laura Ann Mata, Finaye Shelton, Yolanda Smith, Ramona Strickland, Kizzie White, Alberta Stell Williams, and Michelle Williams.

Smith, Nancy (Ohio) (W)

Thirty-seven-year-old Nancy Smith, a mother of four, was a bus driver for the Head Start program in Lorain, Ohio. Accused of taking several young children to Joseph Allen's house and sexually abusing them, Nancy was convicted of molesting four children and sentenced to fifteen to ninety years in prison in 1994. Joseph was sentenced to twenty years to life. At the time Nancy, a white woman, did not know Joseph, a black man, with whom she was a codefendant. As is typical of this genre of wrongful convictions, there was no physical evidence linking her (or Joseph) to these alleged offenses. Their convictions were based primarily on the inconsistent and contradictory testimony of several young children. Nancy spent fifteen years in prison before a judge acquitted her and Joseph in 2009 and released them on $100,000 bail. The judge acknowledged a number of flaws in the original trial, including the use of hearsay evidence, the use of suggestive interview techniques, and withholding exculpatory evidence from the defense. In making his decision the judge commented, "The court has absolutely no confidence that these verdicts are correct." The Ohio Court of Appeals later upheld the authority of the judge to vacate the convictions and sentences.

Smith, Sarah (Florida) (W)

Sarah Smith was a nineteen-year-old mother who on November 14, 1997, was startled when she witnessed Manatee County Sheriff's officers dressed in black masks and raid equipment breaking down the door of her house. Ordering her on the floor, one of the officers claimed that he found a Tylenol bottle containing crack cocaine. The next day social services arrived to take her fourteen-month-old daughter to a foster family. At her February 1998 trial, officers testified that she threw the Tylenol bottle across the room before later confessing to possessing cocaine. Despite her protestations of innocence, a jury convicted her and she was sentenced to a year of house arrest followed by six months of probation. Sarah was additionally fined $400. In lieu of house arrest she agreed to serve thirty days in jail. A subsequent investigation by the FBI of the activities of the Delta Division of the Manatee County Sheriff's Office revealed that drug officers regularly planted evidence on suspected drug users. As a result, prosecutors dropped over seventy cases involving sixty-seven defendants. Five officers were eventually convicted on these charges. After one of the officers admitted to planting the cocaine in the medicine bottle, Sarah's conviction was vacated and the charge was dismissed in February 2000. In 2004 she finally settled a civil lawsuit against Manatee County and the sheriff's officers for an unknown amount. *See also:* Karen O'Dell.

Smith, Shirley Ree (California) (B)

Shirley Ree Smith was a thirty-seven-year-old grandmother who was accused of killing her seven-week-old grandson, Etzel Dean Glass III, by violently shaking him. Etzel had no bruises, no brain swelling, or bleeding of the retina—all symptoms of shaken baby syndrome (SBS). Prosecutors theorized that the baby was shaken so violently that death was instantaneous and therefore no other symptoms were present, a conclusion that is not supported by medical research. Shirley acknowledged that Etzel had fallen from the couch and hit his head on the carpet earlier that day, although he appeared to be unfazed from the fall. The prosecution could not explain why she unexpectedly lost her temper, nor could they explain how it was possible that she could have engaged in the violent behavior without being detected with the child's mother sleeping just a few feet away. Nonetheless, in 1997 Shirley was convicted of second-degree murder and given a sentence of fifteen years to life. On three different occasions the Ninth Circuit Court of Appeals struck down her conviction until in 2011 the US Supreme Court, acknowledging potential problems in the case, upheld her conviction. The three dissenting judges were particularly critical of the ruling stating that "In light of current information [on SBS], it is unlikely that the prosecution's experts would today testify as adamantly as they did in 1997." In 2012 California Governor Jerry Brown commuted Shirley's sentence to time served, indicating that he had significant reservations about her conviction. It was only the second time in his tenure as governor that he commuted a sentence.

Smith, Yolanda (Texas) (B)

In 2000 Yolanda Smith was one of twelve women convicted of drug-related crimes during a predawn raid of the predominantly African American section of Tulia, Texas, on July 23, 1999. Undercover agent Tom Coleman provided false testimony during the trials. In addition, prosecutorial misconduct contributed to this miscarriage of justice. Yolanda was wrongfully incarcerated for two years, six months, and twenty-nine days. On August 22, 2003, the governor of Texas pardoned her and thirty-four other Tulia residents. *See also:* Marilyn Joyce Cooper, Vickie Fry, Denise Kelly, Etta Kelly, Laura Ann Mata, Finaye Shelton, Lawanda Smith, Ramona Strickland, Kizzie White, Alberta Stell Williams, and Michelle Williams.

Sommer, Cynthia (California) (W)

In February 2002 Cynthia Sommer's twenty-three-year-old marine husband became ill and died. The official cause of death was ruled a heart attack. When the military examined some tissues taken from his body in 2003, however, tests revealed the strong presence of arsenic. Cynthia, who had moved to Florida, was arrested and extradited to California in 2006. Although her defense counsel argued that the samples taken from her husband were probably contaminated, the prosecution proved to be more effective in its contention that Cynthia poisoned him to collect over $250,000 in insurance benefits and monthly survivor benefits of $1,900. Convicted in January 2007 of first-degree murder with "special circumstances" (financial gain) she became eligible for a sentence of life without parole. Prior to sentencing, Cynthia was granted a new trial to begin in May 2008. When previously unanalyzed tissue samples were discovered and tested negative for arsenic, the prosecution asked that the charges against her be dropped in April of that year. Forensic errors and ineffective assistance of counsel contributed to her false conviction.

Souza, Shirley (Massachusetts)

Shirley and Ray Souza were accused by their college-age daughter of having molested her when she was young. At the time the daughter was seeing a therapist after having been traumatized by a near date rape. Soon other family members became convinced of the guilt of their parents and believed they had been involved in the abuse of their grandchildren. In 1993 the Souzas' bench trial began. Their judge, Elizabeth Dolan, believed that children were incapable of lying and was willing to overlook any inconsistencies in their testimony. Two granddaughters testified that they had been sexually victimized by Shirley and Ray. Judge Dolan was overtly hostile to the defense's expert witness who expressed skepticism of the interviewing techniques used to elicit past events and the use of anatomically correct dolls. A maladroit defense counsel who neglected to call expert witnesses on behalf of his clients and who failed to prepare Shirley and Ray for their cross-examination contributed to their wrongful conviction. The erroneous outcome was also the result of eyewitness error by the children and prosecutorial misconduct. Consequently, in 1993 the Souzas were convicted and sentenced to nine to fifteen years in prison. They were allowed to remain under house arrest wearing ankle bracelets and using a telephone monitoring system—all of which they were required to purchase—while awaiting their appeal. Despite turning down their appeals on two occasions, Judge Dolan did not impose any restrictions on home visitations and later revised their sentence to nine years retroactive to May 1993. In April 2002 Shirley and Ray completed their sentence at their house, although they were never exonerated of molesting their two granddaughters.

Stallings, Patricia (Missouri) (W)

Wrongly convicted in 1991 of poisoning her three-month-old infant, Ryan, using ethylene glycol (an ingredient in antifreeze), twenty-four-year-old Patricia Stallings was sentenced to life without parole. Lab tests which showed high concentrations of the substance in his blood and the existence of crystalline structures in his brain were presented as forensic evidence during her trial. Additionally, a container with antifreeze was found in her basement. Pregnant with her second child at the time she was arrested, Patricia's baby was placed in foster care upon his birth in February 1990. Although the infant had no contact with his biological mother, he exhibited the same symptoms as Ryan. He was later diagnosed with methylmalonic acidemia (MMA), a rare genetic disorder. When new tests were run using tissue samples from Ryan, it was disclosed that he also had MMA. Patricia's attorney chose to ignore these results and on January 31, 1991, she was convicted of first-degree murder and assault. After the trial forensic experts who tested Ryan found that methylmalonic acid had been misidentified as ethylene glycol. Furthermore, treatments administered by the hospital under the assumption that he had been poisoned could have contributed to the misdiagnosis. After a new trial was ordered because of inadequate legal counsel, Patricia received her freedom on July 30, 1991. On September 20, 1991, the prosecution dismissed all charges. Patricia was wrongfully incarcerated for approximately eight months.

Strickland, Ramona (Texas) (B)

During the predawn hours of July 23, 1999, drug agents descended on the small town of Tulia, Texas. The drug raid, which focused on the African American section of the city, resulted in the wrongful conviction of twelve women of color. Undercover agent Tom Coleman falsely testified against the residents and prosecutorial misconduct further contributed to the miscarriage of justice. Twenty-six-year-old Ramona Strickland was fined $2,000 in 2000 for her alleged involvement in this activity. However, in 2003 she was one of thirty-five residents who were pardoned by the governor when the lies used to convict innocent individuals surfaced. *See also:* Marilyn Joyce Cooper, Vickie Fry, Denise Kelly, Etta Kelly, Laura Ann Mata, Finaye Shelton, Lawanda Smith, Yolanda Smith, Kizzie White, Alberta Stell Williams, and Michelle Williams.

Strickland, Reshenda (Washington) (B)

Twenty-four-year-old African American Reshenda Strickland was wrongfully convicted on February 13, 2004, of third-degree theft and fourth-degree assault for allegedly struggling with a loss prevention officer at a T.J. Maxx store in Vancouver, Washington, on March 21, 2003. At the trial the store manager and loss prevention officer positively identified her as the perpetrator and an all-white jury took less than one hour to reach its verdict. Because she had a past history of theft, the judge gave her a six-month sentence for the shoplifting and assault charges. On May 19, 2004, the charges were dismissed and she was released when her twenty-one-year-old sister, whose skin was several shades lighter than hers, confessed to the crime.

Swain, Lorinda (Michigan) (W)

In 2001 forty-one-year-old Lorinda Swain was convicted of four counts of first-degree criminal sexual conduct for allegedly having sexual contact with her thirteen-year-old adopted son, Ronnie, since the age of eight. There was no physical or even circumstantial evidence to suggest that the crime actually occurred—only the statements of her son and a jailhouse snitch, Deborah Charles, who had twelve aliases and twenty-four felony convictions. Lorinda was sentenced to up to fifty years in prison. After serving eight years, she was released while awaiting an appeal. Since her conviction Ronnie has recanted his testimony, stating that he was afraid that he would be arrested for molesting his three-year-old niece when he was twelve. A school bus driver has testified that Ronnie and his younger brother, Cody, always waited together for the school bus to arrive, yet at the trial Ronnie said that his mother would send Cody outside to wait on the bus while she molested him. The statements made by the bus driver have been corroborated by one of Lorinda's neighbors. Aware of a lack of evidence in this case, the prosecutor appealed the decision to award Lorinda a new trial in February 2013. There are no more recent updates available on the case.

Sykes, Kimberly (Michigan) (B)

Wrongfully convicted in 2002 of larceny by conversion and false report of a felony, Kimberly Sykes was one of three women who worked at a Detroit mobile phone store when two armed men forced them to give them money from the store's safe. Police and prosecutors erroneously believed that the robbery was an inside job and that the women aided and abetted the robbers. In 2003 an appeals court unanimously reversed her conviction due to insufficient evidence. One year later the Wayne County Circuit Court dismissed the charges. Kimberly was awarded $1.31 million by a jury in 2008. *See also:* Tevya Urquhart.

Taylor, Ada JoAnn (Nebraska) (W)

Ada JoAnn Taylor is one of six individuals wrongfully convicted of the 1985 murder and rape of a sixty-eight-year-old widow in Beatrice, Nebraska. Known as the Beatrice Six, three of the falsely convicted were women and three were men. Threatened with the possibility of death in the electric chair, JoAnn falsely testified that she witnessed the rape and murder of the victim and helped hold a pillow over the woman's face while Joseph White and Thomas Winslow sexually assaulted her. For her false confession and testimony, JoAnn received a sentence of up to forty years in prison. After serving nearly twenty years in jail and prison she was released on parole on November 10, 2008, when DNA identified a lone man from Oklahoma as the perpetrator. On January 26, 2009, she was formally pardoned by the state of Nebraska and received $500,000 from that state in September 2012 for her wrongful incarceration. *See also:* Kathy Gonzalez and Debra Shelden.

Taylor, Ruth (California) (W)

This is another Kern County, California child sex abuse case involving multiple individuals falsely accused by children. As is typical of this genre of wrongful convictions, there was a lack of evidence to substantiate the children's outrageous stories. In this situation the prosecutor provided the child witness toys and clothes prior to her testifying. Questionable interviewing techniques were used to elicit testimony from alleged victims. After the first conviction was overturned, Ruth accepted a plea bargain of six years in prison to avoid a second trial. After serving five years she was released early but was required to register as a sex offender. In 2001—sixteen years after her conviction—she was cleared of all charges.

Thomas, Teresa (Ohio) (B)

On September 15, 1993, when Teresa Thomas took the life of her live-in boyfriend, Jerry "Jake" Flowers, she had endured months of physical and emotional abuse. Jake isolated her from others by refusing to allow her to work or go to the grocery store. He denied her food on occasions for up to four days and periodically molested her both vaginally and anally. Teresa had required medical attention more than once after these altercations. Just prior to the shooting, Jake threatened to kill her and would wake her up while she was asleep with his hands over her mouth and nose so that she had trouble breathing. A jury convicted Teresa of murder on December 20, 1993, and she received a sentence of eighteen years to life. That conviction was overturned on January 22, 1997, when the Ohio Supreme Court ruled that she had no duty to retreat from her boyfriend when he attacked her that night in their trailer home. On August 21, 1997, at her retrial Teresa was acquitted of the murder charge.

Thompson, Georgia (Wisconsin) (W)

Wrongly incarcerated in a federal prison in Illinois for over four months, Georgia Thompson was the victim of a politically motivated conviction for fraud. She was accused of awarding a contract to a Wisconsin-based company that supported the democratic governor, although the company's bid was the lowest received and preference was typically given to organizations from Wisconsin. There was no evidence that any political pressure had been exerted on Georgia to award the contract or that any crime had been committed. She eventually resigned her state position and had to sell her condominium and cash in her state pension to pay her legal bills. In 2007 Georgia was cleared when a federal appeals court overturned her conviction and ordered her immediate release on the first day of oral arguments. During the oral arguments one of the federal appeals court judges told the prosecutors that the "evidence is beyond thin" and that she was "not sure what your actual theory in this case is."

Town, Cherie (Washington) (W)

Cherie Town was another victim of the child sex abuse hysteria in Wenatchee, Washington, during the early to mid-1990s. Pressured by the police to confess, she also pleaded guilty to reduce her possible prison time. In 1995 she was convicted of two counts of child rape involving her sons, who were mentally challenged, and was sentenced to five years in prison. Her conviction was overturned when she accepted an Alford plea to one count of child molestation and agreed to drop her appeal of her original conviction in exchange for release from prison. On December 2, 1999, Cherie was released from prison. As of 2012, however, she was still required to register as a sex offender. As was common among those convicted during the Wenatchee child sex abuse scandal, Cherie is poor and developmentally disabled. *See also:* Connie Cunningham, Carol Doggett, Idella Everett, Susan Everett, Sharon Filbeck, Barb Garass, Doris Green, Donna Hidalgo, Laura Holt, Sadie Hughes, and Linda Miller.

Tucker, Dianne Bell (Alabama) (B)

Dianne Tucker (along with Victoria Bell Banks and Medell Banks) was accused of killing a nonexistent infant. Her original charge of capital murder was later reduced to manslaughter. Convicted in 2001, Dianne received a fifteen-year sentence. In 2002 she agreed to a new sentence in which she received credit for time served and included one day of probation. A provision was added that she could never appeal her original sentence nor could she pursue civil charges against the state of Alabama. A coerced false confession, police misconduct, prosecutorial misconduct, and insufficient evidence to support a conviction (there was no body and no one ever saw an infant) were factors in this wrongful conviction. Dianne suffers from a diminished mental capacity. *See also:* Victoria Bell Banks.

Tullos, Nancy (California)

Fifty-six-year-old Nancy Tullos was vice president of human resources at the Broadcom Corporation, a semiconductor company, in November 2007 when she was charged with participating in a stock options back-dating operation. She agreed to plead guilty to a single count of obstruction of justice and cooperate with authorities in their investigation of other executives at the corporation. As the investigation continued, it became apparent that there were improprieties on the part of the government. In particular, questions were raised as to whether Nancy had voluntarily pleaded guilty or if she had been intimidated by the prosecutors. In January 2010, US District Judge Cormac Carney set aside Nancy's guilty plea based on her innocence and government misconduct. She became the last of the Broadcom executives to have their convictions overturned. Had she been sentenced, Nancy could have been incarcerated in a federal prison for up to ten years.

Tyson, Betty (New York) (B)

Betty Tyson was a heroin addict and street prostitute in May 1973 when a fifty-two-year-old white man, Timothy Haworth, was found dead. Police surmised that the victim had been looking for a prostitute when he encountered John Duval, a transvestite prostitute, and Betty. After a twelve-hour interrogation in which Betty was shackled to a chair and repeatedly beaten and kicked by police, she confessed to the crime. Although there was no physical evidence linking her to the crime and the tire tracks did not match that of her vehicle, an all-white male jury convicted her of second-degree murder and robbery. She was sentenced to twenty-five years to life for her role in the crimes. In 1997 one of the teenage witnesses recanted his story and told of police coercion. It was also learned that the police had withheld a statement from another teenage witness in which he confirmed that he had never seen either John Duval or Betty Tyson with the victim. One of the detectives in Betty's case had been convicted earlier of fabricating evidence in another case. In May 1998 Betty had her verdict overturned and prosecutors decided against retrying her case. She was wrongfully imprisoned for twenty-five years. Her codefendant, Duval, was officially cleared in February 2000 when a jury acquitted him of all charges.

Urquhart, Tevya (Michigan) (B)
On March 7, 2002, a Detroit phone store was robbed by two armed men shortly after the business opened. Tevya Urquhart was one of three women present that morning. Police and prosecutors incorrectly assumed that the robbery was an inside job and that Tevya and her coworkers aided and abetted the robbers. Wrongly convicted in 2002 of larceny by conversion and false report of a felony, Tevya was sentenced to five months in jail along with three years of probation. After having served about two and a half months, she was released when an appeals court threw out her conviction because there was insufficient evidence to support the charges. In 2004 Tevya was exonerated when the charges were dismissed by the Wayne County Circuit Court. She was awarded $1.27 million in damages by a jury in 2008. *See also:* Kimberly Sykes.

Walker, Cynthia Geneva (Oregon)
This case is similar to that of Nancy Baker-Krofft and involves two similar statutes passed by the legislature in Oregon. Both cases focused on what constitutes "withhold[ing] necessary and physical care" of a child. Nancy was charged with three counts (one for each of her children) of 1st degree criminal mistreatment based solely on the condition of her household. Her case was heard concurrently by the Oregon Supreme Court along with the Nancy Baker-Krofft case. She was officially cleared of the charges in 2010.

Walpole, Merla (California) (H)
In 1965 Merla Walpole and Antonio Rivera were facing difficult times. Antonio was financially unable to support his family, and their three-year-old, Judy, was extremely ill. The couple decided that they could no longer take care of their daughter and abandoned her at a service station in San Francisco. An article in the *San Francisco Chronicle* the following day confirmed that a little girl had been found in that area. Authorities suspected that Merla and Antonio had killed their daughter, but the case lay dormant until February 1, 1973, when the badly decomposed body of a little girl was found near Fontana in San Bernardino County. On June 3, 1974, Merla and Antonio were formally charged with murder. In March 1975, a jury found the couple guilty of second-degree murder. On April 28, 1975 Superior Court Judge Thomas Haldorsen ordered a new trial to investigate their story

about abandoning their child. In October 1975, an investigation resulted in the location of their daughter. Now thirteen years old, the girl exhibited a strong resemblance to her parents. Blood tests and bone analyses suggested that the teenage girl was indeed their daughter. As a result of these findings, the prosecution dismissed the charges against them on November 22, 1975. Marla and Antonio were erroneously incarcerated for 476 days. The identity of the body was never ascertained.

Ward, Madeleine (Illinois) (W)

Madeleine Ward moved her aging parents from an assisted living facility in Louisiana to her home in Illinois. Her sister and brother-in-law felt that the mother could not make financial decisions because she was mentally incompetent. Madeleine disagreed and felt that her mother was capable of making her own decisions. Eventually, her parents were moved to separate living facilities, where they died. Questions arose regarding Madeleine's use of the money from her mother's estate. In January 2006 she went on trial, accused of theft and financial exploitation. At first the jury was deadlocked and ultimately found her guilty of theft but acquitted her of the charge of financial exploitation. Madeleine received a sentence of six years and seven months and was ordered to pay $320,000 back to her mother's estate. During the trial her defense was never given a list of the specific expenses that were alleged as being fraudulent, making it difficult to defend her against the accusations. Furthermore, the defense was not allowed to have three witnesses testify on Madeleine's behalf. In April 2008 her conviction was overturned by the Illinois Court of Appeals and her case was dismissed. On January 8, 2010, a county circuit judge granted her a certificate of innocence.

Ware, Melonie (Georgia) (B)

This wrongful conviction occurred in Decatur, Georgia, where a day-care provider, Melonie Ware, was babysitting nine-month-old Jaden Paige when he became unresponsive on March 21, 2004. He died, and Melonie was arrested. She was tried for felony murder, aggravated battery, and cruelty to a child. The medical examiner labeled the death a homicide and concluded that Jaden had been the victim of shaken baby syndrome (SBS) while discounting the possibility that his sickle cell anemia (SCA) could have caused his death. Jaden also had a leg fracture, which occurred at the hospital. In November 2005 Melonie was found guilty and subsequently sentenced to life in prison. After a prolonged legal dispute, she finally received a new trial in 2009. New evidence at the trial included medical records revealing that the bruises under Jaden's scalp were probably the result of a failed medical procedure that attempted to insert a probe into his skull.

Furthermore, two prominent physicians testified that the little boy died of complications from his SCA, whose symptoms mimic those of SBS. The jury acquitted her of the charges but not before her family had invested over $700,000 in expert witness and legal fees.

Watkins, Cathy (New York) (B)

On January 19, 1995, forty-three-year-old Baithe Diop, a driver for the New Harlem Car Service and a Senegalese immigrant, was shot to death in the Bronx. Miriam Taveras, a drug addict, identified twenty-seven-year-old Cathy Watkins and five men as the individuals she saw leaving the scene immediately after the gun shots. A police investigation disclosed that the victim had been lured to a building in which Cathy lived after a telephone request for a pick-up at that address. Police asked Cathy to call the New Harlem Car Service and pretend to be ordering a car to pick her up. On the other end was the dispatcher who took the car request that resulted in Diop's death. The dispatcher immediately confirmed that the voice was that of the original caller. At that juncture Cathy and the five men—none of whom she knew—were charged with Diop's murder. Convicted in September 1997 of second-degree murder, she was sentenced to twenty-five years to life. A federal investigation later revealed that a drug gang known as SMM (Sex, Money, and Murder) was responsible for Diop's murder. In October 2012 Cathy received her freedom from prison after posting bond and in December 2012 her case was dismissed. Because she had been held in custody while awaiting her trial, Cathy was wrongfully incarcerated for seventeen years of her life.

Weaver, Mary (Iowa) (W)

Forty-one-year-old Mary Weaver was accused of killing eleven-month-old Melissa Mathes while babysitting. The autopsy revealed that the infant had sustained severe head injuries prior to her death. Doctors who examined the body surmised that the cause of death was shaken baby syndrome (SBS). That diagnosis implicated Mary as the perpetrator since it was believed at that time that an infant would become unresponsive immediately in cases of SBS and Melissa had been under Mary's care for almost forty-five minutes when she became unresponsive. During the investigation Melissa's mother, Tessia Mathes, acknowledged that her daughter had hit her head on a padded footrest from a recliner but had sustained no other injuries. At the first trial a cemetery employee testified that Tessia had called to inquire about the cost of an infant grave approximately one month prior to the incident. In December 1993 the first trial concluded with a hung jury. A bench trial in March 1994 resulted in a guilty verdict and a sentence of life without parole. Mary was successful in obtaining a new trial in February 1997 after obtaining affidavits from three women who said that Tessia told them that Melissa had hit her head on a coffee table and had been knocked unconscious before Mary arrived. The defense also retained an expert witness to refute the contention that Melissa was the victim of SBS. On March 5, 1997, Mary was acquitted of all charges by a jury.

Wentworth, Michelle (New York) (W)

This is a federal case in which Michelle Wentworth and John Arena were convicted in 1995 of extortion for conspiring to spill butyric acid at Planned Parenthood in Syracuse and at the offices of a doctor who provided abortions in East Syracuse. John admitted that he paid Michelle's daughter $100 to dump the acid at each facility. Nevertheless, Michelle was sentenced to three years in prison and ordered to repay $52,062 in restitution. She wasn't cleared until after she had completed her sentence. After a subsequent Supreme Court decision redefined extortion to the obtaining of property and not merely taking away one's right to run a business, federal prosecutors agreed to drop their initial convictions and penalties. As a result of her wrongful conviction, Michelle was forced to sell her home to pay her fine. Her marriage of twenty years failed due to the strain caused by the trial and incarceration. Michelle was fifty-one years old in 2004 when she was exonerated.

Wesson, Michelle (Florida) (W)

Michelle Wesson's fourteen-year-old son, Jimmy, had a genetic condition that made him extremely susceptible to illness from germs. He also was developmentally delayed and had the mental understanding of a three-year-old child. When Jimmy died from septicemia, a blood disease aggravated by harmful bacteria, Michelle's messy, cluttered home immediately became the center of controversy, even though it was impossible to determine the exact cause of death. Accused of child neglect causing great bodily harm, she was sentenced to five years in prison in 2003. Michelle was released in 2005 and exonerated that same year.

White, Kizzie (Texas) (B)

After the predawn drug raid on Tulia, Texas, on July 23, 1999, twelve women of color were arrested and falsely convicted of drug-related crimes. Undercover agent Tom Coleman falsely testified regarding their criminal activity. Prosecutorial and police misconduct led to the wrongful conviction of Kizzie White, who was sentenced to twenty-five years in prison. After serving four years, she was released and granted a pardon from the governor of Texas on August 22, 2003, for her wrongful incarceration. *See also:* Marilyn Joyce Cooper, Vickie Fry, Denise Kelly, Etta Kelly, Laura Ann

Mata, Finaye Shelton, Lawanda Smith, Yolanda Smith, Ramona Strickland, Alberta Stell Williams, and Michelle Williams.

Wilcox, Jennifer (Ohio) (W)

The Huber Heights (Ohio) police department began investigating a possible sex ring involving children in the Glenburn Green housing project during the summer of 1984. Jennifer Wilcox and Robert Aldridge were singled out as possible leaders of this group. Although a search of their apartment failed to reveal any proof of a sex ring, the police continued their investigation. Three brothers—Justin (age eight), Jason (age ten), and John (age twelve)— were brought into the station for intensive interrogations. Justin was told that he would be put in jail if he didn't testify against Jennifer and Robert. Jason was put in a holding cell until he acquiesced. John was charged with rape and taken to the juvenile detention center until he agreed to testify for the prosecution. Numerous other children were subjected to similar tactics. In January 1985 Jennifer and Robert received life sentences for multiple counts of child sexual abuse. Seven years later, the three boys recanted their testimony. During a postconviction hearing additional information disclosed that the prosecutor had "sanitized" the document given to the defense counsel. The inconsistencies in the testimonies of the various children had been altered as well as details of the three boys' interrogations. Furthermore, the prosecutor had withheld exculpatory material, including the results of medical examinations that concluded that there was no physical evidence among any of the alleged victims that they had been sexually abused. In 1997 charges against Jennifer and Robert were dismissed after they had been wrongfully incarcerated for eleven years.

Williams, Alberta Stell (Texas) (B)

In 1999 forty-nine-year-old Alberta Stell Williams was one of twelve women of color accused of drug-related crimes in the early morning drug bust in Tulia, Texas. The following year she was sentenced to ten years in prison based on the false testimony of undercover agent Tom Coleman and prosecutorial misconduct. She was incarcerated for two years, nine months, and five days before being released. On August 22, 2003, Alberta was one of thirty-five Tulia residents who received pardons from the governor of Texas. *See also:* Marilyn Joyce Cooper, Vickie Fry, Denise Kelly, Etta Kelly, Laura Ann Mata, Finaye Shelton, Lawanda Smith, Yolanda Smith, Ramona Strickland, Kizzie White, and Michelle Williams.

Williams, Michelle (Texas) (B)

Twenty-three-year-old Michelle Williams was one of twelve women of color who were falsely convicted of drug-related crimes after an early morning raid on the town of Tulia, Texas, on July 23, 1999. She was wrongly incarcerated for two years, five months, and thirteen days. On August 22, 2003, the governor of Texas pardoned her and other Tulia residents after it was ascertained that undercover agent Tom Coleman had lied about the drug transactions. Prosecutorial misconduct further contributed to this false conviction. *See also:* Marilyn Joyce Cooper, Vickie Fry, Denise Kelly, Etta Kelly, Laura Ann Mata, Finaye Shelton, Lawanda Smith, Yolanda Smith, Ramona Strickland, Kizzie White, and Alberta Stell Williams.

Wilson, (Kathryn) Dawn (NC)

This is a case involving the child sexual abuse scandal at the Little Rascals day care center in Edenton, North Carolina. Overall, ninety children accused twenty adults of 429 instances of child sexual abuse, although only seven individuals were actually arrested as a result of these allegations. Dawn worked there as a cook in 1989 when the series of events began unfolding. Her trial began in November 1992 at Hertford, North Carolina. Convicted in January 1993, Dawn received a life sentence. While serving her sentence, she gave birth to a baby boy. In September 1993 she was released on $250,000 bail while awaiting the outcome of her appeal and put under house arrest. The Appellate Court of North Carolina dismissed her conviction in May 1995, and four months later the North Carolina Supreme Court upheld the decision of the appellate court. Finally, in May 1997 charges against Dawn were formally dismissed by the prosecution. *See also:* Betsy Kelly.

Wilson, Shelia (Kentucky)

This case appeared in the book *In Spite of Innocence: Erroneous Convictions in Capital Cases* (Michael Radelet, Hugo Bedau, and Constance Putnam). Shelia Wilson was wrongly convicted of first-degree murder in Kentucky in 1979. After being imprisoned for four years she was cleared of charges in 1983.

Winston, Joy (Nevada)

Joy Winston, a Las Vegas woman with a checkered past, was convicted of burglary for allegedly stealing CDs from Wal-Mart. The conviction qualified her as a habitual criminal under Nevada law. Consequently, she was sentenced to ten years to life in 2008 and began serving her prison sentence in March. In June 2009 the Nevada Supreme Court ruled that there was insufficient evidence to support her conviction and therefore she no longer qualified as a habitual criminal. The following month the court ordered her release from prison. The order additionally stated that "because our decision was based on a determination that the state had presented legally insufficient evidence to support the guilty verdict, the Double Jeopardy Clause of the United States Constitution precludes a second trial." Joy was fifty-two years old when she was released.

Wright, Patricia (California) (B)

Convicted in 1998 at the age of forty-six years for the murder of her ex-husband, Willie Jerome Scott, Patricia Wright received a sentence of life without parole because this was her third strike. (The other strikes resulted from the theft of two cheap toys and a hand towel from an open house by her son when he was seven years of age.) Jerome, who maintained ties with his family since the divorce, was gay and lived in a motor home in a crime-ridden area of Los Angeles. His decomposing body revealed a knife protruding from his chest and a plastic bag wrapped around his head. In addition to numerous stab wounds, there was evidence that he had engaged in anal sex prior to his death. A drug addict who frequently kept large sums of money on his person, Jerome was an easy target for anyone who might want to harm him. Although he was murdered in September 1981, police did not arrest Patricia until August 1997 after many long years of accumulating questionable evidence. Faced with the possibility of serving twelve years in prison for child abuse, her brother falsely testified to police that a family friend named Larry Slaughter had killed Jerome but that his sister had arranged for the murder. Although her brother recanted his confession after serving an abbreviated prison sentence, Patricia was found guilty of first-degree murder and conspiracy to commit murder. The murder weapon, which did not contain the fingerprints of either Patricia or Slaughter, had been "lost" by the police by the time of the trial. Police misconduct, perjury by criminal justice officials, and forensic errors contributed to this wrongful conviction. By 2012 Patricia's health had deteriorated to the point that she requested a release to be able to die at home under California's compassionate release law. Suffering from Stage 4 cancer in her brain and breasts and incontinence, Patricia, who is legally blind, was denied clemency from Governor Jerry Brown because she had three prior felonies (the previous two offenses were misdemeanors but were charged as felonies).

Yost, Donna (Michigan)

Donna Yost's first-grade daughter, Monique, died of an overdose of antidepressants in 1999. After some legal questions regarding the sufficiency of the evidence, Donna was finally charged with murder. In April 2006 a Bay County, Michigan, jury acquitted her of premeditated murder but convicted her of first-degree felony murder. Donna was sentenced to life without parole and began serving her sentence at the Robert Scott Correctional Facility in Plymouth shortly after her conviction. In 2008 a Michigan Court of Appeals overturned her conviction and vacated her sentence. According to the ruling, Donna, who suffers from a diminished intellectual capacity, had been denied a fair trial by the trial judge when he "abused his discretion" by selectively deciding which evidence could be presented at trial. Bay County Prosecutor Kurt Asbury, undeterred by the decision, appealed to the Michigan Supreme Court. In 2009 the Michigan Supreme Court upheld the ruling of the appellate court. In return for her release, Donna pleaded no contest on March 21, 2009, to first-degree child abuse and was sentenced to three years probation. In 2012 she successfully completed the terms of that probation.

Bibliography

ABC News. (2005, December 27). "Mom's sentence overturned in baby's death." Retrieved on 3/7/2012 from http://abcnews.go.com/GMA/LegalCenter /story?id=1444895.

Acker, J., Bohm, R., and Lanier, C. (eds.). (1998). *America's experiment with capital punishment*. Durham, NC: Carolina Academic Press.

Ahmed, S., and Botelho, G. (2015, March 24). "Debra Milke, who spent 22 years on Arizona death row, has murder case tossed." CNN. Retrieved on 8/19/2015 from http://www.cnn.com/2015/03/24/justice/arizona-debra-milke-death -sentence/index.html.

Alexander, D. (2013, February 3). "Wrongfully convicted: 20 years after infant's death, Mary Weaver's case still gaining national interest." *Marshalltown Times Republican*. Retrieved on 7/25/2013 from http://www.timesrepublican.com /page/content.detail/id/556936/wrongfully-convicted.

Alley, J. (2009, October 28). "Wrongly convicted woman now sues officers." *News-Herald* (Lincoln Park, Michigan). Retrieved on 4/15/2013 from http: //thenewsherald.com/articles/2005/08/21/localnews/20050821-archive1.prt.

"'American Violet' tells story of ill-fated Hearne drug raids." (2009, March 13). *Dallas Morning News*. Retrieved on 6/10/2010 from http:// www.dallasnews.com.

Anastasia, G. (2011, January 8). "Girlfriend of 'Ace Capone' gets two-year sentence." *Philadelphia Inquirer*. Retrieved on 12/27/2012 from http://articles.philly.com/2011-01-08/news/27017216_1_coles-case-sentencing-guidelines-sentencing-hearing.

Anderson, J. (2009, June 5). "Court overturns woman's murder conviction." *West Virginia Record*. Retrieved on 1/19/2011 from http://www.wvrecord.com /printer/article.asp?c=219424.

Asistio, A. (2012, September 14). "Only female exoneree in U.S. speaks in Fresno." KSEE 24 News. Retrieved on 6/12/2013 from http://www.ksee24.com /news/local/Sabrina-Butler—-AAS-169839826.html.

Associated Press. (2005a, April 1). "Conviction in death voided." *St. Petersburg Times*. Retrieved on 1/13/2011 from http://www.sptimes.com/2005/04/01 /news_pf/State/Conviction_in_death_v.shtml.

Associated Press. (2005b, April 18). "Wrongly convicted." WIBW television. Retrieved on 1/16/2011 from http://www.wibw.com/home/headlines /1484032.html.

Associated Press. (2005c, December 21). "Brandy Briggs will soon be out of prison." Retrieved on 3/7/2012 from http://abclocal.go.com/ktrk/story ?section=news/localandid=3745784.

Associated Press. (2008, February 7). "Mother freed from prison for crime she didn't commit." Retrieved on 1/31/2011 from http://truthinjustice.org /jernigan.htm.

Associated Press. (2010, September 30). "Judge overturns Wirt County assessor's conviction." *Daily Mail*. Retrieved on 1/19/2011 from http:// dailymail.com/News/statenews/201009300744.

Associated Press. (2012, April 9). "Man acquitted in Ted Binion's death arrested on DUI charge." *Las Vegas Sun*. Retrieved on 7/28/2014 from http://www .lasvegassun.com/news/2012/apr/09/man-acquitted-ted-binions-death-arrested-dui-charg.

Associated Press. (2015, March 23). "Debra Milke, who spent 22 years on death row, has murder case thrown out." *Huffington Post*. Retrieved on 8/19/2015 from http://www.huffingtonpost.com/2015/03/23/debra-milke-case-tossed_n_6924472.html.

Baldus, D., and Woodworth, G. (2003). "Race discrimination in the administration of the death penalty: An overview of the empirical evidence with special emphasis on the post-1990 research." *Criminal Law Bulletin, 39*, 194–227.

Barrouquere, B. (2000, February 15). "Judge overturns drug conviction." *Sarasota Herald-Tribune*. Retrieved on 7/24/2013 from http://www .mapinc.org/drugnews/v00/n218/a10.html.

Beck, K. (2004, October 28). *Wenatchee witch hunt: Child sex abuse trials in Douglas and Chelan counties*. Retrieved on 7/5/2014 from http://www .historylink.org/index.cfm?DisplayPage=output.cfmandfile_id=7065.

Beckett, K., Nyrop, K., and Pfingst, L. (2006). "Race, drugs, and policing: Understanding disparities in drug delivery arrests." *Criminology, 44*, 105–138.

Bedau, H., and Radelet, M. (1987). "Miscarriages of justice in potentially capital cases." *Stanford Law Review, 40*, 21–179.

Berger, R., Free, M., and Searles, P. (2009). *Crime, justice, and society: An introduction to criminology* (3rd ed.). Boulder, CO: Lynne Rienner.

Bernhard, A. (2001). "Effective assistance of counsel." In S. Westervelt and J. Humphrey (eds.), *Wrongly convicted: Perspectives on failed justice*. New Brunswick, NJ: Rutgers University Press.

Beyerstein, L. (2007, January 19). "Questionable conviction of Connecticut teacher in pop-up porn case." Retrieved on 7/21/2010 from http://www .faithandthecity.org/issues/education/articles/Questionable-conviction.shtml.

Blakeslee, N. (2002, November). "Bust town: It's been two years since Tulia's tainted drug arrests first came to light. How much has changed there? Not nearly enough." *Texas Monthly*. Retrieved on 10/1/2009 from http://www .texasmonthly.com/cms/printthis.php?file=reporter.phpandissue=2002-11-01.

Blakeslee, N. (2005). *Tulia: Race, cocaine, and corruption in a small town*. New York: Public Affairs.

Bluhm Legal Clinic. (n.d. a). *America's first wrongful murder conviction case*. Chicago: Center on Wrongful Convictions. Retrieved on 1/3/2013 from http://www.law.northwestern.edu/legalclinic/wrongfulconvictions /exonerations/vt/boorn-brothers.html.

Bluhm Legal Clinic. (n.d. b). *First DNA Exoneration: Gary Dotson*. Chicago: Center on Wrongful Convictions. Retrieved on 1/2/2013 from http://www.law.northwestern.edu/legalclinic/wrongfulconvictions /exonerations/il/gary-dotson.html.

Bluhm Legal Clinic. (n.d. c). *First DNA Death Row Exoneration: Kirk Bloodsworth.* Chicago: Center on Wrongful Convictions. Retrieved on 1/3/2013 from http://www.law.northwestern.edu/legalclinic/wrongfulconvictions/exonerations/md/kirk-bloodsworth.html.

Blumstein, A. (1993). "Making rationality relevant." *Criminology, 31,* 1–16.

Boggs, C. (2000). "Lerlene Roever (Shasta) update: Bereft, more alone than ever." *Justice Denied, 2* (1). Retrieved on 7/25/2014 from http://justicedenied.org/volume2issue1.htm#Lerlene.

Brecher, E. (1972). *Licit and illicit drugs.* Boston: Little, Brown.

Buckley, S. (1991, July 3). "Prosecutors reject new trial in Sandra Craig abuse case." *Washington Post,* p. C1.

Budd, P., and Budd, D. (2010). *Tested: How 12 wrongly imprisoned men held onto hope.* Dallas, TX: Brown Books.

Bukowski, D. (2008, March 2). "Bad cops cost city millions." *Michigan Citizen.* Retrieved on 1/16/2011 from http://michigancitizen.com/bad-cops-cost-city-millions-p5708-1.htm.

Burns, S. (2011). *The Central Park Five: A chronicle of a city wilding.* New York: Knopf.

Bush-Baskette, S. (1998). "The war on drugs as a war against black women." In S. Miller (ed.), *Crime control and women.* Thousand Oaks, CA: Sage.

Caniglia, J. (2008a, January 22). "Mansfield woman free after drug conviction based on lies." Retrieved on 11/7/2014 from http://www.freerepublic.com/focus/f-news/1958477/posts.

Caniglia, J. (2008b, January 23). "Feds to release 15 more people in botched Mansfield drug case." *Plain Dealer.* Retrieved on July 12, 2010 from http://blog.cleveland.com/metro/2008/01/feds_to_release_15_more_people.html.

Caniglia, J. (2009, May 15). "Deputy Charles Metcalf, who worked with DEA agent Lee Lucas, pleads guilty to lying at drug trial." *Plain Dealer.* Retrieved on 9/22/2010 from http://blog.cleveland.com/metro//print.html.

Caniglia, J. (2012, September 20). "Rogue informant Jerrell Bray, who set up innocent people, dies in prison." *Plain Dealer.* Retrieved on 10/28/2014 from http://www.cleveland.com/metro/index.ssf/2012/09/rogue_informant_jerrell_bray_w.html.

Carter, C. (2011a, September 30). "A three strikes tragedy." *Crime Report.* Retrieved on 8/8/2013 from http://www.thecrimereport.org/news/inside-criminal-justice/2011-10-a-three-strikes-tragedy.

Carter, C. (2011b, October 10). "Three strikes holds dying innocent woman behind bars: Justice for Patricia Wright and her family!" *San Francisco Bay View.* Retrieved on 8/8/2013 from http://sfbayview.com/2011/three-strikes-holds-dying-innocent-woman-behind-bars-justice-for-patricia-wright-and-her-family.

Carter, M. (1998). "The Virginia Larzelere story." *Justice Denied, 1* (4). Retrieved on 10/23/2013 from http://justicedenied.org/v1issue4#Virginia Larzelere.

Carvin, A. (2007, April 25). "Does sentencing delay mean a possible reprieve for Julie Amero?" PBS Teachers. Retrieved on 8/24/2011 from http://www.pbs.org/teachers/learning.now/2007/04/does_sentencing_delay_mean_a_p_1.html.

"The case of Sonia Cacy." (2010, September 29). Retrieved on 2/29/2012 from http://standdown.typepad.com/weblog/2010/09/the-case-of-sonia-cacy.html.

Castillo, A. (2005, May 26). "Marie La Pinta freed at last!" *Newsday.* Retrieved on 1/16/2011 from http://realcostofprisons.org/blog/archives/2005/05/marie_la_pinta.html.

CBS News. (1999, March 5). "$36 million for wrongful conviction." Retrieved on 8/3/2014 from http://www.cbsnews.com/news/36-million-for-wrongful-conviction.

CBS News. (2000). "State of Georgia v. Sheila Bryan: A small-town mom is accused of killing her own mother." *48 Hours*. Retrieved on 1/31/2011 from http://truthinjustice.org/sbryan-1.htm.

CBS News. (2003, September 26). *Targeted in Tulia, Texas?* Retrieved on 5/20/2009 from http://www.cbsnews.com/targeted-in-tulia-texas-26-09-2003.

Center for Public Integrity. (n.d.). "Harmful error." Retrieved on 1/16/2011 from http://projects.publicintegrity.org/pm/default.aspx?sid=sidebarsandaid=38.

Center on Wrongful Convictions. (n.d. a). "About the project." Retrieved on 5/14/2014 from http://www.law.northwestern.edu/legalclinic /wrongfulconvictions/womensproject/about/.

Center on Wrongful Convictions. (n.d. b). "Paula Gray." Retrieved on 3/25/2013 from http://www.law.northwestern.edu/wrongfulconvictions/exonerations /ilGraySummary.html.

Cesare, C. (2005, April 29). "Sandy Murphy: Officially discharged from prison." KLAS-TV (8 News, Las Vegas). Retrieved on 7/25/2014 from http:// www.8newsnow.com/story/3275876/sandy-murphy-officially-discharged-from-prison.

Chapman, S. (2012, May 10). "Greensburg mom speaks out about 1995 arson, murder conviction." WTHR television (NBC affiliate). Retrieved on 7/20/2013 from http://www.wthr.com/story/15325846/greenburg-mom-speaks-out-about-arson-murder-conviction.

Christian, C. (2001, September 11). "Woman testifies in baby sitter's trial." *Houston Chronicle*. Retrieved on 8/14/2013 from http://chron.com/news /houston-texas/article/Woman-testifies-in-baby-sitters-trial.

Christofferson, J. (2006, August 29). "Conn. Supreme Court overturns mother's conviction in son's suicide." Associated Press. Retrieved on 1/31/2011 from http://truthinjustice.org/scruggs.htm.

Clark, M. (1991, April 10). "Craig case prosecutors fear effects of retrial." *Baltimore Sun*. Retrieved on 5/16/2014 from http://articles .baltimoresun.com/1991-04-10/news/1991100029_1_courtroom-maryland-court-howard-county.

CNN. (2000). *Was Texas town's drug sting racist?* Retrieved on 5/6/2007 from http://archives.cnn.com/2000/US/10/drug.sting.protest.

Cohen, S. (2003). *The wrong men: America's epidemic of wrongful death row convictions*. New York: Carroll and Graf.

Colarossi, A. (2010a, September 15). "Woman who says she was wrongly convicted released from jail." *Orlando Sentinel*. Retrieved on 1/13/2011 from http: //articles.orlandosentinel.com/2010-09-15/news/os-convicted-woman-released-20100915_1_malenne-joseph-orange-county-jail-geordany-francois.

Colarossi, A. (2010b, September 17). "Lawyer can talk to Orlando officer in woman's felony conviction case, judge rules." *Orlando Sentinel*. Retrieved on 1/30/2011 from http://truthinjustice.org/malenne-joseph.htm.

Colarossi, A. (2010c, September 28). "Woman to be exonerated in criminal mischief case." *Orlando Sentinel*. Retrieved on 1/13/2011 from http://articles .orlandosentinel.com/2010-09-28/news/os-convicted-woman-exonerated-20100928_1_kittsie-simmons-malenne-joseph-guilty-verdict.

Colarossi, A. (2011, January 23). "Judge's idea to review botched conviction gets squelched." *Orlando Sentinel*. Retrieved on 12/6/2012 from http://articles.orlandosentinel.com/2011-01-23/news/os-no-botched-conviction-meeting-20110118_1_malenne-joseph-wrong-person-wrongful-conviction.

Commission on Capital Cases. (2008, August 7). "Larzelere, Virginia Gail (W/F)."

Retrieved on 8/5/2013 from http://www.floridacapitalcases.state.fl.us /case_updates/Htm/842556.htm.

Connery, D. (1996). *Convicting the innocent: The story of a murder, a false confession, and the struggle to free a "wrong man."* Cambridge, MA: Brookline Books.

Cressy, L. (1991, March 9). "Dentist murdered at office." Retrieved on 5/9/2013 from http://www.toddlertime.com/helpvirginia/breakingnews.htm.

Daecher, M. (1998, August 28). "Forensic fraud: No motive, no witness, and 99 years in jail: The curious conviction of Sonia Cacy." *Texas Observer*. Retrieved on 2/29/2012 from http://truthinjustice.org/sonia4.htm.

Dale, M. (2009, September 21). "Former Pacer testifies in drug case." Associated Press. Retrieved on 12/27/2012 from http://www.wishtv.com/dpp/sports /pacers_and_nba/other_nba/Former_Pacer_testifies-in-drug-case.

Davis, A. (2007). *Arbitrary justice: The power of the American prosecutor*. New York: Oxford University Press.

Death Penalty Information Center. (n.d.). *Innocence: List of those freed from death row*. Retrieved on 4/15/2014 from http://www.deathpenaltyinfo.org/innocence-list-those-freed-death-row?scid=6anddid=110.

Decker, F. (2002, April 24). "Survivor's story: Beverly Monroe on prison, faith, and the future." *Richmond.com*. Retrieved on 1/19/2011 from http://www .truthinjustice.org/survivor.htm.

Denzel, S. (n.d. a). *Cynthia Sommer—California*. Retrieved on 5/28/2012 from http://www.law.umich.edu/special/exoneration/Pages/casedetail.aspx?caseid =3652.

Denzel, S. (n.d. b). *Dominique Brim*. Retrieved on 12/13/2012 from http:// www.law.umich.edu/special/exoneration/Pages/casedetail.aspx?caseid=3050.

Denzel, S. (n.d. c). *Jennifer Hall—Missouri*. Retrieved on 5/28/2012 from http:// www.law.umich.edu/special/exoneration/Pages/casedetail.aspx?caseid=3271.

Denzel, S. (n.d. d). *Lisa Hansen—Michigan*. Retrieved on 1/5/2015 from http:// www.law.umich.edu/special/exoneraton/Pages/casedetail.aspx?caseid=3276.

Dickerson, M., and Kulstad, M. (2002, April 5). "Beverly Monroe released from prison." *NBC 12 News* (Richmond, Virginia). Retrieved on 1/19/2011 from http://www.truthinjustice.org/beverly-bond.htm.

Druse, R. (1887). *Mrs. Druse's case and Maggie Houghtaling: An innocent woman hanged*. Philadelphia: Old Franklin Publishing House.

Duggan, J. (2008, November 11). "Taylor freed from prison." *Beatrice* (Nebraska) *Daily Sun*. Retrieved on 1/16/2011 from http://www.beatricedailysun.com /news/local/article_8c70d52d-70a1-5bca-b967-1c1d8385.

Dunlap, B. (2010a, February 18). "Assessor fined for falsifying record." *Parkersburg News and Sentinel*. Retrieved on 7/15/2013 from http://www.newsandsentinel.com/page/content.detail/id/526747.html.

Dunlap, B. (2010b, September 15). "Dismissal sought in Hennen case." *Parkersburg News and Sentinel*. Retrieved on 1/8/2015 from http://www .newsandsentinel.com/page/content.detail/id/539067/Dismissal-sought-in-Hennen-case.html?nav=5061.

Edds, M. (2003). *An expendable man: The near-execution of Earl Washington, Jr.* New York: New York University Press.

"Ella Mae Ellison." (1980, March 26). *Boston Globe*. Retrieved on 1/16/2011 from http://www.nodp.org/ma/stacks/e_ellison.html.

"Errors at F.B.I. may be issue in 3,000 cases." (2003, March 17). *New York Times*, p. A18.

Estrin, R. (1999, October 21). "Judge frees convicted child abuser." Associated Press. Retrieved on 1/31/2011 from http://truthinjustice.org/lafave.htm.

Executed Today. (2011, January 3). "1786: Elizabeth Wilson, her reprieve too late." Executed Today.com. Retrieved on 8/14/2015 from http://www.executedtoday .com/2011/01/03/1786-elizabeth-wilson-her-reprieve-too-late.

Executed Today. (2014, October 17). "1817: Maggie Houghtaling." Executed Today.com. Retrieved on 8/14/2015 from http://www.executedtoday .com/2014/10/17/1817-maggie-houghtaling.

"The Fair Sentencing Act corrects a long-time wrong in cocaine cases." (2010, August 3). *Washington Post*. Retrieved on 9/15/2014 from http://www.washing-tonpost.com/wp-dyn/content/article/2010/08/02/AR2010080204360.html.

Fang, L. (2014, July 21). "The real reason pot is still illegal." *The Nation*. Retrieved on 9/10/2014 from http://www.thenation.com/article/180493/anti-pot-lobbys-big-bankroll.

"A Fells Acres chronology." (n.d.). *The Amirault tragedy*. Retrieved on 5/29/2014 from http://mysite.verizon.net/vzex11z4/amichron.html.

"A few of Washington's wrongfully convicted." (2013, May 7). *Seattle Weekly News*. Retrieved on 7/8/2013 from http://www.seattleweekly.com /home/946786-129/harris-convicted-served-trial-county-state.

findingDulcinea. (2011, May 26). "On this day: Alse Young hanged for witchcraft in Connecticut." Finding Dulcinea. Retrieved on 8/16/2015 from http://www .findingdulcinea.com/news/on-this-day/May-June-08/On-this-day—Alse -Young-Hanged-for-Witchcraft-in-Connecticut.ht.

Forejustice. (2014, April 20). *Innocents database*. Retrieved on 5/7/2014 from http://www.forejustice.org/search_idb.htm.

Free, M. (1996). *African Americans and the criminal justice system*. New York: Garland.

Free, M., and Ruesink, M. (2012). *Race and justice: Wrongful convictions of African American men*. Boulder, CO: Lynne Rienner.

Free, M., and Ruesink, M. (forthcoming). "Flawed justice: A study of wrongly convicted African American women." *Journal of Ethnicity in Criminal Justice*. doi: 10.1080/15377938.2015.1015199.

Friends of Justice. (2010, January 16). *More about Martha Coakley and the Souza case*. Retrieved on 8/6/2013 from http://bobchatelle.net/more-about-martha-coakley-and-the-souza-case.

Gavett, G. (2011, June 28). "Shaken Baby Syndrome: A diagnosis challenged." *PBS Frontline*. Retrieved on 6/17/2014 from http://www.pbs.org/wgbh/pages /frontline/the-child-cases/shaken-baby-syndrome.

"Georgia Supreme Court tosses teacher's conviction for sex with student." (2009, summer). *Justice Denied, 43*, 14.

Gershman, B. (1991). "Abuse of power in the prosecutor's office." *World and I* (June), 477–487.

Gillham, O. (2010a, April 3). "Records, defender reveal flaws in case." *Tulsa World*. Retrieved on 9/2/2014 from http://www.tulsaworld.com/site/printerfriendly story.aspx?articleid=20100403_11_A1_Jurors901825.

Gillham, O. (2010b, September 20). "Tulsa judge drops charges as result of probe." *Tulsa World*. Retrieved on 1/19/2011 from http://www.tulsaworld.com /site/printerfriendlystory.aspx?articleid=20100920_11_a1_ulns.

Gonnerman, J. (2001, July 31). "Tulia blues." *The Village Voice*. Retrieved on 8/12/2014 from http://www.villagevoice.com/2001-07-31/news/tulia-blues/full.

Goodyear, C. (2000, December 22). "Foster mom convicted of abuse gets new trial/Judge says attorney erred in not calling expert witness." *San Francisco Chronicle*. Retrieved on 7/22/2013 from http://www.sfgate.com/news/article /Foster-Mom-Convicted-of-Abuse-Gets-New-Trial.

Gould, J., and Leo, R. (2010). "One hundred years later: Wrongful convictions after a century of research." *Journal of Criminal Law and Criminology, 100*, 825–868.

"Grand jury investigation results." (2010, September 20). *Tulsa World*. Retrieved on 9/2/2014 from http://www.tulsaworld.com/site/printerfriendlystory.aspx ?articleid=20100920_11_a1_ulnsb.

"Grand Rapids, Michigan woman punished and humiliated, and now exonerated." (2006, August 18). *Detroit Free Press*. Retrieved on 1/31/2011 from http://truthinjustice.org/lisa-hansen.htm.

Green, R. (2008, November 25). "Substitute teacher lost so much in sordid case." *Hartford Courant*. Retrieved on 6/28/2013 from http://articles .courant.com/2008-11-25/news/rgreen1125.art_1_substitute-teacher-julie-amero-pornography.

Greene, D. (2012, March 29). *New evidence in high-profile shaken baby case*. National Public Radio. Retrieved on 7/23/2013 from http://www.npr.org /templates/transcript/transcript.php?storyId=1495.

Grisham, J. (2007). *The innocent man: Murder and injustice in a small town*. New York: Dell.

Grissom, B. (2010, September 29). "Woman charged with murder campaigns for innocence." *Texas Tribune*. Retrieved on 2/29/2012 from http://www .texastribune.org/texas-dept-criminal-justice/innocence-project-of-texas/woman-charged-with-murder-campaigns-for-innocence.

Gross, A. (n.d. a). *Brandy Briggs—Texas*. Retrieved on 5/28/2012 from http://www .law.umich.edu/special/exoneration/Pages/casedetail.aspx?caseid=3812.

Gross, A. (n.d. b). *Brenda Kniffen—California*. Retrieved on 5/28/2012 from http://www.law.umich.edu/special/exoneration/Pages/casedetail.aspx?caseid=3 359.

Gross, A. (n.d. c). *Deborah McCuan—California*. Retrieved on 5/28/2012 from http://www.law.umich.edu/special/exoneration/Pages/casedetail.aspx?caseid=3 426.

Gross, A. (n.d. d). *Marcella Pitts*. Retrieved on 5/21/2014 from http:// www.law.umich.edu/special/exoneration/Pages/casedetail.aspx?caseid=3539.

Gross, A. (n.d. e). *Melonie Ware—Georgia*. Retrieved on 5/28/2012 from http://www.law.umich.edu/special/exoneration/Pages/casedetail.aspx?caseid=3 814.

Gross, A. (n.d. f). *Yvonne Eldridge*. Retrieved on 7/20/2013 from https:// www.law.umich.edu/special/exoneration/Pages/casedetail.aspx?caseid=3999.

Gross, S. (2008). "Convicting the innocent." *Annual Review of Law and Social Science, 4*, 173–192.

Gross, S., Jacoby, K., Matheson, D., Montgomery, N., and Patil, S. (2005). "Exonerations in the United States 1989 through 2003." *Journal of Criminal Law and Criminology, 95*, 523–560.

Gross, S., and Shaffer, M. (2012). *Exonerations in the United States, 1989–2012: Report by the National Registry of Exonerations*. Retrieved on 1/7/2013 from http://www.law.umich.edu/special/exoneration/Documents/exonerations_us_19 89_2012_full_report.pdf.

Gumbel, A. (2007). "American travesty." Common Dreams News Center. Retrieved on 1/8/2010 from http://www.commondreams.org/cgi-bin/print.cgi?file=head-lines020820-06.htm.

Hansen, J. (2008, November 8). "Helen Wilson's killer identified." *Beatrice* (Nebraska) *Daily Sun*. Retrieved on 1/16/2011 from http://www .beatricedailysun.com/news/local/article_ad61b350-4236-52b8-9085-79429b28.

Harper, D. (2013, December 26). "Tulsa reaches $300,000 settlement in police-corruption wrongful imprisonment lawsuit." *Tulsa World*. Retrieved on 9/2/2014 from http://www.tulsaworld.com/homepagelatest/tulsa-reaches-settlement.

Heller, M. (2010, May). "Sandy Murphy's complicated life." *Orange Coast Magazine*. Retrieved on 7/25/2014 from http://www.orangecoast.com/sandymurphy/Index.aspx.

Helmer, J. (1975). *Drugs and minority oppression*. New York: Seabury.

Hensley, J. J., and Collom, L. (2008, February 7). "Mom freed; served 7 years for heist she didn't commit." *Arizona Republic*. Retrieved on 11/24/2014 from http://www.azcentral.com/community/gilbert/articles/2008/02/07/20080207ban krobber0207.html.

Herbert, B. (2002, August 15). "An imaginary homicide." *New York Times*. Retrieved on 4/9/2014 from http://www.nytimes.com/2002/08/15/opinion/an-imaginary-homicide.html.

Hill, F. (1995). *A delusion of Satan: The full story of the Salem witch trials*. New York: Doubleday.

Hill, F. (2000). *The Salem witch trials reader*. Cambridge, MA: DaCapo Press.

Hodson, S. (2009, June 16). "Teacher sex case reversed over consent defense." *Augusta Chronicle*. Retrieved on 1/13/2011 from http://chronicle.augusta.com/stories/2009/06/16/met_527756/shtml.

Hoffman, A. (2008, April 17). "Judge dismisses charges against marine widow." Associated Press. Retrieved on 1/30/2011 from http://truthinjustice.org/cynthia-sommer.htm.

Hopkins, J. (2012, August 23). "Mom convicted in deadly arson free after court ruling." *Chicago Tribune*. Retrieved on 7/20/2013 from http://articles.chicago tribune.com/2012-08-23/news/ct-nw-arson-mother-20120823_1_dep.

Horner, H. (2007, January 22). "The strange case of Ms. Julie Amero." *Service Assurance Daily*. Retrieved on 3/9/2011 from http://www.network performancedaily.com/2007/01/the_strange_case_of_ms_julie_a_1.html.

Huff, C.R., Rattner, A., and Sagarin, E. (1996). *Convicted but innocent: Wrongful conviction and public policy*. Thousand Oaks, CA: Sage.

Humes, E. (1999). *Mean justice*. New York: Simon and Schuster.

Humes, K., Jones, N., and Ramirez, R. (2011). *Overview of race and Hispanic origin: 2010*. District of Columbia: US Census Bureau.

Ibanga, I. (2009, January 27). "Teacher: Wrong computer click ruined my life." *ABC News*. Retrieved on 6/28/2013 from http://abcnews.go.com/GMA/print?id=6739393.

Innocence Project. (n.d. a). *Ada JoAnn Taylor*. Retrieved on 1/19/2011 from http://www.innocenceproject.org/Content/Ada_JoAnn_Taylor.php.

Innocence Project. (n.d. b). *Bad lawyering*. Retrieved on 2/28/2013 from http://www.innocenceproject.org/understand/Bad-Lawyering.php.

Innocence Project. (n.d. c). *Debra Shelden*. Retrieved on 1/19/2011 from http://www.innocenceproject.org/Content/Debra_Shelden.php.

Innocence Project. (n.d. d). *DNA exonerations nationwide*. Retrieved on 4/15/2014 from http://www.innocenceproject.org/Content/DNA-Exonerations-Nationwide.php.

Innocence Project. (n.d. e). *Eyewitness misidentification*. Retrieved on 2/22/2013 from http://www.innocenceproject.org/understand/Eyewitness-Misidentification.php.

Innocence Project. (n.d. f). *False confessions*. Retrieved on 2/22/2013 from http://www.innocenceproject.org/understand/False-Confessions.php.

Innocence Project. (n.d. g). *Forensic problems and wrongful convictions*. Retrieved on 2/28/2013 from http://www.innocenceproject.org/Content/Forensic_Problems_and_Wrongful_Convictions.php.

Innocence Project. (n.d. h). *Informants*. Retrieved on 2/25/2013 from http://www.innocenceproject.org/understand/Snitches-Informants.php.

Innocence Project. (n.d. i). *Kathy Gonzalez*. Retrieved on 1/19/2011 from http://www.innocenceproject.org/Content/Kathy_Gonzalez.php.

Innocence Project. (n.d. j). *Paula Gray*. Retrieved on 1/19/2011 from http://www.innocenceproject.org/Content/Paula_Gray.php.

Innocence Project Northwest. (2013, August 1). *Our clients' stories of innocence.* Retrieved on 7/10/2014 from http://www.law.washington.edu/clinics/ipnw/Stories.aspx#cunningham.

Innocence Project of Florida. (2011, February 14). "Prosecutor refuses judge's request to simply talk about wrongful conviction." Retrieved on 12/6/2012 from http://floridainnocence.org/content/?tag=malenne-joseph.

Innocence Project of New Orleans. (n.d.). *Cheryle Beridon*. Retrieved on 12/3/2012 from http://ip-no.org/exoneree-profile/cheryle-beridon.

Innocence Project of Texas. (n.d.). *Sonia Cacy: An innocent victim of junk science.* Retrieved on 2/29/2012 from http://ipoftexas.org/index.php?action=sonia-cacy.

Jankin, T. (2004). *Bloodsworth: The true story of the first death row inmate exonerated by DNA*. Chapel Hill, NC: Shannon Ravenel Books (Algonquin).

Jenkins, J. (1979). *Early American imprints, a collection of works printed in America between 1662–1800* (vol. 2). Austin, TX: Jenkins.

Johnson, C., and Hampikian, G. (2003). *Exit to freedom*. Athens: University of Georgia Press.

Juarez, L. (2011, October 11). "Judge blocks path for release of inmate with terminal cancer." *ABC News*. Retrieved on 7/13/2014 from http://abc7.com/archive/8388006.

Kemmerer, T. (2010a). *Friends 'til the end presents: Trenda Kemmerer*. Retrieved on 8/13/2013 from http://www.friendstiltheend.com/trendakemmerer.html.

Kemmerer, T. (2010b). *Trenda Kemmerer: The wheels of justice turn slowly.* Retrieved on 3/7/2012 from http://freetrenda.com/MyStory.aspx.

Kennedy, J. (2003). "Drug wars in black and white." *Law and Contemporary Problems, 66*, 153–181.

Kenyon, J. (2009, March 2). "Shirley Kinge suing New York." Retrieved on 1/9/2015 from http://www.cnycentral.com/news/story.aspx?id=267633#.VK_5f3urHP4.

Kershner, J. (1996, June). "Witch hunt in Wenatchee?" *American Journalism Review*. Retrieved on 7/4/2014 from http://ajrarchive.org/article.asp?id=1400.

Kever, J. (2006, June 11). "Freed from prison, young mom's shackled by uncertainty." *Houston Chronicle*. Retrieved on 3/7/2012 from http://www.chron.com/life/article/Freed-from-prison-young-mom-s-shackled-by-1492198.php.

"Key points regarding Kirstin Lobato's Las Vegas wrongful conviction." (n.d.). Retrieved on 1/16/2014 from http://www.justice4kirstin.com/las-vegas-wrongful-conviction.html.

Kiefer, M. (2015, August 3). "Debra Milke's new world after a half-life on death row." *Arizona Republic*. Retrieved on 8/19/2015 from http://www.azcentral.com/story/news/local/phoenix/2015/08/03/debra-milkes-new-world-half-life-death-row/30974639.

Kinge v. State of New York. State of New York, Court of Claims. Claimant's post-trial memorandum on damages. Claim No. 88273, 2009. Retrieved on 1/9/2015 from http://archive.ithacajournal.com/assets/doc/CB133686428.

Klein, C. (2012, October 31). *Before Salem, the first American witch hunt.* History Channel. Retrieved on 8/16/2015 from http://www.history.com/news/before-salem-the-first-american-witch-hunt.

Kobel, R. (2004, April 28). "Woman held in death of her husband." *Baltimore Sun.* Retrieved on 1/27/2015 from http://articles.baltimoresun.com/2004-04-28/news/0404280337_1_arundel-county-anne-arundel-laura-ann.

Konvisser, Z. (2012). "Psychological consequences of wrongful conviction in women and the possibility of positive change. *DePaul Journal for Social Justice, 5*, 221–294.

Koonse, E. (2012, August 23). "Kristine Bunch released after serving 16 years for son's arson death." *Christian Post.* Retrieved on 7/20/2013 from http://www.christianpost.com/news/kristine-bunch-released-after-serving-16-years-for-sons-arson-death-80506.

Kroll, J. (2008a, January 21). "'They stole the truth,' says woman convicted for crimes she didn't commit." *Plain Dealer.* Retrieved on 1/7/2013 from http://blog.cleveland.com/metro/2008/01/they_stole_the_truth_says_woma.html.

Kroll, J. (2008b, January 27). "Drug informant's lies lead to questions about the criminal justice system." *Plain Dealer.* Retrieved on 10/30/2014 from http://blog.cleveland.com/metro/2008/01/drug_informants_lies_lead_to_q.html.

Kroll, J. (2008c, February 3). "Ex-cons face hard times, even though their convictions were based on lies." *Plain Dealer.* Retrieved on 11/1/2014 from http://blog.cleveland.com/metro/2008/02/excons_face_hard_times_even_th.html.

Kroll, J. (2008d, February 13). "DEA case went ahead despite detective's warnings. *Plain Dealer.* Retrieved on 11/1/2014 from http://blog.cleveland.com/metro/2008/02/dea_case_went_ahead_despite_de.html.

Kroll, J. (2008e, August 11). "Mansfield drug case gone wrong: The inside story." *Plain Dealer.* Retrieved on 9/22/2010 from http://blog.cleveland.com/metro/2008/06/drug_prosecutions_gone_wrong_t.html.

Krouse, P. (2010a, February 5). "Jury acquits DEA agent Lee Lucas on all 18 charges related to drug investigation." *Plain Dealer.* Retrieved on 9/22/2010 from http://blog.cleveland.com/metro/2010/02/dea_agent_lee_lucas_acquitted.html.

Krouse, P. (2010b, February 16). "Richland County deputy sheriff sentenced to 12 weekends in jail." *Plain Dealer.* Retrieved on 9/25/2010 from http://blog.cleveland.com/metro/2010/02/richland_county_deputy_sheriff.html.

Lagos, M. (2003, July 14). "Sandy Murphy and Rick Tabish murder convictions voided." *Los Angeles Times.* Retrieved on 7/25/2014 from http://www.truthinjustice.org/murphy-tabish.htm.

Lancaster, C. (1993, May 12). "Virginia Larzelere sentenced to die in electric chair." *Orlando Sentinel.* Retrieved on 8/5/2013 from http://articles.orlandosentinel.com/1993-05-12/news/9305120479_1_virginia-larzelere-palmieri-sentencing.

Laverne Pavlinac. (n.d.). Forejustice.org. Retrieved on 1/19/2011 from http://forejustice.org/db/Pavlinac-Laverne.html.

Law, V. (2012, March). "Absent compassionate release, austerity helps some terminally ill prisoners obtain freedom." *Truth-out.* Retrieved on 8/8/2013 from http://www.truth-out.org/news/item/7176:absent-compassionate-release-austerity-helps-some-terminally-ill-prisoners-obtain-freedom.

Leatherman, F. (2012, January 7). "The Wenatchee sex ring case: Updated." Retrieved on 7/6/2014 from http://my.firedoglake.com/mason/tag/innocence-project-northwest.

Leff, L. (1987, August 25). "Sandra Craig denied retrial on child sex abuse charge." *Washington Post*, p. B1.

Leo, R., and Davis, D. (2010). "From false confession to wrongful conviction: Seven psychological processes." *Journal of Psychiatry and Law, 38*, 9–56.

Leung, R. (2004a, August 13). "A family accused." CBS News: *48 Hours*.

Leung, R. (2004b, August 24). "Part II: Getting it right." CBS News: *48 Hours*.

Levine, H. (2013, November 18). "The scandal of racist marijuana arrests—and what to do about it." *The Nation*. Retrieved on 9/10/2014 from http://www.thenation.com/article/176915/scandal-racist-marijuana-and-what-to-do-about-it.

Levy, N. (2005, April 29). "Bring justice to Hearne." *Texas Observer*. Retrieved on 8/10/2009 from http://www.texasobserver.org/article.php?aid=1935.

Lezon, D. (2005, December 14). "Mom's conviction thrown out on baby death." *Houston Chronicle*. Retrieved on 3/7/2012 from http://truthinjustice.org/briggs2.htm.

Liebman, J., Fagan, J., and West, V. (2000). "Capital attrition: Error rates in capital cases, 1973–1995." *Texas Law Review, 78*, 1839–1865.

Linder, D. (2003). "The McMartin preschool abuse trial: A commentary." Retrieved on 5/27/2014 from http://law2.umkc.edu/faculty/projects/ftrials/mcmartin/mcmartinaccount.html.

Linder, D. (2014). "The witchcraft trials in Salem: A commentary." Retrieved on 6/28/2014 from http://law2.umkc.edu/faculty/projects/ftrials/salem/SAL_ACCT.HTM.

"Little Rascals day care sexual abuse trial." (2013, November 11). *Wikipedia*. Retrieved on 6/4/2014 from en.wikipedia.org/wiki/Little_Rascals_day_care_sexual_abuse_trial.

Littlefield, D. (2008, April 18). "Widow accused of killing husband speaks out." *San Diego Union-Tribune*. Retrieved on 1/6/2011 from http://signonsandiego.printthis.clickability.com/pt/cpt?action=cptandtitle=SignOnSanDiego.com+%3E+News+%3E+Metro+—+Wi.

Longobardy, J. (2006, October 12). "Kirsten [*sic*] Blaise Lobato is accused in a gruesome slaying. Did she do it? *Las Vegas Weekly*. Retrieved on 1/16/2014 from http://www.lasvegasweekly.com/news/archive/2006/oct/12/the-trial.

Love, J.F. (2009). "Mansfield, Ohio DEA drug sting self-destructs when informant admits manufacturing evidence." *Justice Denied, 43* (summer), 8–9.

Lueders, B. (2007, May 17). "Biskupic tried to 'squeeze' Georgia Thompson: US Attorney's office made offers of leniency, tied to her testifying against others." *Isthmus*, the Daily Page. Retrieved on 1/31/2011 from http://truthinjustice.org/thompson-georgia2.htm.

Lurigio, A.J., and Loose, P. (2008). "The disproportionate incarceration of African Americans for drug offenses: The national and Illinois perspective. *Journal of Ethnicity in Criminal Justice, 6*, 223–247.

Lyon, K. (1998). *Witch hunt: A true story of social hysteria and abused justice*. New York: Avon.

MacCormack, J. (1998, November 23). "Woman is paroled despite big sentence." *San Antonio Express-News*. Retrieved on 8/15/2014 from http://truthinjustice.org/parole.htm.

Maguire, K., and Pastore, A. (2001). *Sourcebook of criminal justice statistics*. Washington, DC: US Department of Justice.

"Malenne Joseph files lawsuit for mistaken identity wrongful conviction." (2012, February 13). *Justice Denied*. Retrieved on 12/6/2012 from http://justice denied.org/wordpress/archives/1733.

Manning, L. (2007, January 14). "Nightmare at the day care: The Wee Care case." *Crime Magazine*. Retrieved on 5/31/2014 from http://www.crimemagazine.com/nightmare-day-care-wee-care-case.

Marley, P. (2008, March 6). "Payment OK'd for Georgia Thompson." *Milwaukee Journal Sentinel* online NewsWatch. Retrieved on 3/7/2008.

Marley, P., and Walters, S. (2007, April 7). "Conviction may cost Thompson $300,000; Former state employee in seclusion after release." *Milwaukee Journal Sentinel*. Retrieved on 12/6/2012 from http://www.jsoline.com%2Fnews%2Fwisconsin%2F29354359.html.

Martin, N. (2011, October 7). "Woman freed after another admits to 2000 robbery." *East Valley Tribune*. Retrieved on 1/5/2015 from http://www.eastvalleytribune.com/news/article_f0ced437-8c67-5a2c-b098-e22d89a700e2.html?mode=jqm.

Masters, T., and Lehto, S. (2012). *Drawn to justice: The wrongful conviction of Timothy Masters*. New York: Berkeley Publishing.

Mathews, J. (1989, May 31). "In California, a question of abuse: An excess of child molestation cases bring Kern County's investigative methods under fire." *Washington Post*, p. D1.

Mauer, M. (1999). *Race to incarcerate*. New York: New Press.

McClellan, D. (1994). "Disparity in the discipline of male and female inmates in Texas prisons." *Women and Criminal Justice, 5*, 71–97.

McDanield, G. (n.d.). "Introduction." Retrieved on 5/8/2013 from http://www.toddlertime.com/helpvirginia/currentwriting.htm.

Meissner, C.A., and Brigham, J.C. (2001). "Thirty years of investigating the own-race bias in memory for faces: A meta-analytic review." *Psychology, Public Policy, and Law, 7*, 3–35.

Mello, M. (2001). *The wrong man: A true story of innocence on death row*. Minneapolis: University of Minnesota Press.

Merchant, N. (2014, July 1). "Pecos County woman's murder conviction reviewed by court." Associated Press. Retrieved on 8/15/2014 from http://www.statesman.com/news/news/local/pecos-county-womans-murder-conviction-reviewed-by-court.

Michels, S., Netter, S., Marquez, L., and Ghebremedhin, S. (2009, April 14). "Why do some women kill?" ABC News. Retrieved on 7/9/2014 from http://abc-news.go.com/US/print?id=7326555.

"Michigan state police polygrapher who wrongly accused innocent woman named." (2006, August 29). *Antipolygraph.org News*. Retrieved on 1/7/2015 from https://antipolygraph.org/blog/2006/08/29/michigan-state-police-polygrapher-who-wrongly-accused-innocent-woman-named/comment-page.

Mid-Atlantic Innocence Project. (2010). *Beverly Monroe*. Retrieved on 1/19/2011 from http:www.exonerate.org/other-local-victories/beverly-monroe.

Miller, H. (2011, July 20). "Convicted." *Independent Weekly*. Retrieved on 9/22/2014 from http://www.theind.com/cover-story/8688-convicted.

Mize, J. (2004, May 20). "Woman freed after wrongful theft conviction." *Columbian*. Retrieved on 12/29/2012 from http://msnbc.msn.com/id/5031653.

Moran, G. (2011, November 13). "Prosecutor accused of affairs with defendants." *Union-Tribune* (San Diego). Retrieved on 1/21/2015 from http://www.utsandiego.com/news/2011/nov/13/prosecutor-accused-of-pursuing-romances-with/.

"Mother's conviction thrown out by court." (2006, August 29). *Seattle Times*. Retrieved on 1/6/2011 from http://seattletimes.nwsource.com/html /nationworld/2003233308_ndig29.html.

Muhammad, C. (2011, November 1). *Dying woman's family fights to free her from prison*. Retrieved on 8/8/2013 from http://releasepatriciawright.blogspot.com /2011/11/dying-womans-family-fights-to-free-her-from-prison.

"Murder convictions in Binion case overturned." (2003, July 15). *Las Vegas Review-Journal*. Retrieved on 1/16/2011 from http://www.reviewjournal.com /lvrj_home/2003/Jul-15-Tue-2003/news/21731396.html.

Murphy, W. (1989). "Appeal brief: Court of Appeals of Maryland, Maryland v. Craig." *Issues in Child Abuse Accusations, 1*. Retrieved on 12/22/2012 from http://www.ipt-forensics.com/journal/volume1/j1_3_3.htm.

Murrin, J. (2003). "Coming to terms with the Salem Witch Trials." *Proceedings of the American Antiquarian Society*. Retrieved on 8/17/2015 from http://www.americanantiquarian.org/proceedings/44539519.pdf.

Musto, D. (1999). *The American disease: Origins of narcotic control* (3rd ed.). New York: Oxford University Press.

Myers, M. (2000). "The social world of America's courts." In J. Sheley (ed.), *Criminology: A Contemporary Handbook* (pp. 447–472). Belmont, CA: Wadsworth.

Natapoff, A. (2009). *Snitching: Criminal informants and the erosion of American justice*. New York: New York University Press.

National Registry of Exonerations. (2013, April 3). *Update: 2012*. Retrieved on 4/12/2014 from http://www.law.umich.edu/special/exoneration/Documents /NRE2012UPDATE4_1_13_FINAL.pdf.

National Registry of Exonerations. (n.d. a). *Ada JoAnn Taylor*. Retrieved on 6/15/2013 from http://www.law.umich.edu/special/exoneration/Pages /casedetail.aspx?caseid=3676.

National Registry of Exonerations. (n.d. b). *Cheryle Beridon*. Retrieved on 12/3/2012 from http://www.law.umich.edu/special/exoneration/Pages /casedetail.aspx?caseid=3022.

National Registry of Exonerations. (n.d. c). *Debra Shelden—Nebraska*. Retrieved on 5/28/2012 from http://www.law.umich.edu/special/exoneration/Pages /casedetail.aspx?caseid=3629.

National Registry of Exonerations. (n.d. d). *Kathy Gonzalez—Nebraska*. Retrieved on 5/28/2012 from http://www.law.umich.edu/special/exoneration/Pages /casedetail.aspx?caseid=3247.

National Registry of Exonerations. (n.d. e). *Paula Gray*. Retrieved on 12/17/2012 from http://www.law.umich.edu/special/exoneration/Pages/casedetail.aspx ?caseid=3433.

National Registry of Exonerations. (n.d. f). *The registry, exonerations and false convictions*. Retrieved on 4/15/2014 from http://www.law.umich.edu/special/exoneration/Pages/learnmore.aspx.

Nelesen, A. (2006, August 2). "Charges dropped in Cadigan slayings." *Green Bay Press-Gazette*. Retrieved on 1/31/2011 from http://truthinjustice.org /labatte.htm.

Nevada Innocence Network. (2005, June). *Shasta Roever—Nevada*. Retrieved on 7/25/2014 from http://nevadainnocencenetwork.weebly.com/from-victims-of-the-state.html.

Nevada Innocence Network. (2012). *From letters by Lerlene*. Retrieved on 7/24/2014 from http://nevadainnocencenetwork.weebly.com/lerlene-roever .html.

Newton, C. (1999). "Massachusetts witch trial: Cheryl Amirault LeFave to return to jail." *Justice Denied, 1* (8).

Newton, M. (1996). "Guilty as charged." Paper presented at the International Council on Cultism and Ritual Trauma Conference, April 12–14, Dallas, Texas.

Nieves, E. (1994, December 3). "Prosecutors drop charges in abuse case from mid-80's." *New York Times*, p. 29.

Norton, M. (2002). *In the devil's snare: The Salem witchcraft crisis of 1692.* New York: Alfred A. Knopf.

"N.Y. woman released after 2 decades in prison." (2005, May 25). NBC News. Retrieved on 6/7/2013 from http://www.nbcnews.com/id/7984243/ns/us_news -crime_and_courts/n-y-woman-released-after-decades-prison/#.U72HZrEyn2Y.

Off, G., and Gillham, O. (2010, August 7). "Wrongly accused woman files lawsuit against police officers, Tulsa." *Tulsa World.* Retrieved on 9/2/2014 from http://www.tulsaworld.com/site/printerfriendlystory.aspx?articleid=20100807 _11_A13_Awogyi251260.

Ofshe, R., and Leo, R. (1997). "The social psychology of police interrogation: The theory and classification of true and false confessions." *Studies in Law, Politics, and Society, 16,* 189–251.

O'Hara, J. (2009, July 21). "Shirley Kinge awarded $250,000 for malicious prosecution." *Post Standard.* Retrieved on 1/9/2015 from http://blog.syracuse.com /news/print.html?entry=/2009/07/shirley_kinge_awarded_250000.f.html.

O'Hare, P. (2006, August 29). "Highlands mother won't be retried in baby's death." *Houston Chronicle.* Retrieved on 3/7/2012 from http://www.chron.com /neighborhood/pasadena-news/article/Highlands-mother-won-t-be-retried-in-baby-s-death.

Oregon Judicial Department Appellate Court Opinions. (2009, September 2). *State of Oregon v. Nancy Baker-Krofft.* Retrieved on 1/16/2010 from http://www .publications.ojd.state.or.us/A135939.htm.

Oregon Judicial Department Appellate Court Opinions. (2010, August 19). *State of Oregon v. Nancy Baker-Krofft.* Retrieved on 6/16/2014 from http://www .publications.ojd.state.or.us/docs/S057958.html.

"Orlando woman too short to be criminal exonerated." (2010, October 1). *Justice Denied.* Retrieved on 12/6/2012 from http://justicedenied.org /wordpress/archives/1048.

Parsons, N. (2014). *Meth mania: A history of methamphetamine.* Boulder, CO: Lynne Rienner.

Pasnik, M. (1993, December 6). "Woman sues in rigging of evidence by troopers." *New York Times.* Retrieved on 1/9/2015 from http://www.nytimes.com /1993/12/06/nyregion/woman-sues-in-rigging-of-evidence-by-troopers.html.

Paternoster, R. (1991). *Capital punishment in America.* New York: Lexington.

Paternoster, R., Brame, R., and Bacon, S. (2007). *The death penalty: America's experience with capital punishment.* New York: Oxford University Press.

PBS *Frontline.* (1997, May). "Innocence lost." Retrieved on 5/29/2014 from http://www.pbs.org/wgbh/pages/frontine/shows/innocence/etc/other.html.

PBS *Frontline.* (1998). "Innocence lost: The plea." Retrieved on 1/22/2004 from http://www.pbs.org/wgbh/pages/frontline/shows/innocence/etc/chronology.html.

PBS *Frontline.* (2004, June 17). "Erma Faye Stewart and Regina Kelly." Retrieved on 10/12/2007 from http://www.pbs.org/wgbh/pages/frontline/shows/plea/four /stewart.html.

Pearson, P. (1997). *When she was bad.* New York: Viking.

Pendergrast, M. (1996). *Victims of memory* (2nd ed.). Hinesburg, VT: Upper Access Books.

Perlstein, M. (2003, March 30). "Freedom no cure-all for those wrongly convicted: Jobs and respect often remain elusive." *Times-Picayune* (New Orleans). Retrieved on 1/16/2011 from http://www.truthinjustice.org/no-cureall.htm.

Perry, M. (n.d.). *Laverne Pavlinac—Oregon*. Retrieved on 5/28/2012 from http://www.law.umich.edu/special/exoneration/Pages/casedetail.aspx?caseid=3526.

Pflaum, N. (2005, March 24). "Out of the fire—the Jennifer Hall story." *Pitch* (Kansas City, MO). Retrieved on 1/2/2011 from http://justicedenied.org/issue/issue_28/jd_issue_28.pdf.

Phillips, S. (2012). "Continued racial disparities in the capital of capital punishment: The Rosenthal era." *Houston Law Review, 50*, 131–155.

"Philly drug kingpin Ace Capone's girlfriend released from prison on appeal." (2011, September 24). Retrieved on 1/28/2015 from http://zru-crazy.com/2011/09/24/philly-drug-kingpin-ace-capones-girlfriend-released-from-prison-on-appeal.

Piaskowski, M. (2007). "Beth LaBatte dies in car crash a year after murder exoneration." *Justice Denied, 37* (summer), 16.

Porterfield, E. (1999, September 25). "Judge backs new trial in Wenatchee abuse case." *Seattle Post-Intelligencer*. Retrieved on 7/11/2014 from http://truthinjustice.org/wenatchee.htm.

Possley, M. (2012, October 18). *Sherri Frederick*. Retrieved on 1/8/2013 from http://www.law.umich.edu/special/exoneration/Pages/casedetail.aspx?caseid=4022.

Possley, M. (2015a, March 19). *Debra Milke*. Retrieved on 8/18/2015 from http://www.law.umich.edu/special/exoneration/Pages/casedetail.aspx?caseid=4660.

Possley, M. (2015b, April 20). *Sabrina Butler*. Retrieved on 8/18/2015 from http://www.law.umich.edu/special/exoneration/Pages/casedetail.aspx?caseid=3078.

Possley, M. (n.d. a). *Beth LaBatte—Wisconsin*. Retrieved on 5/28/2012 from http://www.law.umich.edu/special/exoneration/Pages/casedetail.aspx?caseid=3367.

Possley, M. (n.d. b). *Dayna Christoph—Washington*. Retrieved on 5/28/2012 from http://www.law.umich.edu/special/exoneration/Pages/casedetail.aspx?caseid=3869.

Possley, M. (n.d. c). *Gayle Dove*. Retrieved on 7/20/2013 from http://www.law.umich.edu/special/exoneration/Pages/casedetail.aspx?caseid=3947.

Possley, M. (n.d. d). *Karen O'Dell*. Retrieved on 7/20/2013 from http://www.law.umich.edu/special/exoneration/Pages/casedetail.aspx?caseid=3941.

Possley, M. (n.d. e). *Kathryn Dawn Wilson – North Carolina*. Retrieved on 5/28/2012 from http://www.law.umich.edu/special/exoneration/Pages/casedetail.aspx?caseid=3757.

Possley, M. (n.d. f). *Malenne Joseph – Florida*. Retrieved on 5/28/2012 from http://www.law.umich.edu/special/exoneration/Pages/casedetail.aspx?caseid=3343.

Possley, M. (n.d. g). *Margaret Kelly Michaels – New Jersey*. Retrieved on 5/28/2012 from http://www.law.umich.edu/special/exoneration/Pages/casedetail.aspx?caseid=3867.

Possley, M. (n.d. h). *Mary Ann Colomb*. Retrieved on 9/22/2014 from http://www.law.umich.edu/special/exoneration/Pages/casedetail.aspx?caseid=3117.

Possley, M. (n.d. i). *Mary Ann Elizondo*. Retrieved on 7/20/2013 from http://www.law.umich.edu/special/exoneration/Pages/casedetail.aspx?caseid =4019.

Possley, M. (n.d. j). *Mary Weaver*. Retrieved on 7/20/2013 from http://www.law.umich.edu/special/exoneration/Pages/casedetail.aspx?caseid =3954.

Possley, M. (n.d. k). *Rachel Jernigan—Arizona*. Retrieved on 5/28/2012 from http://www.law.umich.edu/special/exoneration/Pages/casedetail.aspx?caseid =3437.

Possley, M. (n.d. l). *Reshenda Strickland*. Retrieved on 12/29/2012 from http://www.law.umich.edu/special/exoneration/Pages/casedetail.aspx?caseid =3668.

Possley, M. (n.d. m). *Sarah Smith*. Retrieved on 7/20/2013 from http://www.law.umich.edu/special/exoneration/Pages/casedetail.aspx?caseid =3942.

Possley, M. (n.d. n). *Sheila Bryan—Georgia*. Retrieved on 5/28/2012 from http://www.law.umich.edu/special/exoneration/Pages/casedetail.aspx?caseid =3066.

Possley, M. (n.d. o). *Shirley Kinge*. Retrieved on 1/9/2015 from http://www.law.umich.edu/special/exoneration/Pages/casedetail.aspx?caseid =3352.

Possley, M. (n.d. p). *Tamara McAnally*. Retrieved on 7/20/2013 from http://www.law.umich.edu/special/exoneration/Pages/casedetail.aspx?caseid =3923.

Possley, M. (n.d. q). *Teresa Engberg-Lehmer*. Retrieved on 7/20/2013 from https://www.law.umich.edu/special/exoneration/Pages/casedetail.aspx?caseid =3952.

Possley, M. (n.d. r). *Teresa Thomas*. Retrieved on 7/20/2013 from http://www.law.umich.edu/special/exoneration/Pages/casedetail.aspx?caseid =4124.

Possley, M. (n.d. s). *Violet Amirault—Massachusetts*. Retrieved on 5/28/2012 from http://www.law.umich.edu/special/exoneration/Pages/casedetail.aspx?caseid =3863.

Pride, M. (1986). *The child abuse industry*. Westchester, IL: Crossway.

Protess, D., and Warden, R. (1998). *A promise of justice: The eighteen-year fight to save four innocent men*. New York: Hyperion Books.

Ramdhan-Wright, P. (2007). "'Cold case' detectives close file by fingering the wrong person—the Patricia Wright story." *Justice Denied, 38* (fall), 3, 19–20.

Rankin, B. (2009, June 15). "Court overturns teacher's sex conviction." *Atlanta Journal-Constitution*. Retrieved on 3/6/2012 from http://www.ajc.com /metro/content/metro/stories/2009/06/15/teacher_consent_sex.html.

Regoli, R., and Hewitt, J. (1997). *Delinquency in society*. New York: McGraw-Hill.

"Release Patricia Wright." (2013, July 12). Retrieved on 8/8/2013 from http://releasepatriciawright.blogspot.com.

Repard, P. (2013, November 15). "Ex-prosecutor dies, was facing civil rights lawsuit." *Union-Tribune* (San Diego). Retrieved on 1/21/2015 from http://www.utsandiego.com/news/2013/nov/15/marugg-district-attorney -lawsuit.

Reynolds, D. (2002, July 9). "Three pleaded guilty to infant's murder, even though infant may not have been born." *Inclusion Daily Press*. Retrieved on 12/12/2012 from http://www.inclusiondaily.com/news/banks.htm.

Rich, E. (2004a, November 10). "Arundel judge frees woman in death of 'horrible' man." *Washington Post*, p. B1.

Rich, E. (2004b, November 13). "Behind the smoking gun: Tormented wife walks free." *Washington Post*. Retrieved on 6/20/2013 from http://seattletimes.com /html/nationworld/2002089923_spousemurder13.html.

Ridolfi, K.N., and Possley, M. (2010, October). *Preventable errors: A report on prosecutorial misconduct in California 1997–2009*. Santa Clara: Northern California Innocence Project.

Roach, M. (1996). *The Salem witch trials*. Boston: Houghton Mifflin.

Roach, M. (2013). *The six women of Salem: The untold story of the accused and their accusers in the Salem witch trials*. Cambridge, MA: DaCapo Press.

Robinson, B. (2003, April 1). "The 'Little Rascals' ritual abuse case, in Edenton, NC." Ontario Consultants on Religious Tolerance. Retrieved on 1/17/2011 from http://www.religioustolerance.org/ra_edent.htm.

Robinson, B. (2005, April 11). "MVMO ritual abuse cases: Bakersfield/Kern County, CA." Ontario Consultants on Religious Tolerance. Retrieved on 1/6/2011 from http://www.religioustolerance.org/ra_baker.htm.

Roever, L. (1999, March 8). "The case of Shasta Roever." *Justice Denied, 1*(2). Retrieved on 7/24/2014 from http://justicedenied.org/v1issue2.htm #ShastaRoever.

Rominger Legal. (2005). *Florida case law and Florida court opinions (Wesson v. State of Florida)*. Retrieved on 6/18/2013 from http://www.romingerlegal.com /floridacourts/court_opinions3/03-3502.html.

Rooney, P. (2011). *Die free: A true story of murder, betrayal and miscarried justice*. Amazon Digital Services.

Rosser, A. (2009). "WV supreme court broadens self-defense to cover battered women." *Justice Denied, 43* (summer), 12–13.

Ruesink, M., and Free, M. (2005). "Wrongful convictions among women: An exploratory study of a neglected topic." *Women and Criminal Justice, 16*, 1–23.

"Rush to judgement." (1993, April 19). *Newsweek*. Retrieved on 12/27/2010 from http://www.newsweek.com/1993/04/19/rush-to-judgement.print.html.

Russo, J. (2009, February 19). "Wrongful conviction: The Choctaw Three of Alabama." *Voices*. Retrieved on 3/20/2013 from http://voices.yahoo.com /wrongful-conviction-choctaw-three-alabama-2664142.html.

Rutledge, J. (2001). "They all look alike: The inaccuracy of cross-racial identifications." *American Journal of Criminal Law, 28*, 207–228.

Ryan, C. (2008, November 18). "Court rejects appeal of Sandra Murphy." *Las Vegas Sun*. Retrieved on 7/25/2014 from http://www.lasvegassun.com/news /2008/nov/18/court-rejects-appeal-sandra-murphy.

Saari, P., and Shaw, E. (2001). *Witchcraft in America*. Farmington Hills, MI: U.X.L.

"The Salem witch trials, 1692." (2000). EyeWitness to History. Retrieved on 6/28/2014 from http://www.eyewitnesstohistory.com/salem.htm.

Salzman, A. (2004, May 15). "Mother of boy in suicide is spared prison term." *New York Times*. Retrieved on 6/13/2013 from http://www.nytimes.com /2004/05/15/nyregion/mother-of-boy-in-suicide-is-spared-prison-term.

Salzman, A. (2006a, August 29). "Court ruling clears mother in son's suicide." *New York Times*. Retrieved on 6/13/2013 from http://www.nytimes.com /2006/08/29/nyregion/29mother.html?_r=0&.

Salzman, A. (2006b, September 3). "The week; a verdict, a reversal and second-guesses." *New York Times*. Retrieved on 6/13/2013 from http:// www.query.nytimes.com/gst/fullpage.html?res=9806EFDB1E3EF93.

Santora, M. (2003, October 29). "Woman guilty in son's suicide says school bully-ing is to blame." *New York Times*. Retrieved on 6/13/2013 from http://www.nytimes.com/2003/10/29/nyregion/woman-guilty-in-son-suicide-says-school-bullying-is-to-blame.

Savidge, N. (2014, September 14). "Despite equal use, blacks cited more." *Sunday State Journal*, pp. A1, A8.

Schadler, J., and Berman, T. (2010, May 5). "Mom served 14 years for arson now called 'impossible'." ABC News. Retrieved on 7/20/2013 from http://abc-news.go.com/2020/arson-investigation-evidence-science/print?id=10550837.

Scheck, B., Neufeld, P., and Dwyer, J. (2000). *Actual innocence: Five days to execu-tion and other dispatches from the wrongly convicted*. New York: Doubleday.

Scheck, B., Neufeld, P., and Dwyer, J. (2003). *Actual innocence: When justice goes wrong and how to make it right*. New York: Signet Books.

Schneider, A., and Barber, M. (2008, February 25). "'Lies, lies, and more lies,' says jailed man." *Seattle Post-Intelligencer*. Retrieved on 7/12/2014 from http://seattlepi.nwsource.com/powertoharm/rodriguez.html.

Shapiro, J. (2011, June 28). *Child death cases repeatedly mishandled*. National Public Radio. Retrieved on 7/7/2014 from http://www.wbur.org/npr/137466756/flawed-child-death-probes-cause-wrongful-convictions.

Shaw, J. (2011, January 8). "Drug dealer's girlfriend trades mansion for cell, gets two years for money laundering." *Philadelphia Inquirer*. Retrieved on 12/27/2012 from http://articles.philly.com/2011-01-08/news/27017198_1_drug-money-money-laundering-drug-kingpin.

Shemeligian, B. (1996, September 7). "Woman battling conviction in boyfriend's death." *Las Vegas Sun*. Retrieved on 8/2/2013 from http://www.lasvegassun.com/news/1996/sep/07/woman-battling-conviction-in-boyfriends-death.

Sherrer, H. (2003, March). "Medell Banks Jrs.' conviction for killing a non-existent child is thrown out as a "manifest injustice." *Justice Denied, 2*(9). Retrieved on 1/6/2011 from http://forejustice.org/wc/choctaw_three_92602.htm.

Sherrer, H. (2004). "Las Vegas Police and prosecutors frame woman 170 miles from murder scene—Kirstin Lobato's 'very peculiar story'." *Justice Denied, 26* (fall), 5, 19–23.

Sherrer, H. (2008a). "Six people cleared of 1985 Nebraska murder that four con-fessed to committing." *Justice Denied, 41* (summer), 16–17.

Sherrer, H. (2008b). "Two women awarded $2.58 million for robbery convictions based on speculation." *Justice Denied, 41* (summer), 8–9.

Siegel, B. (1999, July 11). "Judging parents as murderers on 4 specks of blood." *Los Angeles Times*. Retrieved on 7/23/2013 from http://articles.latimes.com/print/1999/jul/11/news/mn-54984.

Silvers, A. (2008, December 26). "False imprisonment hung over crash victim's head." *Milwaukee Journal Sentinel*. Retrieved on 4/17/2013 from http://www.jsonline.com/news/wisconsin/36767759.html.

Simon, T., Neufeld, P., and Scheck, B. (2003). *The innocents*. New York: Umbrage Editions.

Smith, C. (2011a, July 14). "The Charles Smith blog: 'The child cases'; (4); selected sto-ries; the hardest cases: when children die, justice can be illusive; Propublica, PBS, Frontline, and NPR." Retrieved on 7/7/2014 from http://smithforensic.blogspot.com/2011/07/child-cases-4-selected-stories-hardest.html.

Smith, C. (2011b, July 17). "The Charles Smith blog: 'The child cases'; (7); Summaries of the nearly 2 dozen cases identified by joint investigation."

Retrieved on 12/10/2012 from http://smithforensic.blogspot.com /2011/07/child-cases-7-summaries-of-nearly-2.html.

Smith, E., and Hattery, A. (2011). "Race, wrongful conviction, and exoneration." *Journal of African American Studies, 15*, 74–94.

Smith, K. (1998, November 25). "Expert testimony sways parole board to release woman jailed for 5 years." *Odessa American*. Retrieved on 8/15/2014 from http://truthinjustice.org/sonia112598.htm.

Smothers, R. (1991, August 19). "Child-abuse case is ordeal for a town." *New York Times*. Retrieved on 6/3/2014 from http://www.nytimes.com /1991/08/19/us/child-abuse-is-ordeal-for-a-town.

Somerville, S. (1992, February 5). "Witness: Virginia Larzelere asked slayer if he was Jason." *Orlando Sentinel*. Retrieved on 5/8/2013 from http://articles .orlandosentinel.com/1992-02-05/news/9202050748_1_virginia-larzelere-lom-bardo-gunman.

Spohn, C., and Spears, J. (1996). "The effect of offender and victim characteristics on sexual assault case processing decisions." *Justice Quarterly, 13*, 649–679.

Stecklein, J. (2009, July 19). "Decade after notorious Tulia drug raid, subject still a taboo in town." *Lubbock* (Texas) *Avalanche-Journal*. Retrieved on 9/30/2009 from http://www.lubbockonline.com/stories/071909/loc_465634283.shtml.

Stein, J. (2007, April 6). "Georgia Thompson acquitted, set free." *Wisconsin State Journal*. Retrieved on 1/31/2011 from http://truthinjustice.org/thompson -georgia.htm.

"Stories of ACLU clients swept up in the Hearne drug bust of November 2000." (2002, November 1). American Civil Liberties Union. Retrieved on 11/15/2005 from http://www.aclu.org/drug-law-reform/stories-aclu-clients-swept-hearne-drug-bust-november-2000?tab=legaldoc.

"Sykes, et. al. v. Anderson, et al." (n.d.). Goodman and Hurwitz, P.C. Retrieved on 10/28/2013 from http://www.goodmanhurwitz.com/newspress/falsearrest.htm.

Talbot, M. (2001, January 7). "The devil in the nursery." *New York Times Magazine*. Retrieved on 5/28/2014 from http://www.truthinjustice.org/mcmartin.htm.

Taylor, J. (1908/1974). *The witchcraft delusion in colonial Connecticut (1647–1697)*. Manchester, UK: Corner House.

Taylor, M., and Doyle, M. (2011, March 20). "Investigation rips army's crime lab, analyst." *Wisconsin State Journal*, p. B1.

Tepfer, J., Nirider, L., and Tricarico, L. (2010). "Arresting development: Convictions of innocent youth." *Rutgers Law Review, 62*(4), 887–941.

"Teresa Thomas, the Athens County women [*sic*] who was convicted, then acquit-ted." (n.d.). *Athens News*. Retrieved on 7/25/2013 from http://www .athensnews.com/ohio/article-2474-teresa-thomas-the-athens-county-women-who-was-convicted-then-acquitted.html.

Thevenot, C. (2010, January 27). "Rick Tabish gets parole from prison in Binion case." *Las Vegas Review-Journal*. Retrieved on 7/25/2014 from http://www.reviewjournal.com/news/rick-tabish-gets-parole-prison-binion-case.

Thevenot, C., and Geary, F. (2004, November 24). "Binion trial verdict: Reversal of fortunes." *Las Vegas Review-Journal*. Retrieved on 1/16/2011 from http://www.reviewjournal.com/lvrj_home/2004/Nov-24-Wed-2004 /news/25339516.html.

Thurston, D. D. (2003a, May 3). "Local woman seeks pardon." [Louisiana] *Courier*. Retrieved on 3/20/2013 from http://www.mapinc.org/tlcnews/v03 /n683/a07.htm?212.

Thurston, D.D. (2003b, July 30). "Foster grants pardon to local woman." [Louisiana] *Courier*. Retrieved on 12/3/2012 from http://houmatoday.com /article/20030730/NEWS/307300314?template=printpicart.

Tilghman, A. (2004). "Autopsies by former examiner reviewed." *Houston Chronicle*. Retrieved on 3/7/2012 from http://truthinjustice.org/patricia -moore.htm.

Tollet, T. and Close, B. (1991). "The overrepresentation of blacks in Florida's juvenile justice system." In M. Lynch and Patterson, E. (eds.), *Race and Criminal Justice*. Albany, NY: Harrow and Heston.

Tonry, M. (1994). "Racial politics, racial disparities, and the war on crime." *Crime and Delinquency, 40*, 475–494.

Tonry, M. (1995). *Malign neglect: Race, crime and punishment in America*. New York: Oxford University Press.

Tonry, M. (2010). "The social, psychological, and political causes of racial disparities in the American criminal justice system." *Crime and Justice: A Review of Research, 39*, 273–312.

Tonry, M. (2011). *Punishing race: A continuing American dilemma*. New York: Oxford University Press.

"Trenda Loue Kemmerer." (2011). *Texas Tribune*. Retrieved on 3/7/2012 from http://www.texastribune.org/library/data/texas-prisons/inmates/trenda-loue -kemmerer/76476.

"Tulsa judge overturns conviction." (2010, September 20). *Tulsa World*. Retrieved on 9/29/2014 from http://www.tulsaworld.com/site/printerfriendlystory .aspxarticleid=20100920_11_a1_ulnsbo738575.

"Tulsa, Oklahoma, settles police corruption case for $425K." (2014, January 31). *Insurance Journal*. Retrieved on 9/2/2014 from http://www.insurancejournal .com/news/southcentral/2014/01/31/319049.htm.

"Tulsa police officers subject of photo lineup, sources say." (n.d.). *Tulsa World*. Retrieved on 9/2/2014 from http://www.lineofduty.com/the-blotter/105455- whats-going-on-inside-the-tulsa-pd.

Turner, K. (2007, October 16). "Fallout continues from informant's confession." *Plain Dealer*. Retrieved on 10/29/2014 from http://blog.cleveland.com /metro/2007/10/federal_prosecutors_said_they.html.

Turner, K. (2009, May 13). "Key players in the 2005 Mansfield drug case." *Plain Dealer*. Retrieved on 9/22/2010 from http://blog.cleveland.com /pdextra//print.html.

United Press International. (2009, June 15). "Teacher's sex conviction overturned in Georgia." Retrieved on 1/13/2011 from http://www.upi.com/Top_News /2009/06/05/Teachers-sex-conviction-overturned-in-Ga/30291245085159.

US Department of Health and Human Services. (2009). *Child maltreatment 2009*. District of Columbia: Children's Bureau.

US District Court for the Western District of Texas. (2002). Civ.02-A-02-CA-702JN. Retrieved on 5/12/2014 from www.readbag.com/povertylaw-poverty-law- library-case-55200-55235-55235a.

Vancouver Branch NAACP newsletter. (2004, June). "President's column." Retrieved on 1/7/2015 from www.naacpvanc.org.

Vanderborg, C. (2012, August 23). "Kristine Bunch, Indiana arson offender, released 16 years after fire kills 3-year-old son." *International Business Times*. Retrieved on 7/20/2013 from http:www.ibtimes.com/kristine-bunch-indiana- arson-offender-released-16-years-after-fire-kills-3-year-old-son-photo-754238.

Victims of the State. (n.d.). *CAC-CAP name index*. Retrieved on 2/29/2012 from http://www.victimsofthestate.org/Name/C1.html.

Wallace, H. (1993). "Mandatory minimums and the betrayal of sentencing reform: A legislative Dr. Jekyll and Mr. Hyde." *Federal Probation, 57*, 9–19.

Walsh, A. (1987). "The sexual stratification hypothesis and sexual assault in light of the changing conceptions of race." *Criminology, 25*, 153–173.

Warden, R. (2005). *The snitch system: How snitch testimony sent Randy Steidl and other innocent Americans to death row.* Chicago: Center on Wrongful Convictions.

Warden, R. (n.d.). *Kristine Bunch.* Retrieved on 7/20/2013 from http://www.law.umich.edu/special/exoneration/Pages/casedetail.aspx?caseid=4085.

Warden, R., and Fredrickson, R. (2012). *The role of false confessions in Illinois wrongful conviction cases: Center on Wrongful Convictions special report.* Retrieved on 2/17/2013 from http://www.law.northwestern.edu/wrongfulconvictions/issues/causesandremedies/falseconfessions/False ConfessionsStudy.html.

Warmerdam, E. (2013, July 8). "Creepy prosecutor claims strike chord with judge." *Courthouse News Service.* Retrieved on 7/24/2013 from http://www.courthousenews.com/2013/07/08/59168.htm.

Weinberg, S. (2003, June 26). *Breaking the rules: Who suffers when a prosecutor is cited for misconduct?* Washington, DC: Center for Public Integrity.

West, E.M. (2010). *Court findings of ineffective assistance of counsel claims in post-conviction appeals among the first 255 DNA exoneration cases.* New York: Innocence Project.

West, G. (2014, May 16). "False positive: An introduction to Houston's prosecution problem." *Houston Free Press.* Retrieved on 9/22/2014 from http://www.freepresshouston.com/false-positive-an-introduction-to-houstons-prosecution-problem.

West, N., and Samuels, A. (1991, April 10). "'We all did some learning,' Craig says of ordeal. Criticism voiced about the way the child sexual abuse case was handled." *Baltimore Sun.* Retrieved on 5/16/2014 from http://articles.baltimoresun.com/1991-04-10/news/1991100216_1_michael-craig-sandra-craig-child-sexual-abuse.

"What happened?" (2007, December 19). Retrieved on 5/8/2013 from http://www.toddlertime.com/helpvirginia/what_happened.htm.

Willard, N. (2007, February). "The Julie Amero tragedy." Center for Safe and Responsible Use of the Internet. Retrieved on 12/01/2014 from http://www.drumsnwhistles.com/pdf/amero-tragedy.pdf.

Williams, C. (2011, November 1). "U.S. Supreme Court reinstates conviction in baby's death." *Los Angeles Times.* Retrieved on 7/23/2013 from http://articles.latimes.com/print/2011/nov/01/local/la-me-shaken-baby-court-20111101.

Williams, J. (2012, April 6). "Shirley Ree Smith sentence commuted in shaken baby case." *Huffington Post.* Retrieved on 7/23/2013 from http://www.huffingtonpost.com/2012/04/06/shirley-ree-smith-sentence-commuted-in-shaken-baby-case.

Williams, M., Demuth, S., and Holcomb, J. (2007). "Understanding the influence of victim gender in death penalty cases: The importance of victim race, sex-related victimization, and jury decision making." *Criminology, 45*, 865–892.

Williams, M., and Norton, D. (1995, June 8). "The unraveling of a monstrous secret—sex abuse scandal has Wenatchee reeling." *Seattle Times.* Retrieved on 7/5/2014 from http://community.seattletimes.nwsource.com/archive/?date=19950608andslug=2125346.

Wisconsin Innocence Project. (n.d.). "Wrongful convictions and exonerations in

Wisconsin." Retrieved on 1/11/2011 from http://www.law.wisc.edu/fjr /clinicals/ip/client_profiles.html.

Witchcraft and Witches. (n.d.). "The witch trials—Connecticut witch trials (America, 1647–1697)." Retrieved on 8/16/2015 from http://www .witchcraftandwitches.com/trials_connecticut.html.

"Woman freed from jail after sister confesses to crime." (2004, May 20). *Columbian*. Retrieved on 5/28/2013 from http://www.lexisnexis.com /hottopics/Inacademic/?.

"Woman jailed for vandalism may not be guilty." (2010, September 3). WFTV. Retrieved on 10/12/2010 from http://www.wftv.com/news/24875691 /detail.html.

"Woman wrongfully convicted by mistaken identity sues police." (2005, Summer). *Justice Denied*, *29*, 4.

"Woman wrongfully imprisoned in Tulsa police corruption case files lawsuit." (2010, August 7). *Newson6* (Tulsa, Oklahoma). Retrieved on 9/2/2014 from http://www.newson6.com/story/12940695/woman-wrongfully-imprisoned-in-tulsa-police-corruption-case-files-lawsuit.

Worldwide Women's Criminal Justice Network. (2012, August 22). *Kristine Bunch*. Retrieved on 7/20/2013 from http://www.wcjn.org/Kristine_Bunch.html.

"Yvonne Eldridge falsely accused of harming children." *Kaiser Papers*. Retrieved on 6/18/2014 from http://horror.kaiserpaers.org/eldridge.html.

Index

About the Book

Marvin Free and Mitch Ruesink reveal the distinctive role that gender dynamics so often play in the miscarriage of justice.

Examining more than 160 cases involving such charges as homicide, child abuse, and drug trafficking, the authors explore systemic failures in both policing and prosecution. They also highlight the intersecting roles of gender and race. Demonstrating how women encounter circumstances that are qualitatively different than those of men, they illuminate unique challenges facing women in the criminal justice system.

Marvin D. Free, Jr., is professor emeritus of sociology at the University of Wisconsin-Whitewater. **Mitch Ruesink** teaches psychology at Waukesha County Technical College. The two are coauthors of *Race and Justice: Wrongful Convictions of African American Men*.